INSULL

INSULL

BY FORREST
McDONALD

The University of Chicago Press

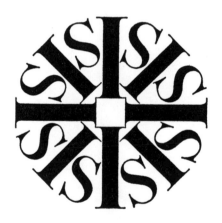

Library of Congress Catalog Card Number: 62–18110

The University of Chicago Press, Chicago & London
The University of Toronto Press, Toronto 5, Canada

© *1962 by The University of Chicago. All rights reserved*
Published 1962. Printed in the United States of America

Designed by Anita Walker Scott

I returned, and saw under the sun, that the race is not to the swift, nor the battle to the strong, neither yet bread to the wise, nor yet riches to men of understanding, nor yet favor to men of skill; but time and chance happeneth to them all.

Ecclesiastes 9:11

to Peggie, for the i.c., and to Ab, for everything

TO THE READER

Do you remember Samuel Insull? Chances are you do if you are an American over forty, or have taken a course in recent American history; but what is it you remember? Isn't he the fellow who went to Greece, the billionaire utility tycoon from Chicago; his empire collapsed, and he was indicted for fraud or something? Or was that Ivar Kreuger, the match king, or Howard Hopson, the holding company manipulator, or Sir Basil Zaharoff, the merchant of death? If your memory is a little better, you may remember headlines in the summer of 1932, telling you of the failure of a gas and electric empire that had operated in thirty-something states, and of a million investors losing two or three billion dollars ("The biggest business failure in the history of the world," you may have read). You may remember Franklin Roosevelt, campaigning in the fall of 1932, denouncing "the Ishmaels and the Insulls, whose hand is against every man's." You may remember 1933, and the battle to extradite Insull from Greece, a battle that shared the front pages with the New Deal and Adolf Hitler and Benito Mussolini and the Lindbergh baby. You may remember 1934, and Insull's trials for use of the mails to defraud, and embezzlement, and violation of the bankruptcy acts.

Chances are you don't remember—though most of this was in the papers, too—that Insull had been in the electric business as long as there had been an electric business; that he had started as Thomas Edison's private secretary in 1881; that he, more than any other man, was responsible for founding the business of centralized electric supply; that he organized the Edison General Electric Company (predecessor of the industrial giant of the same name, sans Edison), and worked out a model of nationwide product distribution that virtually all American industry copied; that he talked, practiced, and popularized "mass production" and selling at the lowest possible cost, long before these ideas were attributed to Henry Ford; that he either formulated or borrowed from others and first successfully applied on a large scale the concepts of the load and diversity factors (on which all utility rates are based) , the "natural monopoly" principle, the open-end mortgage used in financing expansion, and rigorous cost accounting; that he was the father of effective governmental regulation of public utilities and a progenitor of rural electrification; that he pioneered successful welfare programs years before most of business, labor, or government took any significant steps in that direction; that, purely as a matter of good business, he facilitated the growth of important labor unions; that in the development of the idea and techniques of modern public relations, he was the crucial link between Phineas T. Barnum and Madison Avenue; and that he devised methods of marketing securities that made possible gigantic modern corporations, owned by anonymous millions and therefore owned by nobody.

I am not concerned with which of these sets of memories you prefer, if by this is meant your judgment of whether Insull was good or evil, or whether his existence was, in the long run, for better or for worse. But having found out what he did with his life, I am concerned that you know this, and that you know something about what he did to your life and to mine. Yet more crucial, having learned to know him as a man, I am concerned to make you know him. Whether you like him or not, when you get to know him, is a matter of total indifference to me. If only, when you lay down this book, you know Samuel Insull, I shall be content; for then I shall have done all that a historian can hope to do, and all a historian has any right to do.

If I have not failed dismally, getting to know Insull will be considerably easier for you than it was for me. Not that the records were not there, and available. All Insull's personal papers were open to me, his son, acting on the theory that what I might find and report could scarcely be worse than what others had said, turned over all the papers to me, no strings attached, as did virtually every company with which Insull was once connected. But Insull was a man who "specialized in individual cases," and "fixed" things, and arranged matters privately; and so the record he left is but a bare and sometimes deceptive skeleton of the life he lived. The mountainous records of several government investigations—of Insull and of the business he was in—might have added meat to these bones, but as often as not these were as "fixed" as were Insull's own doings. Beyond that, before I could really get to know Insull, I had to talk with many, many persons who had known him. And these—friends and foes and bystanders, executives and elevator operators and cab drivers, lawyers and judges and jurors—proved to be as interested as any in fixing the record.

Do you know Edward Eagle Brown and Abner J. Stilwell? Ned and Ab came to be two of the nation's most powerful bankers, for they were vice-presidents in charge of trouble, and in the 1930's there wasn't anything but trouble. Do you know Harold L. Stuart? Harry Stuart is one of the biggest and best investment banking houses in the world, bar none. Do you know the Duchess, Bertha Baur? Bertha ruled Gold Coast society as subtly and absolutely as Pompadour ruled the society of Louis XV. Do you know Max McGraw? Maybe you've never heard of Max McGraw, but he is the shrewdest financial operator west of Cleveland and the power behind more companies than you can shake a stick at. Do you know Cyrus Eaton, he of the baby blue eyes and nerves of steel, he to whom Khrushchev sends envoys and troikas? With each of these, and countless more, I talked. And each of these, in his way, quaked at the name of Insull. When they praised, they praised in loud voices, and when they damned, they damned in whispers, as if the vengeant ghost of the old man, even yet, stalked their very halls.

And each said, Sit down, I'll buy you a drink (or, I'll take you to lunch, or another equivalent, each according to his way). To me, a kid from the swamps of Texas, these magnates so spoke! From the outset, everyone in Chicago wanted to "buy me a drink." It was obvious from the beginning that guilt (and fear, guilt's most enterprising companion) underlay this uninvited gregariousness, but it was a long, long time before I realized that in buying me a drink each sought in his own way to buy my memory.

For an even longer time I puzzled: Why should anyone, and particularly these giants of the earth, want to buy my memory? And then one day I knew: The reason is that they viewed me not as a person at all but as an institution. They saw my coming as the Day of Judgment, and thus to them my memory was the memory of History; it was the memory of mankind; perhaps it was even the memory of God. This is what everyone, in his own way, sought to buy. Titans and paupers, tycoons and proletarians, those who have won and those who have lost; all wanted to distort or destroy—to fix—that part of the past in which they had lived. This is why they wanted to buy my memory.

But my memory is not for sale. Not for drink, nor money, nor even for love. I am both fallible and corrupt, but my memory, though fallible, is incorruptible.

I owe a debt of gratitude to a large number of persons who, in a more constructive way, helped bring this book into existence.

In the research, I had unrestricted access to the Samuel Insull Papers, to the excellent financial library of Halsey, Stuart and Company, to the manuscript collections at the Edison Laboratory National Monument, to the personal scrapbooks of Britton I. Budd, to all the records of Commonwealth Edison Company, Public Service Company of Northern Illinois, Peoples Gas Light and Coke Company, Middle West Utilities Company, and several of Middle West's operating subsidiaries, and to the private files of the investigation of Middle West and its subsidiaries by the Securities Exchange Commission. For making these generally non-public sources available, and for guiding me through them and patiently answering my endless questions about them, I should like to express particular appreciation to Harold L. Stuart and Miss Virginia Savage of Halsey, Stuart and Company; Miss Kathleen Oliver of the Edison Laboratory National Monument; Willis Gale, John W. Evers, Fred Baxter, and Miss Sophie Goetz of Commonwealth Edison Company; James F. Oates, Robert M. Drevs, and Walter McElligott of Peoples Gas Company; John Osborne of Central and South West Corporation; and Ralph D. Stevenson and Miss Marjorie Graham of counsel for the corporate descendents of Middle West Utilities Company.

Many persons generously gave of their time for interviews. All these are acknowledged in the footnotes, but I should like to add a general word of appreciation here.

Four persons showed special kindness and were of immense service in ways that are not easily described, but for which I am especially grateful: William E. Larsen, C. A. Turner, Abner J. Stilwell, and Miss Edith Malcom.

Dr. Clifford L. Lord, formerly the director of the State Historical Society of Wisconsin and now dean of the College of General Studies at Columbia University, negotiated with Samuel Insull, Jr., a written contract which, though transferred from the State Historical Society to the American History Research Center and finally to the University of Chicago Press, remained intact and provided the conditions under which the Insull Papers were available to me. In brief, Mr. Insull, Jr., agreed to (1) waive all financial connection with the book; (2) make available to me, without restriction, all papers in his possession which related to the subject; (3) do his best to induce the appropriate officials in Insull's former companies to open their records to me; and (4) co-operate in other ways, such as granting interviews and setting up interviews with others. In exchange, it was agreed that Mr. Insull, Jr., should receive fifty copies of the published book, and that he reserve the right to veto the adaptation of the book for television, radio, and motion picture production. Finally, at my request as well as Dr. Lord's, Mr. Insull, Jr., agreed to read and criticize the finished manuscript but to waive any control over the contents. The language of this "academic freedom" clause was as follows:

Prior to any publication thereof McDonald will submit to Insull any manuscript, based upon material secured through Insull's assistance, for Insull's suggestions as to correctness of facts and interpretation. In case of disagreement, after review of the available data, McDonald shall make, independently and in his sole discretion, final decision as to how the text shall read.

Throughout, Insull, Jr., honored the agreement both in letter and in spirit. He helped make all company records available, and he was as diligent in arranging interviews with hostile witnesses as he was in arranging interviews with friendly ones. (One person, a bitter critic of Insull with whom Insull, Jr., arranged an interview, said to me, "My God! I never heard of anybody being so objective. Well, he asked for it"; and then launched into a three-hour indictment of Insull.) In reading the manuscript, he was extremely careful in checking factual data, and arranged for readings by persons who had had closer contact than he with various events recounted in the narrative; but he expressly refused to comment on my interpretation of his father, his mother, his Uncle Martin, and himself, on the ground that no comment he could make could possibly be objective.

The following persons who had special knowledge (in two cases from long study, in the others from personal experience) read, criticized, and helped weed out errors in parts or all of the manuscript: Miss Kathleen Oliver, Miss Sophie Goetz, and John W. Evers, Edward J. Fleming, Leslie E. Salter, Abner J. Stilwell, Arthur Taylor, Cyrus S. Eaton, and Harold L. Stuart.

Five of the best historians I know generously took the time to read the entire manuscript and give me their criticisms of it: Raymond C. Miller of Wayne State University, Thomas P. Govan of New York University, Leslie E. Decker of the University of Maine, and my colleagues at Brown University, James B. Hedges and Natalie Zemon Davis.

If, at any places in this book, I have managed to describe complex technical subjects understandably, accurately, and with an economy of words, the achievement derives in large measure from study of the example of my friend Harland Manchester, the best writer on scientific and technical subjects I know.

The photographs and other illustrative material have been gathered from many sources, including a number of those organizations and individuals acknowledged earlier. My special thanks are due the *Chicago Tribune,* the *Chicago Daily News,* the Chicago Historical Society, the Edison Laboratory National Monument, and Samuel Insull, Jr., for providing a wealth of photographs and documents from which to choose.

Finally, my gratitude to five persons who contributed in ways that few could understand.

With all this help, this book should be better than it is. For its shortcomings, I alone am responsible.

A word of caution: in the pages that follow I make frequent reference to a number of banking, investment, and financial houses as they were during the period with which this study is concerned. Very few, if any, of the men who ran these establishments during the days of Insull are now in control and in some cases even the form of doing business has changed. I refer to these organizations only as they were then constituted, and nothing said here is intended to reflect upon present companies and present managements.

FORREST McDONALD

August 1962

Brown University

CONTENTS

ILLUSTRATIONS

CHAPTER I *London*

An old man leaned against the rail of the S.S. "Exilona," staring blankly into the early morning fog off the New Jersey shore, as the pilot and quarantine boats hove into view and Ambrose Light drew slowly abeam. The twenty-four-day crossing had done little to relieve his aching, exhausted body and had only partially mended his broken spirit. With a sigh born partly of reflection and partly of resignation, Samuel Insull turned and spoke to his State Department guard.[1]

"Berry," he said, "if two men had walked down Fifth Avenue a year ago"—that would have been May, 1933—"and one of them had a pint of whiskey in his pocket and the other had a hundred dollars in gold coin, the one with the whiskey would have been called a criminal, and the one with the gold an honest citizen. If these two men had, like Rip van Winkle, slept for a year and again walked down Fifth Avenue, the man with the whiskey would be called an honest citizen and the one with the gold coin a criminal. I find myself somewhat in this sort of situation. What I did, when I did it, was honest; now, through changed conditions, what I did may or may not

[1] The following dialogue, like all conversations reported in this book, is derived from a composite of recollections, some written, others summoned to mind in the course of interviews. In some instances, here and later, I have made minor corrections in the conversations as reported, to make it conform to Insull's characteristic speech; for example, *Time, the Weekly Newsmagazine* reported, in covering the following exchange, that Insull addressed his son as "Junior"; actually, he always called him "Chappie," and Chappie is used here. Insull's characteristic phrases and words I have learned by reading a vast body of his writings and interviewing persons who were closely associated with him, notably Edward J. Doyle and John W. Evers, who both served as Insull's private secretary; Philip J. McEnroe, who for about twenty years was Insull's close friend and personal bookkeeper; and Samuel Insull, Jr.

be called honest. Politics demand, therefore, that I be brought to trial; but what is really being brought to trial is the system I represented."[2]

A Coast Guard cutter threaded its way through the bevy of tugboats and smaller craft, and two seaplanes hovered overhead. Absently, the old man continued: "This is the first time in thirty years that I've returned to New York without some one of my family to meet me."

One of the passengers said, "But your son is on one of these boats."

"My son is here? Where?" The old man bent over the rail and, through the early morning light, spotted the figure of a young man, also named Samuel Insull, waving from the deck of the cutter "Hudson." "Oh, Chappie! Chappie!" the old man shouted.

"Hello, dad. How are you doing?"

When the young man climbed aboard, the old man, trembling with excitement, turned to his fellow passengers and said, "Gentlemen, my brother—I mean, my son." As the two men embraced, the son thrust a piece of paper into his father's hand.[3]

From everywhere—from the tugs, from the cutter, seemingly even from the air and the sea—newspapermen and photographers swarmed onto the deck of the "Exilona." To still the confusion, the old man barked a command at two photographers who were jostling each other for position: "Keep quiet! There is plenty of time for taking pictures. But this is my mug and I have a proprietary interest in it."[4]

When the newsmen were hushed, the old man spoke again. With the defiant dignity of an aged lion, he announced, "I have a statement for the gentlemen of the press." Raising the crumpled piece of paper given him by his son, he read, in a crisp British accent, from a handwriting he had never seen before:

"I have erred, but my greatest error was in underestimating the effect of the financial panic on American securities and particularly on the companies I was working so hard to build.

[2] Burton Y. Berry, "Mr. Samuel Insull," p. 62. Berry, third secretary of the American Embassy at Istanbul, was Insull's guard on the return trip. This document, a typescript record of all Insull's shipboard conversations on this crossing, was made by Berry in May, 1934, and is now in the Samuel Insull Papers.

[3] *Time*, XXIII (May 14, 1934), 12–13. These events and conversations are summarized in virtually all New York and Chicago newspapers, May 7–8, 1934.

[4] Interview with James Kilgallen, New York, January 3, 1958. Kilgallen, a reporter for the Hearst papers, made the return trip on the "Exilona" with Insull.

"I worked with all my energy to save those companies. I made mistakes, but they were honest mistakes. They were errors in judgment but not dishonest manipulations.

". . . You only know the charges of the prosecution. Not one word has been uttered in even a feeble defense of me. And it must be obvious that there is also my side of the story.

"When it is told in court, my judgment may be discredited, but certainly my honesty will be vindicated."[5]

Later, on the train, came opportunity for a brief conference between the two Samuel Insulls. The ban on privacy—unofficial but rigorously enforced by agents of government and press—was still in effect, but they managed to be alone together for a brief moment in the washroom. Over the noise of the spigot and the train, Insull the elder said, "Where the hell did that statement come from?"

Replied Insull the younger, "A very bright fellow named Steve Hannagan. He's handling our publicity, and it's free. But you've got to do what he says."

Said the old man: "Hmph. All right."

And the Manhattan Limited sped into the sun, taking the two men to Chicago to face trial for a whole age.[6]

Fifty-three years earlier, in the evening of February 28, 1881, Samuel Insull had landed in New York for the first time, having crossed from Liverpool on the S.S. "City of Chester" to become private secretary to Thomas A. Edison. That the eager young Insull of 1881 had talent was obvious; otherwise he would hardly have been called across the ocean to such a job. But that he would grow to become America's most powerful businessman of the twenties—and its most publicized business villain in the early thirties—was no more predictable than that his family and his circumstances could have produced such a man in the first place. His family had for generations been of England's lower middle class—usually in its lowest stratum, sometimes hanging tenuously and tenaciously onto that thin ledge that separated it from the Respectable Poor, sometimes rising into a

[5] Chicago *Daily Illustrated Times, Chicago Daily News, Chicago American, Chicago Daily Tribune, New York Times,* May 7, 1934; *Time,* May 14, 1934.
[6] Interview with Samuel Insull, Jr. Since I have had more than a hundred interviews with Mr. Insull, Jr., no citations of specific dates of interviews with him will be offered here.

status approaching comfort, but never gaining the thrust or having the good fortune necessary for a rise into the upper middle class.[7]

On his mother's side, Insull was descended from artisans and farmers who had plodded their way through the centuries on the strength of their muscles, not their brains. Insull's maternal grandfather, John Short, was the first exception. As a young man he had broken the family ties, left his father's farm on Salisbury Plain, and hiked to London with his belongings done up in a bandana handkerchief. A considerable measure of the traditional English yeoman's tough-mindedness, determination, and practical sense had been accumulating in his line of the Short family, and John Short had enough of each to prosper on a modest scale. Ultimately he became a master mason of some distinction; he was a foreman at the building of the Victoria Tower, at the opposite end of the Houses of Parliament from Big Ben. His eldest son, George, followed his father's trade and became the master mason in the restoration of St. George's Chapel in Windsor Castle. There Prince Albert took an interest in him and arranged for George Short a good position in connection with army fortifications. From all accounts, Insull's mother, Emma Short, inherited the toughness of fiber and the practicality that distinguished this line of the Short family from its collateral branches.

On the Insull side, only in one instance had the family given hope of rising above mediocrity. Insull's paternal grandmother—whose family name was Martin—was descended from a line of successful dairymen. After several generations of toil, good management, and frugality, the Martins had managed to build a thriving dairy and acquire substantial acreage in the heart of what became London County. Thereupon John Martin, Insull's great-grandfather, turned to demon rum and drank up the dairy. Having been thus deprived

[7] Data on Insull's family background are derived from a packet of wills, genealogical statements, and marriage and birth records, collectively described as "Family Materials, 1799–1887," in the Samuel Insull Papers; and from the first six pages of the first draft of Insull's "Memoirs," an unpublished typescript dictated in the summer of 1934 and now in the Insull Papers. In the final draft of the "Memoirs," Insull deleted most of this material. Personal judgments of Insull's parents are my own, based upon the foregoing, interviews with Samuel Insull, Jr., and Edward Doyle, and fifty or sixty letters exchanged between parents and son over the period from 1881 to 1916. Most of these letters are in the Insull Papers; a few, covering the years 1881–92, are in the Edison Laboratory National Monument, West Orange, New Jersey.

of the opportunity for wealth through his wife, Insull's grandfather, William Insull, became a clerk in a lawyer's office, stumbled onto a modest pension, and plodded on in the rut worn by his forebears. His four sons became temperance crusaders.

Insull's father, Samuel (who in a characteristically self-effacing gesture, rechristened himself Samuel, Senior, when Insull entered the business world, so that his son would not have to call himself "Junior") , epitomized both the virtues and the faults of the Insulls. He was imaginative, clever, dedicated, and above all enthusiastic; he had much that it takes to rise above his fellows—except energy, practical sense, and fortitude. He lacked the down-to-earth quality that distinguishes the man of vision from the visionary. He was an idealistic, impractical, intellectual (though not of the university variety, for the universities were reserved to the upper classes) , eager to crusade for every manner of good cause. Unable, like his grandfather, to face or to make out in the world as it was, he re-treated into a theological and philosophical shell, from which he made occasional forays on behalf of one reform or another. Though he was neither good at nor much interested in earning a living, he could and often did campaign enthusiastically for a number of causes, including the Irish, the broadening of the suffrage, dis-establishment, and for various politicians with whom he was in sympathy. His favorite crusades, however, were temperance and religion. A lay preacher in the dissenting Congregational church, to which the Insulls had belonged for several generations, Insull Senior was happiest when he was in the pulpit saving souls or on the plat-form denouncing drunkenness.

It was probably the temperance crusade that first brought Insull Senior and Emma Short together. Her father was a minor hero to temperance workers: Not for theological reasons, but simply because it was not good business to be drunk on the job, John Short had been one of the first nine men in England to take the renowned temper-ance pledge, and he had indoctrinated his children with his own antipathy for strong drink. Whatever the origins of their affection, in 1853, at ages twenty-two and nineteen, Insull Senior and Emma Short were married.

But if Insull Senior married Emma because she espoused tee-totalism, he soon learned that he had made a good bargain, for she was as strong as he was weak and as realistic as he was impractical. The Insulls and the Shorts complemented one another in a way that promised to overcome the deficiencies of each. That which the Shorts traditionally lacked—imagination and a penchant for abstract thinking—was present to a fault in the Insulls. That which the Shorts had in abundance—backbone—was woefully inadequate in the Insulls. During the first six years of their marriage, in addition to keeping the wolf from the door while Sam crusaded, Emma bore him five children. The first three—two boys and a girl—died before the age of ten. The fourth, Joseph (born in 1858), was his father's son. A year later, on November 11, 1859, Samuel was born. Three more were to come—Emma, Martin, and Queenie; and Martin would be a man of great attainment—but Emma and Sam were to have the greatest reason for pride in producing young Sam. He combined all the aggressive toughness of the Shorts with all the enthusiasm and imagination of the Insulls.

Even more important than any of the family characteristics Insull inherited was his physical constitution. An ancient tradition holds that the energy of a family can accumulate for generations, if none expends it, and then, by some mutation, all be released into a single inheritor. So must it have been with Insull. Like the typical lower middle class Victorian, he was small, but his physical endurance was boundless and his energy was inexhaustible. He had a peculiar metabolic make-up. He invariably awoke early, abruptly, completely, bursting with energy; yet he gained momentum as the day wore on, and long into the night. (Later, as an adult, he learned to relax, but relaxation was a learned thing, to be resorted to only when he verged on physical collapse. Relaxation was an act of will; his body always told him to go and go and go.)

Before he was six years old, Sammy's near-demonic energy found a direction and created for him a life habit. Raw energy bred impatience with the lackadaisical way his father worked and thought and admiration for the brisk, efficient way his mother took charge and ran the affairs of the family. Natural love of mother and natural envy of father was thus compounded, and it was compounded still further by the father's preferential treatment of Joe, who was both the eldest son and the child most like his father. As he developed, young Sam grew progressively closer to his mother and away from his father; and in a curious inversion of conventional patterns, he imitated mother instead of father. From a tender age he was the natural leader among the young Insulls; in the absence of mama, he invariably took charge. Rebellion against his father thus seemed destined from the beginning. It was not, however, to be plunged into lightly, for the Victorian rule of absolute paternal authority was honored even in so mother-dominated a household as the Insulls'. The role of Insull's first fourteen years—part of it anyway—was to prepare him for the rebellious step.[8]

During Insull's first six years (1859–66) Insull Senior rented land and operated a small dairy in London. But what with his sporadic excursions to dabble in politics or preach a sermon, leaving to Emma responsibility for the children and the work load, the business was founded on shifting sand. When Insull was six there was enough money to send him and brother Joe to a Dame-school kindergarten —which Insull remembered as an adult only for the beatings the "estimable Dame" meted out in lieu of learning—but in London's great financial panic of 1866 the dairy slipped from Senior's loose grip. The family then migrated to Reading, where Senior found temporary employment and again young Sam and Joe attended a private school for a few months.

Then the family's fortune took a sudden upturn. During Gladstone's first ministry (1866–74) dissenters and temperance workers alike had their palmiest days, their first and only serious round of success. The United Kingdom Alliance, a sort of British national prohibition league, succeeded in electing several champions to Parliament, and though it failed in its main aim of securing a general local option prohibition law, it pushed three temperance measures through Parliament. More important to the fate of the Insulls, it acquired a £150,000 operating fund and was able to engage full-time secretaries in several districts. As a reward for dedicated service, Insull Senior was given a paid secretaryship in the Oxfordshire dis-

[8] The narrative of Insull's childhood is based primarily on his "Memoirs," pp. 5–14. In addition, scattered information is available in the collection of his public addresses in the Insull Papers; many of these were published, as *Central-Station Electric Service* (Chicago, 1915) and *Public Utilities in Modern Life* (Chicago, 1924). Information regarding the external circumstances of Insull's early life was derived largely by reading a file of the *London Times,* roughly for the years 1859–79, in the State Historical Society of Wisconsin.

trict. The job was coterminous with Gladstone's ministry, for when the Conservatives returned to power under Disraeli in 1874 the moment of glory of the United Kingdom Alliance was over. But the job gave the two brothers eight years in a good private school at Oxford, under the tutorship of Oxford students, and it opened the world to young Sam.[9]

Judging by his temperament and taste and the intellectual traits he showed in his teens, Sam's most obvious attributes as a student were by-products of his energy: a capacity for racing through large quantities of reading material, effortlessly perceiving its important assumptions and generalizations, and thoroughly assimilating its salient details. Less obvious was a related quality of mind. Quite unlike his father, who reasoned deductively from abstract principles or generalizations to particular situations or facts, Insull reasoned inductively from particulars to generalizations about them. Himself and his material surroundings—anything he could see or touch, or impalpable things that he could concretize in his mind—he could understand. Very early he learned to see to the heart of relations between things, or between men and things or men and men, and to grasp the underlying principles so clearly that he could perceive ways to shift them around a bit and make them work the better. Except in this practical manner, and in a natural aptitude for quantitative, arithmetic analysis of what he saw—the accountant's way of viewing things—he was never adept at pure abstraction. Hence, in his Oxford days, philosophy was gibberish to him, as was higher mathematics, but of history, political economy, and the classics (in translation) he had an easy ken.

The psychological effects of his years in Oxford were for Insull as important as the educational effects. He received there the first of three key personal rejections in his life that were to wound him deeply and help transform his inherent drive into a burning ambition to achieve Success and Respectability. Oxford was a church city, one in which the established Church of England prevailed, and in the 1860's dissenters there were as welcome as Jews in the Warsaw or Negroes in the Detroit of a later day. From time to time Sam and

[9] Insull, "Memoirs," pp. 4–5; *The Cyclopædia of Temperance and Prohibition* (New York, 1891), pp. 196–97; Arthur Shadwell, *Drink, Temperance and Legislation* (New York and London, 1915), pp. 106–8; "Temperance," in *Encyclopædia Britannica*, XXI (Chicago, 1959), 918–20; Osbert Burdett, *W. E. Gladstone* (London, 1927).

Joe were exposed to taunts because of their religion, taunts Insull recalled with obvious discomfort even in his mid-seventies.[10]

The Oxford experience also had several secondary effects. The exposure to Oxonian orthodoxy at school and the injections of radical Congregationalism at home effectively canceled one another, leaving Insull without much feeling one way or the other on the matter of religion. Without making much fuss about it or allowing it to color his practical judgment, he assumed that there was a God, and that was that. He became almost completely tolerant of the religious or irreligious beliefs of others. Instead of becoming intolerant of intolerance, he learned to weigh religious convictions and prejudices in evaluating others. There were two exceptions, each of which crept into his network of childhood prejudices and rooted deeply there before his religious judgments were firmly molded: a strong affinity for Irish Catholics and a moderate suspicion of Jews. The Irish were of unquestionable goodness because both in Gladstone's Liberal program and in Insull Senior's crusade against the established church, the Irish Catholics were lumped as allies with English dissenters. The Jews were of questionable goodness because Mr. Disraeli was the enemy and also because early Victorian mores had regarded them as untrustworthy.[11]

The Oxford period also gave direction to Insull by providing, in a curious manner, a faith with which he could identify himself. His was a rebellious generation: among others it produced George Bernard Shaw (whom Insull knew when both were in their teens),[12] Sidney and Beatrice Webb, and H. G. Wells, who in turn produced Fabian Socialism. These struck at Victorian stuffiness, at the class structure, and at upper middle class values. Insull was likewise a rebel, but the life he knew was one of lower middle class radicalism, and like the character Samuel Butler proposed to write a novel about,

---

[10] Insull, "Memoirs," p. 6.

[11] Insull's religious attitudes are drawn primarily from study of the patterns of persons with whom he surrounded himself in business; see chap. ix, below. He once explained these attitudes to his bookkeeper, Philip McEnroe (interview with McEnroe, Los Angeles, Sept. 10, 1958).

[12] In the late 1870's Shaw worked as a subordinate, more or less, to Insull in the battery room of the Edison Telephone Company in London; Insull, "Memoirs," p. 18, and "Rise and Development of the Electric Central Station," in *Public Utilities in Modern Life*, pp. 330–40. Shaw described the experience in the preface to the 1905 edition of his novel, *The Irrational Knot*.

Insull rebelled into orthodoxy. At Oxford he imbibed deeply of the classical Victorian values and prejudices, and he never lost them.

He eagerly embraced Victorian platitudes (Idle hands are the devil's workshop; An honest man is the noblest work of God; Time is money) and its prohibitions (Things are simply "done" or "not done"; One reveres one's family; One respects virtuous women and shuns the other kind; One places highest valuation upon a man's word and good name; One never openly displays emotion, affection, or familiarity) , and from these he acquired a strong, albeit imitative, sense of propriety.[13] Equally important to Insull was his own adaptation of hard-boiled utilitarianism (That is good which produces the greatest happiness to the greatest number; Only that which is useful is good; Survival of the fittest, and the devil take the hindmost) and of its sentimental, success-story counterpart, as taught by a Scotch writer with the improbable name of Samuel Smiles. Smiles was the author of a series of "inspirational" books, the most popular of which were his *Lives of the Great Engineers* and *Self-Help*. These books inspired Insull and thousands of other young Englishmen with the notion that if they would but display pluck, diligence, and determination, learn and exercise self-discipline, teach themselves various useful skills, and follow precepts of honesty, thrift, and prudence, then fame and fortune would inevitably follow. Like many others, Insull swallowed Smiles' message without reservation. The only thing that distinguished him from Smiles' other readers was that he applied the formula and made it work.[14]

By the time his Oxford days were over, Insull had embraced Victorianism à la Smiles with the combined fervor of a convert and of an outsider seeking to belong, and he had made up his mind what to do about it. For him the route to Respectability was the classic one, a career in business. Insull Senior had a different idea: he wanted Sam to become a minister. They soon disagreed openly. In February, 1874, when Insull was just turned fourteen, Gladstone's ministry

[13] This morality and outlook pervaded Insull's entire career; statements of it appear in many of his speeches, particularly those to his employees and to groups of young people. One of the clearest and simplest statements of it is in a letter he wrote to his son (Insull to Samuel Insull, Jr., April 25, 1916, in the Insull Papers) .
[14] Insull, "A Quarter-Century Anniversary," and "Looking Backward," in *Public Utilities in Modern Life*, pp. 133–37, 184–98; "Samuel Smiles," in the *Dictionary of National Biography, Twentieth Century Supplement, 1901–1911*, I, 322–25.

failed, and Senior's job with the U.K.A. shortly did the same. In the spring the family moved back to London so that Senior and Joe might have a better opportunity for employment; Sam's course was not yet decided. Joe found a job as a clerk with a chemical company, but his income was far from enough to support the family, let alone educate Sam for the ministry. As yet Senior had nothing permanent himself, but even so he persisted in his insistence that Sam become a minister. Young Sam was convinced that before a man can pray he must eat, and, secretly backed by his mother, he announced that he was going to find a job and would not be ordered or persuaded otherwise.[15]

Unable to cope with his rebellious son, Senior attempted to save face by seeing to it that it was through his own connections that Sam found a job. Thus father and son went to Ludgate Circus to pay a call on Senior's old friend and fellow temperance crusader, Thomas Cook, founder of the celebrated Cook and Sons Tourist Agency. One of the Cooks told them that a place could be found for Sam, but that he would have to wait several months. Senior demanded that Sam wait; Sam insisted that he was going to work immediately. A violent argument ensued. Sam finally ended it by walking out on the discussion and marching straight to the *Times* office to look for a job through the newspaper's want ads. He found one, as an office boy in a firm of auctioneers, at a salary of five shillings ($1.25) a week— two shillings a week less than it cost for railway fare and lunch, had not Sam been prepared to forego these luxuries, and had not mama quietly supplemented his income with pennies pilfered from her household allowance. On July 1, 1874, Insull began his fifty-eight-year career in business.[16]

Insull worked for the auctioneers four and a half years. Though the prime significance of the job itself lay in its termination, in it one of his key talents was first put to work: a capacity for learning the rudiments of one business which would serve him well in another. The firm's principal business was real estate, and what he learned of that business would be of immense use to him in later years. More

[15] Insull, "Memoirs," pp. 6–7.
[16] *Ibid.*, pp. 7–8; "Opportunity," in *Public Utilities in Modern Life*, pp. 199–200; Berry, "Mr. Samuel Insull," p. 21; Venton, Bull, and Cooper to Insull, June 30, 1874, in the Insull Papers.

important, the experience of those years was vital in crystallizing what he already was and in shaping what he was to become. Groping about for guidance, he found it in two men, and between them they shoved him headlong in the direction he was to go.

The head clerk in Insull's office was also the shorthand clerk and a young man of some enterprise and ability. On Sam's first day at work the clerk told Insull that his handwriting was abominable and that he must practice writing "pothooks and hangers" until his penmanship improved. The clerk, immediately impressed by Insull's enthusiasm and the speed with which he learned, began to teach him various subjects that would increase his usefulness around the office. As it happened, the clerk was much interested in music and wanted to devote all his spare time to its study but was unable to do so because he had an evening job as the stenographer of the editor of a weekly newspaper. He decided to free his evenings by teaching Insull shorthand and grooming him to take over part of the secretarial work. Insull leaped at the chance. He was unable to afford evening lessons at the Pitman Institute, but he bought Pitman shorthand instruction books and, under the clerk's direction, set about learning shorthand. Whether because he was really so diligent or because the clerk thrashed him soundly whenever his lessons fell short of what the clerk thought desirable, Insull worked at it long into the night, every night, until he had become an expert stenographer. Soon he was the assistant shorthand clerk in his office and was supplementing his income by work as a stenographer several evenings a week.[17]

After Insull had been with the auctioneers about two and a half years, the clerk arranged for him a regular evening job as stenographer to Thomas G. Bowles, and thus introduced him to a second guiding influence in this period. Bowles was the founder and editor of the highly successful *Vanity Fair,* a weekly magazine that interspersed gossipy paragraphs on finance and diplomacy with notes on society and fashion, cartoons, and spicy biographical sketches of eminent Londoners of the day. In addition to being a man of literary ability, Bowles was well versed in foreign and financial affairs, intimate with many important politicians, and able to gain entrance almost anywhere through his personal and family connections; later

[17] Insull, "Memoirs," pp. 8–10; Berry, "Mr. Samuel Insull," pp. 21–22.

he served a number of years as an influential Conservative in Parliament. From early in 1877 to some time in 1879 Insull went to Bowles' home about four nights a week to take dictation from eight until midnight; waiving sleep as unimportant, he customarily arose at four the following morning and transcribed his notes for delivery to the printers on his way to work. The job gave Insull twelve to fifteen dollars a week over his regular salary, and it gave him a good deal more in the way of intangibles. It sharpened his appetite for good literature, taught him something about influencing popular thinking through the printed word, endowed him with some measure of comfort in the presence of the mighty, and introduced him to high-level political intrigue.[18]

And now Sam began to run. Self-help, under his circumstances, meant self-education. Much of what he sought to learn was practical information: for example, he taught himself bookkeeping by buying standard works on accounting and keeping an imaginary set of double-entry books. He sought, as well, a general education; under Bowles' guidance, he devoured classic works in political economy, history, and literature. But reading, practical or otherwise, was not easy to arrange, for his schedule was crowded and time was short, and if he was to get where he was going—to Respectability and Success—he had to hurry. Accordingly, the mental habits he developed while learning were as important as the substance of what he learned. Because note-taking required too much time, he learned to commit to memory everything he read. Because reading was possible only in off moments—on a train, shaving, walking from place to place—he learned to gulp down and quickly digest what he read, and he developed a flexibility of mind that enabled him, at a moment's notice, to concentrate on a single subject, no matter how trivial, and to completely shut out everything else, no matter how pressing. And most important, because time was more than money —it was his very life—he learned to systematize and render efficient whatever he dealt with.[19]

[18] Insull, "Memoirs," pp. 10–11; "Opportunity," in *Public Utilities in Modern Life*, p. 202.

[19] Insull, "Memoirs," p. 15. Insull's early taste in reading is inferred from various of his reminiscing speeches. His purchases of books a little later (in the early and middle 1880's) , as recorded in bills preserved among Insull's papers in the Edison Laboratory National Monument, indicates a continued interest in the same subjects. Information

Somehow he managed a few diversions; his favorites were opera, cycling, and a literary society. Opera (and to a lesser extent the theater) was both a genuine love and an emotional outlet, for in each he could, without fear of embarrassment, vent his romantic imagination and dream grandiose dreams that ill suited a young London nobody on the make. But, characteristically, he turned his other amusements to useful ends. While cycling he memorized every road, every business establishment, a good many of the buildings in London and the adjoining counties. As a member of the literary society he kept abreast of current events outside the scope of *Vanity Fair*. And two experiences at meetings of the society had a profound effect upon the course of his life.[20]

Insull, who was secretary of the society, persuaded a visiting American celebrity to address the group. The lecture, entitled "The World Upside Down," Insull later described as "screamingly funny," but it was more than that: It was a lecture on publicity and promotion by the world's foremost publicist and promoter, Phineas T. Barnum. From this and subsequent contacts with the circus man Insull learned the principles of public relations, Barnum-style, and he learned them well.[21] Years later he parlayed these principles into efficient public relations techniques, and the popular support he gained thereby made more than one enterprise a success in the face of overwhelming odds. Indeed, Insull may be called the link between P. T. Barnum and Madison Avenue.[22]

A little later—in November, 1878—Insull was asked to address a weekly meeting of the literary society on the subject of self-help. At a loss for anything to say that the other members had not already read in Smiles' book, and as pressed for time as usual, Insull hit upon a short cut. He would find an American publication and draw material from it that would certainly be fresh to his group. At a newsstand he found just what he was looking for: a copy of *Scribner's Monthly*, containing an article about a thirty-one-year-old American

---

on Insull's mental habits, and how he acquired them, is derived from interviews with a score of persons, but particularly with his son and with three of his former private secretaries: Edward J. Doyle (interview in Northfield, Illinois, June 24, 1959) , John W. Evers, Jr. (Chicago, April 25, 1960) , and John J. O'Keefe (Chicago, Jan. 13, 1956) .

[20] Insull, "Memoirs," p. 13.
[21] Berry, "Mr. Samuel Insull," pp. 25–26.
[22] See pages 169–72, 177–86, below.

inventor named Thomas A. Edison. The article served Insull's purpose, and he gave a successful talk. But it also whetted his curiosity,
for if the author was sound in his analysis, Edison was the epitome of
the scientific and inventive spirit of the age, a man destined to tinker
around until he had transformed the world. Insull read everything
about Edison that he could find—and there was a great deal, for
Edison was just then perfecting the carbon transmitter that made
the telephone practical—and everything he read confirmed his
initial impression. Immediately Edison became Insull's hero. In less
than a year he became far more than that.[23]

The instrument of transformation was the second of three devastating blows to Insull's ego. On a Saturday morning just after New
Year's Day, 1879, Insull's boss called him in for an interview. By
this time, at the age of nineteen, Insull was the firm's chief shorthand
clerk and general superintendent of clerical personnel. The boss
reviewed Insull's four and a half years with the auctioneers, com-
mended his diligence, and then fired him. The reason, he explained,
was that an important customer, one worth a hundred pounds a year
to the firm, wanted his son to enter the business, and the following
Monday the son was to begin work as an articled clerk without
wages, eventually replacing Insull. Insull could take his time, of
course, about getting his work up to date before leaving. Doubtless
suppressing an urge to tell the boss where to go, Insull curtly informed him that his work was always up to date, and that he could
terminate his employment at noon.[24]

(Half a century later, Insull was still bitter about this episode.
In most matters he had the capacity to roll with the punches, to
forgive and forget, to endure much before retaliating. But in the
inner folds of his being, where his ego lived, was an untouchable
area, and even a modest affront there was unforgivable and unforget-
table.)

Crushed and humiliated, Insull returned to his desk. His first
impulse was to seek no steady job at all, to earn his way as a free-
lance stenographer, which was more lucrative than office work. But

[23] Insull, "Memoirs," pp. 16–17; "Looking Backward," in *Public Utilities in Modern Life*, p. 185. The article was William H. Bishop's "A Night with Edison," in *Scribner's Monthly*, XVII (November, 1878), 88–99.
[24] Insull, "Memoirs," pp. 13–14; Berry, "Mr. Samuel Insull," pp. 22–23.

on second thought he decided he needed the discipline a regular job would require, and he reluctantly picked up the morning *Times* to look for a job. One advertisement seemed ideal for his needs—an American banker in London needed a secretary, eleven to three daily. Insull wrote out a letter of application and offered his services for thirty shillings a week, which was half again his salary with the auctioneers. This turned out to be the lowest bid, and Insull was hired by the American.[25]

His new employer was Colonel George E. Gouraud, the resident director in London of the Mercantile Trust Company of New York. It soon developed that the hours Insull's services would be required were almost twice the number stated in the newspaper advertisement. It also turned out that Gouraud's principal activity was not banking at all; he was the European representative of Thomas Edison. On learning what he had stumbled into, Insull's heart, imagination, and ambition leaped all at once.

Gouraud found young Insull useful for all manner of duties in addition to those of a stenographer. He made him the head bookkeeper in the office, and he initiated Insull into corporate finance by taking him, as a secretary, to countless conferences with bankers and businessmen. Gouraud also encouraged his secretary to familiarize himself with the details of Edison's affairs, a task for which Insull hardly needed encouragement. He buzzed systematically through every scrap of paper concerning Edison that he could find in the office, and most of it he committed to memory. Consequently, in the fall of 1879, when Edward Johnson, Edison's chief engineer, came to London to supervise the installation of the first European telephone exchange, he found that Insull knew more about Edison's business affairs in Europe than did Gouraud and perhaps even Edison himself.[26]

Soon after Johnson arrived, Edison did something that transformed Insull's admiration into adulation. The Bell Telephone Company, which owned the basic patent on the telephone receiver, was racing to get a London exchange in operation before Edison, who owned the patent on the carbon transmitter, could do so. Edison had a head start, but Bell's lawyers obtained an injunction

[25] Insull, "Memoirs," pp. 14–15.
[26] *Ibid.*, pp. 15–21; Gouraud to Edison, Feb. 17, 1881, in the Insull Papers.

restraining Edison from using any receiver built on the principles covered by Bell's patent. In desperation Johnson and Gouraud cabled Edison, who responded immediately with instructions to proceed; he would, he said, invent a receiver based on entirely new principles and deliver it to London within sixty days. When Edison fulfilled his audacious promise, Insull determined to tie his own fate to that of the inventor.[27]

To do so, he decided, he must do two things: learn everything he could about the technical aspects of Edison's doings, and become intimate with Johnson. He began to spend every available moment with Johnson's engineers, pestering them with questions and making himself as useful a nuisance as possible by working for them in every way he could, from carrying their pliers to stringing wires. When the first small switchboard was installed, Insull temporarily acted as its first operator, and he managed to work in some capacity at every public demonstration of the telephone. After a few months, the opportunity came for closer relations with Johnson. One weekend Johnson, who was ill and sorely in need of secretarial help on some memoranda he was preparing in connection with further patent litigation, was complaining loudly about the laziness of Englishmen who refused to work on weekends. Insull eagerly volunteered to come to Johnson's home and do the work without pay. The engineer accepted the offer, and soon Insull was doing all his secretarial work.[28]

As the two grew closer Insull built well upon the favorable initial impression he had made on Johnson. Observing the young man's keenness, his quickness at grasping the principles underlying technical problems, and above all his ability to systematize complex business affairs, Johnson soon conceived an ideal function for him. While Edison was always doggedly systematic and practical regarding the invention he had on his mind at a given moment, he conducted his personal and business affairs in a slipshod manner that, as often as not, left them hopelessly chaotic. It occurred to Johnson (probably

[27] Insull, "Memoirs," pp. 18–19. According to Edison's most able biographer (Matthew Josephson, *Edison: A Biography*, New York, 1959, p. 150), the feat actually took three months. In an interview with the writer (in New York, March 17, 1959), Josephson confided that Edison's receiver was quite inferior, but the achievement mightily impressed young Insull, nonetheless.
[28] Insull, "Memoirs, pp. 21–22.

by way of a hint from Insull) that Insull was just the sort of fellow Edison ought to have around as a private secretary and general business nursemaid. There ensued a complex bit of minor intrigue (an art at which Insull was precociously gifted and would later become a master); Johnson wrote two of Edison's close associates exactly what he had in mind, and they concurred, but lest they offend Edison they merely told him that Insull was a bright young man he should hire whenever a suitable vacancy occurred. Then Johnson, Insull, and Edison privately agreed that Colonel Gouraud should not be told of Insull's eagerness to work for Edison, lest it prejudice him against Insull. Meanwhile, word leaked out that Insull was anxious to go to America. An American banker in London promptly offered him a job with Drexel, Morgan and Company in New York, but Insull had set his mind on a single goal. In August of 1880, after several months of such confusion, Edison called Johnson home; the telephone mission had been accomplished and Edison needed Johnson to help him with his efforts to develop a workable system of electric lighting. But when Johnson left London, he and Insull had an understanding that should he send for Insull, it would be to become Edison's private secretary.[29]

So now Insull waited, but the wait was neither idle nor long. He reread every one of Edison's European contracts, and he took it upon himself to write weekly letters to Johnson, summarizing the fluctuations in the telephone situation and outlining Edison's shifting interests in connection with it. These letters proved to be the best selling points Johnson could have in recommending Insull. He showed them to Edison and sometimes made Insull rather than the telephone business the topic of conversation. In January, 1881, the break came: Edison's private secretary suddenly resigned. Johnson immediately cabled Insull to come over as soon as possible. His explanatory letter was mailed on a ship that broke a shaft in mid-ocean, and by the time further details reached London Insull was on his way to New York.[30]

[29] *Ibid.*, pp. 22–23; Insull to Edison, April 7, 1880, and Johnson to Edison and Charles Batchelor, June, 1880, both in the Edison Laboratory National Monument. Several months before Johnson left, Edison offered Insull a different job, but it required a speaking knowledge of French, a skill Insull lacked. Insull to Edison, April 7, 1880, in Edison Laboratory National Monument.
[30] Insull, "Memoirs," p. 24; Josephson, *Edison*, p. 253.

Insull's family and friends insisted that he was foolish to leave a good job and excellent connections to chase off to America on the strength of nothing more than a brief cable. It could be somebody's prank, and even if it were from Johnson it contained no promises. It did not even mention salary, and, after all, Sammy was earning, at the age of twenty-one, half as much as did the cashier of the Bank of England.[31] Furthermore, who was Edison? Doubtless a clever fellow, but what future was there in the kind of tinkering he was doing? Besides, had not the world's foremost electrical scientists denounced Edison's alleged electrical inventions as extravagant and visionary claims?[32]

To have been swayed by such objections would have been completely out of character for Insull. One of his most deep-rooted traits—one that derived perhaps from his energy, perhaps from his life history, possibly even from his body chemistry—was that he was absolutely unable, save on an abstract and purely intellectual level, to imagine the possibility of his own failure; he entirely lacked the sense of caution of those who doubt themselves. (Later, he learned to behave cautiously under certain circumstances; but caution, like relaxation, was unnatural to him. His instincts were always so incautious that he could take huge risks without even realizing that he was gambling.)

Besides, his mother was the boss in the family, and she agreed that Sam should go. She imposed only one condition: he must promise never to take a drink of liquor. That promise he cheerfully made and never broke. With her consent, he booked passage and began to make arrangements for the voyage. On February 16 he entrained from London, and the next day he sailed from Liverpool.[33]

---

[31] Insull, "Memoirs," pp. 24–25. Insull was earning about £400 a year; the salary of the clerk of the Bank of England was about £800.

[32] According to Insull, when he first wrote home to a friend that he had seen the Edison system in operation, the friend replied that "it had not taken me very long to acquire the habit of the Yankees to pull the long bow." Insull, "Looking Backward," in *Public Utilities in Modern Life*, p. 194. The *New York Herald*, April 27, 1879, in an article entitled "What Has Mr. Edison Discovered," reported that "well-informed electricians did not believe that Mr. Edison is even on the right line of experiments." W. E. Sawyer, a celebrated electrical innovator, said that Edison's efforts were doomed to "final, necessary, and ignominious failure." For an excellent account of Edison's work on the electric light, and of the skepticism—as well as occasional enthusiastic praise—concerning it see Josephson, *Edison*, pp. 177–250.

[33] Insull, "Memoirs," p. 24.

Until the "City of Chester" landed in New York, Insull's most obvious attributes were self-confidence and enthusiasm. Sixty seconds after he debarked his self-confidence was shaken, and within half an hour the only thing he was sure of was that he had blundered in leaving London. But before the first night was over he knew that a new world was aborning and that he was to have a vital hand in its creation.

The ship arrived at dusk on the 28th of February.[34] Johnson greeted Insull at the dock with the news that he was leaving for London at five the next morning. Insull's heart sank; he had counted on Johnson, as his only friend in America, to pave his way, to ease him into his new job. But there was no time for dismay, even as a reaction, for they had a frantic night's work ahead. They went directly to meet Edison, and as they rode Johnson quickly briefed Insull. Edison had completed his experiments on electric lighting, having demonstrated at his labs in Menlo Park that his light not only worked successfully but could be supplied at a rate cheaper than the equivalent price for gas ("We will make electric light so cheap," he said, "that only the rich will be able to burn candles") . Accordingly, he was closing up his headquarters in Menlo Park and establishing offices for the Edison Electric Light Company at 65 Fifth Avenue in New York in order to start the commercial exploitation of the Edison incandescent lighting system. Simultaneously, he was beginning the construction of what he called an electric central station, a system of dynamos and wires and underground cables through which he proposed to light, from a single source, buildings all over an area of almost a square mile in the financial district in lower Manhattan.

Johnson and Insull pulled up at 65 Fifth Avenue and went in to see Edison. Insull looked at Edison, and Edison looked at Insull, and both were disappointed; each said to himself, "My God! He's so young!" Insull was twenty-one and looked sixteen; he was skinny, popeyed, fuzzy-cheeked; his dress was impractically impeccable and

[34] The following account of Insull's first encounter with Edison is a much-quoted one; it is based upon Insull's recollections, as confirmed by Edison and first published in the "official" Edison biography, Frank L. Dyer, Thomas C. Martin, and W. H. Meadowcroft, *Edison: His Life and Inventions* (2 vols.; New York, 1910) , and republished in Insull, *Central-Station Electric Service*, pp. xxvi–xxxiii. That their mutual reaction was "My God! He's so young!" is not in the published account; it is derived from an interview with Samuel Insull, Jr. The physical description of Edison is Insull's; that of Insull is mine, based upon an examination of photographs of Insull and Insull's statement of his measurements (5' 8", 117 lbs.) in his "Memoirs," p. 12.

his manner was impractically formal. His Cockney accent was so thick that Edison had difficulty understanding him. Mouth agape, he stared at his hero. Edison had just turned thirty-four. He wore a seedy black Prince Albert coat and waistcoat, black trousers that looked as if they had been slept in, a large sombrero, a rough brown overcoat, and a white silk handkerchief around his neck, tied in a careless knot and falling over the front of a dirty white shirt. His hair was long and shaggy; he was beardless but ill-shaven. His manner was as casual as Insull's was formal. His middle western accent was so thick that Insull had difficulty understanding him. Over-all, the only saving feature was "the wonderful intelligence and magnetism of his expression, and the extreme brightness of his eyes." But here was the man who had invented the stock ticker, the multiplex telegraph, the mimeograph machine, the phonograph, and the transmitter that made the telephone practical; the man who said he had invented and was about to give to the world electric lighting, electric power, and electric transportation; the man who would invent, in the next decade, the motion picture and discover the principles that made possible radio and television. Despite Edison's appearance, Insull understandably stood awed.

After the introductions, Johnson showed Insull into an upstairs back room which he would share as sleeping quarters with one of Edison's engineers, then whisked him off to meet Mrs. Johnson and Mrs. Edison and gulp down a quick dinner. By eight o'clock they were back at Edison's office, ready to work all night. Before that night was over, Edison was a bit awestruck himself.

They got right down to business. Edison explained that his financial backers had invested half a million dollars in his electric inventions, but refused to invest any more for manufacturing them or for building a central station to use them, and he was determined to start the enterprises with his own resources. He pulled out a checkbook and told Insull he had a cash balance of $78,000. To finance his new undertakings, he was ready to sell everything he owned. The most valuable thing he owned was his European telephone securities, and he was sending Johnson to Europe to sell them. They wanted Insull's advice on the best place to sell each of the dozens of kinds of securities, how to go about it, and how much could be realized upon them. To the last detail, Insull had the information in his head, together with every other item of potentially useful information about Edison's affairs in Europe. By four in the morning, when Johnson had to leave to catch his ship, Insull had gone through Edison's books and worked out a schedule of Edison's European patent rights, against which additional money could be borrowed. From that moment, Insull was Edison's financial factotum.[35]

At five o'clock Insull put Johnson on his ship and returned to his new home for a few hours of sleep before starting the day's work. The vehicle he returned in was pulled by animals, as vehicles had been pulled when man first devised the wheel. The building he went to was illuminated by fire, as primitive man had illuminated his cave. Most of the machines in it were operated by hand, as machines had been operated when the caveman first employed a fulcrum and lever; a few were relatively modern, being operated by belts attached to steam engines, as they had been operated for the century that steam engines had existed. But all that was about to change.

The next day, which began an hour or two later, Edison asked Insull what salary he wanted; Insull replied that whatever suited Edison suited him. Edison said he would start him at a hundred dollars a month; Insull replied that that would be satisfactory. Edison added that he would probably arrange for him to become secretary, or occupy other executive positions, in the various electric companies he was organizing, and that if Insull did well he would soon be making a good deal more. Only then did he ask how much Insull had been making, and only then did Insull tell him that he had been making almost twice the amount Edison had agreed to pay him. ("If you pushed Edison in money matters," Insull said many years later, "he was as stingy as hell, but if you left the matter to him he was as generous as a prince." At the end of his first year Edison gave him a bloc of stock worth $15,000.)[36]

Insull's duties and hours were as vague as his salary. Edison told

[35] Berry, "Mr. Samuel Insull," pp. 33–34; Josephson, *Edison,* pp. 253–54. The figure Insull stated to Berry is recorded at $82,000, but this was evidently either a slip by Insull or a misrecording by Berry, for whenever Insull told the story he cited the figure $78,000.

[36] Insull, "Memoirs," pp. 31–32; Berry, "Mr. Samuel Insull," p. 34. Judging from letterheads preserved in the Edison Laboratory National Monument, Insull became corporate secretary of virtually all Edison's companies during the first month with Edison; all such jobs paid him a salary.

him simply to take charge of his correspondence and do whatever else was necessary to get his office work running smoothly and systematically. Sometimes he was assigned specific duties, such as supervising the canvassing of the district around the proposed central station and working out careful tables of how many persons would convert from how many gas burners to how many electric lights, how much it would cost to serve them, and the like; such activities were important to the commercial success of Edison's venture. At other times Insull's duties were formal, such as acting as secretary to Edison's various companies; again, they were a hodgepodge, ranging from buying his clothes to financing his business. At all times, Insull held Edison's power of attorney, signed his checks, and answered his mail, at first usually with no more than a cryptic note from Edison ("Yes" or "No") to serve as a guide, later with none at all. Otherwise, he assumed duties as he saw fit, and the more he assumed, the more Edison was pleased. He systematized Edison's office, without attempting to systematize Edison's own activities. "Edison's whole method of work," Insull later recalled, "would upset the system of any business office. He cared not for the hours of the day or the days of the week. I would get at him whenever it suited his convenience. . . . I used more often to get at him at night than in the day time, as it left my days free to transact his affairs." In the regular night-long sessions, Edison might transact business, or set Insull to work watching a meter, or spend the entire night explaining to him the complex technology of what he was about.[37]

The day work was as exhilarating as the night work was instructive. To 65 Fifth Avenue came a continuous procession of curious celebrities, asking to see the inventor and his magic lamp. Famous actors (Sarah Bernhardt, Joseph Jefferson), politicians and heads of state (everybody who was anybody at Tammany, President Diaz of Mexico), newspapermen (James Gordon Bennett, the Pulitzer brothers), and financiers (J. P. Morgan, E. P. Fabbri, J. Hood Wright, Henry Villard) were regular visitors.[38]

And the men around Edison were an exciting band: a lusty, free-

[37] Insull, "Memoirs," pp. 28–29; "Samuel Insull, 1881," folder in Edison Laboratory National Monument, especially letters to Gouraud, June 3, June 11, June 17, July 1, July 8, 1881; and William Carman to Edison, telegram, March 3, 1881, and Insull to John F. Randolph, Aug. 29, 1881, in "Menlo Park, 1881" folder.
[38] Josephson, *Edison*, pp. 244, 252; Insull, "Memoirs," pp. 29–30.

wheeling, hard-swearing gang, readily identifiable by their steady stream of vulgarisms based on insults to their dearest enemy, the gas company (one of the few not obscene: "He lied like a gas meter"). At first, the little Cockney who ran Edison's business was a lonely misfit among them, until he demonstrated that he could learn more quickly, work more furiously, and swear more fluently than any of them, the boss included, and then they accepted him. More important, they respected him: not merely because he was the Chief's favorite, but because they all soon learned—some of them painfully—that Sam Insull could run just as hard and just as fast when the going was rough or there was someone underfoot being trampled as he could on a smooth track.[39]

[39] Descriptions of the men around Edison are legion. The best secondary account is Josephson's; the best primary account—though one marked by numerous errors, some apparently deriving from personal bias—is Francis Jehl, *Menlo Park Reminiscences* (3 vols.; Dearborn, Mich., 1937–41). An excellent description of Insull's role among them is contained in Alfred O. Tate, *Edison's Open Door* (New York, 1938), pp. 52–53, 261–66. Tate became Insull's secretary in May, 1883, and later succeeded Insull as Edison's private secretary.

CHAPTER II *Insull on the Mohawk*

Had Edison's invention been more trivial—had he merely built a better candle or kerosene lamp or gas burner—marketing it would have been simpler, for improvements upon these crude sources of firelight could be immediately used with existing devices. But to make his light usable, Edison had first to invent every component of an electric generating and distribution system, and then to create a manufacturing industry to make them, an engineering organization to install them, and a central station industry to buy them. Furthermore, he had to do so without the aid of his financial backers and, as it turned out, over the almost impassable obstacles they imposed.[1]

[1] The Edison bibliography is large. Full-length biographies include Frank L. Dyer, Thomas C. Martin, and W. H. Meadowcroft, *Edison: His Life and Inventions* (2 vols.; New York, 1910); William A. Simonds, *Edison: His Life, Work, Genius* (Indianapolis, 1934); and Matthew Josephson, *Edison: A Biography* (New York, 1959). Valuable reminiscences include Francis Jehl's *Menlo Park Reminiscences* (3 vols.; Dearborn, Mich., 1937–41); Alfred O. Tate's *Edison's Open Door* (New York, 1938); and, in some ways the most important of all, Insull's unpublished "Memoirs." A number of articles relating to Edison during the years of Insull's direct association with him (1881–92) appeared in *Electrical World* and *Scientific Monthly*. Two recent scholarly works are valuable: Harold C. Passer's *The Electrical Manufacturers, 1875–1900* (Cambridge, 1953) and Arthur A. Bright, Jr., *The Electric-Lamp Industry* (New York, 1949). The following account draws on these sources but is based primarily on manuscripts in the Edison Laboratory National Monument, West Orange, New Jersey; the Henry Villard Papers in the Houghton Library, Harvard University; the Samuel Insull Papers; and Insull's "Memoirs." Useful as their works are, Passer and Bright did not use these vital manuscript sources, and their accounts suffer accordingly. Josephson did use them, and his work is by far the best ever done on Edison. Herein, apart from a few details, I differ with Josephson only in emphasis: he was concerned with Edison, I am concerned with Insull. Our interpretations of the following events are fundamentally in agreement.

As an engineering feat, Edison's achievement is without parallel. When he undertook the building of the pioneer central station, at Pearl Street in lower Manhattan, he had already worked out the three cardinal innovations that made it possible—the incandescent lamp, a relatively efficient dynamo, and the multiple distribution system—but hundreds of minor parts of a complete electrical system had yet to be devised. He had to develop practical switches, sockets, cables, junction boxes, wires, insulators, fuses, meters, filaments, voltage regulators, and scores of other devices, and to teach subordinates how to put them together once he figured out how to make them. He did it all, and for practical purposes he did it alone. He had craftsmen and mechanics to help him, to be sure, but these were simply so many extra arms and legs, not extra brains.[2] All those who might have helped—the world's electrical "experts," such men as Joseph Swan, Professor Henry Morton, Conrad Cooke, and W. E. Sawyer—were unavailable, for they were busily engaged in thinking up reasons why Edison's efforts were doomed to fail.[3]

As a business venture, building the first central station was so audacious as to be called foolhardy, largely because Edison's financial backers so regarded it. Edison's electrical experiments (1878–80) had been financed, and his patents were held, by a syndicate of bankers, notably J. P. Morgan and several of his partners, through a corporation formally styled the Edison Electric Light Company but referred to by Edison and his intimates as "the leaden collar." As soon as a primitive form of the lamp was ready for commercial exploitation, it developed that Edison and his backers had irreconcilable views of the best method of exploitation. The bankers believed that the proper market was for so-called isolated plants: systems designed for lighting a single large building and operated from a "powerhouse" in the basement, much as a steam-radiator heating system is operated. This method had the short-range virtues of requiring small capital outlay and promising quick returns, whereas

[2] For the details of these inventions, Jehl's *Menlo Park Reminiscences* are most valuable, though difficult to follow because of slipshod organization. Josephson, *Edison*, pp. 175–250, and Passer, *Electrical Manufacturers*, pp. 78–128, are balanced accounts and appraisals.
[3] See, for example, the *New York Herald*, April 27, 1879; *New York Times*, Dec. 28, 1879. A good summary of the opinions of "experts" as of 1879 and 1880 is in Insull, *Central-Station Electric Service*, pp. 9–13.

Edison's plan for central stations was slow, risky, and expensive. Edison conceded that isolated plants should be sold to help raise money for developing his first central station, as well as for their incidental publicity; and for this reason he formed the Edison Company for Isolated Lighting, which licensed local organizations in major cities with the exclusive right to sell Edison equipment in their areas. But this was only a stopgap concession, for Edison was unalterably convinced that the great future for electricity lay in central station service. The bankers were as cool toward the central station as Edison was toward isolated plants and, having advanced and received no return on upwards of $500,000, they absolutely refused to advance any more for either Edison's central station or the sizable manufacturing works that Edison's route would entail.[4]

Thus to make his inventions commercially successful, Edison faced an absurd situation. He not only had to do without the aid of his financial backers, but, since they owned the patents, had to pay them for the right to use his limited personal resources and credit to finance a succession of companies which could make, sell, and buy his own inventions. To make the products he formed the Edison Lamp Company, the Edison Machine Works, the Edison Shafting Company, the Electrical Tube Company, and S. Bergmann and Company; to promote and sell them he used the Isolated Lighting Company and also created the Thomas A. Edison Construction Department; to buy them he formed first the Edison Electric Illuminating Company of New York, which built the Pearl Street Station, and then a score of smaller central station companies. Each of these, the manufacturers, the sellers, and the buyers, had to pay patent royalties to the Edison Electric Light Company for its use of Edison's inventions.[5]

The resulting organization was as active and as rational as a queenless beehive, and the confusion was compounded by Edison's own curious personal make-up. Like all persons of colossal creativity,

---

[4] Josephson, *Edison,* pp. 187–91, 201, 222–23, 234, 236–37, 247–48, 293–98, 340–41, 361–65.

[5] Passer, *Electrical Manufacturers,* pp. 84–96; Bright, *Electric-Lamp Industry,* pp. 60, 80; John W. Hammond, *Men and Volts: The Story of General Electric* (New York, 1941), pp. 21, 402. These writers, not having examined the manuscripts in the Edison Laboratory National Monument, do not show the appreciation for Edison's difficulties with his financial backers that Josephson shows.

Edison was possessed of a colossal ego. Hence, systematic as he was when pursuing his own ends, he had an almost pathological hostility to any form of system, order, or discipline imposed from without. Hence his wildly irregular orgies of work and sleep, his sneers at scientists, his cruel practical jokes on his mathematicians, his horror of account books.[6] Hence, too, his invaluable habit of paying careful attention at all points to the economics of his inventions, and his seemingly contradictory habit of abandoning all sensible business methods at unpredictable and sometimes critical moments. (Said Insull, years later, "We never made a dollar until we got the factory 180 miles away from Mr. Edison.")[7] And hence, also, his compulsive need and his almost incredible ability to be simultaneously in the center, at the periphery, and on top of his multifaceted ventures.

As a manager of men Edison was a driver, not a leader, demanding from his subordinates the same single-minded devotion to work that he himself gave. Most of his associates, as a consequence, were simply devoted underlings who did what he told them to do, and only a few, who could work at his own killing pace, were permitted to exercise initiative. Johnson became Edison's promoter-in-chief, Charles Batchelor was made the top executive and given charge of co-ordinating the various companies, and Francis Upton, Ernest Bergmann, and John Kruesi were entrusted with the direct supervision of individual companies. But not even these men were required or allowed to think for themselves. That was Edison's exclusive prerogative. That is, so it was until Insull arrived.[8]

[6] Edison's work habits are well described in the several works cited earlier. As for his sneers at scientists, see his testimony in *Edison Electric Light* v. *United States Electric Company*, Circuit Court of the Southern District of New York, IV, 2571–73, Hearings of June 19, 1890; and Josephson, *Edison*, pp. 278–79, 283, 357. Insull tells an oft-repeated story of Edison and his mathematicians: he once kept a pair of them working all night in a futile effort to learn the exact cubic contents of a 16-candlepower lamp, then showed them how to "calculate" it the next morning. He simply filled a bulb with water, poured its contents into a graduated glass, and announced the results. Insull, "Memoirs," p. 34. On Edison's attitude toward accounting see, for example, Insull to Edison, Aug. 3, Oct. 20, 1887, in the Edison Laboratory National Monument; and Josephson, *Edison*, p. 296.

[7] The capricious side of Edison's business habits has been generally ignored or passed over lightly. For examples of it see Insull to Alfred O. Tate, June 4, Sept. 2, 1887; and Insull to Edison, Jan. 7, Jan. 20, 1888, in the Edison Laboratory National Monument. The quotation is from Alex Dow's report of the Lamp Committee of the Association of Edison Illuminating Companies, Jan. 16–20, manuscript copy in the Insull Papers.

[8] The generalizations in this and the following two paragraphs are based upon the specific events narrated and sources cited in the remainder of this chapter.

Insull's role in this melange was to rationalize it, to make it work. That was not what he had been hired for; he was hired as the personal flunky of the Great Man, and long after he began taking on more important tasks, he continued to answer Edison's mail, write his checks, fetch his umbrella, buy his clothes, and serve as companion, confidant, valet, night watchman, alarm clock, common laborer, financial adviser and trouble shooter. But Edison was ready, after the first day, to entrust him with far more, and in the ensuing months he was quick to perceive three things about the skinny young man from London that qualified him uniquely to take full charge of Edison's business affairs. The first was his absolute devotion to Edison: He could and would mangle anybody, high or low, who stood in Edison's way. The second was that he worked even longer and harder than did Edison himself, and he did so with almost unbelievable speed. The third was that he could render anything— even Edison's kaleidoscopic doings—orderly and efficient.

And that was to be Insull's job, for nearly twelve years with Edison and for forty years thereafter: to make the Edison system work.

For the men around Edison, 1881 to 1885 was a period of frenzied activity and boundless optimism. During the first year and a half, all energies were devoted to building the pioneer electric plant, until September 4, 1882, when Edison completed his engineering miracle by beginning the permanent operation of the Pearl Street Station. Seldom has the dawn of an age been so well heralded, and seldom has the morning after been so anticlimactic. Indeed, there was soon reason to suspect that the whole idea was a mistake. Not because the Pearl Street investment as such was a bad one; though it lost money during its first two years, the publicity attending it was sufficient to rouse another fifty or sixty thousand dollars out of the investors, so that Edison more or less broke even on the venture. But he had planned it as a showpiece, primarily designed to promote central stations everywhere, and in this respect it was a failure. Investors by the score read of the achievement, marveled at it, and kept their money in their pockets.[9]

To Edison's chagrin, the light proved most salable in the form that he considered unsound: the isolated plant proved to be as easy to sell as the central station was difficult. By the spring of 1883, there

[9] Josephson, *Edison*, pp. 251–67; Jehl, *Menlo Park Reminiscences*, III, 1030–88.

were 334 isolated plants in operation and the Pearl Street plant was still almost alone as a central station.[10]

This early trend of the business widened the rift between Edison and his backers and, incidentally, resulted in Insull's first major assignment. The backers, impatient for profits after four years without a return on their investment, now demanded that Edison promote isolated plants. Edison refused, and in the spring of 1883, having demonstrated by six months of successful operation that his central station worked, he set out to found an industry with it as a model. He formed the Thomas A. Edison Construction Department, put Insull in charge of it, and told him to go out and sell and build central stations.[11]

For the next eighteen months Insull traveled the country over, selling the Edison system. Doing so was rarely a matter of simple salesmanship; it was such only when a city had neither a corrupt common council nor a gas lighting company. If the council was corrupt, some kind of personal, extralegal arrangement normally had to be made before a franchise was forthcoming; if there was a gas company, the council had usually been bought beforehand, and promoting an electric company involved outwitting both politicians and competitors. At this form of promotion and salesmanship Insull proved to be extremely adroit, and with others he quickly sold and installed plants in Piqua and Tiffin, Ohio; Sunbury and Harrisburg, Pennsylvania; Fall River and Brockton, Massachusetts; Newburgh, New York, and a score of other places.[12]

[10] Passer, *Electrical Manufacturers*, pp. 112–17, is an account of the growth of the Edison Company for Isolated Lighting; a running account of the progress of the company, as well as of central station sales, is in the *Bulletin of the Edison Electric Light Company* (published periodically in New York); see especially bulletins 11 (June 27, 1882), 14 (Oct. 14, 1882), 15 (Dec. 20, 1882), 18 (May 31, 1883), and 22 (April 9, 1884). Passer sets the number of isolated plants in operation on Oct. 1, 1883, as 221; the *Bulletin* of May 31, 1883, pp. 30–38, lists 334 isolated plants as of that date. See also Letter Books E1730 and E1731, in the Edison Laboratory National Monument.

[11] Third Annual Report of the Edison Electric Illuminating Company of New York (Dec. 11, 1883), published in the *22d Bulletin of the Edison Electric Light Company* (April 9, 1884), pp. 16–19; "Electric Light, 1883, Samuel Insull, Tour of Stations," manuscript file in Edison Laboratory National Monument; Josephson, *Edison*, pp. 268–73.

[12] Josephson, *Edison*, pp. 270–71; Insull, *"Memoirs,"* pp. 39–40; Insull to Tate, Sept. 30, Oct. 10, Oct. 15, Oct. 19, Oct. 23 (2 letters), Oct. 24, Nov. 7, 1883; Letter Books of T. A. Edison Construction Department, 1883, 1884, especially Tate to Insull, Oct. 13, Oct. 29, Nov. 7–9, 1883; and S. B. Eaton to Insull, March 1, 1884; all in Edison Laboratory National Monument; Annual Report of the Edison Electric Light Company,

The success of this activity forced a showdown over control of Edison's various enterprises. Edison's dispute with his financiers now had two interconnected aspects, involving a conflict of interests. On the one hand, as to patent royalties, the major-city companies that were licensed to sell isolated plants made direct cash payments to the parent Edison Electric Light Company, whereas the central stations paid smaller royalties and paid them, more often than not, in stock —for which there was no market—instead of in cash. On the other hand, when the central station business began to take root, Edison's manufacturing concerns began to make money, as Edison had expected. The financiers determined to gain control of the now more lucrative manufacturing companies, and in July, 1884, they made overtures in that direction. At the same time, Edison and his associates determined to shake off the Light Company's leaden collar; to reorganize it, to gain control of it, to make it less burdensome.[13]

Insull had already devised a plan. From the outset he resented the obstructions Morgan and the other bankers placed in the way of his idol, and he soon developed devious means for circumventing many of them. When S. B. Eaton, Morgan's lawyer and the president of the Edison Light Company, caught Insull in this and severely reprimanded him, Insull took it as a special kind of personal affront and immediately swore revenge. Without pausing to dwell on the audacity of a twenty-two-year-old secretary's daring to fight the great J. P. Morgan, Insull began scheming to throw Eaton out. When Edison himself decided to battle the bankers, he found Insull bristling with ideas. Edison and his intimates held only a fraction of the stock of the company, Insull reasoned, but Morgan and his associates held less than a full controlling interest between them, and Edison's prestige among the other minority stockholders was enormous. The suitable tactic was therefore to solicit proxies from the minority

published in *20th Bulletin of the Edison Electric Light Company,* Oct. 31, 1883, pp. 41–50; Passer, *Electrical Manufacturers,* p. 99. The organization through which this work was done was the Thomas A. Edison Construction Department. For an example of Insull's political doings see Insull to Tate, Nov. 7, 1883. For a frank description of the political problems involved see Tate, *Edison's Open Door,* pp. 98–100.
[13] Passer, *Electrical Manufacturers,* pp. 98–100; Insull, "Memoirs," pp. 39–40, 51; Josephson, *Edison,* pp. 294–97; Edison to S. B. Eaton, April 24, 1884; Edison to Henry Villard, April 25, 1884; S. B. Eaton to Edison, April 26, 1884; Notice of Special Meeting of the Stockholders of Edison Electric Light Company, May 8, 1884; Insull to stockholders of Edison Machine Works, Aug. 22, 1884; all letters in Edison Laboratory National Monument.

stockholders. Through the summer of 1884, Insull and two of Edison's other assistants gathered proxies. By the middle of October Edison had more than 3,000 of them in his safe, and only 3,500 were needed. In the face of this strength, Morgan and his associates decided, as Insull put it, to surrender gracefully and "give Edison what he wanted." (Added Insull, gleefully, "There is no one more anxious after wealth than Samuel Insull, but there are times when revenge is sweeter than money.") [14]

At a special meeting of the stockholders of the Edison Light Company held at the end of October, Morgan's man Eaton was replaced as president by a figurehead, Dr. Eugene Crowell, the active top executive position was given to Johnson, and sufficient substitutions were made on the board of directors to give Edison a majority. Morgan himself remained on the board, but for the time being it was Edison's company again.[15]

Then, almost as soon as the pioneering phase was over, the world around Edison abruptly changed. For one thing, as a part of a severe nationwide business slump, the electric business slowed down; for another, a natural psychological anticlimax followed the hectic events of 1881–84. But there was something more. Late in 1884 Edison's wife, Mary Stilwell Edison, died. This gentle, affectionate, simple woman had idolized her husband without pretending to understand him or what he was doing; her naïveté had been exasperating to him, but when he was under enormous pressure she provided that special kind of ballast, of sanctuary, that only an artless woman can give a strong-willed man. And to Insull himself her death was a double blow: because, though only a few years older, Mrs. Edison had been a second mother to him; and because Edison was never again quite the same. Though many great inventions were to come,

[14] Memoranda between Eaton and Insull, February–March, 1884, especially Eaton to Insull, Feb. 18, March 1, 1884, in "Electric Light 1884—65, 5th Avenue Inter-Office Correspondence"; and Insull to Tate, Oct. 27, 1884, in "Samuel Insull, Personal," file; all in Edison Laboratory National Monument. See also Tate to Insull, Dec. 21, 1885.
[15] Insull's letter to Tate, Oct. 27, 1884, summarizes these changes as well as their background, though they were not formally consummated until the director's meeting on the next day. Josephson, *Edison*, pp. 297–98, is a good summary. Passer, *Electrical Manufacturers*, pp. 100–101, accurately describes the organizational changes but mistakenly assumes that Morgan and his associates backed them, failing to realize that the changes were actually the climax of a battle with Morgan.

Edison's creative period as an electric innovator ended with his wife's death, and in the future he not only contributed little to the success of his electric companies, but sometimes actually impeded their progress. From the greatest single asset a collection of electrical enterprises could possibly have, he suddenly became a burden.[16]

Insull did not realize this at the time—if he ever fully realized it —but he did fall into a prolonged depression, during which he despaired of ever making his fortune in the electric business. He had been rewarded well at first; Edison had given him various blocs of stock, and he drew good salaries as vice-president, secretary, or treasurer of various companies. But everyone around Edison sensed that the great opportunity to become rich in the electric business had passed them by. Insull, like many of Edison's other associates, began to dabble in other ventures in his spare time, mostly by backing other inventors. Johnson chose shrewdly: he backed the researches of Frank Julian Sprague, a brilliant engineer too erratic and too temperamental to hold his job with Edison. Sprague began designing small electric motors and then, in partnership with Johnson, developed the first complete and genuinely workable electric streetcar system. Insull's success was more modest: with a gentleman named Edwin G. Bates, he formed the Bates Manufacturing Company to make and sell an ingenious but petty device for handling cash in department stores.[17]

[16] Josephson, *Edison*, pp. 285–90; Insull, "Memoirs," p. 54; Passer, *Electrical Manufacturers*, p. 74. Says Passer, bluntly but accurately: "In 1879, Edison was a bold and courageous innovator. In 1889, he was a cautious and conservative defender of the *status quo*." Curiously—but typically in this otherwise excellent book—Passer attributes the change to objective and institutional circumstances, and neglects the personal ones. The decline of Edison's productivity is clearly implicit in Josephson's biography and in the tables of inventions supplied by Edison's earlier biographers. After 1884, virtually all Edison's inventions were relatively trivial, and some of them were almost foolish. As to his opposition to progress, the clearest example is his opposition to alternating current, which is narrated below. It is also clear from the correspondence between Insull and Edison, cited below in connection with Insull's management of Edison General Electric Company, that in the late 1880's the Edison organization suffered greatly from a lack of engineering talent and from Edison's unwillingness or inability to keep pace with electrical developments.

[17] Regarding Insull's offices see the letterheads of the several Edison companies; on his venture with Bates see the "Insull, Personal" files for 1885 and 1886, the "Bates and Insull" file, and Insull to Charles T. Hughes, March 22, 1885; all in the Edison Laboratory National Monument. On Sprague and Johnson, see Passer, *Electrical Manufacturers*, pp. 237–49, and Harriet Sprague, *Frank J. Sprague and the Edison Myth* (New York, 1947).

As the pace slackened, Insull also took stock of his personal situation. His store of experiences, accumulated in the short space of four years in America (and only twenty-five on earth) , was priceless. Not only had he met virtually all the important figures in the business world and many of those in the political world in both London and New York, but he had dealt with them as a near-equal. Furthermore, he had accumulated a host of minor experiences, all of which could, and most of which ultimately did, prove extremely useful. Too, he knew everybody who was anybody in the electric business in Europe and America; he had gained an intimate knowledge of all parts of the United States; he had picked up firsthand knowledge of urban politics in several sections of the country, of a depth and scale that was rare even among professional politicians; he had learned enough about manufacturing, selling, promoting, administration, and organizing to make a success in any of a variety of manufacturing enterprises. He had also learned the meaning of credit and of what it could do. From the beginning he did minor financing for Edison, and as time went on Edison's need increased and so did Insull's skill and willingness to borrow. (Borrowing in order to build fitted well with Insull's make-up, and it became a deep-rooted habit with him. A dollar, to him, was to be used to buy producing property, against which another dollar could be borrowed for expanding it. "Never pay cash when you can give a note," he said, "and then meet your notes promptly. That's the way to establish your credit.") [18]

But in 1885 and into 1886 such nebulous assets seemed insignificant, for the magic had gone from Edison, and with it from his men. No longer did a host of celebrities drop in regularly; no longer did every flunky around Edison dream of having a million dollars by the time he was thirty. Even Edison himself became discouraged about the future. In a fit of despair, he said to Insull, "I do not know just how we are going to live. I think I could go back and earn my living as a telegraph operator. Do you think, Sammy, that you could go back to earn your living as a stenographer?"[19]

For a time, Insull concentrated most of his energy on his family. He had by no means neglected them earlier; he had written regularly,

[18] This paragraph of generalizations is based upon the voluminous correspondence files in the Edison Laboratory National Monument; the quotation is from Tate, *Edison's Open Door,* pp. 264–65.

[19] Insull, "Memoirs," p. 41.

sent money, visited them, and once had his mother and sister over to visit him. But now he began to do much more. He created a job for his father by making him the paid British representative of the Bates Manufacturing Company, and he brought his two brothers and his oldest sister to America. With Joe, his older brother, he bought a large farm in Manitoba, which Joe farmed for a few years before giving it up, selling out, and coming back East to work in a petty job under Sam. (Ironically, it turned out many years later that the farm was located atop the richest field of oil on the North American continent.) His younger brother Martin came over to take a minor job with Edison, but Sam soon sent him off to Cornell to obtain a degree in electrical engineering. His sister, Emma, came over and served for a time as his housekeeper.[20]

He even indulged himself a bit in personal matters, which to him meant principally his reading and his appearance. He read because he liked to. On his long train trips for Edison he had read a great deal, mainly history, biography, and the works of John Stuart Mill; now he acquired and read a library of more than a hundred books, including all of Dickens, Shakespeare, Thackeray, Fielding, and Emerson, and a wide variety of works in history, economics, politics, philosophy, and the classics. His attention to his appearance derived not from vanity—despite his reputation among the Edison group as a charmer of the ladies—but from his exaggerated sense of propriety. Though he could be ruthless and freewheeling in business affairs, he was, in polite company, always correct in manner and dress. During this period, however, he did make one change in his appearance for personal reasons. Someone brought to his attention that he might do something to offset an unfortunate and misleading expression: When he was startled or puzzled, instead of raising an eyebrow he inadvertently curled his upper lip, as if sneering. His brusque manner and his fierce, hyperthyroid eyes were alone enough to keep people on edge, and the lip-curling made him appear vicious when his reaction was innocent. When he became aware of it, he

[20] Receipt dated June 10, 1882, from J. S. Morgan & Company, London, to Insull; Pardon Armington to Insull, Sept. 1, 1882; Insull to Edison, Dec. 18, 1883; Insull to Joseph Insull, July 2, 1885, May 13, Aug. 4, 1886; Insull to Samuel Insull, Sr., Nov. 2, 1885; Samuel Insull, Sr., to Insull, Nov. 7, Nov. 17, 1885; biographical sketches of Martin J. Insull and Joseph Insull, contained in their applications for membership in the Edison Pioneers; all manuscripts in the Edison Laboratory National Monument.

shaved off his muttonchops and grew a mustache that he wore the rest of his life.[21]

But the dull, despondent days in which one could worry about such trivia as money and mustaches were short-lived: The years 1885 and 1886 turned out to be neither a plateau nor the end of the line, but a major turning point. Partly because of a general upturn in business and partly because of two great technical developments that dramatized electricity anew, the central station business began to expand, and by the end of 1886 a boom was well underway. The technical developments were the first practical electric streetcar system and the first practical alternating current lighting system.

The first commercially successful electric streetcar system was the work of Charles J. Van Depoele, who installed experimental lines in New Orleans, South Bend, and Minneapolis in 1885 before making the world's first permanent installations in Appleton, Wisconsin, and Mobile, Alabama, in 1886. Eighteen months later Frank J. Sprague, the erratic inventor who had gone into partnership with Edward Johnson, completed a superior streetcar system in Richmond, Virginia, and soon the traction boom was on. The demand for electric urban transportation quickly dwarfed that for electric lighting: By the end of 1889 there were 154 electric street railway systems in operation in the United States. At the same time, the impact of traction upon central stations was immediate and enormous. From the beginning, Edison had seen the necessity of a power load to the success of his central stations, for the obvious reason that central station lighting companies were expensive, full-time plants in a part-time business, and the Edison Machine Works manufactured small motors (many of them designed by Sprague) to sell for the purpose of creating a daytime load for central stations. These, however, were of small consequence compared to the huge demand for daytime power that was created by the coming of electric streetcars.[22]

[21] Undated receipt (1885) from D. Van Nostrand for Insull's book purchases; C. E. Spiers to Insull, Aug. 5, 1885; account of Insull with C. E. Spiers, 1886; Insull to Edison, March 22, 1885; Edison to Insull, June 5, 1885; W. Preston Hix to Insull, June 16, and Insull to Hix, July 2, 1885; Tate to Insull, Dec. 21, 1885; Tate, *Edison's Open Door*, p. 53.

[22] Passer, *Electrical Manufacturers*, pp. 216–55; *Electrical World*, XIV (October 19, 1889), 264–65.

The immediate impact of alternating current, though large, was less than that of traction, but in the long run it was far more significant. Until 1886 alternating current (a.c.) was regarded as inferior to direct current (d.c.) because of difficulties in its consumption, and thus Edison had used d.c. Direct current had one serious limitation: For technical reasons, it could be economically transmitted for only about one mile. In 1886 George Westinghouse and William Stanley perfected a device—the transformer—that made it possible to transmit electricity by means of alternating current cheaply for scores, even hundreds, of miles. This opened a new world to the central stations, for it vastly increased their potential service areas and thus made possible the centralization of production in large, economical steam and hydroelectric generating units. A.c. still had many technical flaws, but it would soon make Edison's central stations as archaic as electric transportation made the horsecar.[23]

Jolted out of their lethargy by the combination of new opportunity and new competition, Edison and his men sprang to life. Almost immediately they found themselves, in the fall of 1886, with more business than they had facilities to accommodate. In a matter of months, the space in Edison's shops became inadequate to fill more than a fraction of the orders for his equipment. Accordingly, he cast about for a location with more room, and Insull found and bought for him an abandoned locomotive works in Schenectady; shortly, the Electrical Tube Company, one of the least profitable and most space-consuming of the Edison enterprises, was moved to Schenectady. In the late fall of 1886, a labor problem developed in the Edison Machine Works, and rather than cope with it Edison abruptly decided to move out. He instructed Insull to close up the works on Goerk Street in New York, and move it to Schenectady.[24]

When Insull had completed the move, he asked for further instructions. Edison told him to go to Schenectady and "run the whole

[23] Passer, *Electrical Manufacturers*, pp. 276–95; William Stanley, "The Beginnings of Alternating Current Engineering," in *Electrical Review*, XI (February 15, 1902), 223; C. C. Chesney and C. F. Scott, "Early History of the AC System in America," in *Journal of the American Institute of Electrical Engineers*, LIII (May, 1934), 726.
[24] Insull to Edison, April 28, 1886; Insull to New York Life Insurance Company, Aug. 9, 1886; Insull to Charles Batchelor, Oct. 9, 1886; Insull, "Memoirs," pp. 43–46; Josephson, *Edison*, pp. 340–41; Extract from the Minutes of the Executive Committee of the Edison Pioneers, held at 115 Broadway, April 12, 1921, in the Insull Papers.

thing." He gave no detailed instructions, only a general command: "Do it big, Sammy. Make it either a big success or a big failure."[25]

Insull never doubted which it would be. In two years he quadrupled sales and increased the annual return on the total investment to more than 30 per cent, though he used every nickel of profit to increase the size of the plant. When he went to Schenectady, the $750,000 in stock of the Edison Machine Works was largely water, consisting of rights, good will, and the like; within three years he had written off all the water and had brought the liquidating value of the $100 par common stock from around $25 to almost $150. When he went he took 200 employees with him; when he resigned six years later he was employing 6,000 men.[26]

At the same time he was becoming a manufacturer Insull was forced to become a financier—and at times almost a magician. Despite its rapid growth, or because of it, the Schenectady enterprise was perpetually short of cash. When its assets were $1,500,000, its cash balance was normally around $4,000; and when its assets had doubled, the normal cash holding was still less than $10,000. Morgan and his friends, who were reaping large benefits from the expansion, could have made it profitable to themselves had they been willing to invest new money to capitalize the company's growth, but they refused: indeed, only rarely did they advance money on short-term loans, and as often as not they created new difficulties by calling these loans at inopportune moments. Thus Insull had to raise all the operating capital for the electrical manufacturing as well as to run it, and because Edison renewed his non-electric inventive activity at the same time the Schenectady works was opened, Insull had to raise large additional sums for his research as well. He spent almost half his time going from bank to bank to borrow—often to beg—money on short-term notes and juggling his available cash and credit with

25 Insull, "Memoirs," p. 46; Dyer, Martin, and Meadowcroft, *Edison*, I, 382; K. G. Patrick, "Insull on the Mohawk: A Prelude to Athens," *Schenectadian* (February, 1935) , pp. 7–9.
26 The best record of Insull's work in Schenectady is his regular reports to Edison: Insull to Edison, Aug. 3, Oct. 10, Nov. 5, 1887, Jan. 26, 1888; and the report of Dun and Bradstreet, Oct. 1, 1888, and that of a set of independent examiners, Nov. 1, 1888. See also Patrick, "Insull on the Mohawk"; Insull, "Memoirs," pp. 45–50; Insull to Edison, Aug. 31, Oct. 6, 1887; April 20, May 24, June 26, 1888; Insull to Tate, June 6, 1887; W. E. Gilmore to John F. Randolph, Sept. 23, 1887; Minutes of a Special Stockholders Meeting, Edison Machine Works, Oct. 31, 1887; and (?) to Edison, Feb. 15, 1888; all in the Edison Laboratory National Monument.

extreme dexterity in order to make ends meet. (The experience was frantic, nerve-racking, and disgusting to him. From it Insull developed, and never lost, a deep-seated antipathy for banks and bankers, especially those in New York and particularly those in the Morgan group.) [27]

Then came Henry Villard. This bold, ambitious transportation magnate and financial speculator had been, until he lost his fortune in the financial panics of 1883–84, one of Edison's staunchest backers (he was also one of the earliest; in 1880 he had had Edison install, on his S.S. "Columbia," the world's first nonexperimental incandescent lighting plant). After his financial misfortune he returned to his native Germany for two years and then suddenly showed up again in New York with the backing of powerful German financial interests—the Deutsche Bank, the *Allgemeine Elektrizitats Gesellschaft,* and (electric inventors) Siemens and Halske, all of Berlin, and Jacob Stern, a banker from Frankfurt—and a grandiose plan to form an international cartel to control the electric business the world over. Edison's manufacturing ventures were his first target.[28]

After lengthy negotiations, Villard prepared a plan to consolidate all the Edison companies, including the parent light company, and also to absorb the Sprague Electric Railway and Motor Company. He proposed that the stocks of the various manufacturing companies be exchanged for a total of something over $2,100,000 in stock of a consolidated company and $1,100,000 in cash; that the stocks of the Sprague company and three minor companies be exchanged for another $950,000 in new stock; and that $2,250,000 in stock be sold to Villard's German backers for $1,750,000, which after the cash payment for the manufacturing companies would leave almost $600,000 in working capital. Edison would be given an additional $500,000 in stock in exchange for his incidental inventive services in the future.

[27] See Insull's reports to Edison, cited in note 26, above, and Insull to John F. Randolph, Jan. 7, 1887; Insull to Tate, Feb. 10, 23, March 5, June 4, Sept. 1, Sept. 2, Oct. 6, 1887; June 27, July 5, 26, 1888; Insull to Edison, Oct. 6, 1887; Josephson, *Edison,* pp. 340–41.
[28] Josephson, *Edison,* pp. 236–37, 239–41, 293–94, 298, 351–52; Insull, "Memoirs," p. 50; W. Preston Hix to Marshall & Illsley, Milwaukee bankers, a printed form letter bound in the Minute Book of the Edison Electric Illuminating Company of Milwaukee, in the files of the Wisconsin Electric Power Company, Milwaukee. There is no biography of Villard; the best work on him is James B. Hedges, *Henry Villard and the Railroads of the Northwest* (New York, 1930); his voluminous papers are preserved in the Houghton Library, Harvard University; his *Memoirs* were published in two volumes in 1904.

The $1,500,000 stock of the Edison Electric Light Company, for which Morgan and his associates had actually invested only $779,600, would be exchanged for $2,625,000 in new stock and $1,375,000 in trust certificates, which would be exchanged for stock whenever the company grew profitable enough to pay dividends on them.[29]

J. P. Morgan, without whose consent the consolidation was impossible, thought the proposals interesting but somewhat niggardly as regards the Edison Light Company. He made an exorbitant counter-proposal: that the light company stockholders be given $3,500,000 in stock immediately, and that Drexel, Morgan & Company be allowed to participate in the stock sale. These terms, if accepted, would sandbag the new company with a large amount of stock—40 per cent of the total—in exchange for two sets of dubious assets. The first was about $4,000,000 nominal value of unmarketable central station stocks which the light company had accumulated as royalties. The only other thing it owned was Edison's own patents, which had not yet been upheld in court and which, even if they were sustained, had only half a dozen years to run. The burden could be reduced somewhat, a Morgan man added, by withdrawing the proposed $500,000 payment to Edison.[30]

Piratical as Morgan's demands were, the deal still offered great advantages to Edison and his associates. Edison would receive about $1,750,000 in cash and stocks—and thereby, for the first time in twenty-two years, be free of financial worry and able to pursue his inventive activities without monetary strain. Various of his associates would realize a total of more than $1,000,000 between them (Insull would get $75,000) . Most important, Edison's sprawling manufacturing companies were badly in need of reorganization, consolidation, and liberation from the yoke of the light company, and even more in need of fresh capital to meet a weekly payroll that was now approaching 3,000 workers. Without the consolidation, as Edison wrote, "Mr. Insull and I were afraid we might get into trouble for lack of money. . . . Therefore . . . we concluded it was better to

[29] Printed notice to Edison Electric Light Company stockholders, dated April 26, 1889, in Edison General Electric file, Edison Laboratory National Monument.
[30] C. A. Spofford to Insull, Jan. 23, 1889; Villard to Edison, Feb. 18, 1889; *Chicago Tribune*, March 21, 1889; C. H. Coster to S. B. Eaton, April 19, 1889; Villard to Eaton, April 22, 1889; Villard to Edison, May 22, 1889; Josephson, *Edison*, pp. 354–58.

be sure than to be sorry," and they accepted Villard's and Morgan's terms.[31]

Thus in January, 1889, the Edison General Electric Company was organized, and a few months later the consolidations were formally effected. Four Edison men joined the five appointed by Villard and Morgan on the nine-man board of directors: Edison, Insull, Charles Batchelor, and Francis Upton. Villard himself became president but confined his activities to seeking further mergers with other companies and took no active part in the management of the company. Villard's man J. H. Herrick became first vice-president and chief financial officer. Insull became second vice-president and had full charge of manufacturing and sales, continuing to serve as Edison's personal business manager.[32]

Fortified for the first time with working capital, Insull reorganized and integrated the manufacturing operations, rendering them vastly more efficient. In operating them Insull followed a set of basic principles that he would follow throughout his career. The first was to expand; expand by raising new capital whenever possible, expand by plowing profits back into the business, expand by borrowing every nickel he could lay hands on. The next was to treat his workers (as distinguished from his immediate subordinates, whom he drove like slaves, or like himself) generously and humanely—not out of sentimentality, but for the sound economic reason that discontent breeds stoppages and stoppages are inefficient, irrational, costly. Another was to spread fixed costs as thinly as possible by diversifying operations in order to keep the plant busy at all times. Still another was to sell products as cheaply as possible—not because price competition dictated it; far from it. Rather, it stemmed from Insull's radical belief, which Edison usually shared, that lower prices would bring greater volume, which would lower unit costs of production and thus yield greater profits. (The assumption was borne out by the record.

[31] Edison to Villard, Feb. 8, 1890, in the Villard Papers, Houghton Library; Insull, "Memoirs," pp. 49–51; Josephson, *Edison*, pp. 351–53; Passer, *Electrical Manufacturers*, pp. 102–4; Dyer, Martin, and Meadowcroft, *Edison*, I, 382.

[32] Josephson, *Edison*, p. 353; Edison to Villard, Jan. 30, 1889; letterheads of Edison General Electric Company; A. Marcus' notice to the directors of Edison General Electric Company, undated (*ca.* May, 1890), in Edison General Electric 1890 file; all manuscripts in the Edison Laboratory National Monument.

Insull cut the price of lamps, for example, from $1.00 in 1886 to 80¢ in 1888, to 50¢ in 1890, and to 44¢ in 1891, and the profit rate increased as prices decreased.) [33]

He also rationalized the sales organization. Nationwide sales networks were almost unknown in the 1880's, and the few that did exist were haphazardly thrown together. In working out his organization—a hierarchical system of seven regional sales divisions, each headed by a district manager, and the group co-ordinated by an "intelligence department" and directed by the sales vice-president—Insull established what became a model for American manufacturing companies.[34]

But the Edison General Electric Company contained two weaknesses over which Insull had no control. Villard was on the right side —in favor of central stations instead of isolated plants—but he was exaggeratedly so. He so strongly believed in the future of central stations, particularly if they were operated in combination with streetcars, that he felt that far more money could be made from them than from manufacturing. Accordingly, he visualized Edison General Electric as a holding company that would manufacture and sell only to its own central station companies, "at factory prices, free of all royalties or profits, direct or indirect." Edison G.E. would add to its already large central station holdings by forming central station companies throughout the country and take about four-fifths of the

[33] Insull's policies emerge clearly from study of the Edison General Electric Company files for 1889–91 in the Edison Laboratory National Monument, as well as from the reports to Edison cited in note 26, above. Of the latter, see especially his letters of Jan. 31 and April 20, 1888. Josephson, *Edison, passim,* sheds considerable light on the subject, as does Patrick, "Insull on the Mohawk." See also T. C. Martin, "With Edison at Schenectady," in *Electrical World,* August 5, 1888. Jehl's account, scattered through vol. iii of his *Menlo Park Reminiscences,* is a garbled one; he even has Batchelor and John Kruesi running the Schenectady works.

The three principal writers who have dealt with the subject of cuts in lamp prices—Josephson, Passer, and Bright—cite the cuts to demonstrate the demands of cutthroat competition and infer that Edison G.E. was increasingly in difficulty. They overlook two salient points, evidence for which is included in their own works: 1) that Edison G.E.'s rate of profit (as a percentage of gross sales) increased even more sharply than did its gross business; and 2) that both Insull and Edison repeatedly stated they would sell at the lowest possible price as a matter of policy.

[34] Hammond, *Men and Volts,* p. 176; Annual Report of the Edison General Electric Company, 1890; James F. Kelly to department heads, Edison G.E., Aug., 1890; Edison G.E. "intelligence department," "List of Edison Cash Central Stations in the United States and Canada, Up to October 1, 1890, With Appendix to November 1st, 1890"; H. Ward Leonard to District Managers, Nov. 10, Nov. 19, Dec. 1, 1890; Leonard to Edison, Dec. 10, 1890; all manuscripts in the Edison Laboratory National Monument.

stock of these companies itself (one-third would be paid it for patent royalties) , the remainder and much of the future capital to be raised by selling securities, mostly bonds, to local capitalists. By such means he proposed to control the electric central station business of the United States.[35]

In some ways Villard's approach was even worse than Morgan's. His policy aggravated, by a different method, the problem Morgan had created when he had insisted that the light company's central station securities be capitalized by Edison G.E.; Villard compounded the problem still further by concentrating on buying the stocks rather than the bonds of the operating companies. Because stocks represent ownership and bonds merely represent loans against a mortgage, stocks give control and bonds do not, but stocks are far riskier and, as it turned out, most of them yielded no return through a long period of development. In the day-to-day conduct of business, Villard partially balanced his questionable theory by more realistic practice; but in the main Insull had to continue to borrow to continue to expand. The principal effect of the formation of Edison G.E. was to make this chore considerably easier.[36]

The second weakness was that Edison G.E. lacked engineering talent. This lack was, ironically, a direct function of Edison's character. Having pursued the electric arts with demonic energy until he had worked out a complete system and satiated his own curiosity, Edison was, after 1884, simply no longer interested in electrical inventions. To be sure, some of his greatest achievements were yet to come—among them the perfected phonograph and the motion

[35] This scheme is made explicit in the printed form letter from Edison G.E. salesman W. Preston Hix to Marshall & Illsley, Milwaukee bankers, bound in the Minute Book of the Edison Electric Illuminating Company of Milwaukee, in the files of the Wisconsin Electric Power Company, Milwaukee; Insull, in his "Memoirs," p. 50, says Villard's original view of Edison G.E. was that it should be a "holding company." Edison objected to this approach; Edison to Villard, Feb. 14, 1889, in the Villard Papers, Houghton Library. Villard unrealistically believed that central stations would earn upwards of 20 per cent a year. See vol. cxxviii (Miscellaneous Letters, Aug. 2, 1887, to Sept. 28, 1888) of the Villard Papers.

[36] Villard's concentration on stocks is inferred from Insull's description of Villard's attitude; from several documents in the Villard Papers, notably a copy of an agreement, dated June 18, 1890, between Villard and John A. Hinsey of Milwaukee and vol. lxiv, pertaining to the Edison Electric Light and Power Company of St. Paul; and the minute books and other records of a number of Edison central station companies, including those in Appleton, Milwaukee, Marinette, LaCrosse, and Wausau, Wisconsin, St. Paul and Minneapolis, Minnesota, Menominee, Michigan, and Chicago.

picture—but none of them was in the electric field. Though he was in charge of research and development for Edison G.E. and did considerable research for the company, particularly in traction, this work was singularly fruitless. Furthermore, Edison's corps of technical assistants, always dominated by one man's genius, had an abundance of able technicians but few if any creative engineers. Finally, and most important, Edison's stubborn unwillingness to listen to anyone else's opinion or advice, which had served him so well when he was developing his electrical system, now served him ill: he became a complete reactionary in matters electrical, now fighting rather than causing change.[37]

Both weaknesses showed dramatically in Edison G.E.'s fights with its principal competitors, Westinghouse and the Thomson-Houston Electric Company. With Westinghouse, whose chief asset was its alternating current system, the battle was the celebrated "battle of the currents." Edison was unshakably opposed to alternating current (for personal, psychological reasons, the most insidious form of vested interest). As soon as a.c. appeared, Johnson and Sprague had pleaded with him to work on a.c. equipment, but to no avail. Later, when Insull, who readily perceived the competitive disadvantage at which Westinghouse's a.c. system was placing the Edison central stations, urged Edison to work on alternating current apparatus, Edison reluctantly agreed. The technicians in his laboratories set to work building transformers and a.c. dynamos, and on the strength of Edison's promise, Insull promised the Association of Edison Illuminating Companies that Edison a.c. equipment would soon be forthcoming. But in exchange for his agreement to fight Westinghouse fairly, Edison demanded that it be fought unfairly as well, to which Insull agreed. Then, despite Insull's persistent prodding, Edison dragged his feet in fulfilling his end of the bargain; his men turned out nothing but impractical and inferior a.c. equipment.[38]

[37] Particularly revealing on this matter are Insull's letters to Edison, trying to prod him into action; see, for example, Insull to Edison, Nov. 16, 1887; July 16, Dec. 22, 1890; and John Kruesi to Insull, July 31, 1890. See also Passer, *Electrical Manufacturers,* p. 74, and Josephson, *Edison,* pp. 313–38, 349–50, 361–62.
[38] Josephson, *Edison,* p. 349; Insull to Edison, Nov. 16, 1887; July 16, Sept. 8, 1890; Kruesi to Insull, July 31, 1890; Berry, "Mr. Samuel Insull," p. 49. In this connection,

Accordingly, it was the unfair fight that was waged in earnest. Edison G.E. attempted to prevent the development of alternating current by unscrupulous political action and by even less savory promotional tactics. In both arenas Edison G.E. attempted to damn a.c. on the ground that its high voltage—wherein lay its technical superiority—was dangerous, a menace to public safety. The political activity was lobbying for state legislation that would limit electric circuits to 800 volts, which would have defeated arc lighting as well as alternating current. In at least two states, Ohio and Virginia, Edison G.E. came close to succeeding. The promotional activity was a series of spectacular stunts aimed at dramatizing the deadliness of high voltage alternating current, the most sensational being the development and promotion of the electric chair as a means of executing criminals. The state of New York adopted this innovation in 1888 after a gruesome promotional campaign, conceived by Insull, Johnson, and Edison, and carried out by a German-American named Thurington and H. P. Brown, one of Edison's former lab assistants.[39]

An even more formidable rival than Westinghouse was the Thomson-Houston Electric Company of Lynn, Massachusetts. Thomson-Houston was a cowbird company, one that thrived upon the nests of others. It had been founded (under a different name) in 1880 to exploit the arc-lighting inventions of a pair of Philadelphia high school teachers. Until 1883 its progress was modest, but then it was infused with new capital, new management, and a new policy, and it suddenly became a thriving success. The capital was that of a number of Boston Brahmins who were willing to pour virtually limitless sums into the venture. The new manager was Charles A. Coffin of Lynn, one of the shrewdest and ablest businessmen of his

---

Insull said to Berry (his state department guard) in 1934: "I could tell you hundreds of stories of happenings which occurred before there were such things as Rotary Clubs and business ethics codes . . . but I think that it is best to let them die with me. If I told them I would be accused of sullying Edison's memory and that I certainly have no desire to do."

[39] Berry, "Mr. Samuel Insull," p. 49; Josephson, *Edison*, pp. 345–49; Passer, *Electrical Manufacturers*, pp. 164–75; H. P. Brown, "The New Instrument of Execution," in the *North American Review*, CXLIX (November, 1889), 586; Thomas A. Edison, "The Dangers of Electric Lighting," *North American Review*, CXLIX (November, 1889), 625; George Westinghouse, "A Reply to Mr. Edison," *North American Review*, CXLIX (December, 1889), 653.

generation. The new policy was scarcely distinguishable from theft. Thomson-Houston expanded into every line of electrical manufacturing that promised profit, and it did so by a special means. It spent no money on developing new products, leaving that to the more foolhardy. If the research left the inventor financially strapped, Thomson-Houston would buy up the patents for a minimal sum. If the invention could not be acquired by that means, Thomson-Houston simply infringed on the patent. Being unburdened by developmental costs and investment in machinery and tools, the company was free to work on improving the original; Thomson, an excellent albeit not creative engineer, was a master at thus exploiting other people's innovations. Coffin worked in the same way in developing his manufacturing and sales techniques. While competitors foolishly encumbered themselves with heavy investments in learning how best to manufacture a particular product, he spied upon them, learned their secrets, and improved upon them; similarly, he was adroit at capitalizing on somebody else's publicity and turning it into sales for Thomson-Houston. Through such practices the company "developed" a high-quality, low-cost line of arc lighting and streetcar equipment (by buying, at bargain rates, the inventions of Charles F. Brush and Charles Van Depoele, the pioneer innovators in these fields) and excellent alternating current and incandescent-lighting equipment (by infringing on Westinghouse's and Edison's patents) .[40]

For purposes of short-run success, Thomson-Houston had one other great competitive advantage. Its management was unfettered by any sentimentality about its customers, and it could therefore ruthlessly promote competing central stations, isolated plants, and streetcar companies in the same city, cheerfully disregarding the need of its customers to survive. Like Edison G.E., it often had to use some of its own capital to promote local concerns, but unlike Edison G.E. it concentrated on protecting its investment, not its control, and thus it

---

[40] A good account of the development and growth of Thomson-Houston is contained in Passer's *Electrical Manufacturers,* pp. 26–31, 52–56, 145–46, 233, 249–53, 321–29, 363–64. Said Edison of Thomson-Houston: "The statement that they ask no favors from the Edison Company might be met by the fact that having boldly appropriated and infringed every patent we use, there is very little left to favor them with, except our business, which they are now after." Edison to Villard, April 1, 1889, in the Villard Papers.

normally took bonds instead of stock of the local companies. If its customer-companies got into difficulties, Thomson-Houston therefore inherited property instead of headaches.[41]

Despite the handicaps under which Insull labored, and despite the calibre of the opposition, such was the skill, boldness, and vigor of his management that he was more than able to hold his own. When Edison G.E. was formed, its constituent manufacturing units had gross annual sales of $7,000,000 and net profits of $700,000. Two years later the annual gross was running almost $11,000,000—as against just over $10,000,000 for Thomson-Houston and $5,000,000 for Westinghouse—and, thanks to the efficiencies Insull had introduced, profits had risen thrice as fast, to $2,000,000. (The price of this expansion and rationalization was high. To accomplish it without being able to sell any significant amounts of new securities, Insull had to incur for Edison G.E. a floating debt of $3,500,000. This would prove to be the most significant figure in the competitive equation.) [42]

Insull led the fight, but Villard took the larger view, or at least the view more in keeping with the spirit of the times. Insull fought with better products, more efficient production, lower prices, harder selling. Villard proposed to emulate the legendary tycoon who said "Our business thrives on competition; let us therefore devour some more competitors." Even before the formalities of organizing Edison G.E. were completed, Villard secretly began negotiating with Westinghouse and Thomson-Houston, hoping to effect a consolidation with one or both. (Edison fiercely opposed joining forces with the enemy; Insull held his peace and ran the business.) [43]

[41] This aspect of Thomson-Houston's policies has been traced in records of operating companies that installed Thomson-Houston equipment; see, for example, the minute books of the Ashland Light and Power Company, in the files of Lake Superior District Power Company, Ashland, Wisconsin; Wausau Electric Company, in the files of Wisconsin Public Service Corporation, Milwaukee; and Winona Electric Light Company, in the files of Mississippi Valley Public Service Company, Winona, Minnesota; all for the years 1887–93. For additional details on Thomson-Houston's selling policies see Forrest McDonald, *Let There Be Light: The Electric Utility Industry in Wisconsin, 1881–1955* (Madison, 1957), pp. 20–24, 26–28. Bright, *Electric-Lamp Industry*, p. 94, and Hammond, *Men and Volts*, pp. 404–5, 421–22, describe the United Electric Securities Company, a subsidiary through which Thomson-Houston financed central stations, but neither points out that Thomson-Houston concentrated on holding debt capital rather than equity.

[42] Josephson, *Edison*, pp. 353, 362; Passer, *Electrical Manufacturers*, pp. 104, 150, 328.

[43] Josephson, *Edison*, pp. 359–61; Edison to Villard, April 1, 1889, in the Villard Papers.

But Villard was not nearly so wrongheaded as Insull and Edison were sometimes tempted to believe, despite his great reputation and their friendship for him. He had the foresight to realize that electric power would soon be more important than electric light, and that traction for many years would be more important than either; and for that reason he had brought the Sprague company into Edison G.E. at the outset. Now, in seeking further mergers, he was shrewd enough to go after Westinghouse instead of Thomson-Houston. Westinghouse was small enough to acquire outright, whereas Thomson-Houston was big enough so that in a merger it would have a loud voice. Furthermore, the move was not starry-eyed trust-building for trust-building's sake. Villard realized (with Insull, contrary to Edison) that alternating current equipment was necessary to balance and diversify Edison G.E.'s line of products. Thus in 1888 and 1889, despite the public bitterness of the battle of the currents, Villard and George Westinghouse began meeting privately and made definite strides toward consolidation.[44]

Then a stroke of good fortune broke for Edison G.E. Much of the strategy of consolidation and competition hinged upon patents. Until about 1886, Edison had been lackadaisical about patent infringers, because neither the competition nor the prospects for the business seemed large enough to justify it. In the next three years the Edison organization started prosecuting infringers in earnest, but it was unable to get any serious hearings until 1889. Early in 1889 it met a reversal in a Canadian court, but in the fall Edison G.E. won a series of major victories in American courts, invalidating other lamp patents and confirming Edison's, and it suddenly began to appear that the enemy would be routed. More legal victories followed in 1890, and by the end of that year it was clear that Edison G.E. would soon have the legal power (which it actually won in June, 1891) to force its competitors entirely out of the electric light business.[45]

A lesser man might have played his budding advantage more cautiously, but not Villard. He dropped the negotiations with Westinghouse and shot for the acquisition, on his own terms, of Thomson-

[44] Villard to George Westinghouse, Jr., Sept. 10, 1888; Edison to Villard, Feb. 8, 1890; in the Villard Papers.
[45] Josephson, *Edison*, pp. 354–56; Passer, *Electrical Manufacturers*, pp. 152–55; see also the numerous letters and notes from S. B. Eaton to Insull in the Edison General Electric 1891 file, Edison Laboratory National Monument.

Insull's father, the first Samuel Insull, Sr., was a member of the National Temperance League in 1864 when this photograph was taken at the Crystal Palace. Insull, Sr., is at far right, back row. (INSULL COLLECTION)

The Insull family, about 1866. Samuel Insull, Sr., Emma Insull, and their children, Samuel, Emma, Queenie, and Joseph.

Samuel Insull in his early twenties, about 1882. (INSULL COLLECTION)

Thomas A. Edison gave his proxy to Samuel Insull in 1883 to enable him to attend the annual meeting of the Edison Avenue Milling Company.

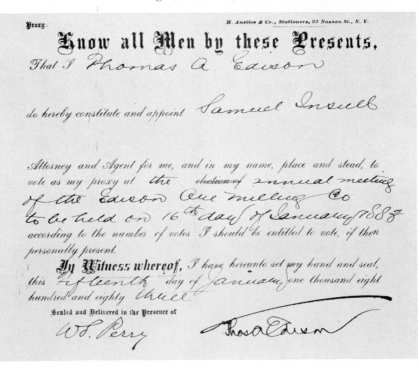

Samuel Insull in his mid-thirties, about 1894. (INSULL COLLECTION)

Gladys Wallis, who became the bride of Samuel Insull, toured the United States in John Drew's renowned theatrical company. About 1896.

(Right) *Byron L. Smith, president of the Northern Trust Company, one of the directors to whom Insull recommended himself as president of the Chicago Edison Company.* (WALINGER STUDIO, CHICAGO)

(Bottom left) *Edward L. Brewster, a member of the board of directors of Chicago Edison, whose financial acumen was at the service of Insull.* (CHICAGO TRIBUNE)

(Bottom right) *Marshall Field, who loaned Insull $250,000 with which to buy stock in Chicago Edison.* (CHICAGO TRIBUNE)

(Top left) *Charles Merz, the British engineer employed by Insull as a consultant. To-gether they lobbied for a uni-fied British power system.* (INSULL COLLECTION)

(Top right) *Roger C. Sulli-van, Insull's principal mentor and closest political friend.* (CHICAGO TRIBUNE)

(Left) *Charles A. Munroe, the first "Insull man," who was vice-president until 1923 of virtually all of Insull's companies except Common-wealth Edison.* (CHICAGO TRIBUNE)

Three generations: the first Samuel Insull, Sr., Samuel In-sull, and Samuel Insull, Jr., about 1902. (INSULL COLLEC-TION)

Insull and his son, about 1904.

Samuel Insull, Jr., and his grandparents, 1905.

Sutton Courteney, country home leased by Insull in the summer of 1905. (ROYAL THAMES STUDIO, ABINGDON)

Gladys Insull and her son, about 1905. (INSULL COLLECTION)

At Hawthorn Farm, near Libertyville, Insull devoted years of study to the breeding of the finest strain of Suffolk horses in the world.

Gladys Insull with one of her few close friends, Mrs. Benjamin Carpenter, at Atlantic City in 1912. (INSULL COLLECTION)

Insull and his son, about 1912, on excursion up the Ottawa River.

Houston itself. With the advantage that would accrue from forcing both competitors out of the incandescent lighting business for the duration of Edison's patents (three more years), he reasoned, Edison G.E. could drive them to the wall. Doing so, however, meant temporarily foregoing his own policies and following those of Insull. Accordingly, in January, 1891, Villard simultaneously determined to sell $3,000,000 in new stock to raise additional working capital and authorized Insull to abandon the program of concentrating on acquiring securities of central stations; thenceforth he was to sell equipment only for cash or on short-term credit. In February, Villard paid his first visit—in secret—to the Thomson-Houston plant and laid the foundations for subsequent negotiations.[46]

After the court decision in June, Villard's contacts with President Coffin of Thomson-Houston became more frequent; by fall they were regular, open, and friendly, and Villard confidently expected that he would soon be dictating the terms of a consolidation.[47] But he made two fatal mistakes: He reckoned without Morgan's capacity for perfidy, and he reckoned without Coffin's capacity for shrewd trading.

Morgan's approval was necessary to any consolidation, both because his banking power was indispensable to the success of a company of the size that would result and because he and his associates were large minority stockholders in Edison G.E. All the same, Villard expected no trouble, for Morgan was in the vanguard of the "trustification" movement, and almost invariably sanctioned consolidations provided (1) they did away with competition and (2) Morgan controlled the financing. In both respects Villard's scheme qualified, and Morgan gave it his tentative approval.[48]

But at what was scheduled to be a routine conference, wrapping up the details of the consolidation, Coffin executed a surprise maneuver. Morgan had asked H. M. Twombly, a Boston member of the

[46] Josephson, *Edison*, pp. 360–61; Circular Letter, Edison General Electric Trustees to Stockholders, Dec. 17, 1890, in the Edison Laboratory National Monument.
[47] Hammond, *Men and Volts*, pp. 191–93; Josephson, *Edison*, p. 362; Passer, *Electrical Manufacturers*, p. 322.
[48] The bibliography on Morgan is sizable, but in none of his biographies does he emerge clearly as a human being, with ordinary human weaknesses. Perhaps the best is Herbert L. Satterlee, *J. Pierpont Morgan: An Intimate Portrait* (New York, 1939). See also Carl Hovey, *The Life Story of J. Pierpont Morgan* (New York, 1912); Lewis Corey, *The House of Morgan* (New York, 1930); John Winkler, *Morgan the Magnificent* (New York, 1930); Frederick Lewis Allen, *The Great Pierpont Morgan* (New York, 1949).

Vanderbilt family who represented their large holdings of Edison G.E. stock, to go over the plant and books of Thomson-Houston, and he reported enthusiastically in favor of the merger. A conference was held at Twombly's house in Boston, and to everyone's surprise, Coffin announced that he had decided not to sell. Coolly, in the manner of a skilled poker player running a bluff, one of Coffin's men said, "We don't think much of the way the Edison company has been managed." This was a kind of audacity that intrigued Morgan, and when Twombly reported it to him, the banker said, "Send them down here to talk to me."[49]

In December, Coffin called on Morgan. He came claiming that Thomson-Houston was the more efficient company and was armed with figures showing that it netted about half again as much on its capital as did Edison G.E. Morgan, consistent in his myopia regarding the electric business, chose to forget that he was personally responsible for Edison G.E.'s excess of unproductive capitalization, barring which the profit rates of the two companies were almost identical. That amnesia was understandable, but another oversight was less so: that almost half of Edison G.E.'s assets were frozen assets in the form of central station securities. On the basis of its actual investment in manufacturing, Edison G.E.'s profit rate was half again that of Thomson-Houston. But Coffin was persuasive, and Morgan was interested only in the comparative balance sheets, and Morgan was sold. He decided on the spot to have Thomson-Houston acquire Edison G.E., rather than the other way around. At Coffin's suggestion, this plan was amended: the companies would be consolidated instead, but for purposes of the consolidation Thomson-Houston would be valued at $18,400,000 and Edison G.E. at $15,000,000, thus giving Thomson-Houston men control.[50]

Having made his decision, Morgan calmly informed Villard that

[49] H. S. Fraser, "Thomas Edison," a manuscript in the Edison Laboratory National Monument; Josephson, *Edison*, pp. 362–63. Passer, in his account of the merger (*Electrical Manufacturers*, pp. 321–29) , treats it—as he does most subjects—as if it were done calmly, rationally, impersonally, and to everyone's satisfaction. Insull, in his "Memoirs," pp. 51–53, mentions ill-feeling and treachery but does not elaborate.

[50] The basic figures and the outline of events here stated are given in Passer, *Electrical Manufacturers*, pp. 150, 328; Hammond, *Men and Volts*, pp. 194–95; and Josephson, *Edison*, p. 363. The statements regarding rates of profit are based upon my own calculations and interpolations, derived from the basic figures cited by Passer and Hammond, and from the data and sources cited earlier in the chapter.

his "courteous resignation would be courteously received." Stunned, Villard wanted to balk, but he could not because of one circumstance: Edison G.E. had a $3,500,000 floating debt, and Morgan was perfectly capable of using it to crush the company if it suited his ends. Villard left quietly. In April, 1892, Morgan's plans for the creation of the new, $50,000,000 corporation, to be called simply the General Electric Company, were completed.[51]

Afterward, there was a noisy scene between the outmaneuvered and defeated Edisonians: Villard, Edison, and Insull, each embittered, each furious, exploded with reckless charges; but tempers soon cooled. Edison, for his part, could hardly complain. He had been forced out of the business he had created, but he had really been out of it for three years and, after all, he made out well financially in the consolidation, ending up with around $5,000,000 in cash. Villard lost power but made money. In his immediate rage he blamed the failure on Insull's borrowing, but he quickly apologized and soon offered Insull the presidency of The North American Company, his biggest concern and one which would one day become a giant in the world of public utility holding companies.[52]

Insull was the only man in the Edison organization who was given a high executive position in the new company. He was offered the second vice-presidency (under Coffin and Thomson-Houston vice-president Eugene Griffin) at a salary of $36,000 a year. Objectively this was no mean station for a thirty-two-year-old, but Insull was in no mood to be objective about it. He had no intention of working under Coffin; for all Coffin's talents, Insull was convinced that Coffin did not understand the business and that he himself should have had the presidency. (Egotistical as this notion was, it was given weight by the early history of General Electric. Forgetting that Thomson-Houston "did not think much of the way the Edison company had been managed," Coffin immediately scrapped his own manufacturing and sales system and adopted the one created by Insull. He retained

---

[51] *New York World*, Feb. 20, 1892; New York *Commercial and Financial Chronicle*, Feb. 6, Feb. 13, Feb. 20, March 12, April 9, April 23, May 7, June 25, 1892; Insull, "Memoirs," p. 52; Josephson, *Edison*, p. 364; Passer, *Electrical Manufacturers*, p. 322.
[52] Tate, *Edison's Open Door*, pp. 260–63; Insull, "Memoirs," pp. 53, 56–57; *New York World*, Feb. 20, 1892; Josephson, *Edison*, pp. 364–65. Villard's continued friendship and respect for Insull is attested by the fact that in the middle 1890's he lent Insull $100,000 on a personal note and carried the loan for him at low interest for several years. This loan is recorded in Insull's personal account books, in the Insull Papers.

his shortsighted attitude toward his customers until he had almost wrecked the entire electrical industry and changed his policy then only after Insull, from the outside, forced him to do so.) Beyond this objection, Insull believed that because of the ill feelings engendered among Edisonians by the merger, and because Insull had, in the end, favored the merger, propriety prevented his profiting in any way from it. Finally, and most important, he had grown increasingly convinced that the central station industry, not manufacturing, was the electric business with a future. Accordingly, he informed Coffin that he would accept the position, but only on a temporary basis; as soon as his services in putting the companies together could be dispensed with, he would resign.[53]

Then he began to look for a job.

Coincidentally, the Chicago Edison Company was just then looking for a president, and two of its directors, Byron L. Smith, the president of the Northern Trust Company, and Edward L. Brewster, head of the brokerage firm of Edward L. Brewster & Company, had written Insull asking him to find them one. Because New York's central station company, being dominated by Morgan, was out, Chicago was the logical place for Insull, and because of a chance

[53] Insull, "Memoirs," pp. 56–57; Hammond, *Men and Volts*, p. 197. Passer, *Electrical Manufacturers*, p. 326, asserts that Edison G.E. was weaker than Thomson-Houston because it never had "a forceful, imaginative, dynamic, and aggressive leader." Here, in my opinion, Passer is grossly uninformed or misinformed; indeed, he shows no awareness that Insull was even running Edison G.E., or that Insull was made second vice-president of General Electric at its formation—an understandable oversight, in view of the fact that he did not use the records at the Edison Laboratory National Monument. But Passer himself points out (p. 324), as does Hammond (*Men and Volts*, p. 176), that Coffin dropped his own manufacturing and sales organization and adopted that of Edison General Electric, which Insull had created. For details of Insull's subsequent relations with General Electric, and the progress he forced that company to make, see pages 60–62, 99–103, and 229–30, below. See also the (privately printed, "not published") Minutes of the Association of Edison Illuminating Companies, 1893–1925, *passim*, especially the activities of the Lamp Committee.

There is a story—one that is widespread in the electric utility industry, but which I have been unable to confirm—that in the original edition of Hammond's *Men and Volts*, the "official" history of General Electric, Insull's vital role in the history of Edison's ventures was given full treatment, but that for political reasons the manuscript was altered, after Hammond's death, to purge Insull from its pages. In the book's preface, it is stated that Hammond died in 1934, at which time Insull was in Greece, a fugitive from justice and the subject of concentrated political attack. Hammond had finished the manuscript in 1922; it was cut considerably and edited and first published in 1941.

remark Edison had once made to him in Chicago ("You know, Sammy," he said, "this is one of the best cities in the world for our line of business"), he had long been interested in the city. The job, if he got it, would be a great comedown from what he had at General Electric, for it would mean leaving a $36,000 job with a $50,000,000 corporation to take a $12,000 job in an $885,000 corporation. But it had a large compensation: He would be allowed to run things (which he had learned to covet as much as money), and thus the opportunity the job offered would be bound only by the limits of Insull's own ability and ambition. Too, if he was to stay in electricity, the only alternatives were Villard's job in The North American Company, in which he would be subordinate to Villard, and Westinghouse, and he just did not have it in him to join Edison's favorite enemy.[54]

Insull felt that it would be improper for him to seek the job directly, and he could think of no suitable way to do it indirectly. As it happened, his mother was visiting him in New York at the time, and he told her his problem. Mama Insull, who always placed far more stock in blunt honesty than in propriety, snorted that there was no problem at all. They asked him in his capacity with Edison G.E. to recommend the best available man, did they not? Well, then, he was the best available man, and he should sit right down and write them a letter saying so. Dutifully, he did so; he wrote identical letters to Smith and Brewster, offering himself as a candidate for Chicago Edison's presidency. They and the other directors eagerly accepted his offer. After some discussion, he agreed to be in Chicago for at least a part of every other week throughout the spring of 1892, and to move there permanently and take up his duties on July 1.[55]

He imposed two conditions. The first was that he would have nothing to do with financing the company; the directors and stockholders, all men of abundant means, would have to satisfy him that sufficient working capital would be available at all times. His harrowing decade of financing Edison's enterprises on a helter-skelter, hand-to-mouth basis had been enough to last him a lifetime.

[54] Insull, "Memoirs," pp. 56–57.
[55] *Ibid.*, pp. 57–59; H. A. Seymour, "History of Commonwealth Edison Company" (typescript, completed in 1935 and now in the files of Commonwealth Edison Company, Chicago), pp. 193–94. Insull narrated most of these events in various reminiscing speeches to his employees; copies are preserved in the Insull Papers.

The second was that the company immediately begin construction of a new plant that would greatly increase its generating capacity and pay for it by issuing $250,000 in new stock, all to be sold to Insull. To buy the stock, Insull borrowed the entire sum from Marshall Field, who in his old age figured the best possible place to invest money was in bright young men.[56]

There was a finishing touch. Just before Insull left for Chicago, the important men in Thomson-Houston and Edison G.E. gave him a farewell dinner at Delmonico's. Forty-nine guests—including, as Insull said, all his intimate friends and all his intimate enemies—gathered, presented him with a handsome silver punchbowl, and heaped laudatory farewell addresses upon him. When the time came for him to speak, he rose, his voice calm but tinged with bitterness, his eyes blazing, and he ventured a bold prediction. He would build his tiny central station rapidly, he said, and one day he would make it bigger than General Electric itself. The assertion, given the occasion, was hardly graceful; it smacked of sour grapes, and it was so far-fetched as to be laughable—except that when Samuel Insull looked like that, nobody ever laughed.[57]

[56] Insull, "Memoirs," pp. 59, 61–62.
[57] Insull described the occasion in his "Memoirs," pp. 60–61. Mementos of the farewell dinner are preserved in the Insull Papers.

CHAPTER III *Chicago*

If Samuel Insull had not existed, it would have been necessary for Chicago to invent him: he became the last and the fiercest of the long succession of restless giants who ruled the city and its surrounding prairie countryside. Chicago had men who built and dared on a colossal scale—Ogdens, Fields, Armours, Wentworths, Pullmans, McCormicks—and it had triumphed on the Great Lakes, and then burst beyond St. Louis and Cincinnati to dominate America's heartland. By 1892, Chicago had set out to overthrow New York as master of the continent. Before it could do so, Chicago itself needed a master. He arrived on July 1.[1]

It was not love at first sight. Even had Chicago been less preoccupied with more important things, it would hardly have been impressed by this skinny, bespectacled, and mustachioed thirty-two-year-old Britisher, arriving from New York to take over one of the thirty-odd companies—and not the biggest one, at that—in a business that had yet to prove itself. To be sure, from the outset Insull had influential friends and contacts in the city; in addition to Brewster and Smith, Chicago Edison's board of directors included Robert

[1] The most important scholarly work on Chicago in the nineteenth century is Bessie L. Pierce, *A History of Chicago* (2 vols. to date; Chicago, 1937, and New York, 1957); older but valuable is Alfred T. Andreas, *History of Chicago from the Earliest Period to the Present Time* (3 vols.; Chicago, 1884–86). More colorful, and quite reliable for a popular history, is Emmett Dedmon's *Fabulous Chicago* (New York, 1953). For background on Chicago, I have read these and a dozen other volumes but have obtained background primarily by reading a file of the *Chicago Tribune* from, roughly, 1892 to 1932. The publishers of the *Tribune* kindly made available to me the files on Insull in their morgue.

Todd Lincoln, John W. Doane, John B. Drake, and others, none of whom was a second-string Chicagoan. And anyone who paused long enough to be arrested by the command in Insull's eyes might have reflected that here was a man with electricity for a soul; and everyone who knew him knew that for a decade he had been Mr. Edison's foremost dynamo. But amidst Chicago's exciting and ambitious undertakings, no one paused to be commanded by any man.[2]

Insull was scarcely more impressed. Despite his determination to fulfil his bold prediction, and the bitter knot of hatred that underscored it, his heart sank when he contemplated Chicago in the flesh. His most vivid image of the city concerned neither its men nor its future, but its filth and its huge rats. On earlier trips to Chicago he had sometimes spent idle evenings sitting on the porch of the old Sherman House, betting with fellow guests upon the number of rats that would emerge from various drains in the street; and this, to him, was Chicago. In short, Insull considered himself a civilized man, albeit one in a hurry, and he feared that while Chicago suited his pace it could hardly accommodate his taste. Indeed, lest he should suddenly decide to chuck it all and return to New York or even to London, he insisted that he be bound to his new job by a three-year contract.[3]

To the naked eye, the most important immediate fact of life for a man in Insull's position was the oncoming Columbian Exposition, the Chicago World's Fair of 1893. In addition to the general boom it would bring, the fair appeared to offer special advantage to any Chicago electric company, for it promised to be the greatest display

[2] Seymour, "History of Commonwealth Edison," pp. 231–32. Although several stories about electricity, the Chicago Edison Company, and the Edison G.E.—Thomson-Houston merger appeared in the *Tribune* in 1892 (for example, May 3, May 4, May 28, June 1, June 14, Nov. 30, 1892), I found no mention of Insull until April 19, 1893.
[3] Insull, "Memoirs," p. 62; interview with Samuel Insull, Jr.; *Minutes,* Chicago Edison Company, directors' meeting, Sept. 17, 1895. The corporate records of Chicago Edison consist of two record books covering minutes of directors' and stockholders' meetings, 1893–1907, and two executive committee minute books, covering 1887–92 and 1893–1907, respectively. There are apparently no records of directors' or stockholders' meetings prior to 1893. Records of Commonwealth Electric Company, Chicago Edison's sister corporation from 1898, when it was created, until 1907, when the two were consolidated, are complete, as are records of the consolidated company, Commonwealth Edison. All are housed in the offices of Commonwealth Edison Company, 72 West Adams Street, Chicago, and were used, without restriction, with the permission of the company. Herein, meetings will be cited by kind and date, without reference to volume number.

of electric lighting and equipment the world had yet seen. Insull's eye, however, was not naked. He knew well that Jackson Park, the site of the Fair, was four miles from the downtown area where Chicago Edison did business, far beyond the practical limits of direct current transmission. He also knew that all the manufacturers would provide their own power for their displays. The Fair was important to him, but only because it would create a climate in which his directors might be more easily persuaded to indorse his ambitious plans to expand.[4]

Insull knew little about how to manage a central station company, but he was sure of one thing: that the only sensible way to sell electric lighting was to have no competition. True, any other operator would also have welcomed a monopoly, but Insull's thinking differed from that of others in one vital respect. To most others, monopoly was desirable because it would enable them to charge higher prices and thus make more money; to Insull it was imperative because it would enable him to build on a broader base of customers and thus expand all the more. All his thinking—or theirs—on central station economics was therefore inverted. Their thinking, as reflected in their operations and their statements at closed-door meetings of fellow operators, was based on the premise that electricity should be considered as a luxury product and that it should be sold at the highest possible price. Insull's thinking, as reflected in his operations and his statements at the same private meetings, was based on the premise that electricity should be considered as for everybody, "even the smallest consumer," and that it should be sold at the lowest possible price.[5]

Insull's attitude derived more from instinct than from reason. He

[4] On the electrical aspects of the Columbian Exposition see Passer, *Electrical Manufacturers,* pp. 142–43; Hammond, *Men and Volts,* pp. 213–19; and Seymour, "History of Commonwealth Edison," pp. 219–25. For a colorful general description of the Fair see Dedmon, *Fabulous Chicago,* pp. 220–37, and the files of the *Chicago Tribune,* May-October, 1893. For an account of the importance of the Fair to the budding central station industry see McDonald, *Let There Be Light,* pp. 30–32.

[5] *Minutes of the Meeting of the Association of Edison Illuminating Companies, 10th Annual Meeting* (1894), pp. 126–27, *11th Annual Meeting* (1895), pp. 49, 78 ff., 92–95. John I. Beggs, the former manager of the Edison central station at Harrisburg, Pennsylvania, and subsequently the man who took the job Villard had offered Insull at The North American Company (and in that capacity became the manager of the Cincinnati Edison Company and later the Milwaukee Electric Railway and Light Company), was the only other operator in the 1890's who consistently maintained with Insull that electricity could compete economically with gas.

could not say at all why he was so sure of his position, nor would he be able to say until the end of the decade, when he had developed one of modern business' first statistical departments and pioneered modern cost accounting. For the present, his faith in the need for monopoly stemmed from his European background, from a utilitarian England which considered monopoly nothing to fear and, through Villard, from a Germany that viewed monopoly under state control as a positive good.

So Insull set out to fashion a monopoly of service in Chicago. Characteristically, he began by gambling his whole financial future on the outcome of his efforts—hence his borrowing $250,000 from Marshall Field to buy Chicago Edison stock. Then he moved into action, and with every major step he blazed a trail that other central station operators were to follow. First he called on Frederick Sargent, a brilliant engineer who had, before opening a consulting office in 1890, worked for Edison (under Insull) and then for Chicago Edison. Insull put Sargent to work designing a new generating plant that inaugurated a radical departure in power-house policy. The engineering features of the plant, contributions of Sargent and Chicago Edison's keen young chief engineer, L. A. Ferguson, were impressive. The plant was located where Harrison Street crossed the Chicago River, far from the center of the company's load. This made it possible to use condensing generators, which required an abundant supply of water. The saving that resulted—halving the amount of coal needed to produce a kilowatt-hour—more than offset the increased investment in distribution lines that the location necessitated. The engineering achievement was widely heralded, but the engineering aspect was second to a subtle economic consideration. At Insull's instructions, Sargent made the plant not only a huge one for the day (1,250-horsepower engines and two 400-kilowatt generators) but expandable to several times its initial capacity. This was Insull's first step toward mastering the complexities of central station economics. As a manufacturer he had learned that the bigger the generating equipment the lower the unit cost of capacity, and as a central station operator he realized that an ever-larger generating plant was the key if investment costs were to be kept within reasonable limits. From 1892 onward he demanded, often in defiance of his own engineers and almost always over the protests of those at General Electric, generators two, three, and four times as large as any others in existence.[6]

Even as the Harrison Street station was taking shape on the drawing board, Insull was moving in another direction. At the very first meeting of Chicago Edison's executive committee, Insull persuaded his directors to buy their second largest competitor, the Fort Wayne Electric Company, together with its two subsidiaries. Three months later, he went after his biggest competitor. The occasion arose when C. Norman Fay, the president of Chicago Arc Light and Power Company, the local Thomson-Houston central station, invited him to lunch to hear a proposal. Over lunch in the Chicago Club, Fay told Insull that his company was about to issue a large amount of new stock, and he asked Insull to join a syndicate to underwrite the issue. Insull responded by following the tactic Coffin had used with Morgan. He did not, he said, believe that Chicago Arc Light was founded on sound economic principles; sooner or later it must fail, and then Chicago Edison would buy or otherwise absorb it. Fay laughed and said that it would be the other way around, since his company was twice the size of Insull's. But Insull knew that Fay's largest stockholder was anxious to sell out and turn to more lucrative enterprises, and that Fay himself was more interested in promoting companies than in operating them. By January, 1893, Insull had induced his directors to offer $120 a share for all the Arc Light stock—its par value was $100, and the market price was about 105—and in February the offer was accepted. Insull had scored a major gain, but again the most important part of his action was that which did not meet the eye. Chicago Edison paid for the stock not in cash or stock, but in 6 per cent debentures; thus even after the $20-a-share premium, servicing the new investment cost the company less than the 8 per cent dividends it was paying on its own stock.[7]

[6] *Electrical Engineer,* XIX (January 23, 1895) , 63–81; *Minutes,* Chicago Edison executive committee meetings, July 14, 1892; July 13, 1893; directors' meeting, Nov. 21, 1893; *Chicago Daily News,* June 10, 1895; Seymour, "History of Commonwealth Edison," pp. 202–7; W. L. Abbott, "The Glory That Was Harrison Street," *Edison Round Table* (a Commonwealth Edison Company house organ) , 1916; Insull, "Memoirs," pp. 73–74.
[7] *Minutes,* Chicago Edison executive committee meetings, July 14, Nov. 29, 1892; directors' meeting, April 19, 1893; Isham, Lincoln & Beale to Insull, April 19, 1893 (bound in minute book of Chicago Edison Company); Seymour "History of Commonwealth Edison," pp. 172–75, 178, 270; Chicago *Economist,* Oct. 8, Oct. 22, 1892; Jan. 21, Feb. 11, 1893; Insull, "Memoirs," pp. 72–73.

Insull's speed in acquiring these companies was not a matter of impatience but the opening plays in a brilliant series of maneuvers which parlayed the General Electric Company's problems and policies into a certain monopoly for Insull. At its formation G.E. was scarcely more beloved by operators of Edison central stations than it was by Insull; after all, Thomson-Houston had been their hated rivals as well as Edison General Electric's. G.E.'s initial actions intensified the hostility. To Edison central station men, the critical question in the merger was its effect upon their exclusive licensing contracts: would competing central stations, licensees of Thomson-Houston, now be able to buy Edison equipment? The new General Electric Company not only answered in the affirmative but with remarkable myopia dealt central stations a double-edged blow. It energetically resumed the promotion of isolated plants, the most serious immediate competitors of all central stations, and to assure sales it increased prices of equipment to central stations and cut the prices of isolated plants, so that the latter were now actually cheaper. In short, G.E. viewed the licensing contracts as one-way agreements that provided them with a number of captive customers.[8]

Then G.E. got into trouble, and to save itself it almost wrecked the entire central station industry. During the boom that attended its first year of existence, G.E. contracted for a large amount of business, and when the first wave of the great financial panic struck in May, 1893, the company was caught with insufficient operating funds and sizable floating debts. Furthermore, as a result of its own bungling and the cleverness of Westinghouse officials, G.E.'s prestige was taking a thorough beating at the Chicago Fair, and orders for new equipment almost completely ceased. The combination of these pressures strapped the company, and its stock plummeted from $114 a share in January, 1893, to 58 in May, and then to 30 in July. Despite the support of the mighty J. P. Morgan, its credit was drying up as rapidly as its obligations were coming due. In desperation President Coffin and the directors turned in August to the most sacrosanct

[8] Association of Edison Illuminating Companies (A.E.I.C.) *Minutes,* 1894, pp. 95 ff., 160 ff., 166–68; 1895, pp. 21–39; 1897, pp. 12–16. It should be emphasized that the discussions recorded in the A.E.I.C. *Minutes* were private; the volumes were printed and privately circulated to members only. See also F. P. Fish (G.E.'s general counsel) to Insull, Sept. 12, 1895, and Insull to Fish, Sept. 14, 1895 (bound in minute book of Chicago Edison Company).

item in their treasury, the $10,000,000 in stocks of Edison central station companies. They tried to create an affiliate and sell the stocks to it, but so weak was the market and so small was the faith of their stockholders that the effort collapsed, despite offers of a 100 per cent preferred stock bonus to be guaranteed by G.E. itself. G.E. held on desperately until November, and then, facing interest and preferred stock payments coming due on December 1, it dumped its entire portfolio (save a handful of choice items) onto the open market at less than a fourth of its face value. Among the choice items G.E. retained was the stock of Chicago Edison, and because none of the latter's investors sold, the stock held firm at 200 throughout the year.[9]

Thus while most of the betrayed operators could only stagger and curse in the storm, to Insull these events spelled opportunity, and he moved swiftly to take advantage of it. His first action was immediately practical. When the Fair closed at the end of October, 1893, G.E. had on exhibit in Chicago a 1,200-horsepower engine and two 800-kilowatt generators, the largest and most efficient in existence. In November, just as the financial crisis was coming to a head, G.E. was faced with the problem of doing something with this equipment. Chicago Edison was the logical buyer and, since G.E. was at that very moment destroying the money-raising potential of virtually all other prospective buyers, Insull was able to dictate both the price and the terms. The price was $50,000, only a fraction of the manufacturing cost, and the terms were even more liberal: Chicago Edison gave G.E. an interest-free, one-year note and extracted a replacement guarantee for the equipment for the same period. The machinery was installed at Harrison Street, and when that plant began full-time operations in 1894, Insull was running what was by far the largest electric power station in the world. He continued to do so for forty years.[10]

What followed was again less obvious but counted for more. Having temporarily destroyed the central station market, G.E. had no recourse after the panic but to promote more isolated plants, and

---

[9] New York *Commercial and Financial Chronicle,* Aug. 5, Aug. 19, Aug. 26, Oct. 28, Nov. 25, Dec. 9, 1893; Chicago *Economist,* Dec. 23, 1893; Hammond, *Men and Volts,* pp. 220–26, 407–8; Passer, *Electrical Manufacturers,* pp. 328–29.
[10] *Minutes,* Chicago Edison executive committee meeting, Nov. 8, 1893.

while all central station men protested, most were too weak to do anything about it. Insull was not, and G.E. found that Chicago was not a fertile field for its isolated promotions, but rather, that in Chicago the necessities of immediate policy dictated that it follow its long-term best interests. The key to Insull's position was his early purchases of the Fort Wayne and Chicago Arc Light companies. By buying these two companies, Chicago Edison had obtained exclusive rights to use every major kind of American-made electrical equipment except that of Westinghouse, and early in 1894 Insull even took the precaution of buying the company which had the Illinois rights to use the equipment of the great German manufacturers, Siemens & Halske. The policy quickly paid off: caught between bad times and difficulty even in buying replacement light bulbs, six of the small central stations in Chicago gave up in 1894–95 and sold out to Chicago Edison, and others were soon to follow. (When he won, Insull was always generous to the losers, paying them more for their plants than they were worth. This was not beneficence but good business; Insull recognized that while money may not buy friends it will keep many a man from becoming an enemy.) This meant that no one but Insull could operate a central station in Chicago unless prepared to use Westinghouse equipment, and since, as a result of the Fair, Westinghouse equipment was immensely popular in the Chicago area, G.E. found that to cross Insull was to play into the hands of its most dangerous competitor. Meanwhile, Westinghouse, to get a foothold in the area, established a lighting company in Evanston and endowed it with an exclusive licence for Cook County; later, Insull was able to buy that company and thereby to assure his complete monopoly.[11]

What was being won on the corporate chessboard, however, was not business but the exclusive right to do business, not customers but the opportunity to make customers. Chicago Edison was not yet a public utility company, nor would it be for many years to come; Insull had simply won for it a solid corporate base on which to work toward becoming a utility. The value of the winnings depended

[11] A.E.I.C. *Minutes*, 1895, pp. 30, 34, 38; Chicago *Economist*, Jan. 6, 1894; Seymour, "History of Commonwealth Edison," p. 270; *Minutes*, Chicago Edison executive committee meeting, Dec. 6, 1898; *Minutes*, Commonwealth Electric directors' meeting, Nov. 15, 1898.

upon Insull's ability and his ambition. The potential was enormous: In 1892 Chicago had more than a million inhabitants and less than 5,000 users of electric lights. Optimists were figuring that in a city of Chicago's size, as many as 25,000 might one day use the product. Insull intended to serve the million.[12]

He did not know just how to go about it. When he came to Chicago he knew what the best American operators knew about selling and pricing, but that was not much; the elusive economics of central station supply was a territory as untouched as electric technology had been a decade earlier. The business had one vital technological attribute that made it fundamentally different from all other kinds: for all practical purposes, electricity could not be stored but had to be manufactured, sold, delivered, and consumed at the same instant. Accordingly, it seemed impossible, even in theory, to develop the business along the more or less rational, tried and true lines of conventional manufacturing. An ordinary manufacturer could compensate for fluctuations in his market by storing his product, and thereby produce on a reasonably regular and thus economical basis, no matter how irregular the demands of his customers. The central station man, on the other hand, had to build a plant large enough to be ready, at all times, to supply the electricity to light every lamp a system served; but since his customers used their lights only a few hours a day and in varying combinations, electric plants were in use only a small fraction of the time. Edison had foreseen this difficulty and attacked it in typical common-sense fashion: he tried to increase daytime consumption by promoting department store and office lighting and small power applications, principally elevators. Neither was easy, for

[12] For general attitudes of Insull and other central station men toward the expectations for the future see the A.E.I.C. *Minutes*, 1892–1900, and the *Proceedings of the Annual Meeting of the National Electric Light Association* for the same period. I have relied largely upon these two sources on this matter, as at all points in this work where I have made general comments about the general state of attitudes, information, ideas, and progress in the industry. I have supplemented them, however, with interviews with a hundred or more men whose experience in the industry extended back to the late 1880's, and over scores of companies in half a dozen states. In addition, several recent company and industry histories shed light on the question; these include Raymond C. Miller's *Kilowatts at Work: A History of the Detroit Edison Company* (Detroit, 1957), which is by far the best of the lot; Charles M. Coleman, *P.G. and E. of California: The Centennial Story of Pacific Gas and Electric Company, 1852–1952* (New York, 1952); Wade H. Wright, *History of the Georgia Power Company, 1855–1956* (Atlanta, 1957); and my own *Let There Be Light: The Electric Utility Industry in Wisconsin, 1881–1955*.

daytime users proved to be the most eager buyers of isolated plants. Even beyond that, the pioneer central station operators soon learned, the problem was more complicated than Edison had expected, if only because they rarely knew whether they were making money or losing it.[13]

One of the principal mysteries of the business was that the total expenses of a central station seemed to stay about the same no matter how much electricity it delivered. By 1892, Insull and a handful of the members of the Association of Edison Illuminating Companies (an organization Insull had promoted in 1885 for the exchange of information on just such matters) had formulated a loose explanation of this enigma. It arose, they reasoned, from the need to build plants large enough to accommodate the maximum momentary demand. Because of this need, and also because the cost of laying cables and wires for transmitting and distributing energy was four or five times as large as the cost of powerhouse equipment, building plants was relatively expensive and operating them was relatively cheap. Indeed, the fixed costs, those that vary with the investment but not with the amount of electricity sold—interest, maintenance, depreciation, taxes, and insurance—were even higher than total operating costs, which vary with the volume of sales. The ratio was lopsided even with crude generators that consumed twelve pounds of coal to produce a kilowatt-hour of electricity, as Chicago Edison's new Adams Street plant did in 1892, and it seemed axiomatic that any technological improvements in the direction of greater efficiency would only increase the imbalance between fixed and operating costs. It also seemed to follow, in a vague and paradoxical way, that adding new customers increased investment and thereby made it

[13] The indispensable source for the development of Insull's thinking on central station economics—and, because he so often showed the way, of the industry's thinking on the subject—is his published speeches, in *Central-Station Electric Service* (Chicago, 1915) and *Public Utilities in Modern Life* (Chicago, 1924). See particularly his presidential address before the A.E.I.C., "Problems of the Edison Central-Station Companies in 1897," "The Development of the Central Station" (1898), "Possibilities of the Central-Station Business" (1907), "Elucidation of Electric Service Rates for Business Men" (1908), "The Larger Aspects of Making and Selling Electric Energy" (1909), and "Massing of Energy Production an Economic Necessity" (1910), in *Central-Station Electric Service*, pp. 1–7, 9–34, 48–53, 54–64, 73–96, and 127–43. See also the discussions on rate-making at the A.E.I.C. meetings from 1895 to 1905; and Insull, "Memoirs," pp. 70–71.

more expensive (and thus less profitable) to provide electricity, whereas keeping the number of customers small and inducing them to pay more or buy more made it less expensive (and thus more profitable).

Accordingly, many men in the industry had concluded that except for arc lighting of city streets, electricity was doomed forever to be a luxury product. In view of the conditions—typical ones—that Insull faced when he went to Chicago, such thinking is understandable. Chicago Edison's total investment was roughly a million dollars, and its generating capacity was 2,800 kilowatts. This meant that the fixed costs on the investment would be close to 2 cents a kilowatt-hour even if the plant operated at full capacity all the time. But it actually operated for an average of only about a sixth of the time, and thus fixed costs alone were almost 12 cents a kilowatt-hour, nearly as much as the equivalent cost for gas. Then in the early 1890's the gas industry introduced the Welsbach gas mantle, which vastly increased the efficiency of gas lighting. Thereafter, almost all central station men resigned themselves to the conviction that price competition with gas was over, and that gas had won. Electricity would continue to have a place, for it had some advantages over gas—arc lighting was better adapted for lighting large spaces, and the incandescent lamp produced a softer, more pleasant light—but it would always be more expensive.

At first Insull adopted the kind of selling and pricing policy used by his fellow operators, but he soon parted company with them. Almost all operators sold on the general premise that the more a customer bought, the less he should have to pay for it; and shortly after Insull's arrival Chicago Edison abandoned its flat-rate lighting charge of 1 cent per lamp-hour (about 20 cents a kilowatt-hour) and substituted a schedule beginning at 12 cents and sliding downward through quantity discounts to 5.4 cents. But this experiment did not last long, for the conventional method was too passive for a man as aggressive as Insull. The old way was aimed primarily at increasing the consumption of existing users, and Insull did not intend to wait for his business to grow at his customers' leisure. Impatient for results, he soon scrapped the innovation and, while he continued to experiment with rate schedules, he now gave his salesmen but one order: sell. If the prospective customer will not buy at the published rates, cut the rates and sell anyway; sell at whatever price it takes to get the business.[14]

The new order was immediately put to the test. Chief engineer Louis Ferguson (who, apart from a former meter reader named John Gilchrist and Insull himself, was the company's most eager salesman) found a big and prestigious prospect, the Great Northern Hotel, an elegant establishment just being built. Its owners were willing to wire the building and give electricity a try, but only at a price far below Chicago Edison's announced rates. The price they asked, said Insull, was "ridiculously low," but he instructed Ferguson to give it to them—taking the precaution of binding them with a five-year contract—and thenceforth long-term private contracts at low rates became Insull's basic method of acquiring the big lighting customers. As he added the big ones he cut rates as fast as possible in order to take on more little ones.[15]

The aggressive sales policy yielded results that dazzled other central station operators. During Insull's first forty-two months, two-thirds of which were attended by major economic depression, Chicago Edison quadrupled its connected load and increased its annual sales from 2.8 to 13.7 million kilowatt-hours; by 1895 its annual operating revenues were larger than its total capitalization had been in 1892.[16]

But Insull must have felt increasingly like a sailor without a compass, sailing fast but not sure where; for neither he, nor Ferguson, nor, for that matter, anyone else in the industry knew for sure how much it cost to produce the light they were selling so well. Insull had assumed that his intuitive ken in such matters—his abnormal quickness at penetrating the jungle of superficialities that obscured the fundamentals of a business problem—would see him through, but

[14] The A.E.I.C. fairly regularly printed comparative rate schedules of companies around the country; at first, Chicago Edison's were about in the middle among the several Edison central stations, but later only those in Cincinnati and Detroit could compare with Chicago in their published rates, and none could compare with Chicago Edison's contract rates. For schedules of Chicago Edison's rates during the period see Seymour, "History of Commonwealth Edison," pp. 214–18, 280–81. See also Insull's remarks at the 1895 A.E.I.C. meeting (*Minutes,* 1895, pp. 104–6) .
[15] Insull, "Memoirs," p. 71. Biographical data on Ferguson and Gilchrist is contained in Seymour, "History of Commonwealth Edison," pp. 123–47.
[16] Seymour, "History of Commonwealth Edison," pp. 192, 208–10, 290.

after two and a half years he knew little more about how to charge a customer than he did when he started. He and most other operators were groping uneasily for a clue that would help unravel the industry's odd economics; but only one of them, W. S. Barstow of Brooklyn Edison, was groping in the right direction, and he was not at all sure of himself. Then, quite by chance, Insull stumbled across the answer.[17]

Toward the end of 1894, Insull went back to England for Christmas vacation and spent a few days by the sea at Brighton, on the southern coast. On his first evening in Brighton he saw an unfamiliar sight: Every shop, even the smallest, seemed to be burning electric lights, and no one appeared to be squeamish about the abundant use of electricity. As curious as he was amazed, Insull looked up the city official who managed the plant—like many small central stations in England, Brighton's was owned by the municipality—and found an unassuming young man named Arthur Wright. Wright attributed his success to a device that he had invented and which he called a demand meter. The idea was simple. The cost of producing electric light, he explained to Insull, is really two costs, fixed costs and operating costs, each of which varies from customer to customer. Accordingly, said Wright, it is no more sensible to have a uniform rate than it is to have a uniform flat charge. Suppose, he said, that you have a customer who owns a vacation cottage wired for twenty lamps, but he burns them only three or four weekends a year. Because you have to invest so much money in equipment to be ready to serve him any time he flicks his switches, it costs more than half as much to serve him those few weekends as it would to serve him day and night throughout the year. Now suppose, Wright continued, that you have another customer who has the same number of lamps but uses them for several hours every night. To charge these two customers the same rate would be absurd; you make more money out of the second customer at a nickel a kilowatt-hour than you do out of the first at four times that rate. Wright measured every customer's use of electricity in two parts, each corresponding to a part of the cost: one

---

[17] See Barstow's paper on rate-making in the A.E.I.C. *Minutes* for 1895, pp. 78 ff., and the discussion that followed. Another man, A. S. Knight of Boston Edison, made important contributions on the subject after 1897 in papers delivered before the A.E.I.C.

part to see how much equipment the customer necessitated, and one part to see how much he used the equipment. The charge for the service was a combination of the two: a given rate for the first few hours of use of the maximum demand, somewhat less for the next few hours thereof, still less for the next few, and so on.[18]

Exhilarated by Wright's brilliant insight, Insull returned to Chicago and forthwith launched the central station business in a new direction. He had fully perceived, as Wright apparently had not, the next step in the logic: that profits depended not upon load, but upon what came to be called load factor—not, that is, upon the total amount of energy sold but upon the percentage of the time one's plant investment was in active use. That fact, in turn, confirmed three policies Insull had adopted without knowing why and without seeing that they were connected: that one should extend service to as many customers as possible, that isolated plants were economically unsound, and that competition was absurd. Since all customers used their equipment only a fraction of the time, but not all at exactly the same time, it followed that a single investment could supply several users, and thus that any two customers could always be supplied more cheaply than one. Conversely, two stations could not possibly serve as cheaply as one; competition must invariably result in greater investment and higher cost in areas of greatest consumption, and virtually no service in other areas. Building on these principles—by sending Ferguson to Brighton, by working with Ferguson to refine Wright's system for use in Chicago, by bringing Wright to the United States to lecture to other central station operators, and by testing each principle and measuring the results statistically—Insull would, in a few years, establish the pattern for rate-making throughout the world.[19]

---

[18] Insull, "Memoirs," p. 88. Insull dated this episode as 1896, obviously a memory slip. In the 1895 discussions at the A.E.I.C. (*Minutes*, 1895, pp. 92–95), Insull talks about Wright in some detail, and at the National Electric Light Association convention in 1897 (N.E.L.A. *Proceedings*, 1897, p. 196) Insull said his meeting with Wright had happened three years earlier. Circumstantial evidence also supports December, 1894: Insull was present at Chicago Edison's executive committee meeting on November 7, 1894, absent from the December and January meetings, and present again on February 5, 1895.

[19] N.E.L.A. *Proceedings*, 1897, pp. 159 ff.; A.E.I.C. *Minutes*, 1895, pp. 92–95; *Minutes*, Chicago Edison executive committee meetings, Feb. 1, April 19, 1898; Insull, *Central-Station Electric Service*, p. 41 (address of June 7, 1898). Another system, the so-called Hopkinson demand system, later supplemented the Wright system; modern rate systems, as they finally evolved, were built on a combination of the two.

But the immediate significance of the discovery was that having learned how to charge, Insull now knew how to sell. Soon after his return to Chicago, he reorganized the sales department, placing at first five, then twenty-five, full-time men under Gilchrist. Gilchrist and his men, armed with precise knowledge of costs, could calculate the exact amount any prospective customer was paying for gas lighting or isolated electric lighting, and offer the service for less. Even more important, they could now bid for a power market as well as a lighting market. In 1894 three-fourths of the electricity Chicago Edison sent out was used for lighting; five years later almost half of it was used for small power applications. In that same five years, the company trebled its customers and its total kilowatt-hour sales and doubled its load factor.[20]

Even as the new economic understanding killed off one set of problems, however, it bred a new one. Insull was now expanding into a much larger area than Chicago Edison, as a direct current company, could serve from a single central station. Alternating current seemed the obvious answer, but the company's investment in d.c. equipment, as well as that of its customers, was already large enough to discourage the change. Furthermore, superior as a.c. was for purposes of transmission, it was distinctly inferior for purposes of consumption. The trouble was that a.c. motors did not perform reliably except at low frequencies—16 cycles was best, and 25 cycles was the maximum decided upon—and at such frequencies incandescent lamps flickered continuously. The problem could be resolved by using one frequency for light and another for power, but this was an awkward and uneconomic procedure.[21]

Then Ferguson, viewing the problem in two parts, as Wright had, asked why not use alternating current for transmission and direct current for distribution to consumers? To do so, he devised an ingenious method. He ordered two machines called rotary converters, which were in effect 25-cycle motors directly connected to d.c. gen-

[20] Seymour, "History of Commonwealth Edison," pp. 238–41, 272–80, 321; John F. Gilchrist, "Campaigning for Business," a paper presented before the A.E.I.C. (*Minutes*, 1902, pp. 322 ff.) .
[21] For a good discussion of the early problems with alternating current see Passer, *Electrical Manufacturers*, pp. 276–95. Full and colorful descriptions of the operators' problems with these technical difficulties are contained in two sets of tape-recorded interviews (January and May, 1954) , with a large number of veteran Wisconsin utility men, now in the possession of the State Historical Society of Wisconsin at Madison.

erators. He had one of the rotary converters wound backward, so that it was a direct current motor operating an a.c. generator. When it had been installed at the Harrison Street plant, he could generate at d.c., change over to a.c., step up the voltage and send the energy anywhere in town, step down the voltage and reconvert to d.c. through the other rotary at a substation, and distribute d.c. from the substation as if it were a power plant. This solved the problem; all Chicago could now be served from a single generating plant, without a prohibitive investment in wire. So successful was Ferguson's distribution system, indeed, that it would soon be necessary to have generating plants larger than it was then possible to build.[22]

As Chicago Edison grew, so grew Insull's prestige among the financial men on LaSalle Street. The subtleties of his achievements were quite beyond them, but two aspects were not: after a half dozen years of severe depression, Insull's company was ten times as large as it had been when he took it over, and during that period it had paid twenty-four consecutive quarterly dividends of 2 per cent.[23] And then, by a single spectacular action, Insull moved into the big leagues.

In the summer of 1896 William Jennings Bryan captured the Democratic Party's presidential nomination and launched his crusade for 16-to-1 silver, a panacea that promised to double the prairie farmer's prices and halve his debts. As if by command (as perhaps it was), the American money market responded by ceasing to exist. From Bryan's nomination in July until McKinley's election in November, bankers stopped lending, and investment houses stopped buying bonds, notes, or debentures. The "Bryan panic" severely curtailed all business activity, but it squeezed tightest in the Middle West and on enterprises to whom credit during that summer and fall was absolutely necessary. Among the principal sufferers were electric central stations and their affluent big brothers, streetcar and elevated railway companies. All these had expanded during

---

[22] Insull, "Memoirs," p. 72; Hammond, *Men and Volts*, p. 238; Seymour, "History of Commonwealth Edison," pp. 308–9. Apparently W. S. Barstow had the idea independently at about the same time and installed rotary converters in his company's system. The rotary converter had been invented in the early 1890's (Passer, *Electrical Manufacturers*, pp. 300–301), but was virtually unused until Ferguson and Barstow thought of using it in this way.

[23] Seymour, "History of Commonwealth Edison," pp. 192, 290; *Minutes*, Chicago Edison executive committee meeting, Aug. 31, 1896; dividends are recorded in the minutes of the directors' meetings throughout the period.

thc upturn in business in the summer of 1895, and most, finding the market for their securities still shaking from the storm of '93, had financed through bank loans. Most of these floating debts came due during the freakish panic of 1896, and companies perished by the score. In Wisconsin not a single major central station or streetcar company survived the year, and those in Michigan, Minnesota, Indiana, and Illinois fared scarcely better.[24]

Chicago Edison had likewise accumulated sizable floating debts in 1895, and it had committed itself to considerable capital outlay in 1896. In the spring, Insull, demonstrating for the first time an uncanny sense of political timing that would often appear again, tried to induce his directors to action. First, he argued, they should authorize a bond issue with an ultimate limit of at least $25,000,000, enough to accommodate expansion for several years to come. Then, because money was already somewhat tight in Chicago, they should go immediately to London and try, before summer came, to sell $1,200,000 of the bonds, enough to take care of all present needs. The secret attraction of London was that it offered the only alternative to appealing to the despised bankers in New York, but there were more logical reasons as well. For one thing, Insull and some of the board members had good financial connections in London and, more important, England would not react to the financial disturbances of American politics until late July, whereas stringency in the United States could begin six to eight weeks earlier. Insull's directors agreed that London was the proper market, but when they placed a $6,000,-000 ultimate ceiling on the proposed issue—leaving, after financing immediate needs and funding the outstanding debentures, only $2,000,000 for future expansion—he threw up his hands in disgust. When they dallied until late June before sending the bonds to an agent in London, he suspected that he would, after all, have to abandon his original intention and become the company's financier as well as its operator. His guess was confirmed when the news came from London, for when the bonds were offered the market for American securities had vanished.[25]

But instead of acting immediately he let his directors stew for two months. Then, late in August, he summarily announced to the execu-

[24] Insull, "Memoirs," p. 69; Chicago *Economist*, July–September, 1896; *Chicago Tribune*, Sept. 2, Sept. 6, Sept. 11–13, 1896; McDonald, *Let There Be Light*, chap. 2, *passim*.
[25] Insull, "Memoirs," pp. 69, 83–85; *Minutes*, Chicago Edison directors' meetings, June 5, July 23, 1896.

tive committee that he was going to London to sell the bonds himself.[26]

He sold the bonds by a means that epitomized salesmanship, Insull-style. Before departing he sent to the prospective buyers, the Scottish American Trust, a financial statement that was as disarmingly frank as it was overwhelmingly detailed. Then he committed the details to memory and sailed, and upon arriving he discussed finance not at all. Instead, he called upon Amyass Northcote, an erstwhile Chicago real-estate operator now heading a London firm specializing in American investments, and suggested to him that he, Samuel Insull, was more or less the protégé of Edward Isham, senior member of Chicago Edison's law firm, Isham, Lincoln & Beale, and one of Northcote's oldest and dearest friends. Then he called upon the chairman of the trust and simply reminded him that they had met when Insull was working for Gouraud. (Insull could do this in such a way as to suggest that it was somehow the early exposure to the chairman's genius that had inspired him, a plucky young Englishman, to go off to the colonies and make a name for himself. If Insull was merely up to par that day, the chairman felt that not to buy the bonds would be to disown a young man he had all but started in business himself. If Insull was at his very best the chairman probably felt a vague uneasiness lest rejecting the bonds would somehow be disrespectful to the Queen.) To both men Insull added just one point: that the mortgage under which the bonds were issued contained an unprecedented, superconservative safety feature that he had devised, namely a built-in depreciation reserve system, replacing the sinking fund of the conventional mortgage, which had proved advantageous to neither buyer nor issuer of bonds. (This feature was the first step in a plan Insull had for revolutionizing bond financing; it was not in keeping with Insull's own theory of depreciation, which was so advanced as to be unintelligible. But it was just the *doucier,* the sweetener, for the buyers of bonds.) [27]

[26] Insull, "Memoirs," pp. 84–85; *Minutes,* Chicago Edison directors' meeting, Aug. 18, 1896; *Minutes,* executive committee meeting, Aug. 31, 1896.
[27] Insull, "Memoirs," pp. 85–86; Insull to London Scottish American Trust, Sept. 11, 1896 (bound in Chicago Edison minute book) ; *Minutes,* Chicago Edison executive committee meeting, Aug. 31, 1896. On the mortgage and Insull's depreciation theory see pp. 91–93, 126–27, below. Insull's ability and techniques as a salesman were mentioned during interviews with dozens of his former associates.

Then Insull waited, allowing the buyers to sell themselves. In less than a week he was able to cable home that all the bonds had been sold at par, and that $800,000 in gold, the initial payment, was on its way to Chicago.[28]

The reaction of the financial community was immediate and enthusiastic. "Such a sale had been thought an impossibility," crowed Chicago's leading financial editor. Others heralded the achievement with adjectives ranging from "brilliant" to "astounding." And a considerable number of Middle Western financiers raced to London to emulate Insull.[29]

But Chicago had seen nothing yet. Keener still than his political ken, more profound than his organizational ability, was Insull's sense of public relations. To him the moment of applause was the moment for action, and act he did. He followed his 1896 triumph with several major, albeit seemingly unconnected, achievements, each of which would have been sufficient monuments for the lifetime of most men. He initiated and brought to a successful conclusion a movement for utility regulation, and thereby effected a fundamental alteration in the relationship between government and business in the United States. He devised a financial innovation, the open-end mortgage (one without a ceiling), and thereby began a revolution in the financing of American business enterprise. He worked out a set of financial policies that altered a century-long pattern of American business development, and thereby built a multi-billion-dollar empire.

But these were long-range doings, and like most successful revolutionaries Insull lived his life not as a lifetime but as a succession of days. Thus in 1896 it was the immediate personal aftermath of the London episode that counted most with him, for with this achievement in international finance he began, for the first time, to deal as an equal with those who ruled Chicago.

The perceptive among them must soon have sensed that they stood to him roughly as the second and third consuls stood to Napoleon: he would not deal with them as equals very long.

[28] *Minutes,* Chicago Edison executive committee meeting, Oct. 6, 1896; Memorandum of Agreement between Chicago Edison and London Scottish American Trust, Sept., 1896 (bound in Chicago Edison minute book); Insull, "Memoirs," p. 85.
[29] Chicago *Economist,* Sept. 12, Sept. 19, 1896; *Chicago Tribune,* Sept. 13, 1896; *Chicago Record,* Sept. 14, 1896; Insull, "Memoirs," p. 86.

CHAPTER IV *Intimates*

Until about 1897 only his mother and Thomas Edison had a deep personal influence on Insull, his thinking, and his career. To be sure, he had learned from others—he learned from everyone he met and from everyone he saw—and he continued to depend upon others for information, ideas, suggestions, advice, and their specialized skills. Ferguson, W. L. Abbot, and Sargent contributed their operating and engineering savvy, Gilchrist his shrewd salesmanship and keen sense of public relations, William Fox (first Insull's, then the company's, secretary) his skill in office management, and Brewster, Smith, and Edward Russell their financial acumen; and Insull learned from exchanging ideas with other central station men, John W. Lieb of New York Edison, W. S. Barstow of Brooklyn Edison, John Edgar of Boston Edison, and John I. Beggs of Cincinnati Edison. But no one made up his mind for him, and except for his mother and Edison, he had not opened up his heart to anyone, and no one had persuaded him against his judgment.

After 1897, however, intimates became both numerous and influential. In order of importance as well as of appearance, they were Gladys Wallis, Samuel Insull, Jr., Roger Sullivan, William G. Beale, and Charles A. Munroe. The latter three represented types who were to play major roles in Insull's life. The first two were unique.

Though he had a million dollars, more or less, Gladys Wallis did not marry Sam Insull for his money. Nor did Sam marry Gladys because of her beauty, although women so beautiful are considerably less common than millionaires.[1]

[1] General chronological data on Gladys Wallis Insull are derived largely from sketches that appeared from time to time in newspapers; for example, *Chicago Herald and*

Her beauty ripened quickly, and it never faded (at the age of fifty-six she dazzled Chicago as the eighteen-year-old Lady Teazle in Sheridan's *The School for Scandal*), but it was of an immensely deceptive kind, appropriate for an immensely deceptive lady. Dimpled, exquisitely featured, standing less than five feet and weighing less than ninety pounds, she was dainty, almost fragile in appearance. Actually she was not at all fragile: she was as tough as a South of Ireland Presbyterian.[2]

Which she was. Like Insull, she was born of parents who espoused the wrong religion at the wrong place and time. When Douglas Bird and Katherine Mitchell were married in Ballysadare, County Sligo, in 1867, Douglas was teaching school, fighting his Catholic neighbors, and drinking too much. When they moved to New York a year later, just in time for the birth of the first of three daughters, he was working and fighting somewhat less and drinking somewhat more. In order to support the family while her husband made a series of vain and halfhearted stabs at seeking his fortune, Mama Bird converted their large rented dwelling on Eleventh Street into a boarding house for actors. In 1869 they had a second daughter, Margaret Anna Bird, who was to change her name to Gladys Wallis at the age of eight when, with the help of one of the boarders, she began a career as an actress. A year or two before Margaret/Gladys began her career, Papa Bird went West to see if he could become rich in the gold and silver fields. He never came back, he never wrote a line, he never sent a dollar. After six years—during which

Examiner, Oct. 23, 1925, Oct. 2, 1932; *Chicago Daily News,* Feb. 10, 1926; *Chicago Tribune,* May 21, 1925; and the obituary that appeared in the *New York Times* and all Chicago newspapers, Sept. 24, 1953. Personal data are taken primarily from her letters to Insull and to her son, about eight hundred of which, covering the years 1897–1945, are preserved in the Insull Papers. Factual data on her ancestry was supplied by Samuel Insull, Jr. My analysis of her personality and character is based upon these sources and upon interviews with several of her friends and acquaintances, particularly Miss Anna Nicholas (Chicago, Dec. 31, 1959), Mrs. Tiffany Blake (Chicago, Feb. 4, 1958), Mrs. Bertha Baur (Chicago, Dec. 8, 1957), Edward J. Doyle (Northfield, Illinois, June 24, 1959), R. H. James (Chicago, May 20, 1958), Philip McEnroe (Los Angeles, Sept. 10, 1958), Carlos Drake (Los Angeles, Sept. 11–12, 1958), Arthur Meeker, Jr. (New York, Jan. 3, 1958), and Samuel Insull, Jr. The interview with Miss Nicholas—who for many years was Gladys' dressmaker, intimate friend, confidante, and in some ways emotional stay—was particularly revealing. All judgments expressed here, of course, are presented as my own.
[2] The physical description is based upon photographs in the Insull Papers; regarding the performance in *The School for Scandal,* see pages 233–35, below.

Gladys saw, in the boarding house, enough of sex to make it repugnant to her forever—the family heard from someone that he had died, apparently of pneumonia, somewhere in the mountains of Utah, Nevada, or Colorado.[3]

Unlike Insull, Gladys was impelled by no drive to achieve Respectability. To her respectability was spelled with a lower-case "r," and it was an attribute one simply had or did not have; it was the small, steel-tough ball of something inside one that stood between humanity and the gutter. Though the gutter was never more than one misstep away, the traumas of her early home life armed Gladys with impenetrable defenses against two of its most insidious entrances, sex and liquor. Protected by these (but also hampered, for they precluded her taking the bedroom route to success) and blessed with a considerable measure of talent and an abundance of fiery determination, she worked and fought and clawed her way toward the nebulous security of stardom. At fifteen she occasionally drew top billing; soon after she was twenty she was making seventy-five to a hundred dollars a week, first with the renowned W. H. Crane Company and later with the even more renowned company of John Drew.[4]

Along the way, as she learned her art she also learned much about life, but what she learned was not always perfectly balanced. Socially—that is in polite society—she fared brilliantly; her beauty and her wit and charm got her gracefully through most situations, and when these failed, she could use her quick talent for mimicry to bluff her way. But she was both cursed and blessed with a built-in,

[3] On Mrs. Insull's reactions to matters of sex much can be inferred from the sources cited in note 1, above. Precise information, however, was obtained from persons to whom she confided more or less explicitly, but who, for personal reasons, requested they not be named before giving the information to me. That condition seemed an argument for omitting the subject entirely—on the grounds that it is technically not documentable—even though what I learned from them is logically consistent with what I learned elsewhere of the lady. Nonetheless, despite this reservation, I have included it here because, as will be narrated later, it came, in my best judgment, to be a critical factor in Insull's life.

[4] *Chicago Herald and Examiner*, Oct. 23, 1925; *Chicago Tribune*, May 21, 1925; Insull, "Memoirs," p. 99. Figures on Gladys Wallis' income are from occasional remarks in her letters to Insull in 1897. The *Chicago Daily News*, Feb. 10, 1926, cites the reminiscences of a veteran Canadian journalist and drama critic (Hector Charlesworth, in *Candid Chronicles*, published in Toronto in 1926) about Gladys Wallis' early career. Charlesworth discusses several of her performances and says that "her grace, charm and intelligence amounted to something like genius"; he believed that had she not married Insull, she would have become one of the great stars of the age.

foolproof phoniness detector. Consequently, she never learned to like other women —she rarely had more than one female friend at a time, though these friendships were as deep as they were rare—and only by deliberate effort was she able to get along with women at all. And though she had learned at a tender age how to gather men around her like iron filings around a bar magnet, she had not found one she could trust or love.

Her drive to reach the top paled the ambition that drove Sam. She thought she was seeking the heights because of the secure, comforting warmth that applause and money would afford her, and because the artist in her commanded that she do so. What she really wanted was a father.

Enter Samuel Insull, engaged in the male counterpart of the same pursuit. It is said that strong men who are dominated by their mothers grow up to marry them; Insull more or less consciously intended to do just that. But this was one thing about which he was in no hurry. Sooner or later the right lady would show up. But for the time being he never lacked lady friends, and besides, his mother and sister Emma were around often enough to satisfy his need for proper feminine company.[5]

Superficially, Gladys resembled his idealized mother-image not at all, but she conquered him in less than a week. They met in February, 1897, at a small dinner party given by Insull's friend Eugene Lewis (erstwhile partner of Insull's old enemy, S. B. Eaton) and his fiancée, actress Amy Busby. Gladys was Insull's third choice among Miss Busby's friends for a dinner partner, but that was his last free choice in the matter. He called the next day, and the next, and the next. When her company left a week later, she owned him. He was determined to make it the other way around.[6]

---

[5] My information on Insull's attitudes on this subject in the 1890's is based upon hearsay, but it is, I believe, reliable: in the 1920's, when Insull's son occasionally showed a streak of the playboy, Insull discussed the matter with his good friend and attorney, Daniel Schuyler, and commented upon his own twenties and thirties. At least one such discussion was held in the presence of George W. Lennon, then a young lawyer in Schuyler's firm; Lennon reported the conversation to me in an interview in Chicago on August 21, 1959. Much can be inferred from his correspondence with Gladys, 1897–99; from his private correspondence and letters about him during the 1880's, in the Edison Laboratory National Monument; and from his letters to his son, in the Insull Papers. For an excellent statement of his attitude toward marriage and the family, see Insull to Insull, Jr., April 25, 1916.

[6] Insull, "Memoirs," p. 99; Samuel Insull, Jr., to the writer, July 8, 1959. The remainder

It would be no easy task. Gladys had been pursued by some of the ablest pursuers in New York, Chicago, and points between. Too, Insull had certain handicaps. The most obvious was that she was on the road and he was in Chicago. Again, during the courtship he was hardly unoccupied, either of time or of mind; his work day remained at sixteen hours throughout, and for a variety of reasons, largely political, he was under greater pressure than he had yet experienced in Chicago. And to make his position particularly challenging, he simultaneously occupied the active presidency of his industry's two top organizations, the Association of Edison Illuminating Companies and the National Electric Light Association. Finally, he was physically somewhat less than a matinee idol. He was no longer skin and bones, as he had been when he went to Chicago, but his general appearance was one of ultra-sternness, better designed to instil fear than flutters in a maiden's heart.

Nonetheless, Insull was well equipped for the game of love. Though he looked more like a mustachioed, mortgage-holding villain than a hero, he had one commanding physical attribute, his eyes. His eyes could persuade, command, demand, or hypnotize; they could disarm with gentleness or overwhelm with blazing passion; they could sear the soul with a crackling fire or dissect it with an icy scalpel; they were eyes that few men could face, and few women could resist.[7] As for his disadvantages, he knew how to turn disadvantages into advantages, and he would transform these, too. The problems of time and distance were problems only if one so regarded them: any seasoned male knows that thoughtfulness in absentia and appropriate correspondence (and Insull wrote marvelous letters) can be utilized to breed interest and desire, making personal contact a delicious climax to long anticipation. As for his pressing preoccupations, it was typical with him (as well as revealing) that when he was under greatest duress his need for a strong, understanding

of this account of Insull's courtship is based upon approximately five hundred letters from Gladys Wallis to Insull, written between February, 1897, and May, 1899, all in the Insull Papers; I have read them all, most of them twice. Because they are so voluminous, and because so much to be learned from them is implicit (for example, the evolution of her feelings, as indicated by the measure of affection expressed in the salutation and complimentary close), no specific citations will be offered here.

[7] This feature of Insull's appearance is to some extent apparent from his photographs; significantly, almost every one of the scores of persons I have interviewed commented on the quality of Insull's eyes.

woman was greatest. Hence while his essential wooing tactic was to appear as Gladys' tower of strength and ever-reliable crutch, he could at the same time sincerely demonstrate his own need for her. Some women can resist a man who supplies every need, and some can resist a man who convinces them that they alone are needed, but no woman can resist both. And though Gladys was an extraordinary person, she was first a woman.

It took him about a year to convince her that he was the only man for her. As it happened, her career took its worst turn during the first year they knew each other. She had left the Drew Company, partly because the presence of Maude Adams and Drew's young niece, Ethel Barrymore, virtually precluded opportunity for starring roles with that company, and partly because (or so she suggested in one of her letters to Sam) Drew, a married man, seemed rather more interested in her as a woman than as an actress. She then joined the much less respected and seemingly less respectable company of William Frawley. In starring roles for Frawley she met with considerable success before critics and before audiences, but she was unable to get along with either Frawley or his cast. During the first half of 1897, as she was growing increasingly discontented with her lot, Sam wrote regularly, made several trips East to see her, and overwhelmed her with his thoughtfulness. By midyear he had won a position as most nearly trusted friend, and she had become, far more than she realized, dependent upon his daily letters as a solace against loneliness.

It was in the late fall, however, that he first had opportunity to demonstrate to her that he had become indispensable. In November, while she was playing in San Francisco, the manager of the Tivoli Theatre offered her a permanent engagement in starring roles at $100 a week and costumes, with no travel and only half the work involved in the Frawley Company. She tentatively accepted, then changed her mind when Frawley countered with an offer of $125. But Frawley, smarting under her condescension, his dependence upon her, and the several tastes she had given him of her explosive temper, took this as a final humiliation, and a few weeks later—as soon as the Tivoli opening had been taken by someone else—summarily fired her. She was stranded in San Francisco without friends, funds, or a job. Sam raced to the rescue with money, lawyers, and advice, and the gentleness and tact with which he handled the delicacies of the role melted the last of her resistance.

All save one. They became engaged in February, 1898, after she had returned home for a rest (at Sam's expense) and then resumed work, for the rest of the season, in the traveling company of a play called *The Circus Girl*. But no date was set, for she wanted, first, to satisfy her overpowering need to prove that she had been a success, that she was to marry Sam because she so elected and not because he offered an easy way out.

The proof came suddenly in the fall of 1898 when she received, almost simultaneously, an offer to rejoin the Crane Company and an offer to go into vaudeville on a long-term contract at $400 to $500 a week—approximately the same as Sam's salary as president of Chicago Edison. Her inclination was to accept the lucrative offer, but Sam, alarmed into being at his persuasive best, convinced her that vaudeville was indecorous if indeed not bawdy. At his urging, she accepted Crane's offer instead, and in May, 1899, after the close of the season, they were married.[8]

Though they both had tempers somewhat too violent to permit uninterrupted harmony, they were otherwise beautifully matched in every way except one. Sam, like many men of great creativity and energy, had sexual drives as powerful as his need for success; Gladys, on the other hand, never outgrew that part of her childhood which made her view sex with fear, hostility, and disgust. Nonetheless, the first years of their marriage were the happiest in Sam's life, and during that period he came—for a moment—close to contentment, all but ready to stop running.

On April 12, 1900, Samuel Insull, Jr., was born.[9] Like Dombey's son, he was an institution first and (until proved otherwise) a human being only second. As such, he served as an added bond of affection between his parents, and later as a bridge whenever they seemed about to grow apart. They lavished such love upon him that he

[8] Two huge scrapbooks in the Insull Papers, called "Insull-Bird," contain an abundance of clippings about the wedding and about the bride and groom.
[9] Data on the childhood of Insull, Jr., is derived from interviews with him; from an interview with his closest childhood friend (Carlos Drake, in Los Angeles on Sept. 11–12, 1958); from a reminiscence by another of his childhood friends (Shreve Cowles Badger, "Recollections of the Distinguished Twenties," in Chicago *Townsfolk*, Feb., 1949, pp. 11–27); and from letters between parents and son, 1907–17, in the Insull Papers.

tended, albeit timidly, toward the complete smart aleck, but they
tempered their love with firm discipline (Spare the rod and spoil the
child, said Sam with such conviction that he might have coined this
platitude) as well as with their own personal contributions. Sam
spoon-fed Junior the morality of Samuel Smiles and encouraged conviction in the practicality of the traditional virtues—responsibility
toward one's family, community, country, respect for established
authority, for one's elders and betters. Gladys taught him something
of her unerring talent for perceiving quality even in the most unlikely humans, and this talent's counterpart, a quickness to detect and
to despise the pretentious fraud. And though there were those who
maintained that she lacked this grace herself, she planted in Junior
the seed of that most precious of human qualities, humility. (He did
not learn humility easily, nor did he learn it precociously—indeed
he did not learn it until it became a condition of survival—but he
learned it nonetheless.)

But like many strong-willed parents to whom an only son is initially
an institution, the Insulls competed for his affection on a level far
different from the character-molding aspect on which they co-
operated. Gladys feared and envied only the world of business as a
rival for her husband's love, and she determined, so secretly that it
was a long time before she confessed it even to herself, that the same
preoccupations should not take her son from her. As secretly and as
determinedly, Sam set out to make Junior into a duplicate of himself.
Had it not mattered so much to the parents, this competition would
have amused them both: Sam cluttered Junior's quarters with every
manner of mechanical toy, from steam engines to electric trains, and
terrified him by taking him at the age of three to witness the operation of a monstrous steam-electric turbine; Gladys sought to interest
him in plays and poetry long before he could read and almost before
he could talk. In both arenas he learned quickly and felt deeply,
but throughout his childhood Gladys had the better of it. She got a
flying start because she recognized her son as a human being, a discovery Sam himself did not make for many years. Junior was his
mother's son until he was in his late teens. Then, in a sudden and
painful breach—signaled by the composition of a poem called "My
Brother the Turbine"—he decided to abandon all notions of a career
in the arts and follow his father into business. Later, that decision

would seem almost as important to the course of American business development as it did to the young man who made it.

During the first year of his courtship Insull received his initial bath of fire in Chicago's political inferno. Wooing Gladys all the while, he thwarted an effort to cremate him and emerged fire-proofed. For the next thirty-five years, barring one major and costly blunder, he was perhaps the most consistently successful and power-ful political operator in American business. For most of these years his principal mentor and closest political friend was Roger Sullivan, a man whose career ranged from ward heeler to statesman. Ironically, when first they met, Sullivan was heading one of several political groups who were attempting to blackmail Insull as a by-product of an effort to scalp traction magnate Charles Tyson Yerkes.

The faction in Chicago politics headed by Sullivan was called variously the Ogden Gas Crowd and the Sullivan-Hopkins faction of the Democratic Party. This group had introduced a new dimension into the business of urban politics and in so doing had established a new pattern for "the ethics of graft" in Chicago. It was a new dimension because it postulated that politicians should keep their hands out of the public till and earn their livelihood from non-civic activities, those for which, all the same, political power was an indispensable asset. Such activities must inevitably be what the academicians describe as "affected with a public interest": public utilities, or such quasi-utilities as the coal, building supply, and junk businesses. As it happened, Sullivan and most of his friends began with neither capital nor credit and had to resort to political influence to acquire them. The logical sources of the stake they required were the owners of existing enterprises, who might be happy to finance new ventures as a means of avoiding costly legislation. This was, to be sure, extortion pure and simple. It was nonetheless an elevation of the ethics of urban politics, for it was merely extortion, not theft, and it involved the conveyance of nothing that belonged to the people—no dipping into the public treasury, not even the sale of the votes of aldermen. Besides, the victims were public utilities, and as every urban politician recognized, "the people" instinctively re-garded public utilities as their natural enemy.[10]

[10] The most important single source on Chicago politics during this period—and one of the most important on urban politics anywhere—is the autobiography of Carter

Sullivan, along with George Brennan and erstwhile Mayor John P. Hopkins, had derived their Ogden Gas epithet from their maiden enterprise in the acquisition of credit and capital. In 1895 they had caused the passage of an ordinance granting a more than liberal franchise to the Ogden Gas Company. The company was one they had created for the purpose, and one whose stock they distributed in eleven equal blocs to various individuals, among whom the most prominent were themselves. The existing gas monopoly, the Peoples Gas Light and Coke Company, relished the liberal franchise of Ogden as much as it did not relish the notion of having a competitor. The Ogden group generously offered to sell out to the Peoples Company for a paltry $7,333,333. When Peoples Gas gratefully accepted, the holder of each bloc had two-thirds of a million dollars he could call his own. Everyone gained from the transaction: the politicians, the company, and in a way they would never have suspected, even the people. Subsequent variations on the franchise theme were similarly rewarding to all concerned.[11]

Should anyone be disposed to suspect, after this, that the Ogden Gas Crowd was the least savory of Chicago's political groups, he need only look at the others. Indeed, except for the decent and therefore powerless element, the Sullivan group stood at the head of the list. Next came the other major Democratic faction, that headed by Mayor Carter H. Harrison II, son of the martyred (by an anarchist's bomb in 1893) mayor of the same name. The father left the son

Harrison II, *Stormy Years* (Indianapolis, 1935). Harrison, mayor of Chicago from 1897 to 1905 and again from 1911 to 1915, pulled no punches in his description of the inner workings of Chicago politics, though he is occasionally demonstrably in error and he is understandably at pains to present himself in the most favorable light. Also useful are Lloyd Wendt and Herman Kogan, *Lords of the Levee* (Indianapolis, 1943); Charles E. Merriam, *Chicago: A More Intimate View of Urban Politics* (New York, 1929); and Harold L. Ickes, *Autobiography of a Curmudgeon* (New York, 1943). The files of Chicago newspapers, especially the *Tribune* and the *Inter-Ocean*, are indispensable. Ickes, in his *Autobiography*, p. 36, says that it was Sullivan who in 1912 made possible the nomination of Woodrow Wilson for president.

[11] This transaction is detailed in Harrison, *Stormy Years*, pp. 192–99; see also Ickes, *Autobiography*, pp. 36–37; the corporate aspect has been traced in the minute books and annual reports of Peoples Gas Light and Coke Company, in the offices of the company, Chicago. The account here is oversimplified, generally following Harrison's. Though this is in substance accurate, the transactions were actually extremely complex, involving several other pieces of legislation, leases rather than sales, assumption of certain debts, and so on. (For some of the salient details, see Peoples Gas Company's annual report for 1902 and the *Minutes* of the directors' meetings, Jan. 25, 1907, and Sept. 25, 1913.)

comfortably endowed, though not embarrassingly rich, in money and talent, and as mayor, Harrison the younger was reasonably efficient and not particularly concerned with the opportunities for loot that the position afforded. But the organization of his party was firmly held by Sullivan and Hopkins, and Harrison had an unquenchable thirst for popularity and an urge to become mayor of Chicago. The first of these desires he satisfied by practicing an artful species of demagoguery, the second by welding a coalition among what might be styled the pimp element in Chicago politics: the bosses of the wards dedicated to gambling, prostitution, extrapolitical crime, and related pursuits. In exchange for their political support, Harrison arranged to save these gentlemen sizable sums by tolerating their various activities, thus making it unnecessary to carry legions of policemen on their payrolls. (In this perverse fashion Harrison, too, helped elevate the ethics of Chicago politics. Before Harrison, the scholars who populated the city's poolrooms were fond of pointing out that "Our cops are not for sale, though it is easy enough to lease one for a time.") [12]

Powerful as these groups were, neither they nor the Republicans' Blond Boss, Billy Lorimer, dominated the city council. The balance of power in the council belonged to a bipartisan group of aldermen known as the Gray Wolves. In their wards the Gray Wolves ruled in the fashion of feudal barons, but in the common council they paid homage to the requisites of modern commercialism by selling their votes according to a regular schedule of bribes, ranging from $300 to $25,000. They were so corrupt that on controversial issues Alderman "Johnny De Pow" Powers, leader of the pack, often found it difficult to prevent their selling out to both sides at once. [13]

Reasonably enough, the central figure in this melange was not a politician at all but the city's leading public utility magnate, Charles Tyson Yerkes. Yerkes' unqualified and undiscriminating contempt

---

[12] Harrison, *Stormy Years, passim;* Wendt and Kogan, *Lords of the Levee, passim;* Ickes, *Autobiography,* pp. 35–36.

[13] Harrison, *Stormy Years,* pp. 131, 192–93; Dedmon, *Fabulous Chicago,* pp. 259–60; Sidney I. Roberts, "Chicago Civic Profiles: The Chicago Franchise War," *Men and Events* (July, 1958), p. 18; Sidney I. Roberts, "Portrait of a Robber Baron: Charles T. Yerkes," *Business History Review,* XXXV (Autumn, 1961), 344–71. Robert's articles contain much useful information but suffer, in my opinion, from lack of understanding of some of the intricacies of contemporary corporate finance, and for that reason are not always reliable in their interpretations.

for politicians, customers, and stockholders spoke so loudly that his superior abilities and solid achievements as an entrepreneur were scarcely remarked on. He unified, electrified, and modernized the city's archaic transportation system and rendered it more extensive, more comfortable, faster and cheaper than any then existing in any large American city; but then, with consummate dexterity, he regularly wiped out any popularity these accomplishments might have won him. (Typical of his disdain for public relations was his answer to the request of a group of citizens that he add additional cars during rush hours. "Preposterous," he said. "It is the straphanger who pays the dividends," an observation as true as it was imprudent.) [14]

Far from being the wellspring of political corruption in Chicago, as he was generally regarded, Yerkes was its principal victim. Early in his efforts to put together his traction system, he made the fatal blunder of yielding to a demand that he buy certain necessary ordinances, and thereafter no legislation was free to him, even when it happened to be ardently desired by populace or politicians. [15]

Boodling, Yerkes' career, and Insull's political novitiate came to a climax in 1897, when Yerkes initiated what might be loosely termed a preventive war. Mighty as he was, Yerkes' footing was made

[14] The best source on Yerkes is a pair of celebrated novels, *The Titan* and *The Financier*, by Theodore Dreiser, in which almost every character is taken directly from life. Until about 1957, copies of these novels were in the library of Peoples Gas Company in Chicago. The fictitious names had been struck out, the real names penciled in, and some of Dreiser's minor factual errors corrected. The volumes have since disappeared.

The bibliography on Yerkes and Chicago traction is sizable. In addition to Harrison's *Stormy Years*, pp. 103–208, 240–47, Roberts' "Chicago Franchise War," *Men and Events*, (July and August, 1958), and his "Portrait of a Robber Baron," *Business History Review* (Autumn, 1961), see Harry Weber, *Outline History of Chicago Traction* (Chicago, 1936); Chicago *Economist, Street Railway Supplement for 1896;* Henry Demarest Lloyd, *The Chicago Traction Question* (Chicago, 1903); Burton J. Hendrick, "Great American Fortunes and Their Making: Street Railway Financiers," *McClure's Magazine* (November, 1907).

[15] Each of the sources cited in note 14 mentions Yerkes' blatant use of bribery; none fully shares my belief that Yerkes was the victim rather than the wellspring of corruption. In my opinion, none shows adequate appreciation of the fact that bribery as an instrument of political corruption was in full bloom in almost all large American cities from about 1870 to 1900, and that the stakes grew high as utilities grew large with the advent of electric-powered transportation. It is clear from study of company records and newspapers of Milwaukee, Chicago, Boston, and Providence, and from secondary works concerning New York, Philadelphia, and San Francisco, that operators of public transportation systems in the nineties had to pay off venal politicians or be destroyed.

perpetually precarious by two distinct yet intimately related problems: franchises and finances. Under Illinois law, city councils could
enfranchise public utilities for a period of only twenty years at the
maximum. Because his system had been fashioned from a host of
smaller companies, Yerkes had to seek a renewal of the franchise for
one part or another of the whole every few years, a fact that repeatedly made him vulnerable to costly and troublesome political
sniping. What was worse, most of his more important franchises
were to expire in 1903, a scant six years away.[16]

Had the franchise problem been merely costly and troublesome,
Yerkes might not have bothered to take drastic steps; after all, the
common council was for sale, and Yerkes had bought it often enough.
But the problem was somewhat more involved than that. Yerkes
commanded great financial resources, and his quick credit was also
great, but not even he could mobilize enough capital to finance an
ever-expanding utility business without the aid of long-term credit.
True, he might have mitigated the problem had he been more
scrupulous about issuing watered securities, but he could not obviate
it. The ability to sell bonds was indispensable, and the ability to
sell bonds was inseparable from franchise security, simply because
no one was anxious to buy thirty-year bonds from a company which
might cease to exist in less than a decade.[17]

In the early and middle nineties Yerkes had made several halfhearted attempts to alter the situation through state legislation,
only to find Democratic Governor John P. Altgeld invariably poised
with pen in hand, eager to veto any measure that Yerkes was even

---

[16] Roberts, "Chicago Franchise War," *Men and Events* (August, 1958) , p. 16; Harrison,
Stormy Years, pp. 109–10.

[17] None of the voluminous writings on traction and political corruption in the nineties
—of which the sources cited in note 14, above, are only a fraction—shows any understanding of the economics of the franchise problem, nor do any of the contemporary
newspaper accounts. Newspapers, muckrakers, and politicians—the corrupt and the
honest reformers alike—tended to take the position that the streets belonged to the
people, and that a franchise for their use by a private corporation should be awarded
only for limited periods and with provision for compensation to the city. What they all
apparently overlooked was that municipal compensation would simply be passed on to
passengers in increased fares, and that long-term franchise security did make possible
lower interest rates and thus lower cost of service, if lower costs could be enforced.
The solution ultimately worked out was to grant indeterminate franchises and provide
for regulatory commissions to enforce standards of rates and service. Rather than attempt to argue the subtleties of the question, most operators apparently observed that
city councils were for sale and simply bought them.

suspected of approving. In 1896, however, Yerkes became convinced of the urgency of the need for action, for that summer's financial storm came within an ace of wrecking all his enterprises on the shoals of short-term credit. Immediately after this unnerving experience, it appeared that perhaps the moment was as propitious as it was urgent, for the fall elections saw the defeat of Altgeld at the hands of the amenable if indeed not purchasable Republican, John R. Tanner.[18]

As soon as the legislature convened in February, 1897, Yerkes moved into action. Through one of his kept politicians, Senator John "Farmer" Humphrey, he introduced a set of bills which together promised not only the solution to all his problems but constituted, as well, one of the most progressive pieces of legislation ever considered by the state of Illinois. In essence, the Humphrey bills contained three proposals: (1) they would extend for fifty years all existing streetcar and elevated railway franchises, (2) they would require companies to pay to the cities they served an initial franchise compensation of $2,000 a mile and additional annual compensation of a percentage of gross revenues, beginning at 3 per cent and sliding upward over the years until it reached 7 per cent, and (3) they would remove control of local transportation companies from corrupt city councils and place it in the hands of a state regulatory commission that would, at least by design, be tough, expert, and nonpartisan. Together the measures were identical in almost all important respects to the renowned legislation by which Wisconsin created its pioneer utility commission in 1907, and where the Humphrey bills differed from the Wisconsin law they were more exacting upon companies. Had they passed, the history books would say that the Progressive movement was launched by Illinois in 1897 rather than by Wisconsin in 1901.[19]

[18] *Chicago Tribune*, Sept. 2, Sept. 11, Sept. 17, 1896; Harrison, *Stormy Years*, pp. 136–37.
[19] Illinois Senate and House *Journals*, 1897, Senate Bills Numbers 148, 149, 150, 258; *Chicago Tribune*, Feb. 19, Feb. 20, 1897; Roberts, "Chicago Franchise War," in *Men and Events* (August, 1958), p. 20; Harrison, *Stormy Years*, pp. 114, 140. Roberts and Harrison suggest that Yerkes had the Humphrey bills introduced only as a ruse, not expecting to be able to have them passed. Both writers, as well as contemporary newspapers, viewed the bills as a steal; all overlook the similarity to the much-praised laws creating the Wisconsin Railroad Commission. For an excellent brief account of the latter see *Census of Electric Light and Power, 1912*, pp. 162–64; for details of the creation of the Wisconsin commission see acts of 1905, 1907, 1911, and 1913, all of which are summarized in the *Wisconsin Blue Book* for 1929, pp. 79–96.

Having framed such legislation, Yerkes now cheerfully set about the business of bribing the legislators to pass it. He reckoned that the price would be high; after all, he was bribing politicians to pass laws that would make it unnecessary for him to bribe them again. Even so, he grossly underestimated the cost, for he was shortly buried in a public furor headed by as bizarre a collection of political bedfellows as Chicago had ever seen. Apparently a reporter for the *Chicago Tribune* set off the protest when he speculated in print (and later confirmed) that Yerkes had established an escrow fund of half a million dollars in cash to be exchanged for the votes of state senators and representatives. Carter Harrison, who was just then being elected to his first term as mayor, seized upon the issue and threw all his political might against the bills, and most honest reformers of all shades (who though not particularly numerous were extremely vocal) and most of Yerkes' enemies (who though not particularly vocal were extremely numerous) quickly joined the fray. Even this phalanx would have been hardly sufficient to defeat the Humphrey bills but for the support of Chicago's business elite. These leaders, having occasionally toyed with political reform through such organizations as the Chicago Civic Federation and the Union League Club, chose this peculiar occasion to take a firm stand, and their stand was decisive. Thus in what is surely one of the most ironic fits of righteous indignation on record, Chicago perpetuated the law of the jungle for its utilities.[20]

Yerkes did not panic in retreat, and he did manage to secure the passage of the so-called Allen Law, which extended no franchises but authorized city councils to grant them for up to fifty years. The effort was in vain, for Yerkes was politically dead, and after a year even the Allen Law was expunged from the statute books.[21]

All the while Sullivan-Hopkins and the Gray Wolves sat watchful, waiting, poised to strike, if only as scavengers after the battle. The Allen Law seemed the logical weapon, and since Yerkes was dead and the Gas Trust had been so recently victimized, Samuel Insull

[20] *Chicago Tribune,* Chicago *Inter-Ocean, Chicago Record, Chicago Daily News,* Feb. 17 to June 10, 1897; Harrison, *Stormy Years,* pp. 136–44; Roberts, "Chicago Franchise War," *Men and Events* (July, 1958), p. 12 (August, 1958), pp. 16–20.
[21] *Chicago Tribune,* Chicago *Inter-Ocean, Chicago Daily News, Chicago Record,* May 20, June 8, June 9, June 10, 1897; Harrison, *Stormy Years,* pp. 145–82; Roberts, "Chicago Franchise War," *Men and Events* (August, 1958), pp. 22–23.

seemed the logical prey. He was small fry, but he might be able to dig up a few hundred thousand, maybe a million, to prevent the creation of a competitor with a fifty-year franchise covering the entire city. On May 28, 1897, the Allen Law was passed, and within the week the Wolves dispatched couriers to inform Insull how much it would cost him to prevent the enfranchisement of a competitor. Insull, anticipating their demands, began to sweat the cold, premonitory sweat of dread, but when the messengers arrived he faced them calmly and refused. Baffled but undaunted, the Wolves simultaneously created and voted a fifty-year franchise to a corporation they styled Commonwealth Electric Company. Insull would not yield. Sullivan-Hopkins and the Wolves, experienced in wars of nerves and equipped with abundant capital, countered with the next and ordinarily decisive step, transforming the dummy corporation into an active competitor. Only then did they learn the reason for Insull's show of contempt for their efforts: because Insull had quietly acquired the exclusive rights to buy the electrical equipment of every American manufacturer, Commonwealth could hold its franchise for eternity but could never light a single bulb. After four months the politicians capitulated and sold Commonwealth and its franchise to Chicago Edison for $50,000. When the Allen Law was repealed in 1898—and for decades thereafter—Insull was the only electric utility operator in the state with a franchise for more than twenty years, and his franchise would not expire until 1947.[22]

To Insull not the least valuable fruit of the year's doings was the grudging respect he had won from Chicago's political professionals. Yet being among wary enemies is scarcely an improvement over being among unwary ones; and neither this change nor the fact that the events of 1897 made blatant corruption obsolete was enough for Insull. He sought nothing less than the friendship of all his foes—at least all the important ones. The one vital conquest on this front, the friendship of Roger Sullivan, was won with a maneuver as undramatic as it was shrewd. A few years after the franchise debacle,

[22] *Chicago Tribune, Chicago Daily News,* May 20–29, June 18, June 22, 1897; May 18, May 19, 1898; Chicago *Economist,* May 21, 1898; *Minutes,* Commonwealth Electric Company directors' meetings, June 10, July 21, 1897; March 3, May 9, 1898; *Minutes,* stockholders' meeting, Dec. 24, 1897; A.E.I.C. *Minutes,* 1895, pp. 30, 34, 38 (Insull's remarks therein); Insull, "Memoirs," p. 79; Harrison, *Stormy Years,* p. 159; Seymour, "History of Commonwealth Edison," pp. 264–65; interview with Samuel Insull, Jr. The figure $50,000 is from Samuel Insull, Jr.

Insull arranged to bump into Sullivan in London. Insull invited Sullivan to meet his mother, and Sullivan accepted. The visit would take only a few minutes, Insull said, but they stayed all afternoon. When they left, Sullivan said, "Insull, I've never trusted you. But any son of that woman must be all right." In this casual fashion was born an intimate personal friendship that lasted until Sullivan died in 1920.[23]

For thirty of his seventy-nine years Insull had near him at least one man who could say no and make it stick. The first of these was William G. Beale, the active partner of Chicago Edison's law firm, Isham, Lincoln & Beale. But for Beale that firm's stock in trade would long since have degenerated into little more than expensive respectability. By the late 1890's Edward Isham, the senior partner, had ceased to be active, and Robert Todd Lincoln, son of Abraham Lincoln and vice-president of Chicago Edison, had always been rather more abundantly blessed with name than with talent. Not that Beale lacked prestige in his own right: between the mayoralties of John P. Hopkins and Carter Harrison II Chicago had witnessed an almost unprecedented aberration, two years of honest administration, and during these years Beale had earned renown as corporation counsel under the Puritan mayor, George B. Swift. But it was as a working lawyer, and one with brains, that Beale was useful to Insull. Beale was adroit in functions ranging from the intricacies of corporate law to the rough and tumble of politics, but he had a specialty. He was one of those rare souls who become prematurely wise, and though he was only seven years older than Insull, he looked and played the role of the old counselor. Whenever Insull's aggressiveness, daring, or violent temper threatened to lead him into rash action, it was Billy Beale—and for a decade, Beale alone—who deterred him.[24]

When they were both at their best, only Beale could make safe what only Insull dared to do. They were both at their best in the Commonwealth Electric affair, and they were at least close to their

[23] Interview with Samuel Insull, Jr.; Insull, "Memoirs," pp. 157–58.
[24] Albert N. Marquis (ed.), *The Book of Chicagoans, 1911* (Chicago, 1911), p. 47; Insull, "Memoirs," pp. 157, 174; interview with Harry J. Dunbaugh, Chicago, Nov. 19, 1957. Mr. Dunbaugh, who had been with Isham, Lincoln & Beale since 1903, had for some years been working on a history of the firm.

best when they followed up that victory. The franchise implied as many problems as it did advantages. For one thing, politics precluded, for the moment, extending its benefits to Chicago Edison through a merger. For another, while the franchise made extensive as well as intensive development possible, technical obstacles stood in the way: Chicago Edison was a direct current company, and direct current could not be economically distributed all over Cook County, even with the use of rotary converters. Insull therefore decided to continue to operate Chicago Edison under its old franchise, but to limit its operations to an area within about a mile of the Loop, and develop Commonwealth Electric separately as an alternating current company operating in the rest of the city. Since Chicago Edison could not legally own the stock of another corporation, Insull held Commonwealth's stock as a nominee. Commonwealth and Edison would be interconnected at every appropriate point, and the operations of the two would be integrated.[25]

The operating problems and opportunities afforded by the franchise, however, were trifling compared to the financial. Insull, like many others in the utility business but like almost no one out of it, saw that the one supreme advantage of long-term franchise security was that it permitted long-term, low-cost financing. And like very few in the business, he recognized two other things about utility finance: first, that vast quantities of debt capital would be necessary if the City of Chicago was to have the kind of electric service that Insull would see that it demanded; second, that electric companies, like modern governments, borrow money that they cannot and do not intend to repay except by perpetually refinancing. Furthermore, he understood that electric companies, not having the taxing power which is government's capital, must see to it that the money borrowed is turned into and protected as perpetual capital.[26]

Beale agreed. Insull's directors, on the other hand, were a good

[25] Insull, "Memoirs," pp. 79–81; minute books of Chicago Edison and Commonwealth Electric companies, 1898–1907; contract between Commonwealth Electric and Chicago Edison, July 11, 1898 (bound in Chicago Edison minute book); Seymour, "History of Commonwealth Edison," pp. 265–71.
[26] For examples of Insull's thinking on the relations of franchises and politics to financing see his comments at a luncheon of the City Club of Chicago, March, 1908, reproduced in *Central-Station Electric Service*, pp. 62–64, and his address to the Investment Bankers Association of America, October 30, 1913, published in the same volume, pp. 427–44.

board of directors, which means they were rich, eminently respectable, and (with two or three notable exceptions) not cursed with an
excess of intelligence or even of financial acumen, as they had demonstrated in the 1896 financing. Insull foresaw an ultimate need of at
least $100,000,000 in bonds, but he had to convince a board that just
a year earlier had balked at $6,000,000. Then H. H. Porter, a friend
experienced in railroad financing, suggested to Beale and Insull
that, boards being what they are, to them a mortgage with no limit
might seem much smaller, more conservative, than one with a limit
of $100,000,000. Insull proposed to them a mortgage with no limit,
and they accepted. Under this mortgage, Insull would issue half a
billion in bonds before he was through.[27]

Billy Beale drew up the necessary document, and thereby the two
men contributed the open-end mortgage to American finance
capitalism. The mortgage contained several other innovations in
addition to that of having no stated limit. The bonds to be issued
under it were for a term of forty-five years (which, though not unprecedented, was twice as long a period as that for conventional utility
bonds) ; they matured all at once instead of being retired serially;
instead of providing a sinking fund for the bonds, the mortgage
provided the equivalent of an annual depreciation reserve to be set
aside out of earnings—that is, the theory was that one should protect
the investor not by paying back or setting aside some of his money
each year, which was senseless because both borrower and lender
would then have to look again for investment, but by protecting the
property covered by his mortgage. As further protection—actually a
guarantee that no bonds would be issued except to cover bona fide
investment—it provided that bonds could be issued from time to
time to capitalize no more than 75 per cent of actual plant facilities
already constructed.[28]

To create such a mortgage was one thing, to sell bonds under it was
another. Insull soon had opportunity to find out whether they could

[27] Insull, "Memoirs," pp. 80–81; *Minutes,* Commonwealth Electric directors' meetings,
Aug. 10, Aug. 22, Sept. 6, 1898; stockholders' meeting, May 31, 1898; annual report for
the year ending March 31, 1899; Seymour, "History of Commonwealth Edison," p. 288.
[28] The original copy of the mortgage is bound in the minute books of Commonwealth
Electric, at the stockholders' meeting, May 31, 1898; for a lengthy discussion of it and
of its significance see the Chicago *Economist,* June 30, 1898. See also Stock and Bond
Circulars issued by Russell, Brewster & Company, 1901–13 (a bound volume in the Insull
Papers) , pp. 3, 6, 8, 11, 15.

be sold. To launch the new company, he arranged to purchase a handful of companies on the South Side, which he had previously allowed to operate because they were outside the practical service area of Chicago Edison. To effect this purchase and initiate active business by Commonwealth, Insull needed about $2,000,000, and the company issued bonds in that amount. Bankers were so afraid of them that none would take them except on a contingent basis, but their fears proved unjustified. Partly because of the abundance of cheap money that appeared after McKinley's inauguration and partly because of the reputation Insull was rapidly earning in Chicago financial circles, the 5 per cent, forty-five-year bonds were sold at 92 per cent of par within two weeks, to yield a net interest of 5.22 per cent. The sale was all the more noteworthy because the wide territory Commonwealth proposed to serve—the largest yet undertaken—made it, in the eyes of investors, distinctly a risky venture.[29]

Marketing of bonds under the Commonwealth mortgage found Insull a second trusted friend and adviser very much like Beale, and it also established some financing patterns that he was to follow until the end of his career. The adviser and friend was John J. Mitchell, president of the Illinois Trust & Savings Bank. Mitchell was a banker's banker, and yet, despite Insull's antipathy for anybody's banker, he was the ideal banker for Sam. Superficially, they were poles apart: professionally and in private life Mitchell was so conservative with money that even his closest friends regarded him as stingy. He never moved rashly, he never gambled, he rarely made a major mistake. But his conservatism was in large measure a pose affected as a means of accumulating a reserve of prestige on which he could draw when bold or even audacious action suited his purposes. Mitchell could sit as interminably and as noncommittally as any banker, but as he sat he was no more inactive than is a still, silent cat stalking a bird. And like a cat stalking a bird, he moved only when his movement would be decisive.[30]

[29] *Minutes,* Commonwealth Electric directors' meetings, Aug. 10, Sept. 6, 1898; Insull, "Memoirs," pp. 79–80.
[30] For a biographical sketch of Mitchell see Marquis (ed.), *The Book of Chicagoans, 1911,* p. 483; for a picture of him in action see F. Cyril James' excellent work, *The Growth of Chicago Banks* (2 vols.; New York, 1938), *passim.* Much characterization and information was obtained from interviews; especially informative were interviews

In making up his mind about Mitchell, Insull decided at once. In addition to the obvious value of his support in coping with other Chicago bankers, Mitchell had, in Insull's eyes, one priceless virtue: he was as determined as Insull was that Chicago should become a seat of vast financial power, independent of New York. Furthermore, he not only knew how it might be made so, as did Insull, but was also able, as Insull was not, to go about it without arousing enmity in New York. Indeed, by the turn of the century, whenever J. P. Morgan—which is to say, New York—visited Chicago, he bypassed the twin giants of the First National, James B. Forgan and sometime Secretary of the Treasury Lyman B. Gage, and called upon Mitchell; and all the while Mitchell was openly inciting Chicago bankers to take Middle Western business away from New York.[31]

In making up his mind about Insull, Mitchell was even more cautious than usual. Mitchell became a director of Chicago Edison early in 1896, but for two years he appeared to be just another respectable businessman, sitting on the board and giving or withholding sanction of the actions of management. Actually, he spent the time studying Insull. (Mitchell was skeptical of, and singularly qualified at evaluating, boy wonders of the business world, having been one himself; in 1873 he had gone to work as a twenty-year-old messenger in his bank, and seven years later he had become its president.) After watching the 1896 financing and the 1897 political maneuvering, Mitchell decided that Insull was his kind of businessman: a thoroughgoing radical, but one who knew exactly what he was about. Having decided, he backed Insull without reservation. He helped Insull sell the open-end mortgage to the other directors, and thenceforth Mitchell joined Gladys, Sullivan, and Beale as fixtures in Insull's inner group.[32]

---

with Arthur Meeker, Jr. (New York, Jan. 3, 1958); Edward Eagle Brown, former chairman of the First National Bank in Chicago (Chicago, Oct. 21, 1958); and several interviews with Abner J. Stilwell, former vice-president of the Continental Illinois National Bank and Trust Company.

[31] James, *Growth of Chicago Banks*, vol. ii, *passim;* interviews with Abner J. Stilwell; *Chicago Evening Post*, Dec. 9, 1908; *Chicago Tribune*, Dec. 10, 1908. See also the *Chicago Inter-Ocean*, 1901–13, where Mitchell is regularly quoted as Chicago's expert on all matters financial.

[32] Marquis (ed.), *The Book of Chicagoans, 1911*, p. 483; *Minutes*, Chicago Edison directors' meetings, Feb. 18, 1896, and thereafter; Insull, "Memoirs," p. 175. The evidence of the importance of Mitchell to Insull is boundless; in almost every one of Insull's major undertakings, from 1897 to 1927, Mitchell was along as a director.

With Mitchell at one elbow and Beale at the other, Insull worked out the long-range pattern he was to use in financing his enterprises. The first rule was that New York was out of it. The second was that financing was always done in Chicago whenever Chicago could and would accommodate him. The third was that when Chicago could not or would not, he would look to London for credit. Until World War I this arrangement proved adequate. It was not entirely satisfactory, for though it made him independent of New York it still left him dependent upon bankers somewhere. But in giving him a choice of bankers, it gave him far more flexibility than was enjoyed by most utility operators. A third choice, one that would make him the master of bankers, was soon to come in the person of a twenty-six-year-old Rhode Island Scotsman named Harold L. Stuart. But Stuart was the bridge to the future.[33]

This prudent woman, this prudent politician, this prudent lawyer, and this prudent banker whom Insull had made a part of himself were to serve not as brakes but as regulators, like chains of leaden shields about an atomic reactor. The next person to join the group came by a different route and served a different function. This was Charles A. Munroe, a man who dared raid the nascent empire.

At the time of this venture, Munroe was twenty-six years old, a lawyer with an almost demoniacal craving for wealth and a comparable talent for pursuing it. Like many before him, he had, as a young man, fled the barren hills of Vermont—those hills so prolific of stones and men as hard and inarticulate as stone—to seek his fortune in the Middle West. Munroe shared his predecessors' hardness, but there the resemblance entirely ceased. No tight-lipped puritanical bumpkin was he; indeed, Munroe was so elegant in taste and manner and dress that, but for the steel in his eyes and his backbone, he might easily have been mistaken for a dandy. And the stereotyped Vermonter's notion of accumulating this world's goods a nickel at a time was incomprehensible to him. His eyes were on the main chance, and he had the imagination to see it and the courage to seize it.[34]

[33] Insull's financial patterns are made more or less explicit in his "Memoirs," pp. 82–83; I have studied them in records of scores of his companies.
[34] Marquis (ed.), *Who's Who in Chicago*, 1931, p. 706; obituaries in *Chicago American* and *Chicago Tribune*, Dec. 29, 1957; interview with Munroe and Samuel Insull, Jr., New York, May 16, 1956.

In 1901 he thought he saw it. For a year or so Munroe had been working with a client in Joliet who owned, among other things, the rights to a small water power site on the Illinois River. Munroe knew virtually nothing of the economics of hydroelectric power, but like millions of his fellow citizens he was intrigued by the recent and spectacular harnessing of Niagara Falls, and like them he had a vague notion that water power was free power. The client entertained no such delusions, and he sold Munroe an option on his water power rights. Munroe quickly learned the first two principles of hydro economics: that a good deal of money is needed to develop even a small hydro site, and that power, no matter how cheap, is worthless unless one has a place to sell it. He also recognized that the second comes first, and on the theory that it would be easy enough to raise the money for the development if he could sell the power, he began to look for a market. Chicago, alas, was unavailable, and Munroe began to acquire franchises from villages in the vicinity of his power site. He soon realized that he was getting in over his head in a business he did not understand.[35]

Then suddenly the break came, in Yerkes' departure from Chicago. In 1901 the great man had had enough, and under pressure from discontented stockholders and amid considerable talk of indictment, he sold all his holdings and removed to London. The general citizenry exhaled a sigh of relief. Newspaper editors and reformers, spoiled by years of having so convenient a symbol of corruption in their midst, began the search for a new root of all evil. Venal politicians exhaled a sigh of nostalgia for the good old days. Sam Insull exhaled a sigh of new-found comfort, confident that Yerkes' departure would make politics less hectic for all utility men. Charlie Munroe sighed not at all: he sprang into action, for here was the main chance. In Chicago, as elsewhere, the power consumed by streetcars and elevated railways dwarfed the power consumed for all other purposes. In Chicago, as elsewhere, traction companies generated their own power. But in Chicago the practice had derived neither from economics nor from necessity, but from the fact that

[35] This account of Munroe's attempted raid, except when otherwise documented, is based upon the interview with him, May 16, 1956. Munroe's account was checked against the corporate records of Commonwealth Electric, Chicago Edison, Economy Light and Power, and North Shore Electric companies, all in the files of Commonwealth Edison Company.

Yerkes had a large personal stake in the business of selling power equipment. It was no secret that Yerkes had used his own transportation companies as a captive market for his power equipment company. Munroe shrewdly calculated that as a result the transportation companies' power costs were probably high, and that with Yerkes gone their managers might be eager to rectify this matter. His first call on the president of the Lake Street "El" yielded results: an informal agreement to buy all the power Munroe could deliver, from Joliet or elsewhere.[36]

Munroe was quick to visualize the implications of this triumph. So was Insull, as soon as he learned of it. It meant that Munroe threatened to become, by virtue of one brilliant stroke, the leading supplier of electric power in Chicago. Careful investigation, and reflection upon his findings, would have demonstrated to Insull that his fears were groundless, for Munroe had neither money nor a real source of power, and no more grasp of the economics of what he was doing than he could derive from reading Hearst Sunday supplements. But on this and all subsequent occasions when he was faced with a raid, Insull reacted instinctively: act first and think about it later. The action called for was to buy out Munroe. (Munroe had nothing to sell, but being a shrewd bargainer, he made Insull pay well for the privilege of finding this out.)

Having bought, Insull thought. The first and most obvious fruit of his reflection was that he should do what Munroe had seen could be done, develop the huge market for power that the traction companies afforded. Landing contracts for supplying all this power would immediately double Insull's sales, and it would do more, for the traction load was an off-peak load. Chicagoans got up in the morning and used electric lights supplied by Insull's generators. Then they went to work, using conveyances not supplied by Insull's generators. All day long they used lights and power furnished by Insull, then they returned home, again on conveyances not powered by Insull's generators. When they got home they again used Insull-

---

[36] On Yerkes' financial interests in manufacturing companies, see the *Chicago Tribune, Chicago Record,* and Chicago *Economist,* 1894–98, random references; for a delightful account of his departure from Chicago, see Harrison, *Stormy Years,* pp. 204–8. The Co-operative Electric Light Company, which Insull had bought for its rights to use Siemens & Halske equipment, had had exclusive rights only for the use of central station equipment; Yerkes had retained control of rights for traction equipment.

supplied energy, and there the day's peak rate of consumption was reached. When they rode, they not only used someone else's power but used it at a time when Insull's equipment was relatively idle, waiting for its next round of use. The implication of this diversity in time of use was that, given the traction load, Insull could supply twice the power with only half again the equipment. Given the high ratio of fixed costs to operating costs in the production of power, the traction companies, not having Insull's alternate market for power, could not possibly produce it as cheaply as Insull could. Insull armed himself with statistics demonstrating this fact and started winning as customers every traction company in Chicago. (Insull soon began describing what he was doing as massing production, a phraseology which his publicists shortened to mass production and contributed in that form to the American language, long before historians mistakenly ascribed it to Henry Ford.) [37]

The next fruit of Insull's actions and cogitations was a revolution in the technology of electric supply, one fully as important as Edison's inventions and the transformer in making technically possible cheap and abundant electricity. Committed as he was to the economy of increasing the size of his generating units as he increased his sales, Insull was ready for a bigger generating plant the moment he signed his first contract for supplying a traction company. He was rudely awakened by his engineers, who told him he was already pressing the limits imposed by the reciprocating steam engine. The generators in the Harrison Street Station were using engines of 4,000 kilowatts, and, the engineers explained, if the engines were made larger the problems of stress in a push-pull action would be almost insurmountable. And even if the stress could be overcome, size could not; a power plant with 50,000-kilowatt generating units, the usefulness of which was already imaginable, would occupy a plant as big as Chicago's entire Loop. Theoretically, a turbine engine could overcome both problems and could be built to any size, but the number of tinkerers martyred trying to perfect a steam

[37] For Insull's thinking on this subject, and statistics and graphs detailing its workings, see *Central-Station Electric Service,* pp. 54–96; for the power contracts with traction companies see *Minutes,* Commonwealth Electric directors' meetings, Nov. 15, 1904; April 15, 1905; and *Minutes,* Chicago Edison directors' meetings, Jan. 15, 1902; Feb. 13, 1906. As early as the turn of the century, Insull used the term "massing production"; in a speech preserved among Insull's speeches in the Insull Papers, Louis A. Ferguson refers to "centralizing production, or as Mr. Insull calls it, massing production."

turbine would populate the army of a second-rate nation. Very well, then, said Insull, let us build a new plant with huge steam-electric turbines.[38]

There ensued a sequence of events that was to be endlessly repeated, though never again on quite so grand a scale. Insull's own engineers, even Fred Sargent, told him it could not be done. The engineers at General Electric (who, sneered Insull, carried slide rules with which they could prove anything was impossible) also, but more confidently, adjudged it impossible. Insull's confidence remained unshaken; it was based upon several years of observation of European efforts to build a turbine, and particularly of British engineer Sir Charles Parsons, who had had considerable success building small steam turbines for racing boats. He called upon Charles Coffin, General Electric's resourceful president. Coffin offered to try an experimental 3,000-kilowatt turbine. Insull retorted that he could get 3,000-kilowatt reciprocating engines that would probably be more efficient; what he wanted was size, and if G.E. could not do it, then he would go to England, for he was confident that Parsons could. The thought of the competitive advantage a foreign manufacturer would gain if he should succeed was too much for Coffin, and he offered a counterproposal. General Electric would attempt to build a 5,000-kilowatt turbine, not as filling an order from a customer, but as a joint-risk venture with Insull's Commonwealth Electric Company. Insull agreed, and in April, 1902, the contracts were signed.

Seventeen months later, Commonwealth Electric's new Fisk Street Station was dedicated, and the world's first large steam-electric turbine was ready, after appropriate pomp and ceremony, to be fired. When the engines started, they vibrated madly, and visiting dignitaries were hastily shuffled off to a safe distance and the engines stopped. The trouble was located and rectified, and Sargent, as engi-

[38] The following account of the development of the steam turbine is based upon Insull, "Memoirs," pp. 74–78; Hammond, *Men and Volts*, pp. 275–84 (an account that contains several errors) ; Seymour, "History of Commonwealth Edison," pp. 318–21; Insull, "Chicago Central-Station Development—1892–1922 and Thereafter," in *Public Utilities in Modern Life*, pp. 368–74; *Minutes*, Chicago Edison directors' meetings, April 16, 1901; Jan. 15, Oct. 21, 1902; and *Minutes*, executive committee meetings, Jan. 7, Oct. 7, 1902; July 18, 1904; B. E. Sunny (of General Electric) to L. A. Ferguson, Dec. 28, 1901, confirming memorandum of agreement, Dec. 27, 1901, between Insull, Ferguson, and Sargent for Chicago Edison and Commonwealth Electric and Messrs. Rice, Lovejoy, Emmett, and Sunny for General Electric; and *Minutes*, Commonwealth Electric directors' meetings, Dec. 17, 1901; July 9, 1902.

neer in charge, prepared again to start the engines. Then he noticed that Insull was apparently intent on standing at the engineer's side throughout the test operation. Sargent immediately urged him to leave.

"Why?" said Insull.

"This is a dangerous business," said Sargent.

"Then why don't you leave?" asked Insull.

"Look, Mr. Insull. It's my job to stay here. I have to. But you don't. Don't you understand, this damned thing might blow up."

Insull looked at Sargent, then looked at the turbine. "Well," he said, "if it blows up, I blow up with it anyway. I'll stay."

He stayed, and it did not explode, and thereby a new age of power dawned. In another eighteen months Insull had the 5,000-kilowatt units at Fisk Street torn out, and the General Electric engineers, finding courage in their success, built him units twice that size. Within a decade he would be demanding, and getting, single units of 35,000 kilowatts, and within another decade he would be using generators five times that size.

The chain of events Munroe had set off by his attempted brigandage did not stop there. For several years Insull had been urged by one of his friends, Frank J. Baker, to form a company to develop electric service in Chicago suburbs. Munroe's effort did what Baker's arguments could not: Though no one had yet demonstrated that interconnected suburban utilities were economically feasible, the experience with Munroe suggested that they could be valuable as buffers against predators. Accordingly, Insull organized the North Shore Electric Company and, soon thereafter, four other small companies to form a defensive network around Chicago.[39]

Then there was Munroe himself. Insull appreciated the obvious fact that a man who could conceive such schemes as Munroe had conceived could be taught to execute them and would be a priceless addition to the fold. Thus Insull clasped Munroe to his bosom and

[39] Insull, "Memoirs," p. 94; Imogene E. Whetstone, "Historical Factors in the Development of Northern Illinois and its Utilities" (mimeographed by Public Service Company of Northern Illinois, Chicago, 1928), *passim;* "Important Papers" of North Shore Electric Company, Economy Light and Power Company, Kankakee Gas and Electric Company, Chicago Suburban Light and Power Company, and Illinois Valley Gas and Electric Company, all in the files of Commonwealth Edison Company; Insull, *Public Utilities in Modern Life,* p. 184n.

trained him, and inside a decade, under the tutelage of Ferguson, Gilchrist, and Insull himself, Munroe emerged as Insull's chief suburban lieutenant and, in many respects, his right arm as well. Others had higher ranks in the Insull command, but they were all specialists of one sort or another; Munroe was the only man in the organization who represented Insull himself in miniature.[40]

Munroe's example also alerted Insull to another advantage of expansion: In acquiring a new property one might also acquire able young men. He devised methods for detecting such talent, and thenceforth, with the sole exception of Insull's succession of private secretaries, new properties were the most prolific producers of executives inside the growing Insull organization.

[40] On Munroe's education as an Insull man, the source is the interview with Munroe, May 16, 1956; his importance to the Insull organization is implicit in the corporate records of the several Insull companies to 1923 and was attested by interviews with various former Insull executives, including Britton I. Budd (Chicago, June 22, 1959), Edward J. Doyle (Northfield, Illinois, June 24, 1959), Fred Scheel (New Lenox, Illinois, Sept. 3, 1959), and Samuel Insull, Jr.

CHAPTER V   *The Big Shot*

Because he had descended from the ranks of the mighty, Insull became a towering figure in the central station industry even as he entered it. Thus upon taking control of Chicago Edison in 1892 he had taken, simultaneously and automatically, a seat in the high councils of the Association of Edison Illuminating Companies. To the surprise of many, he also began to attend the meetings of the more or less rival industry association, the National Electric Light Association. Before long he had brought the other leading Edison operators—many of whom had worked directly under him when he was Edison's right hand—into N.E.L.A. with him, and thenceforth Insull and a handful of his friends dominated both organizations and through them the industry. The most important of his associates were John I. Beggs (Villard's man in Milwaukee and Cincinnati), Charles L. Edgar, W. S. Barstow, John W. Lieb, Joseph B. McCall, and, a little later, Alex Dow, Henry L. Doherty, and Sidney Z. Mitchell.[1]

Insull and this young managerial elite quickly reshaped the two organizations, making them complementary instead of competitive. In essence, the N.E.L.A. became the industry's voice in public matters and the A.E.I.C. its forum for private matters. To N.E.L.A., as overseer of public policy, fell such tasks as public relations, political activity, and advertising. To A.E.I.C., as overseer of private policy, fell the tasks of working out operating problems and keeping a

[1] See the *Minutes* of the meetings of the Association of Edison Illuminating Companies, 1894–1910 (privately printed, not published, annually), and the *Proceedings of the Annual Meetings of the National Electric Light Association* for the same period.

watchful eye upon member companies themselves and upon General Electric. The A.E.I.C. intrusted its policing functions to an executive committee and a "lamp committee"—Insull, Lieb, Barstow, Edgar, and Beggs, and later, Dow and Doherty—and for almost four decades these committees formed the *de facto* governing bodies of electric utilities in the United States.[2]

But Insull's place in the industry did not rest long upon past performance and current committees. Though he began at the top, that was only the beginning. What followed resulted from success at home and aggressive, radical leadership in the industry at large.

His success at home is reflected—but only reflected—by figures on the growth of Chicago Edison and Commonwealth Electric companies. Production, having quadrupled during Insull's first three years and doubled again in the next three—to 26 million kilowatt-hours in 1898—soared to almost a hundred million kilowatt-hours by the time Insull went after the electric railway load, and then it skyrocketed. By 1905 annual production had doubled for the seventh time in the thirteen years Insull had been in Chicago, and in another five years production again quintupled, to more than the combined output of New York Edison, Brooklyn Edison, and Boston Edison. By 1907, the year Chicago Edison and Commonwealth Electric were consolidated, the company was sixty times larger than it had been when Insull took over. And despite the enormous expansion, it had paid dividends of 8 per cent every year.[3]

The traction load carried most of the increase during the decade after 1902; in 1909 two-thirds of the output of Insull's companies was used for transportation. Even so, Insull viewed it as merely a steppingstone to bigger things. He saw traction as a base load, vital because it saved twenty years in building loads big enough to permit taking full advantage of the economies of massing production and

[2] In the 1890's the executive committee was the broader governing body and the lamp committee watched only General Electric. Judging by the *Minutes*, after 1900 the influence of the former diminished and the lamp committee became the actual seat of power in the industry. According to Samuel Insull, Jr., by the early 1920's, when he entered the business at his father's right hand, this transition was complete.

[3] Seymour, "History of Commonwealth Edison," pp. 192, 287, 321, 377; Ralph W. Liddle and John W. Evers, Jr., "History of Commonwealth Edison Company" (a typescript volume prepared by the company in connection with a rate hearing before the Illinois Commerce Commission in 1934), p. 172–A; *Minutes*, Commonwealth Edison stockholders' meeting, Nov. 9, 1908, and its *Annual Report* for 1912; Insull, *Central-Station Electric Service*, pp. 332–33, 411.

distribution. With each traction customer he added, he could cut the rates for, and thus expand, all other kinds of service. "Sell at the lowest possible price," he preached; sell "ridiculously low," he preached; sell so low that no one can afford not to have electric service. And he practiced what he preached—not out of altruism, but out of hardheaded practicality: he knew that the electric man's promised land lay in the almost unimaginably vast potential market in industrial power and commercial and residential lighting. At the turn of the century electric central stations produced less than one-thirtieth of the power consumed in factories; and gaslit shops and residences outnumbered those lighted by electricity by more than twenty to one.[4]

To win customers, Insull sold electricity at rates so low they appalled other central station men. His traction rates started at less than a cent a kilowatt-hour and scaled down to as little as four-tenths of a cent. To get power and light customers he used the same formula he used in getting traction customers: one part quality service, two parts hard selling, and three parts rate cuts. He continued to sell to large power customers by offering special contracts at whatever price was necessary to get the business. For commercial and residential customers he used uniform rate schedules and cut them as fast as possible. The first across-the-board rate cuts for these customers came in 1898; another followed in 1905, and new cuts were made every year thereafter for the next decade. Average rates for these customers, having been 20 cents a kilowatt-hour when Insull began in Chicago, were down to 10 cents by 1908, and thenceforth they fell steadily by about a cent every two years. Average rates for all classes of service fell from around 20 cents in 1892 to 10 cents in 1897, to 5 cents in 1906, to 2½ cents in 1909. The cost of electricity in Chicago was far below that in most comparable cities; the cost in New York, Brooklyn, Philadelphia, Boston, Milwaukee,

[4] Insull, *Central-Station Electric Service,* pp. 99–101, 140, 255–307, 325–27, 340; A.E.I.C. *Minutes,* 1895, pp. 104–6; Seymour, "History of Commonwealth Edison," p. 323. The relative figures on industrial power, gas, and central station electricity are estimates, based upon surveys made by the National Electric Light Association in 1890 and 1900; the *Census of General Electric Light and Power Stations,* 1902; *Historical Statistics of the United States, 1789–1945* (Washington, 1949), pp. 156–59; and comparisons of figures on relative production and customers of Commonwealth Edison and Peoples Gas companies in Chicago—for example, in 1900 Chicago Edison and Commonwealth Electric combined had 16,000 customers and Peoples Gas had well over 300,000.

and Baltimore ranged from roughly two-fifths higher to almost three times as high. And the reduced rates and hard selling brought in the customers: the company acquired its 10,000th customer in 1898, its 50,000th in 1906, its 100,000th in 1909, its 200,000th in 1913.[5]

As Chicago Edison and Commonwealth Electric broke ahead of other companies, blazing trails that all followed, Insull's stature among his fellows grew apace. By the turn of the century, few men in the industry could be regarded as his equal. By 1910, all men in the business walked in his shadow; others in the industry sometimes spoke of him, as did his employees, as "The Chief."[6]

(So successfully did Insull lead, and so diligently did other operators follow, in capturing the huge power and light load that in retrospect it seems simple, logical, even inevitable. But it is easy to forget that before electric companies could sell manufacturers on using central station power, they had first to become able, and then to convince factory owners they were able, to deliver power so much cheaper than factory-generated, belt-distributed steam power that they could justify replacing with electric motors every piece of power equipment in the United States. It is also easy to forget that from the early 1890's, when the Welsbach gas mantle was introduced, until 1911, when the tungsten-filament incandescent electric lamp became generally available, gas was as good as electricity for lighting,

[5] Rate cuts are summarized in Liddle and Evers, "History of Commonwealth Edison," pp. 83–84, and Seymour, "History of Commonwealth Edison," pp. 280–87, 432–33; see also *Minutes,* Chicago Edison directors' meetings, April 19, 1898, May 9, 1905, June 19, July 3, Nov. 20, 1906, and *Minutes,* executive committee meetings, June 3, 1902, May 19, 1905. For comparative rates, see A.E.I.C. *Minutes,* 1898–1910; Payson Jones, *A Power History of the Consolidated Edison System, 1878–1900* (New York, 1940) ; and the company histories cited in note 12, chap. iii, above. For growth of customers in Chicago, see the *Annual Report* of Commonwealth Edison Company for 1912. Extrapolating from company records and the electrical censuses of 1902 and 1912, it would appear that the national average rate in 1902 was about one-eighth higher than the average Chicago rate, and a decade later it was half again as high as the average Chicago rate.

[6] Insull's subordinates became presidents of the industry's principal associations: L. A. Ferguson, for example, became president of the Association of Edison Illuminating Companies in 1901, a year before he became vice-president of Chicago Edison; later, he was president of both the National Electric Light Association and the American Institute of Electrical Engineers; John F. Gilchrist became president of the A.E.I.C. while still only a department head in Commonwealth Edison; and several of Insull's vice-presidents became presidents of the several national electric and gas industry associations.

and that unless central stations could drastically reduce costs, gas was cheaper. Finally, it is easy to forget that the transformation occurred more slowly in other countries and only to the extent that their governments forced an imitation of the American experience; and, what few ever knew, that the two countries that created the most praised and emulated government-owned systems—Canada and England—learned how by calling on Samuel Insull to teach them.) [7]

Insull's aggressive exploitation of the economics of mass production only partially explains his spectacular success. Underlying it was his own irresistible drive, his daring spirit of innovation, and his exhaustive attention to details, tempered by an ability to synthesize mountains of data into fundamental principles. In his twenty-fifth year in America—as in his fiftieth—he continued to work as many hours as he had in his first. Throughout, he not only accepted change, he demanded it. "In my business," he said, parroting Edison, "the best asset is a first-class junk pile," and his junk pile was heaped with obsolete ideas as well as obsolete machines. From his own engineers and outsiders he demanded, and got, a vast array of technological improvements, all leading to increased efficiency or economy of operations; he formulated, or borrowed and first applied on a large scale, virtually every concept basic to the industry's development. [8]

But a more important attribute underlay even these, one difficult to define and illustrate: a keen sense of what might be loosely styled business ecology. Most successful central station operators were aware by 1900 that the welfare of electric utilities was inseparable from the welfare of the cities they served, but Insull went a good

[7] On the difficulties confronting the owners of central stations the best single source is the *Minutes* of the A.E.I.C., from 1900 to 1917; the several company histories cited earlier shed much light, as do Seymour's unpublished "History of Commonwealth Edison" and the tape-recorded interviews with veteran Wisconsin utility men, now in the possession of the State Historical Society of Wisconsin. On Insull and Canada, the published sources are limited. One recognition of Insull's importance to Canadian development is John H. Dales, *Hydroelectricity and Industrial Development: Quebec, 1898–1940* (Cambridge, 1957), pp. 16, 21–24. On Insull and the British Grid System see pp. 220, 276, 335–36, below, and the sources cited there.

[8] The analysis of Insull's way of thinking and of doing business is based on conclusions drawn from all the sources used for this book. Most useful for survey purposes, though only superficial in their treatment of labor and politics, are his *Central-Station Electric Service* and *Public Utilities in Modern Life,* and the *Minutes* of the A.E.I.C. The quotation is from *Central-Station Electric Service,* p. 73.

deal further. He perceived that all aspects of life in a large city were closely interrelated, that a development in any part of the organism must inevitably affect all other aspects and the whole.

Given Insull's compulsion to render human affairs orderly and efficient—and thereby manageable—it followed that he should attempt to reduce to predictability that part of the whole which he and his companies touched directly. And with the aid of E. J. Fowler, a brilliant young pioneer statistician on his personal staff, he developed effective methods for determining in advance such things as the rate of consumption at a given place and a given time. Indeed, largely because of Fowler and Insull, electric utilities became more successful in the application of actuarial techniques than any other kind of business save life insurance companies. Such activities were in the rationalizing spirit of the age, the same kind of things that many other men in business, labor, and politics were doing.[9]

At the same time, however, Insull did not completely worship a machinomorphic god. He was far too sensible to limit his activity by what could be reduced to statistics or even to logic; he knew and understood far more about human behavior than could ever be captured by formulas. He would let scientific method teach him, but he would not let it master him, for stronger even than his aversion to disorder was his aversion to entrapment by institutions of his own making. Thus he accepted the slide rule and utilized it to the fullest, but when it contradicted what experience, common sense, or intuition told him, he invariably disregarded the instrument.

[9] For an account of the origins of Chicago Edison's statistical department see Seymour, "History of Commonwealth Edison," pp. 244–46; for brief biographical sketches of Fowler see Marquis (ed.), *Who's Who in Chicago, 1931*, p. 333, and *Edison Round Table* (the company house organ), June, 1943. For a few examples of his work see the statistics, graphs, and charts in Insull, *Central-Station Electric Service*, pp. 56, 59, 77–91, 131–33, 259–307, 322–30. For years, Insull required Fowler to prepare pocket-sized handbooks containing every conceivable kind of statistic on electricity in Chicago, down to hourly tables of consumption by districts, and required all executives and important salesmen to carry them; a file of these is preserved in the Statistical Services Department of Commonwealth Edison Company. None of the recent studies of the history of accounting, such as S. Paul Garner, *Evolution of Cost Accounting to 1925* (University, Alabama, 1954), and James D. Edwards, *History of Public Accounting in the United States* (East Lansing, 1960), shows a proper appreciation for the pioneering work of utilities (led by Insull and Fowler) in this field. According to one former Insull man, A. G deClercq (interview in Chetek, Wisconsin, Aug. 24, 1959), Insull's vice-presidents regularly maneuvered to have Fowler shifted to their departments, in the expectation that he would continue to remain in Insull's favor and they would benefit.

His feeling for the ecology of human relationships and his un-
common measure of common sense often led Insull to do things that
defy categorization. Much of what he did might be hailed by progressives as enlightened and denounced by conservatives as radical; some
things he did might be viewed by moralists as the ultimate of corruption, others as the ultimate in morality. Actually his "method"
was none of these, but simply what an intelligent man does in an
unintelligent world. One can pick up Insull's trail anywhere, and
move along it in any direction, and find a sensible, sometimes surprisingly sensible, anticipation of future needs.

Start with coal. Insull was in the power business, which means he
used a large amount of coal to feed his steam engines. By 1890 every
urban political machine not operated by morons had in it, somewhere, a coal company. In Chicago the political coal company was
operated by Francis S. Peabody, sometime ward heeler, sometime
sheriff, usually Democratic national committeeman from Illinois.
Because Peabody was an important politician, Insull began to
patronize him as a coal man; because Peabody happened also to be
an intelligent coal man, Insull began to rely increasingly on his
judgment. By about 1903, Insull began to foresee a regular need for
what was then an almost unimaginably large supply of coal. At about
the same time, Peabody began to aspire to become a large-scale miner
as well as distributor of coal. Peabody needed, but did not have, a
considerable quantity of capital; Insull could get capital but needed
coal. Accordingly, Chicago Edison and Peabody Coal Company
struck an agreement: Peabody would furnish Chicago Edison all the
coal it would need, for generations to come, at cost plus a reasonable
profit. Having that contract, Peabody could then raise the money to
buy mines and fulfill his side of the agreement.[10]

Almost immediately, Insull learned that a large part, perhaps the
largest part, of the price of coal was the price of carrying it from the
mines to the point of consumption. The cost of transportation involved operating costs over which he had no control and interest
costs on an investment which was inflated. Accordingly, Insull

[10] Marquis (ed.) , *The Book of Chicagoans, 1911*, p. 529; *Chicago Tribune*, Aug. 28, 1922;
Harrison, *Stormy Years*, pp. 195–96; Seymour, "History of Commonwealth Edison,"
p. 290–91, 456; Insull, "Memoirs," pp. 63–65, 157; *Minutes*, Chicago Edison directors'
meetings, Dec. 19, 1905, Dec. 23, 1913; Insull, *Public Utilities in Modern Life*, pp.
345–46.

bought a small railroad which would haul nothing but his coal, and keep forever busy doing it. Over the years, the savings that resulted from buying coal from Peabody paid for the railroad and amounted, in addition, to a small fortune for the Edison company stockholders. The contract made Peabody, and thereby all important Democratic politicians, happy. The railroad, in turn, brought Insull other savings, but the effects of the venture, for a moment, stopped there.[11]

The effects of going into the coal business, on the other hand, had hardly begun. The coal business involved dealing with the organized labor business, which could have been difficult, for the organized labor business, in turn, involved dealing with the young, imaginative, fearless, and incorruptible representative of the Illinois mine workers' union, John L. Lewis. But Lewis was as realistic and sensible as were Peabody and Insull, and no trouble was forthcoming. Peabody, upon expanding into activities on the scale which the Insull contract brought, had the foresight to take on a partner. The partner was Fred Upham, who by no coincidence happened to be the senior Republican national committeeman from Illinois. Peabody and Upham approached the young Mr. Lewis. John, they said, you are a reasonable man. John agreed. John, they continued, you'd like to have your union recognized, wouldn't you? John reckoned that he would. You'd also like, they continued, to have some legitimate mine safety laws. Again, John agreed.

Here, then, said Upham and Peabody, is what we'll do. They agreed to recognize the union in all their mines, and exert every effort to have it recognized by all other Illinois mines, a task they would simplify by facilitating the organization of the Illinois Mine Operators Association. They also agreed to "cause the passage" of legislation by the state of Illinois, whereby certain standards of mine safety must be maintained, and whereby an enforcing commission would be established, on which miners—Lewis' men—would have equal representation with owners. In exchange, they asked only one thing of Lewis: that all contracts between mines and unions be set to expire on April 30 each year. (The advantage to the operators was that if there were strikes, they would normally come during the

---

[11] Seymour, "History of Commonwealth Edison," p. 291. The name of the railroad was the Chicago and Illinois Midland Railroad; the corporate records are in the files of Commonwealth Edison Company.

summer months when there was little demand for coal.) Lewis agreed, and peace and prosperity was enjoyed by all.[12]

The key to Insull's labor relations was his compound of realism, good sense, and shrewd understanding of men. Privately, he felt strong sympathy for organized labor—as the only way labor could deal with organized capital or management—but he was obviously on the other side of the fence. To deal with unions, he viewed them as two kinds, each expressing the character of its business managers. One kind was a shakedown racket, to be dealt with in the most expedient manner—whether by paying protection to a corrupt business manager or, if there was a chance of winning, by choosing to fight. The other was the kind dominated by business managers who, after taking care of themselves, sincerely had the interests of their men at heart. These were to be dealt with as equals.[13]

The most important of the second type was Mike Boyle of the International Brotherhood of Electrical Workers. Boyle, who wore the epithet "Umbrella Mike" for his alleged practice of collecting bribes and graft in an umbrella, was—no matter what else he might do—a man who first took care of his workers. Mike was also (1) tough, (2) sensible, and (3) eminently suspicious of bosses. Insull met Boyle in 1905. In an age in which wide gulfs separated rich and poor and unbridgeable gulfs separated capitalists and union organizers, he won Boyle's trust with a dramatic demonstration of respect for Boyle as a social equal and man of worth. Boyle's

[12] The details of these negotiations and their outcome is derived from an interview with Samuel Insull, Jr. Apparently the statute resulting from the agreement was the act of June 10, 1909, creating the Illinois Mining Investigating Commission, *Illinois Laws of 1909*, p. 55. A great number of revised safety laws for mines was passed in Springfield in the 1911, 1913, and 1915 sessions of the legislature. For a summary of these laws see J. W. Thompson, *Illinois Mining Statutes Annotated*, Department of the Interior Bulletin 169 (Washington, 1919). Cecil Carnes, in his more or less "official" biography, *John L. Lewis: Leader of Labor* (New York, 1936), p. 11, mentions Lewis' success in obtaining mine safety legislation, but because such negotiations were always private and unrecorded does not, understandably, explain how this success was achieved. For data on Upham see Marquis (ed.), *The Book of Chicagoans, 1911*, p. 683; Upham had retail coal outlets of his own and was vice-president of Commonwealth Edison's railway subsidiary.

[13] Information on Insull's attitude toward organized labor is derived principally from interviews with the two men who handled such relations for him from about World War I to the end of his career: A. G. deClercq (in Chetek, Wisconsin, Aug. 24, 1959) and Britton I. Budd (in Chicago, June 22, 1959). Much additional information was obtained from a set of scrapbooks of Budd's own career, in his possession, which contains numerous clippings from labor newspapers, as well as from Samuel Insull, Jr.

workers, unrecognized and only loosely organized, had walked out on a construction job at Commonwealth Electric in a dispute involving jurisdiction. Louis Ferguson, who handled such matters, was unable to cope with Boyle and his men, and antagonism on both sides was growing strong. Insull conceived a sensible proposal for long-range peace, one Boyle would welcome, but before he could offer it he had to overcome Boyle's hostility, suspicion, and distrust. To do so, he decided to deal with Boyle personally, a procedure rare enough in itself. Then, instead of summoning Boyle to his office, as most would have done, to be duly impressed, and angered, by the plush offices, Insull went out to the site of the strike to talk with Boyle in Boyle's own makeshift quarters. Most important, and most Insull-like, when Boyle did come to Insull's office, Insull had five-year-old Junior with him. After greeting Boyle, he turned to Junior and said, "Junior, shake hands with Mr. Mike Boyle and remember him. He will be a very important man in your life. Mr. Boyle, I'd like you to meet my son." Boyle was so pleased by Insull's gesture of respect that he was immediately ready to listen to the proposals Insull was prepared to make.

The outcome was an agreement that settled the problem to everyone's advantage. Insull agreed to recognize the union on his construction jobs, including the wiring of homes and buildings, and to try to see that only union labor was used on all such construction in the area, even when it was not that of his own companies. The union, once recognized, would be dealt with at arm's length, and Boyle and his union could resort to anything in the labor repertoire, including strikes, without fear of protest from Insull. In exchange for this concession, Boyle agreed to make no effort—indeed, to thwart any effort—to unionize the operating personnel of Insull's companies. The rationale for the agreement, on Boyle's side, was that in the electric business far more workers were used in construction than in operation; under this arrangement, Boyle consistently got larger all-union jobs than any man in a comparable position in the United States, and often his union local had the largest closed-shop construction jobs in the country. On Insull's side, the rationale was that it was vital that the operating personnel be non-union, for his companies were becoming utilities, performing a service that could not be subjected to strike without immeasurable damage to the public interest. The personal consideration, and therefore the more important one, was that the arrangement gave Insull the freedom to manage operating affairs as he saw fit.[14]

This agreement, in turn, was only a beginning for Insull in his labor relations; now he became one of the leading practitioners in a movement that came to be called welfare capitalism. Boyle's men periodically wanted wage increases and fringe benefits, and since, under the agreement, they always outnumbered the non-union workers, Boyle was able to demand and get what they wanted. To keep his own employees happy, Insull had to keep up with, or even keep ahead of, what Boyle was able to demand. Accordingly, Insull emulated Bismarck and tried to kill his workers with kindness. His employees worked forty-four hours a week at a time when sixty and seventy were the norm. He initiated programs offering free medical benefits, profit-sharing, company-financed night schools, unemployment compensation, voluntary employers' liability benefits, workers' savings and loan associations, a retirement plan, mutual benefit associations, and a host of others. In installing most of these he showed a keen awareness that they would work, if properly established, where employment was stable and the labor turnover was slow, whereas they might well be worthless schemes in other businesses. To guide himself in their proper establishment, he studied —sometimes through industry associations, sometimes at his company's expense, sometimes at his own expense—programs for each of these kinds of employee benefits as he found them all over the world, whether operated by governments or private industry. Finally, he took the first, tentative steps toward employee-ownership by encouraging employee associations which would acquire stock in his companies at a cost well below the market price. And every time he arrived at a decision regarding a new program of labor benefits, he urged it upon the rest of the industry.[15]

[14] Information regarding the origins of this arrangement is derived from an interview with Samuel Insull, Jr.; confirmation of its existence and details of its nature are derived from interviews with A. G. deClercq and Britton Budd. Lloyd Wendt and Herman Kogan, *Big Bill of Chicago* (Indianapolis, 1953), p. 204, makes reference to Boyle as "Umbrella Mike."

[15] Seymour, "History of Commonwealth Edison," pp. 417–25, 460–65, 498–511; *Minutes*, Commonwealth Edison, directors' meetings, May 18, June 15, Nov. 9, 1909, Nov. 21, 1911, Dec. 10, 1912, May 19, 1914; *Edison Round Table*, 1909–1920; Insull, "The Final Test of Welfare Work," in *Central-Station Electric Service*, pp. 193–96; N.E.L.A.

Insull with Theodore Roose-
velt at a rally in 1917. (CHI-
CAGO HISTORICAL SOCIETY)

The State Council of Defense
of Illinois, headed by Insull
throughout World War I.
(CHICAGO HISTORICAL SOCIETY)

Members of the State Council of Defense of Illinois and Governor Lowden
1917-1918

Bottom row, [*left to right*]—Samuel Insull [Chairman], Frank O. Lowden [Governor of Illinois], Mrs. Joseph T. Bowen, John P. Hopkins' [Secretary], Fred W. Upham
Center row—David E. Shanahan, B. F. Harris [Vice-Chairman], John A. Spoor, Charles H. Wacker
Top row—John H. Walker, Victor A. Olander, J. Ogden Armour [Treasurer], John G. Oglesby, Levy Mayer, John H. Harrison, Dr. Frank Billings

*Died October 13, 1918, and was succeeded as member and secretary by Roger C. Sullivan

Republican boss Billy Lori-mer. (CHICAGO TRIBUNE)

(Bottom left) *Michael J. Boyle, head of the International Brotherhood of Electrical Workers.* (CHICAGO TRIBUNE)

(Bottom right) *John J. Mitchell, president of the Illinois Trust & Savings Bank, who backed Insull without reservation.* (CHICAGO TRIBUNE)

Hawthorn Farm, the house near Libertyville. (CHICAGO TRIBUNE)

Britton I. Budd, president of Public Service of Northern Illinois. Insull named Budd as head of Chicago Elevated Railways when Commonwealth Edison became owner of its biggest customer. (MRS. BRITTON I. BUDD)

John G. Shedd, chairman of Marshall Field & Company, one of Insull's most trusted advisers. (CHICAGO TRIBUNE)

George A. Cooke, former chief justice of Illinois, who in later years was nearest to being Insull's personal attorney. (CHICAGO TRIBUNE)

James A. Patten, a celebrated grain speculator, member of the board of Peoples Gas, and another of Insull's trusted friends and advisers. (CHICAGO TRIBUNE)

George F. Mitchell, Insull's private secretary, who later became president of Peoples Gas. (G. F. MITCHELL)

Edward J. Doyle, another private secretary, who succeeded Insull as president of Commonwealth Edison. (INSULL COLLECTIONS)

Samuel Insull at the races with Milton J. Foreman, prominent Chicago lawyer, at one time chairman of the local transportation committee of the city council. (CHICAGO TRIBUNE)

(Bottom left) Edward W. Lloyd, the one man in the world who knew more about the economics of industrial power sales than Insull did. (CHICAGO TRIBUNE)

(Bottom right) John F. Gilchrist, a former meter reader, who became Chicago Edison's most eager salesman and vice-president of Commonwealth Edison, Public Service of Northern Illinois, and Middle West Utilities. (CHICAGO TRIBUNE)

*In 1922, on the verge of a
nervous breakdown, Samuel
Insull went to Europe to rest.*
(INSULL COLLECTION)

*Samuel Insull, Jr., in 1925,
the year before his marriage
to Adelaide Pierce.*

The Chicago Gold Coast as it was in 1926. (CHICAGO HISTORICAL SOCIETY)

Insull's manifold business interests, as caricatured by John T. Mc-Cutcheon in 1927. (CHICAGO TRIBUNE)

Insull with Stanley Field, nephew of Marshall Field, at the opening of the Chicago Civic Opera House, November 4, 1929. (CHICAGO TRIBUNE)

"Insull's throne" was the irreverent name given the forty-two-story office building Insull constructed on the bank of the Chicago River to house the Chicago Civic Opera Company. (CHICAGO HISTORICAL SOCIETY)

Nowhere was the interplay between Insull and the industry more pronounced, nor was his practical ecological approach to business problems more clearly demonstrated, than in his activities in public relations and governmental regulation.[16]

Insull had fared well in the local political storm of 1897–98, but it required little foresight to realize that the tempest had but temporarily subsided. The clouds were gathering anew: popular feeling against Yerkes in Chicago and against steam railroads everywhere was mounting, and when the storm broke it would almost certainly affect other utilities as well as transportation companies. Furthermore, reform or no reform, the vicissitudes of Chicago politics were always uncertain and often deadly. Consequently, Insull initiated and executed decisive courses of action on two fronts: in the industry at large and at home in Chicago.

As early as June, 1898, in his presidential address before the National Electric Light Association, Insull proposed that the electric utility industry seek to have itself regulated by state commissions, clothed with full power to fix rates and standards of service, and seek to alter the conditions of franchises so that if a company failed to render satisfactory service, the municipality it served would have the right to acquire its plant at cost less depreciation. These proposals actually differed little from those Yerkes had espoused in 1897, but Insull had learned from Yerkes' troubles that public opinion counted, and he put his proposals quite differently. To make his ideas publicly and politically salable, Insull emphasized not monopoly but the rate-making power, not franchise security but provision for municipal acquisition.[17]

The assembled central station men greeted Insull's proposals with the enthusiasm a Bryan Democrat might have expected from

Proceedings, Reports of the Committee on Public Policy (of which Insull was the dominate figure), annually, especially the report for 1911; interview with Miss Helen Norris, long-time Dean of Women of Commonwealth Edison Company, in Chicago, July 16, 1958.

[16] The following account is an elaboration—including several corrections of earlier errors and imprecise statements—of my article, "Samuel Insull and the Movement for State Utility Regulatory Commissions," delivered at the Midwest Conference of Business Historians, Madison, Wisconsin, February, 1958, and subsequently published in the *Business History Review,* XXXII (Autumn, 1958), 241–54.

[17] N.E.L.A. *Proceedings,* 1898; Insull, *Central-Station Electric Service,* pp. 34–47. Insull reiterated the plea in speeches published in the same volume, pp. 60, 119, 155, 178, 188, 246, 340, 399, 408, 441, 473.

the American Bankers Association. (After all, this was 1898, a decade before the establishment of the first state utility commission given the power to fix rates.) Anticipating a hostile reaction, Insull had attempted to slant the convention's program to suggest that the alternative to regulation would be something a good deal worse. He did find a few supporters: Alex Dow of Detroit, Samuel Scovil of Cleveland, H. M. Atkinson of Atlanta, and Ernest H. Davis of Williamsport, Pennsylvania; and he appointed these men to serve with himself as the N.E.L.A.'s Committee on Legislative Policy, a committee he established by executive decree. But his recommendations were premature. The 1898 convention took no action on his proposals, and for the next half-dozen years the committee floundered for lack of support.[18]

Meanwhile, Insull set out to win public favor at home. From the outset, he displayed a conspicuously advanced concept of public relations. "I care not," he said, "how good may be the franchises under which you operate . . . , how able may be the management of your property . . . , or how good may be your engineer and how perfect your plants, unless you can so conduct your business as to get the good will of the community in which you are working, you might just as well shut up shop and move away." Convinced that the vulnerability of utilities derived as much from a lack of popular understanding as it did from the public character of the business, Insull attempted, on an ever-broadening basis, to educate his customers. In 1894—fifteen years before it began to be standard practice —he started publishing annual financial reports, disclosing details of the business of his companies. In 1897 he began making public appearances at every opportunity, and by 1900 he was instructing employees in public relations. In 1901 he established an advertising department, which he soon expanded into one of the first full-fledged public relations departments in existence. This department published a magazine called *Electric City*, which the Edison and Commonwealth Electric companies distributed free of charge by the tens of thousands in stores all over Chicago. (To induce storekeepers to distribute the magazine, Insull rented space and provided display racks illuminated with free electricity, which in turn led not a few stores to convert from gas to electric lighting.) In *Electric*

[18] N.E.L.A. *Proceedings*, 1898–1904, *passim*.

City, lessons in the economics of electric supply were sugar-coated with instructions on ways to save money in the use of electricity.[19]

By far the most effective device Insull had for winning public favor, however, was rate cuts. To be sure, the cuts were dictated simply by good economics, but they also had immense publicity value—who ever heard of a public utility voluntarily cutting its rates?—and Insull exploited it to the full. Furthermore, he announced his cuts with an extraordinary sense of timing. Every time Chicago politicians threatened to channel popular feeling against Yerkes, the steam railroads, or the local gas companies into a wave of anti-utility ordinances, Insull acted. By the time politicians turned their batteries on Chicago Edison or Commonwealth Electric, they invariably found that Insull had just cut his rates. Only once, in 1906, were rates cut by contract ordinance. This ordinance was vetoed by Mayor Edward F. Dunne, a doctrinaire advocate of municipal ownership, whereupon Insull installed the rate cut anyway—with, of course, considerable publicity in his favor.[20]

These moves did no harm to Insull's reputation among professional politicians. To transform their respect into dependable friendships, he employed considerably more subtle means. He won individual friendships individually, as he had with Sullivan and with Peabody, but he also worked out a number of general rules to govern his dealings with politicians. The first was that politicians must be regarded as not for sale. Insull never bribed anyone, not so much because he considered it unethical but because he believed it expensive and impractical: If the word ever got around among politicians that Insull had paid for a particular piece of legislation, he would have to pay for all legislation he sought, no matter how much it might have been in the public interest. Yerkes had violated

[19] Insull, *Central-Station Electric Service,* pp. 204–5; *Chicago Daily News,* June 11, 1894, June 10, 1895, and Chicago *Inter-Ocean, Chicago Tribune,* June 12, 1894, June 11, 1895 (and all Chicago newspapers for the second Tuesday in June thereafter until 1908, after which the time of the annual stockholders' meeting and the publication of the annual report was changed); *How Commonwealth Edison Company Works* (privately printed by the company, 1914), pp. 157–62; *Electric City,* 1903–1917 (complete file in the offices of the company); Seymour, "History of Commonwealth Edison," pp. 241–44.

[20] See, for example, *Minutes,* Chicago Edison executive committee meeting, Jan. 2, 1906, directors' meetings, June 19, July 3, 1906; *Chicago Tribune,* Chicago *Inter-Ocean,* June 11, June 19, June 26, June 27, 1906.

this rule and thenceforth could never do otherwise, and Insull learned from Yerkes' mistakes.[21]

Insull's second rule was that one must view politics as a business, as did the professionals, and respect the right of politicians to earn a living. Insull thoroughly understood the unusual economics of the business of urban politics. Structurally they resembled the economics of the periodical press, in that "customers" (whether voters or subscribers) were not the source of income, but the means by which one qualified to make an income. As newspapers must win subscribers before being able to earn money from advertisers, so must politicians win votes before they are able to exploit public office for profit. In dealing with politicians, one must view the two aspects of the business separately. The best way to deal with the second aspect —how politicians made money once in office—was to regard it, Insull thought, as none of his affair. Dealing with the primary aspect was more difficult. One must make regular and large campaign contributions to all candidates in all important elections, irrespective of party, and recognize that such contributions were more welcome when the politicians needed them than they were when the contributor had a favor to seek. One must be ready to make other contributions, such as providing jobs—never important ones, and always with the reservation that the jobs must be justified from a business point of view—for the ward bosses to distribute. Most important, one must respect the rules under which politicians themselves operated. This required that one never ask a politician (1) for anything that one was not legitimately entitled to, or (2) for anything that would embarrass him politically. Finally, one must expect and accept public denunciations by one's political friends, whenever

[21] This analysis of Insull's political policies is based upon study of incidents to be narrated below, particularly in this chapter and chaps. vii and x; and upon interviews with persons who were intimately associated with Insull in his political activities or otherwise had direct knowledge of them. Principal among these were Samuel Insull, Jr., to whom Insull taught his rules of politics; Britton I. Budd and Charles A. Munroe, who were, as Insull men, highly skilled political operators themselves; John W. Evers, Jr., and Philip McEnroe, who as Insull's private secretary and personal bookkeeper, respectively, were aware of much of Insull's political activities; George W. Lennon, who was a lawyer in the firm headed by Daniel Schuyler, Insull's "political" lawyer; William H. Sexton, sometime corporation counsel of Chicago and long-time important Democratic politician; Francis L. Daily, long-time member of the firm of Cooke, Sullivan & Ricks, attorneys for Peoples Gas Company; and William H. Stuart and Nate Gross, two veteran Chicago newspapermen.

political expediency necessitated it. By faithfully observing these principles, Insull was almost always able to obtain whatever his companies in Chicago needed (which most of the time was simply to be left alone), no matter how the political climate varied.

During the years from 1898 to 1905, as other utility operators experienced less success in urban politics than did Insull, increasing numbers of them came to view expert, nonpolitical state regulatory commissions as a prospective sanctuary. But it was something else that gave Insull the opportunity to spur them to action: the specter of municipal ownership.

The movement for municipal ownership of electric utilities, given birth in the 1880's by electrical equipment salesmen and nourished in many places by the owners of gas companies who thought that municipal ownership would stifle the competitive growth of electric lighting, came to maturity in the decade after 1896. Personally, Insull neither feared municipal ownership in Chicago nor objected to it as a matter of principle; indeed, he lobbied for twenty years to bring about a government-owned system for England and occasionally spoke in favor of municipal ownership in the United States. But most men in the industry were terrified of it, and in their fear he saw a means of gaining support for state regulation. With other men who advocated regulation, he set out to play upon and aggravate this fear and to pose regulation as the only alternative. In 1904 the N.E.L.A. established a Committee on Municipal Ownership, which two years later was transformed into a dynamic new Committee on Public Policy. On the new committee were Insull, most of the men who had been on his earlier Legislative Policy Committee, and the elite corps from the A.E.I.C.'s executive and lamp committees: H. L. Doherty, John W. Lieb, Alex Dow, and C. L. Edgar.[22]

The Public Policy Committee energetically studied, worked out the principles of, propagandized, and lobbied for the establishment of state regulatory commissions. The 1907 N.E.L.A. report became the foundation of the industry's position on the subject. This report warned the N.E.L.A. that "it should be impressed upon the officials controlling public-utility corporations that the public will is that

[22] Insull, "Memoirs," pp. 89–90; Insull, *Central-Station Electric Service*, pp. 46, 217–18; Carl D. Thompson, *Public Ownership* (New York, 1925), pp. 268–89 and *passim*; N.E.L.A. *Proceedings*, 1904. For an example of early promotion of a municipally owned plant see the *Milwaukee Sentinel*, May 16 to July 1, 1888, especially June 16.

these companies shall exist, not primarily to make dividends upon certain investments of capital, but as the most efficient means of supplying the public needs." If companies could not fulfil that function, or even if they did but were not soon under adequate regulation, public ownership would inevitably follow. Self-preservation therefore dictated (1) that the industry, through the N.E.L.A., "should favor properly constituted general supervision and regulation of the electric light industry"; (2) that regulation should be vested in state commissions, whose members should be appointed in a manner "that will give them the greatest freedom from local and political influences"; and (3) that commissions should have power to control franchises, protect users against unreasonable or discriminatory rates, enforce a uniform system of accounting, and make public all pertinent information about the affairs of the regulated companies. The work of the committee was so successful—and the prestige of its members so large—that, while many in the industry still regarded regulation as merely the lesser of two evils, and while support was not entirely unanimous, the 1907 report was accepted without modification and adopted as the working policy of the association.[23]

In 1905 and 1906 the municipal ownership movement gained such momentum that it began to appear that regulation actually was the only way to stop it. A main source of strength of the movement was the low cost of money and the favorable market for municipal bonds that prevailed after the demise of the free silver movement. From 1897 to the spring of 1907 the yield on high-grade municipal bonds fluctuated between 3½ and 4 per cent. Furthermore, after 1902, when the Treasury Department began allowing national banks to use municipal bonds as collateral security against government deposits, even small municipalities began to find good markets for their bonds. Able to finance projects on an unprecedented scale, city after city held referendums and voted for municipal ownership, and city after city voted into office advocates of municipal ownership. In Chicago, a mayor was elected in 1905 on the strength of a campaign whose sole major promise was immediate municipal ownership of the city's traction companies. Everywhere, it is true, transportation companies were the principal targets of the movement, but the

[23] N.E.L.A. *Proceedings*, 1907.

impact was distinctly felt by electric central station companies, particularly in the Middle West. In 1896 there had been less than 400 municipally owned electric plants in the United States; a decade later the number was more than 1,250. This rate of increase was more than half again as fast as the rate of increase of privately owned plants. In the years from 1902 to 1907, the rate of increase was more than twice as fast.[24]

Almost as suddenly as it came, the municipal ownership movement collapsed. Early in the summer of 1907 the bond market began to sag, and at the end of June, when the City of New York failed dismally in an effort to sell a 4 per cent bond issue, the bond market snapped. New York City's financial crisis during the rest of the year, the receivership of one of the major traction companies in that city, and the financial debacle in October combined to make the market for municipal bonds all but disappear. After about a year the market for high-grade municipals was restored and stabilized, but the popularity of the bonds of smaller cities was over and would not be recovered for fifteen years. Since the municipal ownership movement had been most successful in the small cities—more than 80 per cent of the municipally owned electric plants were in cities of less than 5,000 population—its life's blood had been drained.[25]

Advocates of regulation quickly seized the opportunity to redirect the energy of the derailed municipal ownership movement into support for regulation. That this was successfully accomplished was due in part to the work of Insull and other members of the N.E.L.A.'s Public Policy Committee and in part to the work of the National Civic Federation, another organization in which Insull had an important hand.[26]

[24] Thompson, *Public Ownership*, pp. 268–89; Wisconsin Utilities Association, "Municipal Ownership" (mimeographed by the association, Milwaukee, 1925); James, *Growth of Chicago Banks*, II, 736–39; *Chicago Tribune*, Chicago *Inter-Ocean*, *Chicago Daily News*, March-April, 1905.

[25] James, *Growth of Chicago Banks*, II, 750–68; *Wall Street Journal*, *New York Times*, *Chicago Tribune*, Chicago *Economist*, June (throughout), Oct. 16–Dec. 4, 1907; the municipal bond market has been traced in the files of the New York *Commercial and Financial Chronicle*, the Chicago *Economist*, and the *Wall Street Journal*, covering the years 1907–1927.

[26] Scholarship on the National Civic Federation has been far from satisfactory. Useful but disappointing is the most recent, Marguerite Green, *The National Civic Federation and the American Labor Movement, 1900–1925* (Washington, 1956); extremely valuable are the early chapters of John R. Commons' autobiography, *Myself* (New York, 1934).

The National Civic Federation was the outgrowth of the Civic Federation, a Chicago organization established in the 1890's to cope with some of the city's more pressing problems. The board of the national organization consisted equally of businessmen, leaders of organized labor, and a group theoretically defined as the public; on its executive committee were Insull, President John Mitchell of the United Mine Workers, Louis Brandeis, a handful of progressive corporation presidents (including Insull's friend C. L. Edgar of Boston Edison Company), and a wide range of other persons. The federation was influential in bringing about a number of far-reaching reforms, especially in the fields of labor legislation and business regulation. For two years it studied utility regulation and municipal ownership, and in 1907 it published a three-volume document on the subject. Its recommendations were:[27]

First: Public utilities, whether in public or in private hands, are best conducted under a system of legalized and regulated monopoly.

Second: Public utilities in which the sanitary motive largely enters should be operated by the public.

Third: The success of municipal operation of public utilities depends upon the existence in the city of a high capacity for municipal government.

Fourth: Franchise grants to private corporations should be terminable after a fixed period and meanwhile subject to purchase at a fair value.

Fifth: Municipalities should have power to enter the field of municipal ownership upon popular vote under reasonable regulation.

Sixth: Private companies operating public utilities should be subject to public regulation and examination under a system of uniform records and accounts and full publicity.

Seventh: The Committee takes no position on the question of the general expediency of either private or public ownership. The question must be solved by each municipality in the light of local conditions.

The recommendations of the federation, in short, were exactly coincident with Insull's view and, except for lacking the unqualified

---

The indispensable sources are the monthly magazine, *National Civic Federation Review*, which was published in New York from April, 1903, to November, 1920, and the several reports of the federation's investigations.

27 National Civic Federation, *Municipal and Private Operation of Public Utilities* (3 vols; New York, 1907). The summary quotation is from the introduction to Vol. I. For one newspaper's reaction see the Chicago *Inter-Ocean*, July 22, 1907.

indorsement of private ownership, with the views expressed in the
1907 N.E.L.A. report.

The report of the National Civic Federation provided the general
outline on which most regulatory laws were based. In at least one
instance the report was the direct source of the law: that creating the
Wisconsin Railroad Commission, which itself became a model for
many commissions that followed. John R. Commons, the distinguished University of Wisconsin economist and labor historian who
drafted the Wisconsin law, had served as one of the chief full-time
investigators on the committee (sometimes working directly with
Insull), and he drew up the Wisconsin law on principles derived
from that experience.[28]

During the 1907 state legislative sessions, the movement for regulatory commissions bore fruit in two other states, Massachusetts and
New York. Each of the three pioneer commissions was of extraordi-
narily high caliber and as a result the regulatory movement was off to
an auspicious start. By 1909 most people who were concerned with
the subject, in and out of the industry, had begun to look favorably
upon regulation by state commissions. In that year President Bal-
thesar Meyer of the Wisconsin Railroad Commission asserted that
the Wisconsin commission had taken utilities out of politics, eliminated feuds between cities and the managers of public and private
plants, raised public morality through the removal of discrimination,
introduced new stability into the business, and was working a revolution in business management by its uniform system of accounting and
its regulation of rates. This view was widely accepted, and the movement for state commissions spread rapidly. Within nine years after
the establishment of the first three commissions, thirty more had
come into being. Almost invariably, regulation was opposed by other
utilities but actively supported by all the leading electric central
stations.[29]

In Illinois the creation of a commission was considerably more
complex than in most states, largely because of the confused situation
of local transportation. In 1903 the franchises of the companies formerly controlled by Yerkes expired, and the state legislature, anticipating a move for municipal acquisition of the properties, passed ap-

[28] Commons, *Myself,* pp. 111–28.
[29] *Census of Electric Light and Power Stations,* 1912.

propriate enabling legislation. The new proprietors of the Union Traction Company—a holding company under which Yerkes had consolidated most of his elevated railway properties—promptly headed off action by throwing the company into a friendly receivership and thereby under the protection of the federal courts. The Chicago City Railway Company, the largest streetcar firm, chose a different course: It began negotiating for a new franchise by offering concessions to satisfy all but its most doctrinaire enemies. The champions of municipal ownership regarded both actions as delaying tactics and began gathering strength for an all-out campaign.[30]

The battle came to a climax in the spring of 1905, with action both in Springfield and in Chicago. From the state capital came a new law authorizing the city to fix rates, through contract ordinances, for all utility service, and another law authorizing the city to expand its tiny street-lighting plant into a full-scale electric system directly competitive with Insull's companies. In the city, Edward F. Dunne was elected mayor on a platform of immediate acquisition by the city of all local transportation companies.[31]

An operator less daring than Insull might have been panic-stricken by such thinning of the ice, and most would certainly have resorted to the courts in an effort to stave off political action. Insull did neither; he executed a series of maneuvers that left both politicians and businessmen breathless. First he immediately announced a rate cut, effective July 1, 1905. Almost simultaneously, he secretly negotiated a verbal contract with the City Railway Company, to furnish all its future power needs, beginning in November. In the next six months, as the city council pondered means of acquiring the various traction companies, Insull quietly contracted with all but two—those in receivership—to furnish all their power needs; these agreements would be binding no matter what the political disposition of the properties. In January, 1906, the city council began an investigation of the gas company's rates and turned to Insull's companies in February. Frustrated because Insull had already cut his rates, the council was at a loss until Insull made a presumptuous proposal. He offered to

---

[30] Harrison, *Stormy Years*, p. 207; *Growing Up with Chicago* (Chicago, 1944), pp. 295–99; Ickes, *Autobiography*, pp. 101–8, 111–12.

[31] *Minutes*, Chicago Edison directors' meeting, May 9, 1905; Seymour, "History of Commonwealth Edison," p. 427; *Chicago Tribune*, Chicago *Inter-Ocean*, *Chicago Evening Post*, *Chicago Daily News*, March-May, 1905.

cut rates still further, in exchange for official sanction of a merger of Chicago Edison and Commonwealth Electric, under the latter's franchise. As one alderman observed, the companies could legally merge without permission, simply by causing Commonwealth to acquire Edison. What Insull was asking was that the merger come about by the action of an administration dominated by reformers and avowedly anti-utility in attitude.[32]

William G. Beale drew up a contract ordinance incorporating the proposals. The reform aldermen, aiming at the traction companies (and not knowing of Insull's power contracts with the traction companies), regarded Insull's business as relatively unimportant. Too, since he was offering to cut his rates and since they felt it would be difficult to force him to do so, they were willing to settle on his terms. After some debate, they joined a coalition of Insull's friends on the council and passed the measure. Mayor Dunne, humiliated by Insull's maneuver, vetoed the measure. The city's press, previously solid in support of Dunne, moaned; the only way to reduce rates now, they speculated, would be to cut them by ordinance and pray that Insull would be unable to defeat the measure in court.[33]

Then Insull played a trump card. With a great flourish, he announced that he was granting the rate cut in spite of Dunne's veto. Dunne attempted to save face by calling in accountants from New York, in the hope that they could turn up some irregularity in Insull's books, making it possible to "prove" that he should actually have cut his rates more than he had. After a quick inspection, the accountants told the mayor that a full audit would be embarrassing, since Insull's books were in order and his rates were, on the average, probably the lowest in the world. Dunne never made public their report, and he dropped the subject. Not surprisingly, he was one of the few Illinois politicians who never became Insull's friend.[34]

Political pressure eased off during the next four years. The trac-

[32] *Minutes,* Chicago Edison directors' meeting, Feb. 13, 1906, executive committee meetings, May 19, 1905, Jan. 2, May 1, 1906, and stockholders' meeting, June 11, 1906; Commonwealth Electric directors' meetings, Nov. 15, 1904, April 15, 1905; *Chicago Tribune,* Chicago *Inter-Ocean,* Chicago *Evening Post,* Feb. 6, Feb. 7, June 12, June 17, June 19, June 26, June 28, 1906.
[33] *Chicago Tribune,* Chicago *Inter-Ocean,* Chicago *American,* June 11, June 19, 1906.
[34] *Chicago Tribune,* Chicago *Inter-Ocean,* Chicago *American,* June 26, June 27, June 28, 1906; Chicago Edison directors' meetings, June 19, July 3, 1906; Insull, *Central-Station Electric Service,* 54–55.

tion problem was settled with a series of compromise ordinances in 1907, and in the same year Fred Busse, a no-reform Republican, began a four-year term as mayor. The climate had so calmed that, after prefacing his action with another 10 per cent cut in June, Insull decided to proceed with the merger of his two companies. In September, 1907, stockholders approved and Chicago Edison and Commonwealth Electric were consolidated as the Commonwealth Edison Company.[35]

The consolidation was, in the main, easily effected. The lines and power plants of the two companies were already interconnected and operated as a unit, and their officers and operating personnel were virtually the same. The corporate details were complex, for Commonwealth was the subsidiary and Chicago Edison the parent company, and yet they had to be treated as if the reverse were true so that the new company could operate under the franchise and open-end mortgage of Commonwealth. After all the necessary exchanges of stocks, bonds, and debentures, the new company had outstanding $44,963,000 in securities—$24,000,000 in stock, the remainder in bonds and debentures.[36]

The most ticklish problem, for both political and economic reasons, was establishing an accurate valuation to place on the new company's property and plant. Before, the two companies had recorded their property on their books at cost less depreciation. Politically this was the safest method, for it was the simplest and most conventional sys-

[35] *Chicago Tribune*, Chicago *Inter-Ocean*, April 3, June 11, June 19, July 16, Sept. 9, Sept. 17, 1907; *Minutes*, Chicago Edison directors' meetings, June 11, June 25, 1907; stockholders' meeting, Sept. 16, 1907; Commonwealth Electric directors' meeting, June 25, 1907.

[36] *Minutes*, Chicago Edison directors' meetings, June 25, Sept. 16, 1907; Commonwealth Electric directors' meetings, June 25, Sept. 9, 1907; stockholders' meetings, both companies, Sept. 16, 1907; Articles of Consolidation between Chicago Edison and Commonwealth Electric companies, Sept. 16, 1907. The articles were drawn so that the new company could operate under the franchise and open-end mortgage of Commonwealth; this included payment of an annual municipal compensation of 3 per cent of gross revenues, a feature that was not contained in the Chicago Edison franchise. Otherwise, Commonwealth was treated as a subsidiary in the transaction. Insull was nominally Commonwealth's sole stockholder, but he held the stock in trust for Chicago Edison. Accordingly, in the consolidation Chicago Edison's stockholders get everything, Commonwealth's got nothing; in effect, Chicago Edison's shareholders received 1.6 shares of Commonwealth Edison for each share they held of Chicago Edison. The dividend rate was reduced to 5 per cent, that being the equivalent of maintaining the 8 per cent rate on the old stock; the rate on the new stock was gradually increased until 1917, when it reached 8 per cent.

tem, and in the event of subsequent inquiries like Mayor Dunne's, simplicity and conventionality would be advantageous. But the system was misleading. Sometimes it overstated values: When Insull bought smaller companies he almost invariably paid more than they had originally cost. Too, since what he was buying was a business, not equipment, and since the equipment of acquired companies was generally not serviceable in a larger system, he usually scrapped most of the equipment he acquired soon after he bought the company.[37]

On the other hand, in two important respects Insull's books understated the value of the investment. The first involved real estate. Insull bought sites for generating plants and substations many years before he expected to use them; as the years passed, the realty owned by his companies steadily—and sometimes spectacularly—increased in value, but the increase was never recorded on the books. The other was also a bookkeeping peculiarity. Building most major facilities in the electric business required one to three years, during which time a sizable investment was entirely unproductive. The interest paid on that investment was part of the cost of building the plant and thus properly chargeable as capital investment. Insull, however, always had his companies treat interest-during-construction as an operating expense, chargeable against income instead of capital, and thus new plant facilities were regularly valued on the books at 10 to 20 per cent less than their actual cost.[38]

To arrive at a fair initial valuation for the property of Commonwealth Edison, the company employed H. M. Byllesby & Company, a distinguished electrical engineering firm—in which Insull was an inactive partner—to make an appraisal and inventory. Byllesby's method was to appraise all current assets (equipment and supplies) at their original cost and permanent assets (property and plant) at their replacement cost less an allowance for depreciation, based upon

[37] For a summary of the details of such purchases see Seymour, "History of Commonwealth Edison," pp. 267, 270; records of the individual transactions are scattered through the minute books of Chicago Edison and Commonwealth Electric companies.

[38] On land purchases see, for example, *Minutes,* Commonwealth Edison directors' meeting, Dec. 21, 1909, recording the acquisition of a fifty-nine-acre site at Roscoe and California streets (3400 North and 2600 West) for only $275,000. Twenty years later, the property was worth many, many times that but was still carried on the books at the original cost. Some general information on Insull's bookkeeping practices appears in the A.E.I.C. *Minutes* from time to time; otherwise, however, there are no short cuts; one must study the property accounts of the company, either in the company's files or the files of the Illinois Commerce Commission, Springfield.

the age and estimated future life of every item of property. After several months, Byllesby made his report: He found the property and plant of the company to be worth $51,975,549 and its current assets an additional $3,590,157, or a total of more than $55,000,000, against which just under $45,000,000 in securities were outstanding.[39]

Equally ticklish was the question of how to keep books now that an initial property valuation had been established. At the turn of the century, big business in America—that is, the corporation with a huge permanent investment—was only in its second generation, and businessmen had not yet worked out accounting methods that would accurately tell them the state of their companies' affairs. Particularly vexing was the question of devising a method that would reliably reflect depreciation. One generation of businessmen had gone broke learning something about depreciation that might appear obvious: that if a company earned, say, 10 per cent annually on its investment, but in doing so wore out its equipment in ten years, it was only breaking even; if it treated the earnings as profits and paid them out as dividends to its stockholders, it would be broke in ten years. Learning how much of a company's income to set aside to replace worn equipment took more than another generation. What came to be conventional among manufacturers was to employ the straight-line depreciation theory. Under this system, it was held that property begins to depreciate the moment it is put into service, and that properly one should reckon the annual depreciation of each piece of equipment by estimating its useful life and compensate for it by setting aside an equivalent sum from income, to be held in reserve or spent on replacement equipment.[40]

[39] *Minutes,* Commonwealth Edison stockholders' meeting and annual report, Nov. 9, 1908; Seymour, "History of Commonwealth Edison," p. 413. Insull's partnership with Byllesby is implicit in his personal account books, in the Insull Papers. That Insull and Byllesby were partners would not necessarily bias the appraisal. Since there was no commission regulating utilities in Illinois, the company had nothing to gain by padding values to enlarge a rate base; indeed, for tax purposes it might even have been advantageous to have understated values—which may well have been a consideration in keeping land values on the books at cost. But the important point is that Insull and the directors did not know what the property was worth, and they wanted to know for their own private, corporate purposes. The appraisal was not intended to be made public or used for rate-making or bond-selling purposes.
[40] For a summary of utility depreciation theories see Federal Trade Commission, *Utility Corporations, Summary Report,* Senate Document 92, Vol. 72A (Washington, 1935), 496–504. This description is admittedly biased in favor of straight-line depreciation—it is actually an argument for it—but, however unfavorably stated, the general

Insull believed that in the electric central station business it was impossible to estimate the life of property, for technological change was so rapid and unpredictable that equipment was normally scrapped as obsolete long before it wore out. Accordingly, Insull developed an alternate depreciation theory called the retirement reserve system, which was later employed in one form or another by most utility men who learned at Edison's feet. This theory held that as long as a piece of property was maintained in good operating condition, it did not depreciate at all; on the day the equipment was retired, it depreciated all at once and the investment in it should be replaced out of future earnings, over a time equal to the period it had actually been in service. To provide a cushion against large, unexpected replacements, Insull set up retirement and replacement reserves, taken from income. As long as plants grew obsolete faster than they wore out, the retirement reserve system gave operators a more reliable picture of their affairs, for it compensated for the actual cost of replacing equipment, not an estimated cost. During long periods of relative technical stability, however, this system would require that less be set aside from earnings than did the straight-line method, and thus, if measured by the conventional manufacturers' system, would impair investment and overstate income.[41]

As Insull's methods for dealing with such corporate and accounting problems became established—and as the period of political peace in Chicago continued—his vested interest in the status quo increased and his enthusiasm for a regulatory commission might well have declined. But by 1911 he had a new reason for wanting a commission: he had expanded his operations into well over a hundred

---

principles of the retirement system are intelligible. This report, it should be noted, was written not only in a climate of intense political hostility to utilities—the Public Utility Holding Company Act of 1935 was being debated when it was published— but also during the heart of the Great Depression; in times of deflation or depression, the virtues of straight-line depreciation are most obvious; the reverse is true in times of rapid expansion and inflation. In 1922, the National Association of Railroad and Utilities Commissioners had recommended a uniform classification of accounts for electric utilities, in which the retirement reserve system was endorsed.

[41] Federal Trade Commission, *Summary Report*, p. 569, citing a brief filed by Insull attorneys with the Interstate Commerce Commission, Docket 15, 100 (1924). The F.T.C.'s statement is a persuasive denunciation of the Insull theory; the I.C.C. brief is an equally persuasive indorsement and explanation of it. The retirement reserve system used by Insull is also clearly implicit in the printed annual reports of his various companies.

suburban communities, and he now had to deal with as many city councils. Early in 1911, with the help of Sullivan, he was instrumental in inducing the legislature to create a joint committee to study "the relations of the public utilities of this State to the people thereof." Recalling that Yerkes' advocacy had killed the Humphrey bills, Insull played his cards carefully during the ensuing months. Testifying privately before the committee, he advocated a commission modeled after the Wisconsin Railroad Commission, and through every political connection he lobbied for such a commission; but publicly he kept silent, and when asked by newspapers for comment, he made deliberately ambiguous statements. Early in 1913 the committee did exactly as he had recommended: It proposed a measure designed to create a commission modeled after that in Wisconsin. Ironically, the only opposition came from persons calling themselves Progressives and from the remaining old-style boodlers, both of whom preferred, for different reasons, that control remain in the hands of the city council.[42]

In June the legislature passed the bill, and under it the State Public Utility Commission of Illinois went into operation on January 1, 1914. One important feature of the Wisconsin law, one which Insull had advocated from the outset, was omitted: that placing utilities under franchises of indeterminate duration, perpetual unless revoked for cause, and providing for municipal acquisition if the voters of a city adjudged unsatisfactory the performance of a company. The absence of this feature left control of franchises in the hands of city councils and was a perpetual handicap to the effective working of the commission. Otherwise, however, the Illinois commission got off to a good start and seemed destined to be a worthy emulator of its Wisconsin prototype.[43]

[42] Whetstone, *Historical Factors in the Development of Northern Illinois and Its Utilities,* pp. 39–50, 142–43, 147–53, 167–69; *Minutes,* Public Service Company of Northern Illinois directors' meetings, Oct. 26, Nov. 2, 1911 (minute books on file in the offices of Commonwealth Edison Company); *Report of the Special House Committee Appointed to Investigate the Charges of Corruption Concerning Traction Legislation* (Springfield, 1903) ; *Majority and Minority Report of the Special Committee on Public Utilities . . . Together with a Draft of a Bill to Provide Local Control of Public Utilities in Chicago* (Springfield, 1917) ; Illinois Senate Committee on Public Utilities, *Reply of Public Utilities Commission to Criticisms . . .* (Springfield, 1919) ; William H. Stuart (ed.) , "Memoirs of State Senator Richard Barr" (unpublished, copy in possession of William H. Stuart, Chicago) ; Chicago *Inter-Ocean,* Sept. 16, Sept. 26, Sept. 27, 1913; *Chicago Tribune,* April 16, April 17, 1913.

[43] Stuart (ed.) , "Memoirs of Senator Barr"; all Chicago newspapers, June, 1913.

Insull's successful efforts in the fields of regulation and employee relations, as well as in electric power development, were radically altering relations between business, labor, and government; and the changes he would cause or evoke in all three areas were only beginning.

But Samuel Insull was, after all, a man pursuing Success, and the means, however radical, however they affected the lives of men or the life of man, were only means. The goal was Success, and one of the principal attributes of that goal was money.

Confident though he was regarding the ultimate future of the central station business, Insull quickly lost any illusions he might have had about its being a quick road to wealth. Competitive conditions and the peculiar economics of the business dictated that both dividends and executive salaries remain disproportionately low, at least compared with dividends and salaries in other kinds of businesses. During the forty years Insull operated electric companies in Chicago, the companies invariably paid 8 per cent dividends (or the equivalent) on their common stock—never more, never less. As to salaries, Insull began in 1892 at $12,000 a year, was raised to $16,000 in 1895, and to $25,000 in 1898. After 1900 he was paid an additional $5,000 for serving as president of Commonwealth Electric, and when the two companies were merged in 1907 his salary became $50,000 a year. While such salaries were by no means trifling, they were far from lavish; presidents of manufacturing companies of comparable size sometimes received ten times these amounts. Furthermore, to become a millionaire on such salaries and dividends would take half a century, more or less, and Insull was hardly prepared to wait that long.[44]

His earnings from stock in Chicago Edison were boosted by a peculiarity in Illinois law, one that always made the return on the stock somewhat more than it appeared to be. Under Illinois law, corporations issuing new common stock first had to offer the new issue to existing stockholders at par. If the corporation was growing rapidly and regularly issuing new stock, and if the market price of the stock was above its par value, the result was a considerable bonus for stockholders. In 1903, for example, Chicago Edison increased its

[44] Dividends recorded in annual reports and directors' meetings, 1892–1932, and in *Moody's Public Utilities* for any given year; salaries recorded in Insull, "Memoirs," p. 60; *Minutes*, Chicago Edison directors' meetings, Sept. 17, 1895, Aug. 16, 1898; Commonwealth Electric directors' meetings, April 28, 1903, June 11, 1907; Commonwealth Edison directors' meeting, Sept. 17, 1907.

stock by $2,276,210, or 30 per cent. Each stockholder was given the right to buy thirty shares for each hundred shares he owned. The price of the new stock was its par value, $100, whereas the market price was $140. Each stockholder's "rights" were thus worth ($40 × 30 shares =) $1,200 for each hundred shares held, or $12 a share. Adding this to the $8 annual dividend, the actual income in 1903 was $20 a share. Since new stock was offered frequently—keeping pace with the expansion of the company—these pre-emptive rights were immensely valuable. But while Chicago Edison was thus an excellent investment, Insull rarely owned enough stock to yield a net income to match his salaries.[45]

In the nineties Insull's principal income supplement came from a minor venture in manufacturing. After the merger creating the Edison General Electric Company, Sigmund Bergmann, who had manufactured fixtures for Edison, had begun to form several manufacturing companies in both New York and Berlin. One of these was the General Incandescent Arc Light Company; by exploiting recent technical developments in arc lighting, it quickly became a profitable venture. In 1895 Bergmann decided to retire from all American activities and concentrate on his German concerns, and he offered to sell Insull the General Incandescent Arc Light Company. To finance the purchase Insull sold more than half of his Chicago Edison holdings and borrowed about $100,000 from Henry Villard and another $100,000 from Chicago banks and Edward L. Russell, his broker. Having gone this far into manufacturing, Insull decided to go a step further. After the original Edison patent expired in 1894, anyone could enter the business of manufacturing incandescent lamps, and Insull either formed or purchased the General Incandescent Lamp Company for this purpose. He financed both ventures with his personal credit, returned virtually all earnings into expansion, and operated them in absentia through his brothers. (For older brother Joe it was a way of providing a job; for younger brother Martin it was a way of learning whether Sam's investment in his education had been wasted. Martin showed real talent, and in the future Sam used him as a trouble shooter for several of his small ventures outside

---

[45] This feature is explained in Seymour, "History of Commonwealth Edison," pp. 409–11; it was commented upon regularly (as "slicing melons") in all Chicago newspapers in the late 1920's and early 1930's.

Chicago.) In 1903 he sold both companies, through a complex series of transactions, to General Electric, realizing a net profit of something like a quarter of a million dollars.[46]

After this, however, and except for an occasional unsuccessful flier in fields entirely unrelated to his own (his special weakness was the backing of inventors and magazines), he stuck to the central station business. As his stature in the industry rose, more and more central station operators, large and small, called on him for help, and these undertakings became increasingly lucrative. In addition, bankers often asked him to take over the temporary management of companies they had financed and which were in trouble because of mismanagement; the firm of Trowbridge & Niver, Chicago investment bankers who financed many small-town electric and streetcar systems, repeatedly used Insull's managerial skill to bail them out of troubled investments. Finally, electrical engineering firms sometimes acquired small companies for non-payment of construction bills and, forced to reorganize the companies before they could retrieve their investments, asked Insull to assume control or advise on the reorganization and management. Normally, Insull took his compensation in securities of the companies involved, securities that were virtually worthless unless he succeeded in putting the companies on a solid footing. By such means, at one time or another, Insull came to be an officer, director, and stockholder in utilities in Wisconsin, Indiana, Kentucky, Pennsylvania, Louisiana, and California.[47]

Insull held these securities until the companies were stable and he could sell advantageously; he regarded his efforts solely as a means of making money, and he had no urge to take on the headaches and re-

[46] These transactions are recorded in Insull's personal account books, in the Insull Papers. For a brief note on the General Incandescent Arc Light Company and the General Incandescent Lamp Company see Bright, *Electric-Lamp Industry*, pp. 146, 214; for data on Bergmann see the sources cited in chap. ii, above.

[47] These doings can be only loosely traced. Insull's trail as a trouble shooter can be followed through the *McGraw Central Station Lists* for 1900–1916, the annually published directories of directors and officers of all central stations in the country. Insull's financial relations with Trowbridge and Niver and his holdings in scattered companies are reflected in his personal account books. In folders in the Insull Papers, headed "Samuel Insull, Biographical," are contained a few newspaper clippings about some of these activities. In two cases I have traced Insull's activities in corporate records: those of the complex of companies in Winona, Minnesota, and LaCrosse, Wisconsin (in files of Mississippi Valley Public Service Company, Winona), and those of two Wisconsin River hydroelectric companies, Southern Wisconsin Power Company and Wisconsin River Power Company (in files of Wisconsin Power and Light Company, Madison).

sponsibilities of permanent managerial posts outside the Chicago area. He made two exceptions. He invested in and became a director of, but did not actively manage, the United Light and Railways Company, a small holding company that operated traction lines in and through a number of small Middle Western cities; and he became a partner of H. M. Byllesby. Byllesby had once been Insull's employee under Edison; later, a rival as a vice-president of Westinghouse; and, finally, a consulting engineer in Chicago, where he and Insull became close friends. Byllesby, like many other engineers who built central stations and hydroelectric plants, often found himself owning his customers because they went broke, and he soon owned a handful of little companies scattered around the country. Instead of selling such companies as quickly as possible, Byllesby expanded and established a general engineering, managerial, and financial service to take charge of them and to serve other small companies as well. Byllesby invited Insull to become his partner in this enterprise, and Insull accepted. From 1902 to 1912 he and Byllesby were equal partners and co-owners in H. M. Byllesby & Company.[48]

Through such means Insull built his fortune. After the formation of Commonwealth Edison he held 6,044 shares of company stock, worth, at the market price of $135 a share, about $815,000. His salary was set at $50,000, and his yearly dividends were just over $30,000. His total net worth was about $1,500,000; his total annual income, not counting capital gains, was just under $100,000.[49]

[48] Insull's personal account books, 1902–1912, and United Light and Railways Company, circular dated August, 1913, both in the Insull Papers; interview with Samuel Insull, Jr. Biographical data on Byllesby is scattered through the eighty-three volumes of the Federal Trade Commission's *Utility Corporations* investigation; in Passer's *Electrical Manufacturers;* and in the records of the several Byllesby companies, two sets of which I have studied at length: those that became the Wisconsin Public Service Company (offices in Milwaukee) and Northern States Power Company (offices in Minneapolis and Eau Claire, Wisconsin). In using the F.T.C. documents, care must be exercised to distinguish between the activities of Byllesby companies before and after 1924, for in that year Byllesby died, and the companies soon moved in different directions, normally less savory ones. This distinction is not often made in the F.T.C. documents.

[49] Insull's holdings of Commonwealth Edison stock are recorded in *Minutes,* Commonwealth Edison stockholders' meeting, Sept. 16, 1907; his salary is recorded in the directors' meeting of Sept. 17, 1907; the market price of the stock is from the *Chicago Tribune;* the estimate of his net worth and annual income is from his personal account books.

CHAPTER VI *The Success; Or, The Short, Happy*
Life of Samuel Insull

By 1907, at the age of forty-eight, Samuel Insull had
achieved Success. He had everything by which Success can be measured: the love of a beautiful wife; a healthy and intelligent son; a
million dollars; the presidency of a huge business that he had created
from almost nothing; the respect—and even the affection—of his
employees and associates; prestige in his community; international
renown as the foremost leader of his industry. And it was no hollow
success. He had won it by his own imagination, industry, and intelligence, and no man could charge that he had compromised himself in
the winning.

Insull could mark 1907 as the year of Success for a variety of reasons, the most important being a symbolic achievement and two
symbolic acquisitions. The achievement was the formation of Commonwealth Edison Company, the formal realization of his fifteen-
year goal, a unified power supply for all Chicago. The acquisition
was a country estate. (Before long he also had a yacht, another symbol of English Respectability; to the lower classes, the land identified
the respectable gentleman and the yacht the respectable man in
trade, much as in America the private railroad car identified the
tycoon.)

Surrounded by so many symbols of success, Insull could, for the
first time, comfortably let his guard down and become a human
being. But he had hardly done so when he abruptly learned that Success was not what he had been pursuing, after all.

Having become a Success, Insull found to his surprise that he had to play at being one. In some respects the role ill-suited him: he slipped into it as one slips into a pair of new shoes a size too small. Even so, he plunged vigorously and methodically into the task, even when his heart was not in it. Thus, feeling that one of the attributes of Success is that the successful man rubs shoulders with the mighty, he set about doing so, assiduously. He met presidents and kings and lords and ladies and liked precious few of them; he made a point, for example, of getting to know every American president from McKinley to Hoover, but all but Theodore Roosevelt, whom he admired and supported, bored him.[1]

Another aspect of the role, as he played it, was personally more rewarding, that of giving away money. He gave little to formal, organized charities, rarely more than two or three thousand dollars a year, for "I specialize," he said, "in individual cases." Sometimes his benefactions were open and direct. Already he had a long list of pensioners—close or distant members of his and Gladys' families, old friends, anyone who could claim a connection with Edison, and families of deceased employees, even some he had not seen in twenty years. The list would grow in time to cost him more than $50,000 a year. Too, he was invariably an easy mark for those persons who made direct appeals for loans, which they rarely repaid, or investments which never panned out: veterans of service in British armed forces, other Britishers down on their luck, unemployed actors, inventors, journalists, and drunks vowing to make a fresh start, roughly in that order of priority.[2]

[1] At his son's suggestion, Insull mentioned in his "Memoirs" (1934) a large number of Very Important Persons he had known, and references to them are scattered through the volume. Although the correspondence in the Insull Papers was considerably thinned out after Insull's death, at least one letter from each of the presidents from Taft to Hoover was saved. In 1934, Insull made several candid judgments of the presidents in conversation with Burton Y. Berry, his State Department guard on the return trip from Greece, and these are recorded in Berry's transcript, "Mr. Samuel Insull," pp. 9–10, 12, 28–29, 41–42, 43. The same document contains numerous references to important political and business figures in Europe.
[2] Insull's personal account books; "Family Letters" file in the Insull Papers; Berry, "Mr. Samuel Insull," pp. 27–28; interviews with Philip McEnroe (Insull's personal bookkeeper), Los Angeles, Sept. 10, 1958; Edward J. Quinn (Insull's tax lawyer), Chicago, Nov. 21, 1957; Charles Stuart (head of the New York branch of Halsey, Stuart, the investment banking house with which Insull did a great deal of business), New York, July 30, 1957; and many others. Because of Insull's secretiveness in giving, it is primarily through interviews that details of his charities are to be learned. Stuart, for example,

But he found greatest pleasure in giving money anonymously. The joy of secret charity derived in part from his upbringing and in part from a childlike delight in mysterious and conspiratorial doings, but it came also from playing a role. His favorite image of himself was that of a character out of Dickens: the Englishman of good heart and lowly origins who has somehow made his pile in the Colonies or the States and then, like Oliver Twist's Mr. Brownlow or Pip's Magwitch, spends his declining years as someone's unknown bene-factor. Every December he sent from $500 to $2,500 to his sister Emma, who served as his almoner until the task grew too large, whereupon she farmed out the task to various sub-almoners. Emma interested herself in the welfare of the Respectable Poor and dis-pensed largesse accordingly: a pair of glasses for an old proofreader, unemployed because his eyes were failing; a traditional Christmas dinner for a hard-working widow and her children, together with gifts for the children and cash to pay her debts; a set of books for a young laborer who aspired to improve himself. And in Chicago on many a cold January evening, Insull sat alone before a crackling fire-place, reading and rereading, sometimes tearfully, the detailed re-ports Emma sent him—a scene that would have brought a warm smile from a Dickens ("Such a good, kindly gentleman") or a sneer from a Shaw ("the smug hypocrisy of rich little men").[3]

In still another phase of the role, Insull turned something initially imitative into a personally satisfying and, later, creative and produc-tive activity: his life as a country gentleman. Sometime in 1906 he found a farm with a large house and a hundred and sixty acres of rich prairie land, located outside Libertyville, thirty-eight miles north-west of Chicago. Early in 1907 he made the first payment on the

indicated that for years he served as Insull's almoner in the New York area and in that capacity parceled out thousands upon thousands of dollars to support various persons and causes; yet no one I interviewed in Chicago had any knowledge of these doings. Some of the gifts are recorded in random letters in the Insull Papers; see, for example, Insull to Gladys Insull and Samuel Insull, Jr., and Insull to Frank and Annie Rose, Dec. 20, 1919, providing a pension for two old employees.

[3] These gifts are ordinarily recorded in Insull's personal account books as drafts to his sister Emma; several of her reports are contained in the Insull Papers under "Family Letters" and "Miss Emma H. Insull." See, for example, Emma H. Insull to Insull, Dec. 15, 1915; Jan. 12, 1916; Emily C. Servanté (a sub-almoner) to Insull, Dec. 13, 1915; and Ella L. Mundy to Emma H. Insull, Jan. 3, 1916. Insull's sentimentality was attested by several of his intimates, notably Philip McEnroe, John J. O'Keefe, and Howard Ketting.

property, and in the spring the family moved in. They maintained a large apartment in the city, but thenceforth Hawthorn Farm was the principal residence and the subject of Insull's unwavering devotion. Ultimately he bought all the surrounding farms, extended his land-holdings to 4,000 acres, and (in 1914) built a mansion on the place.[4]

Developing a vast country seat was once the affectation of British gentry, and experiments in scientific farming and cattle breeding continue to be affectations of American gentry, but Insull's interest in the farm was entirely personal, the satisfaction of a childhood fancy. There are some things a man wants to do, and has wanted to do, and has secretly promised himself he would do since he was five years old. As a five-year-old in London, Insull had been thrilled at the sight and sound of the massive Suffolk draft horses that pulled milk wagons around the city and dreamed of owning such a team one day. On his farm, he devoted years of study and care to the breeding of the finest strain of Suffolk horses in the world. By the time Insull had perfected his string of horses, there was neither use nor market for Suffolks; the advent of the tractor had rendered them obsolete. Insull disregarded considerations of utility and market value and simply enjoyed himself.[5]

Yachting was the same—in part affectation, in part the fulfilment of a childhood fancy. But both horse-breeding and yachting filled an always serious need, the need to relax. Insull's demonic pace took its toll even on so strong a constitution as his, and the increasingly public nature of his work tore at his nerves. Periodically, he had to have time to uncoil, to let down his guard, and if anything serves that function better than the sod, it is the sea.

[4] The financial records of Hawthorn Farm are recorded in the ledger volumes of Insull's account books. The estate is described in most of the biographical sketches of Insull that appeared in serial form in virtually all Chicago newspapers in July and August, 1932. I have toured the estate through the courtesy of John F. Cuneo, who acquired it after Insull lost it in 1932.

[5] For examples of reports of Insull's activities as a gentleman farmer see Chicago *Journal of Commerce*, Dec. 2, 1927; Sept. 8, 1928; *Chicago Herald and Examiner*, Aug. 24, 1929; *Chicago Tribune*, March 21, 1928; June 15, June 29, Oct. 6, 1929; *Chicago Evening Post*, Sept. 8, 1928; Nov. 16, 1931; *The Chicagoan*, Sept. 28, 1929; *Chicago American*, Nov. 27, 1929; *Chicago Daily News*, Nov. 27, 1929; Nov. 16, 1931. Miscellaneous comments regarding them are contained in Insull's letters to his wife and son, especially from about 1909 to 1923. Regarding the origin of his love of Suffolk horses, information was derived from Jesse D. Scheinmann, Los Angeles, Sept. 11, 1958, and Sam Alcover (Insull's former farm manager), Libertyville, April 20, 1960. Mr. Alcover provided many insights into this aspect of Insull's life, as did William E. Larsen.

But Insull soon learned what others before him had discovered—
that success first breeds more success, and then more work. In what
began as little more than a fit of self-indulgence on Hawthorn Farm,
he discovered a missing element in the economics of electric supply,
and in doing so contributed the most conspicuous part of the electrical revolution in America: the sprawling, gigantic transmission-line
systems that serve villages and farms in every corner of the land.

Libertyville, like most country towns in the Middle West, was
without electricity, or virtually so. In 1896 it had dusk-to-midnight
electric lights on its main street, but by 1907 the service had, if anything, grown worse, and no electricity was available a mile or so out
of town, where Insull lived. An isolated plant would have satisfied the
needs of the farm, and so would a small local central station, but
for a man like Insull either possibility ran against the grain. The
proper solution was a transmission line that would tap power from a
nearby community already served by an Insull company; and he had,
in fact, chosen a farm near Libertyville because there it would be
convenient to extend a transmission line.[6]

So he ran a line from Lake Bluff to draw power from his small suburban company, North Shore Electric. And then one thing led to another. Little was done for several years, for an expensive, six-mile
transmission line to serve Insull and a handful of customers resulted
in rates that hardly threatened the local reign of the kerosene lamp.
But something piqued Insull's curiosity—possibly nothing more
than the acquisition of a new automobile in the summer of 1908
while Gladys and Junior were in Europe; for the first time he had a
chance to tour Lake County. In any event, he began to wonder, at
first idly, then systematically, then enthusiastically, about the possibility of electric service for rural areas. In 1909 he began a thorough
survey and completed it early in 1910; by April he was ready to conduct an experiment. If it was economically sound to serve all the customers in a city from a single power source, why was it not also sound
to string together a number of villages into what was, in effect, one
city and supply their power needs from a single source?[7]

[6] Lowell Nye, "Our Town," a booklet (24 pp.) published by the town of Libertyville,
ca. 1941, p. 8; interview with Samuel Insull, Jr.; Whetstone, *Northern Illinois and Its
Utilities, passim.*
[7] *Ibid.;* Insull to Insull, Jr., fourteen letters between June 14 and Sept. 12, 1908. What
Insull was groping toward was the extension of the principles of what has come to be

The only way to find out was to try it. But to do so was to flaunt the judgment of everyone who heard of the experiment. In spite of Insull's prestige in Chicago, most Chicago financial men who learned of the venture shared the opinion of the financial writer who suspected that Insull was slipping, that he was trying to make money by wiring up a "collection of junk piles." In spite of Insull's stature in the industry, and his reputation as a man who profited from radical innovations, most utility men considered it foolish, flying in the face of rather than complementing the known principles of central station economics. And as usual, Insull cared not a jot for what other people thought.[8]

In the area were twenty-two towns with more than 300 inhabitants. Ten of these towns had dusk-to-midnight lighting, and twelve had no electricity at all; in addition, a handful of farms received electricity from the isolated plant of a gentleman farmer. This was the unpromising territory Insull proposed to electrify. He bought the ten part-

called the diversity factor. The diversity factor is the ratio of the load factor of any group of customers to the average load factor of the individual customers in the group. Suppose, for example, there are twenty residential customers in a block, each of whom uses lights and appliances in such a way that his personal demand is one kilowatt. If the maximum demands of all customers should come at the same time, the maximum demand, or peak load, for the system would be twenty kilowatts. But in all likelihood these customers would use their lights and appliances in such combinations that the peak load for the group would be no more than perhaps ten kilowatts. Thus while the load factors of the individual customers might average around 7.5 per cent, the load factor for the group would be twice that figure. The diversity factor in this example would be 2. Obviously, the greater the number and kind of customers and the greater the number and kind of appliances used by the customers, the greater the diversity factor.

Insull had been working on this problem—a matter as central to the economics of electric supply as was rate-making and the load factor—for some time. One of his engineers, Harry B. Gear, worked out the details of the concept. Though it had been floating around in the industry for three or four years, Gear became the recognized authority on the subject. His textbook, *Electric Central Distribution Systems, Their Design and Construction* (New York, 1911), in collaboration with Paul F. Williams, appeared in several editions and was a standard work in engineering schools. For a brief summary of Gear's work on the diversity factor see Seymour, "History of Commonwealth Edison," p. 403; for a clear statement of Insull's thinking on the subject see his 1909 A.E.I.C. address, published in *Central-Station Electric Service*, pp. 73–96; and the address he gave to New England central station men, delivered on February 25, 1910, and published in the same volume, pp. 127–43.

[8] For examples of the general skepticism of central station men regarding small town and rural electrification see the several discussions on central station economics in the A.E.I.C. *Minutes* and the N.E.L.A. *Proceedings* (between about 1905, when it first began to be mentioned, and about 1912). The quotation from the financial writer is from Insull, "Memoirs," p. 95.

time local plants and then set out to build a transmission-line net-work to connect twenty of the twenty-two towns and about 125 of the farms in the area.[9]

Optimistic as Insull habitually was, the success of the experiment surprised him. As he had expected, the investment in transmission lines more than doubled the previous investment per kilowatt of capacity in the area, but the diversity of the demand on the system and the increased generating efficiency of large units more than compensated for the increased investment. Insull found that he was able to extend full-time service to the entire area, slash rates, reduce both fixed and operating costs, double the load factor within two years, and earn a handsome return on his investment in the bargain.

The long-range implications of this discovery were immense. The economics of systematized rural electrification—as depicted on the tables, prepared by Insull's statistician E. J. Fowler[10]—were such that, as time passed, rates would necessarily fall and profits would rise almost as a matter of course. The initial investment in transmission lines would always be high, but once it was made, the cost would be diluted with every increase in output, with every customer added. Furthermore, as the experiment demonstrated, the peak seasonal demand in rural areas came in midsummer, instead of in midwinter as in cities; if country areas were interconnected with urban areas, the same generating plant investment could, in effect, service both loads.

The Lake County experiment was the first demonstration anywhere that systematized electric service was economically and technically possible in large areas, rural as well as urban. The news of it exploded upon the industry. Many other central station men, having

---

[9] The entire experiment is described in detail in Insull's address before the Franklin Institute in Philadelphia, March 19, 1913, published in the *Journal of the Franklin Institute,* CLXXV (June, 1913), 561–600, and in *Central-Station Electric Service,* pp. 357–91. Some of the working papers are preserved in the files of Commonwealth Edison Company. The experiment is reflected in the minute books of the several suburban companies involved, notably the Illinois Gas and Electric Company, North Shore Electric Company, and Public Service Company of Northern Illinois, as well as the "Important Papers" files of these companies, all in the offices of Commonwealth Edison Company. It is described from the point of view of the small communities in Whetstone, *Northern Illinois and Its Utilities;* a brief account is contained in Insull, "Memoirs," pp. 95–97.

[10] The tables as well as the foregoing statistics are from Insull's Franklin Institute address (1913), which he was invited to make because of the radical nature of the experiment and its startling success.

been shown the way, were quick to follow Insull; even before the experiment was formally completed, the more imaginative of them had begun to duplicate it, and by 1914 lines had begun to emanate

TABLE 1

LAKE COUNTY EXPERIMENT, GENERAL STATISTICS

	SEPARATE MANAGEMENT (1910 CONDITIONS)	UNIFIED SYSTEM (1912 CONDITIONS)
Population Served	15,395	22,188
Number of Towns Served	10	20
Number of Customers	1,422	3,457
Connected Load in Kilowatts	2,033	4,503
Kilowatt-Hours Sold	699,574	1,898,978
Kilowatt-Hours Sold Per Capita	45	86
Income	$62,371	$136,694
Income Per Kilowatt-Hour	8.9¢	7.26¢
Income Per Customer	$43.86	$39.54
Income Per Capita	$ 4.05	$ 6.16
Maximum Kilowatts	573	963
Annual Load Factor	14.6%	28.9%

TABLE 2

LAKE COUNTY EXPERIMENT, COMPARISON OF COST OF ENERGY

	1910	1912
Investment Per Kilowatt of Maximum Demand		
Generating Station	$178	$122
Substation	...	70
Transmission	...	190
Total	$178	$382
Fixed Charge on Investment Per Kilowatt of		
Maximum	$20.85	$42.60
Maximum Kilowatts	573	963
Load Factor	14.6%	28.9%
Costs Per Kilowatt-Hour at Local Plant or Substation		
Fuel	2.04¢	.61¢
Other Operation, including Substation and		
Transmission	3.42¢	.56¢
Fixed Charges on Investment	1.62¢	1.68¢
Total Costs*	7.08¢	2.85¢

* Showing a saving in supplying the district from unified power supply and transmission system of 4.23 cents per kilowatt-hour.

from cities all over the Middle West to electrify villages and hamlets in the surrounding countryside. In another five years the systematization movement had gained such momentum that—along with the new automobile industry—it would dominate, and then carry, the American economy for better than a decade. By the time it was over, electric power would be so abundant and cheap in the United States that people who had never expected to use it found it as natural and as necessary as breathing.[11]

In the process Insull launched another movement which would ultimately result in the electrification of virtually every farm in the Middle West and four-fifths of the farms in the United States. As he began operating in Lake County, Insull pushed the formation of a new committee of the National Electric Light Association: the first Committee on Electricity in Rural Districts. He was supported by the Rochester Railway and Light Company, which (like a few other interurban electric railway companies) had experimentally run distribution lines from its railway power lines to adjacent farms; by companies on the west coast, where extensive rural electrification for purposes of irrigation had already begun; and by friends of Insull who were as eager to work for new uses of electricity as he was, the Boston Edison Company, General Electric, and a handful of utilities in Colorado. Otherwise, support was far from enthusiastic; the chairman of the eastern division of the N.E.L.A. committee prefaced his 1913 report in this manner: "I have some hesitancy in presenting a Report on the subject mentioned, which has, to some extent, always been considered a joke." Farmers shared the apathy, and when In-

---

[11] The spread of the systematization movement in the wake of the Lake County experiment has been traced in the works cited earlier for utilities in Georgia, California, Michigan, and New York, and in the corporate records of utilities that were based in Milwaukee, Racine, Green Bay, Kilbourn, Eau Claire, and Chippewa Falls, Wisconsin; Minneapolis, Duluth, and Stillwater, Minnesota; and all over Kentucky, Indiana, Oklahoma, and Texas. In order to study it, I constructed maps based upon data in the *McGraw Central Station Lists*, showing the spread of interconnected systems. An excellent map of the entire country, showing the extent of interconnections above 11,000 volts, is published in the *Supplement* to *Electrical World*, January 5, 1924. This map demonstrates clearly that it was in areas served by Insull companies, by those of his erstwhile partner, H. M. Byllesby, and by those of his friends among utility operators in the Middle West that systematization and rural electrification proceeded most rapidly. If one compares this map with the several maps in the F.T.C.'s *Utility Corporations, Summary Report* (1935), showing ownership of systems, and, in addition, recalls (as is shown in the *McGraw Central Station Lists* for 1912–16) that Insull was a director in companies operating in California and western Pennsylvania, it becomes clear that companies with which Insull was associated were ten to twenty years ahead of the rest of the nation—or the world—in developing systematized electric supply. The obvious inference, I believe, is that systematization and rural and small-town electrification were advanced almost a generation through the efforts of Insull.

sull's committee called upon Secretary of Agriculture James Wilson to seek government help in a program of rural electrification, they were greeted with an enthusiastic yawn. Nevertheless, the committee continued to study and gather useful information, and Insull extended electricity to as many farmers—several thousand—as he could induce to take it. And in 1920 one of Insull's men in the field began almost singlehandedly to vitalize the farm electrification movement.[12]

Insull himself, hoping to discover how far the newly discovered principles could be pushed, applied them in his own neighborhood. He sought to learn, in detail, what gains could be made by unifying supply for different kinds of power users scattered over fairly large areas. For example, in Illinois a huge quantity of energy was used to pump water in villages and cities and to make ice, mine coal, run interurban railways, and perform a multitude of other functions; and each user supplied his own power. It seemed reasonable to suppose that, since many used power at different times, the same investment could be made to serve several at once. Upon thorough study, Insull learned that the waste resulting from the use of obsolete and inefficient equipment was enormous and the waste resulting from duplicated equipment was staggering. For all Illinois outside Cook County, the combined demand for power was just over 300,000 kilowatts, and various users had installed about 437,000 kilowatts to cover it, though they never used more than about 225,000 kilowatts at the same time. If they were connected as an integrated system, they could easily be served with a total capacity, including abundant reserve, of about 270,000 kilowatts, thus saving more than half of the $43,000,000 that was invested in power supply in the area. The waste of fuel under the existing systemless arrangement was incalculable, but Insull believed that at least three to four times as much coal as necessary was being burned.[13]

[12] N.E.L.A. *Proceedings*, 1910, *passim*; 1912, pp. 262–329; 1913, pp. 136, 137–297; Insull, *Public Utilities in Modern Life*, p. 236; McDonald, *Let There Be Light*, pp. 271–92; Farm Electrification Papers, in offices of Wisconsin Power and Light Company, Madison. The man in the field was Grover C. Neff of Wisconsin Power and Light Company.
[13] The records of these studies are scattered through the files of Commonwealth Edison, Public Service Company of Northern Illinois (both in Commonwealth Edison Company offices), and Middle West Utilities Company's Illinois subsidiaries (in offices of Central and South West Corporation, Chicago). Some of the resulting data are sum-

Even as he gathered this knowledge, he began to apply it. In 1910, as soon as he knew where the Lake County venture was leading, he began working on a systematized electric power supply to serve every Illinois community within fifty to seventy-five miles of Chicago.[14]

North of the city he was already operating the North Shore Electric Company in ten villages along the lake, as well as two each to the south and west, and now he was electrifying Lake County.

Southwest of the city, his young lieutenant, Charles Munroe, erstwhile raider, enthusiastic and brilliant promoter, and one of the few Scots ever to enter Insull's inner circle of confidence, already controlled the small utility serving Joliet and four nearby hamlets, and now Insull turned him loose to pave the way for electrification of the Illinois River valley. Within the year, Munroe bought up fifteen limited-service plants and got franchises to serve the fifty-six villages in the area which had no service.

West of the city, Insull joined forces with L. E. Myers, an old friend, a canny and daring construction engineer, and one of the few Jews ever to enter Insull's inner circle of confidence; Myers had already acquired and developed a set of suburban utilities operating in Cicero, Berwyn, and Oak Park.

South of the city, Insull encountered for the first time, but by no means the last time, a pair of financiers and promoters from Grand Rapids, Charles Kelsey and Joseph A. Brewer; they had bought, patched up, and expanded a utility serving Kankakee and two neighboring villages. For the first but not the last time Insull bought them out (over the next two decades the Kelsey-Brewer organization engaged regularly in the business of buying and developing strategically located properties and selling them to the highest bidder, usually Insull).

---

marized in Insull's 1913 Franklin Institute address; others are in his 1914 address before the Finance Forum of the New York City Y.M.C.A., published in *Central-Station Electric Service*, pp. 445–75. See also Insull's 1921 lecture at Princeton, "Production and Distribution of Electric Energy in the Central Portion of the Mississippi Valley," in *Public Utilities in Modern Life*, pp. 263–303.

[14] The following summary of the consolidation of companies is based upon the "Important Papers" files and the minute books of the several constituents, all on file in the offices of Commonwealth Edison Company; Whetstone, *Northern Illinois and Its Utilities, passim;* interview with Charles A. Munroe, New York, May 16, 1956; interview with L. N. Boisen (Myers' onetime right-hand man), New York, July 21, 1954; and the *McGraw Central Station Lists* for 1910–12.

In August, 1911, Insull merged these five cores into a new corporation, the Public Service Company of Northern Illinois. Altogether, thirty-nine predecessors went into the new company; altogether, they had served about 6,700 customers in about fifty communities, mostly only part time. In its first four years the company extended service to no less than a hundred new communities, to 65,000 new electric customers and to 56,000 gas customers; and as it did so it cut rates nearly in half.[15]

From the outset Public Service was a financial success. It paid common stock dividends from the beginning; it started as a $23,000,000 corporation, and five and a half years later, when the United States entered World War I, it had become a $50,000,000 firm. Even so, despite quick success and favorable connections, Public Service was difficult to finance during its early years. Investors proved more ready to bet on Insull than upon his smaller companies; whenever favorable permanent financing could not be arranged, Insull borrowed for the company on his personal credit $100,000 to $500,000 at a crack. The cost of money so borrowed was high, 5 or 6 per cent, but on its own credit the company had to pay even more, sometimes almost 8 per cent.[16]

The relationship between Public Service and Commonwealth Edison formed a pattern that prevailed among Insull companies until they grew into a vast empire. Insull himself was at first the largest single financial backer; he was joined by a dozen or two of the larger stockholders of Commonwealth Edison, a handful of employees, several of his old friends in New York and London, and the two or three London financial houses which had profited from financing his Chicago operations. Physically, Public Service was interconnected with the Edison company at several points, and energy was exchanged (by contract) whenever it was mutually advantageous. The officers

15 *Minutes*, Public Service of Northern Illinois directors' meetings, Aug. 31, Oct. 19, Oct. 26, Nov. 2, 1911; stockholders' meetings, Aug. 31, Oct. 20, 1911; Feb. 28, 1916; and *Annual Report* for 1915; Whetstone, *Northern Illinois and Its Utilities*, pp. 138, 147–48. Growth statistics for this company, as for most companies discussed in this work, may be traced over the years in *Moody's Public Utilities*, published annually.
16 On dividends and growth see Public Service's *Annual Reports* for 1912–17; on Insull's personal borrowing for the company see his personal account books for the same period; on this and on the cost of money and problems of financing in general see, for example, *Minutes*, directors' meetings, April 22, May 27, Sept. 23, Oct. 15, 1912; March 3, March 17, April 11, May 26, July 12, Sept. 29, Oct. 15, 1913; Jan. 21, Nov. 30, 1914; March 28, Oct. 10, 1916.

and directors of the suburban company were Insull's young lieutenants Munroe, Ferguson, Gilchrist, Gulick, and others—in the Chicago company. Thus the companies were intimately related through management, ownership, and operation, but had no formal corporate connections.[17]

In 1911, that was as far as Insull intended to go. Much as he abhorred waste and excited as he was about having found a means of eliminating a great deal of it, he was not yet ready to dominate or reform the world, not even the world's power supply. He preached the gospel of systematization to everyone who would listen, but his own province was Chicago and the area around it, and he intended to confine his operations to that province. Samuel Insull, the Success, would help others succeed, but he had no desire to run their affairs for them. In another eight or ten years he would be approaching retirement, and already he was beginning to think of himself as the elder statesman, the grand old adviser of the electric industry. Thus it was that he reorganized, but rejected opportunity to control, utilities from Wisconsin to Louisiana and from Pennsylvania to California.[18]

But the short, happy life of Samuel Insull was almost over. Insull was, after all, a man like other men, and like other men he had to face his moment of corruption. His moment came in the spring of

[17] Stockholders can be only approximately ascertained. Stock transfer books apparently no longer exist, but the holdings of many important stockholders are recorded in the minutes of the annual meetings. The backing of Insull's friends in Chicago and New York is reflected in those minutes, in the minutes of the directors' meetings cited in note 16, and in Russell, Brewster and Company's Stock and Bond Circulars, 1914–1921, a bound volume in the Insull Papers. On the backing of the London houses of Robert Benson and Robert Fleming see Insull, "Memoirs," pp. 104, 167–70; on the patterns of management in general see the same volume, pp. 174–76. Directors and officers are recorded in the *Annual Reports* as well as in the *Minutes* of the directors' meetings following the annual stockholders' meetings. The patterns are also stated in the several volumes of the F.T.C.'s *Utility Corporations* reports that deal with Insull's companies, especially Vols. XXXVIII and XLIV.

[18] The addresses cited in note 13 are the best samples of Insull's preaching. Much more is contained in the A.E.I.C. *Minutes* and the N.E.L.A. *Proceedings* for the period; in those volumes, the papers and remarks of Insull's subordinates—Ferguson, Gilchrist, and others—should not be overlooked. Still more is contained in the file of Insull's speeches in the Insull Papers. Insull never explicitly stated in public, as far as I am aware, that he intended to confine his active operations to the Chicago area, but it is clear from his refusal to accept power outside Chicago and implicit in his actions and words, that this was his intention.

1912. It grew, as do the moments of corruption of all incorruptible men, out of love and the purest goodness, and it came because he was only a man. He survived it, but after it had passed he was a different man. He had the same birth and antecedents as the earlier Samuel Insull, but he was a different man, and he was not going, he could not go, where the other had been going.[19]

In January, 1912, Gladys had gone to Atlantic City on a holiday with one of her few close friends, Mrs. Benjamin Carpenter. A message greeted her there, announcing that Junior had scarlet fever. She rushed home and found things at Libertyville in great disarray: Quarantine kept Insull from his son, and he was at wit's end. Gladys was also forbidden to go near him, but she plunged in anyway, for her only child lay dying; where Sam had been sensible and left it to experts, Gladys was a mother and left it to nobody.

For three long months Junior lay precariously between life and death. Three nurses stood by: Miss Kaeburg, who had seen Congressman Lowden's children through a siege of polio, assumed command as head nurse; a dedicated nobody named Miss Cole bravely took on a shift as the second nurse; and a third came in from time to time. But to take a scarlet fever case in 1912 was roughly tantamount to taking a large draught of strychnine, and all others feared coming near the child. All save one. Mrs. Samuel Insull, the delicate, temperamental, babied, former actress, the wife of the most powerful man in Chicago, undertook the daily task of scrubbing the house from wall to wall, downstairs and up, with formaldehyde; for in those days, antisepsis was of the few safeguards known, and no one else dared do the scrubbing.

Time dragged on like an endless nightmare, and Junior got neither

---

[19] For the following, I have pieced together a general account of the sequence of events from records of the movements of Insull and his wife during the period in family letters, corporate records, and newspapers; and I have obtained personal information from interviews with several persons, notably those cited in note 1, chap. iv, above, and also Miss Helen Norris, who in 1912 was librarian of the Commonwealth Edison Company and subsequently became the company's Dean of Women. I had already inferred, from these sources and from general study of Insull and comments by several of his old associates on his changed behavior after 1910, that in one form or another the episode related below took place. Explicit confirmation was given me by persons in whom Mrs. Insull confided, who, for personal reasons, made anonymity a condition of giving the information to me. It is narrated here, although I cannot divulge my sources, on the grounds that it is critical to an understanding of Insull's subsequent behavior and that I have no doubts whatever as to its accuracy.

better nor worse. Then early in April his fever began to rise and would not stop rising, and then his heart stopped beating. For sixty seconds, or a hundred and twenty, he was clinically dead; then Miss Kaeburg seized him and beat him frantically until, by some miracle, the heart started again. Within a day the main source of the fever was discovered; immediately, the fever started to fall, and within a week it was gone. All that remained was the anticlimactic wait through the final weeks of quarantine.

The while, Insull came daily to talk to Gladys, calling up to a second-story window. There was not much to say (what can one say?), and the daily meeting became an ordeal for both. To keep himself busy, he worked outside the house. As Junior's crisis came and went, the spring thaw came also, and Sam began to plant trees. (The trees wanted planting; they had been ordered for Junior's birthday. Besides, what else could he do—stand outside the window with a long face and say, There, there?)

Shut inside, Gladys had time to think. Indeed, she had time for nothing else save her bleeding hands and the continuous scrubbing that kept them bleeding. Already, perhaps at the instant Junior's heart stopped beating and began again, she had realized that he had ceased to be their son and had become hers alone. Now, during his recovery, she thought of herself. But of the decision she was making, she need not have thought, for her heart had made up her mind. Each day, as she watched Sam arrive and go off to plant trees, she made it again: The intimate part of their marriage, the part she had accepted only with gritted teeth, must end.

She had considered ending it once before, in 1909, when it seemed that she could bear that part no longer, especially with a man who loved work more than he loved her. But Sam detected that all was not well and won her anew on a second honeymoon. Now, however, it was simple. By the time Sam re-entered the house, it had been five months since they had shared a bedroom. All she had to do was close her bedroom door, quietly but firmly, and keep it closed. So quietly and so firmly did she close it that Sam, for a time, did not realize that it was closed forever.

She did not know what she was doing to him. He was fifty-two years old, an age at which a man's ego most wants feeding, an age at which a man's masculinity most wants confirmation, an age at which a man can least accommodate rejection. But to Gladys, to tiny, beautiful, sometimes steel-tough, disdainful Gladys, sex was a dirty word, and what her husband was now experiencing would have been incomprehensible to her, even if he had been able to explain it.

To Sam it was comprehensible enough, but comprehending it made it none the more bearable. To be sure, one could find ways to avoid self-doubts for moments at a time. One could find confirmation in other women, but their solace was as short-lived as it was easy; or one could worry and travel and work all the harder; but when these were dropped for even an instant, the doubt returned. The only lasting escape was to find a means of becoming immune to pain.

The answer was that somewhere there was a seat of power so great that from it Insull could be more human, and reach out and touch more human beings more deeply, than he had ever dreamed possible, and yet do so in the security of knowing that his Self would not be vulnerable. Perhaps he had been moving in this general direction since birth; but, until now, he had welcomed the approaches of others, always at his invitation; and until now, much as he loved to run things, he had resisted the temptation to accept new power, save when it was along the direct route to Success. Now, from the spring of 1912, he began moving straight to that place of power, with unconscious but infallible instinct.

Money ceased to be important to him; henceforth, he gave it away almost as fast as he earned it. Indeed, he began dissolving the connections from which he had made a great deal of money without actively running things—his directorships of electric companies in California, Pennsylvania, and Louisiana, his interest in the United Light and Railways Company, his partnership with Byllesby—and by 1917 he was out of all such ventures. At the same time, he began broadening the scope and number of concerns under his direct command. The companies he ran in January, 1912, had assets of around $90,000,000; they were almost exclusively in the electric utility business in and around Chicago. Five years later the companies he ran had assets of over $400,000,000; they were in gas and traction as well as the electric business, and they were operating in thirteen states.

It was not that he launched a campaign to increase his power. Each step toward it was taken separately and each was dictated by circumstances, the kind of circumstances that push a successful man around. Each seemed the only sensible thing to do in response to the demands of immediate conditions, of responsibility to family or friends or community or nation. Each was taken because there seemed to be no one else able and willing to assume the responsibility. Yet all, from 1912 to 1919, pointed in the same direction, and that direction was increased power. For Insull, in his great ego, now was certain of something he had once only suspected: that in public and in private matters, he was power's safest repository.

Within a month after Junior's illness, Insull made his first major move outside Chicago. There was a pressing practical reason, the strain imposed on his personal credit by his involvement in the development of Public Service Company of Northern Illinois. In 1902, at the behest of Chicago bankers Trowbridge and Niver, he had reorganized various properties around New Albany, Indiana (across the Ohio from Louisville). To give his younger brother Martin a chance to prove himself in a major managerial job, he departed from his usual custom and acquired a controlling interest in the companies. Martin displayed surprising brilliance as a manager and a penchant for expanding over everything in sight; by the summer of 1911 he was operating local electric, gas, and streetcar companies capitalized at around five million dollars. Then, under Sam's guidance, he began to duplicate the Lake County experiment, and before long he was expanding his operations so rapidly that the little companies needed all the money that Sam's credit resources could provide, just at the time when Public Service of Northern Illinois was imposing the same demand.[20]

Now was the time to get out, to liquidate with a handsome profit, as Insull had done with the General Incandescent Lamp Company a half-dozen years earlier, and with each of his minor ventures outside Chicago since. But this time he had no intention of getting out; he

[20] Insull's investment in the New Albany properties first appears in his account books in 1902; the development of the properties can be generally traced in the *McGraw Central Station Lists;* it is summarized in Insull, "Memoirs," pp. 103–4. Information on Martin Insull's years in New Albany is derived from his application for membership in the Edison Pioneers, a manuscript in the Edison Laboratory National Monument; from Marquis (ed.), *Who's Who in Chicago, 1931,* p. 493; and from an interview with Martin Insull's daughter, Mrs. Virginia Insull Rafferty, in Morocco, Indiana, Aug. 20, 1959.

proposed to become involved all the more. The only problem was how to finance it. In May, 1912, at a meeting attended by Junior (who at twelve was thus present at his first major business conference) and Edward P. Russell, Insull's broker, who was an old friend and a director of Commonwealth Edison Company, Russell suggested that the way to finance the new undertakings was to form a holding company and to turn over all of the New Albany properties in exchange for its securities. Because the holding company was new, its securities would not be worth much at first, but even so, simply because it was Insull's company, it could probably finance its future expansion by selling its own securities, albeit at a large discount. If the company should fare well, Insull and such friends as might participate in it stood, in the long run, to profit greatly from the appreciation of its securities. Should it not work out—well, nothing ventured, nothing gained.[21]

And thus, almost with a shrug of the shoulders, was born the Middle West Utilities Company. The organization was easily effected. Insull had invested about $800,000 in cash in the New Albany properties, an investment worth perhaps $1,000,000; to acquire the properties necessary for rational expansion from its original base, Middle West needed about $3,500,000 in cash. Accordingly, Middle West raised the equivalent of about $4,500,000 by issuing its own securities. Insull thereby got cash and securities equal to his investment, and the company got the properties and its operating capital.[22]

These transactions were simple but, in a manner that was to be typical of the company and its operations, they were recorded on the company's books in a way that would forever leave accountants' heads swimming. Middle West took in from Insull and recorded as assets securities with a face value of $3,900,000. To pay for these and various lesser assets it issued to Insull and duly recorded as liabilities $5,000,000 par value of preferred stock and $7,000,000 par value of

[21] Insull, "Memoirs," pp. 104–5; interview with Samuel Insull, Jr. Insull also testified as to the origins of Middle West in his 1934 trial for use of the mails to defraud; *U.S.* v *Samuel Insull, et al.,* p. 4266, transcript in the Insull Paper.

[22] F.T.C., *Utility Corporations,* XXXVIII, 424–37; Middle West Utilities, *Annual Report,* 1913; *Minutes,* Middle West Utilities, directors' meeting, May 6, 1912. The corporate records of Middle West are in the offices of Central and South West Corporation, Chicago; an abridged minute book, containing records of all financial transactions, 1912–32, is in the Insull Papers.

common stock. Insull then returned $1,000,000 of each class of stock to the treasury and also gave the company $3,600,000 in cash. Then he raised the cash by selling to various friends and friendly houses— in general, the group which had invested in Public Service of Northern Illinois—all the preferred stock at a nominal price of $90 a share, but with a bonus of one share of common for each share of preferred they bought. Then the company nominally returned $330,000 in cash to Insull, with which he in fact became one of the purchasers of the stock he was selling. The securities Middle West acquired were written down on its books from $3,900,000 par value to $383,000. That left the company showing what appeared to be essentially water of something over $6,000,000. This amount was not capitalized but set up as a deferred asset (discount on stocks sold), to be written off whenever earned surplus should become large enough.[23]

The reason for all this financial hocus-pocus, in addition to the usual confusion of corporate bookkeeping, lay mainly in the legal requirement, then in force in all states, that all stock have a par value (usually $100), and that stock must at least technically be issued at par, no matter what its market value; otherwise it would be legally assessable for the difference between the issuing price and par. Under that condition, issuing and trading stocks would become virtually impossible, for no one would buy a stock at a market price of, say, $50, if he would thereby become legally liable to pay another $50 any time the corporation should demand it. Accordingly, until no-par stock became legal (1912 in New York; after World War I in other states), it was general business practice—and the only honest way to reconcile market realities with legal requirements—to treat all stock as if it had been issued at par and to adjust one's account books appropriately, usually by creating a credit entry (such as "value as a going concern," "deferred assets," or "good will") to balance the dif-

[23] These transactions are recorded in the *Minutes,* directors' meeting, May 6, 1912, and in F.T.C., *Utility Corporations,* XXXVIII, 424 ff. For a part of their explanation see the testimony of F.T.C. examiner Asel R. Colbert, who prepared the commission's exhibit on Middle West, *ibid.,* pp. 15–85. I have also interviewed Mr. Colbert (Madison, April, 1957) and two men who discussed the transactions with Insull: Edward J. Doyle, his secretary, and Samuel Insull, Jr. Even after these interviews and after studying the transactions off and on for four years, I did not understand them until I consulted certain entries in Insull's personal account books for May and June, 1912, which provided the clue I needed to untangle the matter.

ference between the actual and the nominal issuing price of the stock.[24]

Another reason lay in what Insull intended, in the long run, to do with Middle West. This was, in essence, to extend the Lake County experiment all over the middle western states, to extend systematized electric supply to large rural areas which then had little or no electricity. A holding company, Insull knew, could make money in three ways, none of which had much to do with operating its subsidiaries; all had to do with profiting from their growth. The first two Insull regarded as piracy: charging exorbitant fees for the construction of growing plant facilities or for the financing of the captive operating companies. The third was to build the operating companies into valuable, money-making concerns and thus to profit from the natural rise in the value of their securities. If one followed this route, it was advantageous to understate rather than to overstate the value of newly acquired properties and to record new securities of the parent company at par value rather than market value. Such bookkeeping maximized profits, whether these were book profits created by writing up the value of securities to reflect increased market values or actual profits realized from the sale of securities.[25]

Sometimes Middle West made profits spectacularly, when it ac-

[24] For a brief discussion of no-par stock see Henry W. Ballantine, *Ballantine on Corporations* (Chicago, 1946) , pp. 468–75, 796–801. Lack of understanding or lack of awareness of this problem has been a widespread source of confusion in studying the history of American business, particularly during the period from about 1880 to about 1910. This kind of bookkeeping is sometimes related to, but is quite a different thing from, "watered stock," for which it has often been mistaken.

[25] Insull's purpose is stated both implicitly and explicitly in his "Memoirs," pp. 104–5; in several of his addresses, especially his 1913 Franklin Institute address and his 1914 Finance Forum address, in *Central-Station Electric Service*, pp. 357–91 and 445–75; and in the record of what Middle West actually did. Negative information—that the Insull organization did not contain privately owned construction or security marketing companies—is clear from the United States government's first investigation of utilities, the F.T.C.'s *Control of Power Companies*, 69th Cong., 2d sess., Senate Document 213 (Washington, 1927) , pp. 251–59. The subsequent F.T.C. investigation, resulting in the eighty-odd volume *Utility Corporations Reports* (Washington, 1928–35) shows a curious lack of understanding of the principal means by which holding companies exploited operating companies, despite the fact that the commission was unrestrained in its denunciation of the evils of holding companies. The Securities Exchange Commission, in its investigation of holding companies, was more penetrating. Interviews with C. A. Turner of Chicago, former statistician for the S.E.C., made the foregoing generalizations possible, as did his copies of several of his unpublished reports—for example, on the American Gas and Electric Company system—which he kindly made available to me.

quired securities at a large discount and quickly created a market for them, but normally profit-making was a long and tedious process. Typical in both respects was the early history of Central Illinois Public Service Company (CIPSCo). Middle West made a cash profit of $131,946 and a nominal stock profit of almost $4,000,000 merely by creating that company and lending its credit to it. The nominal profits would become real, however, only if Middle West could repeat the success Insull had had with Public Service of Northern Illinois. In a decade, it did just that.

Middle West acquired Central Illinois in 1912, when it was operating a streetcar line in Mattoon, a twelve-mile interurban line to Charleston, and small, part-time central stations in these towns and the village of Kansas. Middle West began by buying the electric plants in every hamlet in central Illinois and, soon thereafter, southern Illinois—in all, the lighting plants in fifty-six rural communities. But from then on, CIPSCo expanded not by buying existing companies but by extending "high-lines" into places where electricity had never been before. In the next five years, Middle West bought and built into the CIPSCo system plants serving twenty villages and extended service to fifty-five other villages; in the dozen years after that, it extended CIPSCo's lines into nearly five hundred communities, almost none of which had had service of any kind. In 1912 about 15,000 customers in the area had some kind of electric service, usually limited and unreliable; they bought about 15,000,000 kilowatt-hours of electricity a year and paid more than fifteen cents a kilowatt-hour for it. Five years later, almost 40,000 customers had full-time and generally reliable electric service; they were buying more than fifty million kilowatt-hours a year, commercial and residential lighting customers at a dime a kilowatt-hour and power users at about three cents. (When the Insulls were through, 150,000 customers in the area would buy almost 400,000,000 kilowatt-hours a year, lighting customers for less than seven cents and power customers for less than two.) [26]

Almost without exception, the towns served by CIPSCo were farm

[26] *Minutes*, Middle West directors' meetings, May 6, May 28, July 10, Oct. 7, Oct. 28, Dec. 12, 1912; Jan. 8, Feb. 10, April 8, April 30, June 13, June 24, July 29, Dec. 9, 1913; F.T.C., *Utility Corporations*, XXXVIII, 37–49, 461–70; S.E.C. Hearings, 1940, Central Illinois Public Service Company, Integration Data, Exhibits I to X (typescript, copy in files of Central and South West Corporation, Chicago).

villages; only half a dozen had more than 5,000 inhabitants, and none had more than 10,000. This was not, however, entirely by design. Insull hoped to simplify the task of electrifying rural areas by developing a sprinkling of urban bases in each territory, but all efforts to acquire such bases in Illinois were frustrated. The streetcar systems and, only incidentally, franchises to do an electric business in virtually all the larger cities in downstate Illinois were controlled by a large network of concerns owned by a congressman and businessman named William McKinley. McKinley not only refused to sell the electric properties in these cities to Insull but refused to develop them himself, and spoke loudly, condescendingly, of Insull's efforts to electrify rural areas; furthermore, he said as much to prospective insurance-company investors in Insull companies. (This was hitting Insull in his area of no forgiveness, and from it was born a personal enmity between the two men which ripened over the years into a deep hatred. Insull could swear and denounce with remarkable fluency, but when genuinely involved emotionally, he used extremely simple language. For McKinley he reserved his strongest condemnation: "That man is no good." Ultimately, after McKinley became a senator in the 1920's, this hatred would lead Insull to make his most costly political blunder.) [27]

In still another respect the development of CIPSCo presaged the pattern of things to come, this one a pattern of weakness in Middle West's way of doing business. Though Middle West's aim was to systematize, to rationalize, electric power supply, the way it went about it sometimes resulted in irrational expansion. For one thing, since many local plants provided gas, water, streetcar, or ice service as well as electricity, CIPSCo often found itself wandering into these businesses while buying an electric plant. At first, Insull encouraged this diversification because he had the mistaken notion that as long as he was supplying power for making ice, pumping water, and running streetcars he might as well own companies in these businesses if they could be bought cheaply. It did not take him long to learn the folly of this view.[28]

[27] All sources cited in note 24; Central Illinois Public Service, *Annual Report*, 1927; Insull, "Memoirs," p. 161; interview with Britton Budd, Chicago, June 22, 1959; interviews with Samuel Insull, Jr.; *McGraw Central Station Lists*, 1912, 1913; Carroll H. Woody, *The Case of Frank L. Smith* (Chicago, 1931), pp. 7-10 and *passim;* see also below, pp. 262-70.

[28] See *Minutes*, Middle West directors' meetings, 1912-21, and the annual reports of the company for the same period.

Again, to buy electric property in a desirable location it was often necessary to pay for property of no great value which had been made a part of the "package." For example, some of the more important holdings necessary to CIPSCo's development were owned by A. H. Bickmore, a New York investment banker. Bickmore, like Trowbridge and Niver, had backed a number of small utility companies, only to find himself with a portfolio of sour investments. He had dumped them all into a subsidiary called National Light, Heat, and Power Company, and now he was eager to dispose of the subsidiary. National's holdings included five key Illinois properties and one company necessary to the expansion of Middle West's Indiana holdings, but they also included electric plants in two small communities in Missouri and a company that served electricity to five towns in New Hampshire, four in Maine, two in Vermont, and one in upstate New York, as well as gas in two places and a street railway in another. Bickmore offered to sell all National's holdings, but not a part of them. Middle West accepted, and as a result owned properties in upper New England and Missouri, far from its base of operations. In similar fashion, Middle West also acquired central stations in Kentucky, Oklahoma, Nebraska, and Michigan.[29]

As long as Middle West remained small enough so that Sam Insull could supervise it, this Topsy-like growth was not particularly dangerous. Insull developed Middle West's peripheral properties only so far as was necessary to render adequate service and, with one exception, permitted expansion only in Illinois, Indiana, and Kentucky. Thus restricted, Middle West grew steadily, but it did not mushroom into a financial giant. After five years it was still capitalized at $32,-000,000 and probably even that figure was a third more than the actual value of its assets. Its subsidiaries had grown remarkably: on the eve of World War I, they served 131,000 electric and 43,000 gas customers in four hundred communities and in thirteen states. They were accomplishing their purpose of extending reliable central station electric service over large rural areas to people who had never been served before and at rates roughly half those paid by

[29] *Moody's Manual of Railroad and Corporation Securities,* 1912; *Minutes,* Middle West directors' meeting, Oct. 7, 1912; Insull's testimony in *U.S.* v. *Insull,* p. 4267 (Nov. 1, 1934); Middle West Utilities Company, *Annual Report for the Year Ending April 30, 1913.* Similar transactions are recorded in *Moody's* and the Middle West minute books and its annual reports for subsequent years.

lighting customers in small towns in other parts of the country.[30]

As a business, Middle West was expanding and keeping afloat, meeting its interest payments, amortizing the discounts on its stocks, making the payments on its preferred stock, and occasionally paying modest dividends on its common stock. But though hopes for its financial future might be bright, it would have been clear to anyone less optimistic than Samuel Insull that Middle West would never be as strong as its subsidiaries and would always be better at building utilities than at making money.

Between 1911 and 1914 Insull also emerged, by default, as Chicago's leading traction magnate. The Chicago transportation system had always been in a snarl, but it began to appear that something might be done about it after the departure of Yerkes. The sound and fury attending the municipal ownership movement soon subsided, and in 1907 traction settlement ordinances were passed. Early in 1910, at the instigation of Mayor Fred Busse, groups of citizens interested in solving the problem began to hold conferences with the operators of the multitude of transportation companies in the city. It was soon clear that the only solution lay in a consolidation of all elevated railways and surface lines. By the end of 1910, the presidents of the elevated companies had agreed that a merger between them should be effected, and Henry Blair, president of the largest of the streetcar companies, indicated that he would go along with the plan. Accordingly, by early 1911 the El companies decided to proceed with their part of the merger.[31]

Because of a long history of political and financial shenanigans, the credit of the El companies was sorely limited, and few investors believed that the legislation necessary for the over-all merger could be obtained. The El companies needed about $6,000,000 in cash to begin integrating their facilities, and no one knew where to find it. Here Insull entered. Because Commonwealth Edison had so much at

[30] Middle West Utilities Company, *Annual Report for the Year Ending April 30, 1917; Moody's,* 1917; S.E.C. Integration Hearings, 1940, statements of the several subsidiaries of Middle West Corporation, copies in the files of Central and South West Corporation, Chicago.

[31] *Chicago Tribune,* Feb. 16, March 2, May 23, 1910; May 20, May 21, 1911; *Chicago Evening Post,* May 7, 1910; Feb. 6, May 21, May 22, 1911; *Chicago Daily News,* May 4, 1910; *Minutes,* Commonwealth Edison directors' meeting, April 26, 1911; Insull, "Memoirs," p. 192; Seymour, "History of Commonwealth Edison," pp. 434–35.

stake in the power business of the transportation companies, and because its credit was superb, the El operators hoped that Insull might be willing to underwrite a loan for the needed amount. He was. In April, 1911, the Chicago Elevated Railways Collateral Trust, a voluntary association of the various El companies, was organized. Insull, for Commonwealth Edison, agreed to guarantee $6,000,000, in exchange for stock of the trust, should it turn out that the merger between the El and surface lines could not be accomplished within three years. The guarantee enabled the El companies to borrow the sum. Before the three years were up, Chicago politics had taken a new turn, and the merger never materialized. Thus in July, 1914, Commonwealth Edison had to put up the cash. To provide the El companies with working capital it advanced a little more; as a result, it now held four-fifths of the common participating shares in the trust. In short, Commonwealth Edison Company owned its biggest customer.[32]

It was destined to be so from the formation of the trust. Insull had been unwilling to enter the scheme except on condition that should it become necessary he would control it, and it was common talk even as the trust was being formed that Insull was the power behind it. It was on his terms that the trust was formed, and it was under his supervision that the elevated railway companies of Chicago grew.[33]

In choosing the operating head of the El companies, Insull picked a man who became one of his most reliable arms and one of the most powerful and able figures in his inner circle. The man was Britton I. Budd, the forty-year-old president of the Metropolitan Elevated Railway Company, who had worked his way in fifteen years from assistant storekeeper to head of the company. (According to Budd, Insull picked him to head the combined organization because his salary was lower than that of the other presidents. Insull's own recollection was more flattering. "I got all the heads of the elevated lines together and looked them over," he said. "Budd was by far the most likely looking of them." In either event, it was one of the wisest choices Insull ever made.) Insull and Budd worked closely together, and Budd, more quickly and perhaps even more thoroughly than any

[32] *Minutes,* Commonwealth Edison directors' meetings, April 26, Nov. 21, 1911; Aug. 19, 1913; May 19, June 9, 1914; Seymour, "History of Commonwealth Edison," pp. 434–36.
[33] *Chicago Record-Herald, Chicago Daily Journal, Chicago Evening American,* Aug. 9, 1911; *New York Times,* Aug. 10, 1911; *St. Louis Post-Dispatch,* Aug. 13, 1911.

other Insull man, understood how to conduct a business Insull-fashion.[34]

Under Budd's management, the El companies began for the first time to make sense. Just after the trust was formed, a reporter asked Insull about dividends. Insull replied, "Who ever heard of El stock paying dividends?" Nobody had, and the new El stock did not pay dividends. But nobody in Chicago, at least, had heard of reduced rates and universal transfers and clean stations and courteous conductors; nor had anyone heard of labor relations so favorable that labor newspapers would attack politicians who said unkind things about the company for which members of the unions worked. Under Budd and Insull, people heard all these things and more. Budd managed the properties so skilfully that he was heralded by financial writers as far away as Boston as a "Moses for the tractions." Letters to the *Chicago Tribune* stopped denouncing the El companies and began to praise them; one enthusiastic subscriber went so far as to proclaim, "Praise Budd from Whom All Blessings Flow."[35]

Soon afterward, Insull began acquiring, modernizing, and co-ordinating the interurbans connecting Chicago with its suburbs. Neither this step toward rationalization, it turned out, nor Budd's farsighted management, nor what people were coming to regard as Insull's magic would completely solve the city's transportation problem. It would plague Chicago long after Samuel Insull was dead. But upon assuming the responsibility for one reason Insull took it seriously for another, and with his first efforts the situation began to improve.[36]

Insull assumed one other major position at this time: chairmanship of the board of directors of Peoples Gas Light and Coke Company.

---

[34] All Chicago newspapers, August–September, 1911; Marquis (ed.), *The Book of Chicagoans*, 1911, pp. 98–99; interview with Britton Budd, Chicago, June 22, 1959; Budd's scrapbooks, covering his career from the 1890's to the 1940's, in his possession.

[35] *Chicago Evening Post*, Sept. 5, 1911; Oct. 29, 1913; *Chicago Tribune*, Oct. 29–Nov. 3, 1913; Sept. 28, 1922; *Electric Traction*, July, 1921; an unnamed Boston newspaper (clipping in Budd's scrapbooks), Nov. 9, 1920; *Electric Railway Journal*, Sept. 23, 1922; *Manufacturers News*, Sept. 7, 1922; Budd to all employees (form letter in Budd scrapbooks), Dec. 16, 1920; *Chicago Unionist* (undated clipping, ca. October, 1923); *Chicago Union Leader*, Nov. 17, 1923.

[36] On Insull's expansion to the interurbans see *Chicago Tribune, Chicago Examiner, Chicago Daily News,* Aug. 16, 1916; April 27, 1919; April 26, 1920; October 11, 1923; January 16, 1924.

As was the case with the traction companies, people in trouble turned to Insull to bail them out, on the theory that he was the only man who could do so, and Insull could think of no reason—nor did he try very hard—to avoid doing so. But this time the motivation was quite different, and the intentions were somewhat less than honestly stated.

If the political and financial affairs of Chicago's transportation companies were muddled, those of the gas company were chaotic. After surviving an orgy of political franchises and shady trusts during the nineties and a prolonged strike in 1903, the several gas companies of Chicago were finally put on a solid legal footing through laws and ordinances that permitted them to consolidate into one, the Peoples Gas Light and Coke Company. But in the wake of the political storm over Yerkes and his traction legislation, public utilities became open game for every manner of crusader, and Peoples Gas had no man of Insull's political acumen to steer it through the troubled period that followed. At last, in 1913, the owners made a belated effort to rectify this weakness by asking Insull to assume the chairmanship. They had no intention of letting him run the company; they merely wanted him to perform his political arts in its behalf.[37]

They approached him the wrong way. Assuming that every man is for sale, they offered Insull $50,000 a year to become chairman of the board, a position that involved no responsibility for the active management of the company. Insull refused.

Then someone in the gas company had a clever notion. If Insull would not rent his political influence for $50,000 a year, perhaps he could be persuaded by a power play. The one thing Insull guarded most jealously was the gains he had made as the supplier of Chicago's motive power, and the one thing that might induce him to do something he otherwise would not was to threaten his control of the city's power supply. Gas hardly threatened to supplant electricity as the most economical source of industrial power, but the management of the gas company decided to bluff. Playing upon Insull's awe before

[37] The general history of the company prior to 1913 has been traced in its minute books and annual reports and in Chicago newspapers. The details on the motivations and actions of the company's management in inducing Insull to assume the company's chairmanship are derived from an interview with Francis L. Daily (long a lawyer with the firm of Cooke, Sullivan, and Ricks, counsel for the Gas Company), in Wilmette, Illinois, Nov. 18, 1957.

the claims of inventors—an attitude born of his adulation of Edison
—they had some of the company's engineers and mechanics build a
model gas engine and display it prominently (behind a guard rail,
so that it could not be inspected closely) in the company showrooms.
With great fanfare, they announced that they were entering the
power market with a revolutionary new motor. It was completely
portable, they claimed, and could be manufactured cheaply in any
size; they released fictitious operating figures that were calculated to
suggest that the engine would be more efficient and cheaper than an
electric motor.[38]

Insull went for the bait. Childlike, he stole into the company building to have a look. He could not get close enough to be sure, but he
became convinced that it was at least possible that the engine could
be as valuable as the gas company claimed. Thus what an offer of
money could not do, a threat to his supremacy in the power business
did. In September, 1913, Insull became chairman of the board of the
Peoples Gas Company.[39]

Despite the deception that brought him into it, and despite the fact
that he went in only part of the way, Insull did not enter the venture
with his eyes completely closed. He knew the company had political
troubles aplenty and was under enormous political and popular pressure to reduce its rates. But he also knew that though the company's
management on the upper levels left much to be desired, management on the operating level was excellent. Insull brought to the
board with him two of his most trusted business friends, John J.
Mitchell and James A. Patten, thus insuring control of the five-man
directorate, and he immediately set out to improve the company's
affairs. Doing so did not prove difficult; within a year or two, both
major problem areas seemed well in hand.[40]

Nonetheless, Insull was making what would prove to be a dangerous mistake. Because he deceived himself that he could have the
power without much attendant responsibility, he took over without
fully informing himself of what he was getting into. When he became

[38] Interview with Francis L. Daily. The salary figure is from *Minutes*, Peoples Gas directors' meeting, Oct. 14, 1913.
[39] Insull, "Memoirs," pp. 184–85; *Minutes*, Peoples Gas directors' meetings, Sept. 24–25,
1913; *Chicago Tribune*, Chicago *Inter-Ocean*, *Chicago Daily News*, Sept. 25–26, 1913.
[40] *Minutes*, Peoples Gas directors' meetings, 1913–14, and all Chicago newspapers for the
same period.

undeceived, it was almost too late. What he did not know was that underlying the obvious weaknesses of the company were others that were far worse. The company was in a peculiar squeeze between politics and technology that might prove fatal even under superb management. But as events were to demonstrate, the company was weak, if not rotten, at the core. Insull's rehabilitation of the Peoples Gas Company was to be one of his most spectacular business achievements.[41]

[41] Insull said in his "Memoirs" (pp. 184–85) that the company had a reputation for being well managed; he doubtless referred to the operating aspect of the business, not the financial. For its weaknesses, see pp. 206–8, below.

CHAPTER VII   *The War*

Insull went to war when Great Britain did, in August, 1914. Although he had been an American citizen since 1896, he violated American neutrality even before President Wilson made his famous plea for "neutrality in thought and deed" a month after the war in Europe began. Until the United States entered the war in April, 1917, Insull had to operate under cover, for had he been found out, he might have gone to jail. When his adopted land joined his native land he began to work publicly for the allied cause, and he did so with a vigor, enthusiasm, and effectiveness that earned him world-wide commendation. In the process, he acquired a reputation and a pair of tools that afterward made possible a rise to dizzying heights of power. Perhaps they also made it inevitable, for, in the next decade and a half, most of Chicago would agree that he was power's safest repository.

Insull's unhesitating actions on behalf of England stemmed from intellectual as well as emotional reasons. Not only did he have family, business, and social ties in his native land, but he also believed that American participation in the war was inevitable. His opinion was well informed: Few Americans were as well versed in international affairs, for he had made a lifelong study of the subject, and friends in high places on both sides of the Atlantic had enriched his study with inside information. Thus, for example, he knew that Britain would declare war before the British people knew it. From an English railroad president he had learned the timetable for the mobilization of transportation, and when he read in American newspapers an apparently innocuous announcement concerning British railroads, he knew that war was less than seventy-two hours away.[1]

Convinced that America would necessarily be drawn into the war, and knowing that he and other former Englishmen would strive to see that the involvement was on the side of Great Britain, he was also convinced that the German-Americans in the Middle West would make equal efforts to promote the cause of Germany. As William Hale (Big Bill) Thompson, the mayor of Chicago, said, "It is possible that a portion of the citizens of Chicago might not be wildly enthusiastic" for the Allies, for "Chicago is the sixth largest German city in the world. It is the second largest Bohemian city, the second largest Swedish, the second largest Norwegian, and the second largest Polish." Insull did not believe that such groups could induce the United States to join the Central Powers as a belligerent; the cultural and economic ties between England and America were too strong to permit that. But he was afraid that, by playing upon traditional American isolationism and pacifism, they could keep America neutral so long that the Allies could not win.[2]

To Englishmen in Insull's position the task ahead was thus one of swaying public opinion, and at a time when "public relations" and mass selling were in their infancy, in this art Insull had few peers. Said a former Morgan partner, Robert Bacon, to a Frenchman: "In America . . . there are 50,000 people who understand the necessity of the United States entering the war immediately on your side. But there are 100,000,000 Americans who have not even thought of it. Our task is to see that the figures are reversed and that the 50,000

[1] Said Insull: "Medill McCormick, Melville Stone, and Mr. Freud were the only men in Chicago when I went there with whom I could discuss foreign affairs with as much understanding as would be shown by the average men you would meet upon the highway in England." In London, he had necessarily followed international affairs, and he continued to do so in New York. (At one time he lived with Arthur Brisbane, who became, for the *New York World*, one of America's first foreign correspondents.) Berry, "Mr. Samuel Insull," pp. 35–37. Other statements in the same document refer to his contacts in high places in European governments. Later, Insull became a close friend of Cardinal Mundelein, whose hobby was study of international governmental finance, and he and Insull spent countless evenings together discussing the subject. The incident regarding the railroad man and mobilization is narrated in Insull's "Memoirs," pp. 112–13. The railroad man was Sir William Guy Gronet, general manager of the Midland Railroad, later chairman of the London Scottish and Midland Railroad.

[2] Insull's thinking on the subject is clear from the several letters to and from his father, 1913–15, in the Insull Papers; his "Memoirs," pp. 112–16; and Berry, "Mr. Samuel Insull," pp. 15–16, 27, 45. The quotation is from William H. Stuart, *The Twenty Incredible Years* (Chicago, 1935), p. 41.

becomes the 100,000,000. We will accomplish this." Insull's role in accomplishing this was of considerable importance.[3]

The official British propaganda agency, Wellington House, was established in September, 1914, and from the outset it had an American branch, headed by Sir Gilbert Parker. In the beginning, however, Parker aimed at trying to win supporters only among America's elite—Bacon's 50,000—and he tried to win them individually: he worked through personal correspondence and literature sent out on a mailing list compiled from *Who's Who*. Insull's keen sense of public relations told him this was an absurd way to go about it, that broad-based propaganda and consequently full utilization of American newspapers was absolutely necessary. But there was a barrier to this. The British, ever concerned with propriety, traditionally refused to send newspaper correspondents to the battle front under official auspices and never granted them interviews with cabinet ministers. Insull understood American newsmen, and he believed that to befriend them by favoring them would so influence their reporting that the entire American press would become a propaganda agency for the British government.[4]

In January, 1915, Insull called on Sir Edward Grey, the British Minister of Foreign Affairs, to sell him on the idea. Grey was flabbergasted, almost horrified. "Mr. Insull," he said, "you, born an Englishman, come here and make the suggestion that His Majesty's Minister for Foreign Affairs should be interviewed by a newspaper reporter. It seems impossible." But Insull persisted and had a number of long conversations with Grey and David Lloyd George (then Chancellor of the Exchequer), in an attempt to arrange interviews with cabinet ministers for Edward Price Bell of the *Chicago Daily News*, the dean of American correspondents in London. This effort failed, but ultimately Insull convinced Grey of the merits of his general plan, and by April Grey and the rest of the cabinet had consented. Thereafter, the American newspapers became one of the most

[3] James D. Squires, *British Propaganda at Home and in the United States from 1914 to 1917* (Cambridge, 1935), p. 43. The quotation is worded slightly differently in several books on the war. The original source is Gabriel Hanotaux, *Histoire Illustrée de la guerre de 1914*, IX (Paris, 1914–24), 56.
[4] Squires, *British Propaganda*, pp. 26–34; H. C. Peterson, *Propaganda for War: The Campaign against American Neutrality, 1914–1917* (Norman, Oklahoma, 1939), pp. 12–70; George S. Viereck, *Spreading Germs of Hate* (London, 1931), *passim*; Insull, "Memoirs," pp. 115–16; Berry, "Mr. Samuel Insull," p. 15.

effective organs of British propaganda, propaganda that was vital in shaping American attitudes toward the war.[5]

(Insull's understanding of American newspaper readers enabled him to see ways of influencing public opinion that would have occurred neither to British propagandists nor to American public relations men. For example, in describing some of his methods years later, he said, "You would have thought that the 'Lusitania' affair [May 7, 1915] would have provoked a declaration of war, if anything would, but it did not. However, a few days after that disaster the German Government published an order that American ships must comply with certain rules in order to pass the German submarine blockade. There were to be only two ships allowed to pass each week, and there were many other similar regulations, but the important point was that those ships that passed had to be painted in such a way as to suggest the old prison uniform—those striped things that were used before the uniform was changed to one of a neutral color. This gave us a wonderful opportunity, and we used it for all that it was worth. We saw to it that cartoons appeared in every small paper throughout the land showing Uncle Sam wearing a prison uniform at the Kaiser's bidding. This struck home to the man in the street much more forcibly than had the 'Lusitania' disaster and it really cast the die for America's entrance into the war upon the allied side.")[6]

At home, Insull worked directly in propaganda activity. The first aim of British propaganda was to appeal to the Anglo-American heritage and community of interest; the second was to paint the Germans as barbarians and to seek support for Britain through pleas to justice, mercy, and similar sentiments. To paint the Germans black, Insull helped arrange for the regular distribution of strongly biased war information to 360 American newspapers which had no press service and contributed nearly $250,000 toward financing this effort. To appeal to American sentimentality, he helped organize a series of

[5] In his "Memoirs," p. 116, Insull admits that it was he who persuaded Grey to exploit American newspapers in this fashion. See also "Memoirs," p. 144. The background of the shift is made clear in the several accounts cited in note 4; the effects of it are visible in many American newspapers, January-June, 1915.

[6] Berry, "Mr. Samuel Insull," p. 16. Insull was probably mistaken in referring to the "Lusitania"; from the context it would appear that he was thinking of the sinkings after the Germans resumed submarine warfare in February, 1917.

allied bazaars throughout the nation. The allied bazaars—unlike German bazaars, which were espionage centers—were strictly charitable, but they were more effective for propaganda purposes for just that reason. They asked Americans for medicine, food, and other aid for Britain, and thereby invoked the desired image of the allied cause. Too, as Insull said, "You get people interested in running a bazaar, and they finally get interested in the cause for which the bazaar is run."[7] (To supplement these activities, Insull ran an "underground railroad" which recruited men from all over the United States, sent them to Canada, and enlisted them under British colors. He also personally bore the expense of financial assistance to the families of men so recruited and in addition contributed large sums for direct relief in England.)[8]

By the middle of 1916 the majority of Americans were clearly and strongly pro-Ally; but in spite of the effectiveness of British propaganda, in spite of President Wilson's strong private convictions in favor of Britain, and in spite of the economic stake a large segment of American business had in an allied victory, the American people, in general, still had little urge to go to war. As a matter of political expediency, Wilson's advisers found it prudent for him to run for re-election on the slogan, "He kept us out of war." And as 1916 wore on, it became increasingly evident to informed persons that Britain and France were nearing the point of collapse.[9] (During the war Insull's

[7] Insull, "Memoirs," pp. 114–17; Berry, "Mr. Samuel Insull," pp. 14, 15, 27. The general aspects of these activities are described in the works cited in note 4, above, although Insull's part is mentioned in none of them. Insull's activities were so secretive that but for his admissions in his unpublished "Memoirs" and to Burton Berry, they would scarcely be recognized. With those admissions, however, the trail becomes visible; for example, Insull's mysterious expenditures, as recorded in his account books, become explicable, as do his extensive travels, certain references in letters to his father, and occasional absences from board meetings. A file of newspaper clippings spanning the years 1914–17, preserved in the Insull Papers, covers Insull's public doings, such as the allied charities bazaars. The person through whom Insull gave £50,000 was Sir Arthur Vincent.

[8] Berry, "Mr. Samuel Insull," p. 15; Insull's letters to his father and Emma H. Insull, 1914–16, in the Insull Papers; interview with Colonel Ralph H. James (wartime head of the British Home Defense Office), Chicago, May 20, 1958; Sir Auckland Geddes to Insull, May 29, 1920, and Insull to Geddes, June 4, 1920, in the Insull Papers.

[9] The historiography of America's entrance into World War I is so confused and biased that little beyond these generalizations is agreed upon. The bibliography is huge; a good bibliography for works and documents available up to 1939 is in Charles C. Tansill's *America Goes to War* (Boston, 1938), pp. 664–79, though the book itself is hardly bias-free.

parents, over eighty years old and in delicate health, died, at least in part for want of a proper diet. To him this personal tragedy, particularly the loss of his mother, sharply dramatized, and perhaps even symbolized, the imminent possibility of the defeat of his native country.) [10]

Germany, having the upper hand but hard pressed, seized the moment to launch an effort to bring about a negotiated peace and asked Wilson to serve as the intermediary and arbiter. In the face of this prospect English agents faced an enormous task that had to be executed quickly and without fail. Wilson, a man accustomed to titanic struggles inside his conscience, had to be badgered unmercifully and incessantly to reject the German peace overtures. Sir William Wiseman, head of British secret service in America and chief, *sub rosa,* of British propaganda, had the ear of Colonel House, Wilson's most trusted adviser; Insull himself had the ear of Joseph Tumulty, Wilson's private secretary; the House of Morgan, which had a huge financial stake in the allied cause, had the ear of everyone who was anyone; and through these and countless other voices the beleagured President was subjected to persuasion. Efforts to persuade him failed, for within a month or two after his re-election Wilson determined to try to negotiate peace, but they helped delay his decision, and when Wilson decided, it was too late. By January, 1917, Germany was ready to gamble on an all-out effort to win the war before America could mobilize. A necessary part of this campaign was the resumption of submarine warfare. In the face of so great a provocation, the road to American entry into the war was a short one. On Friday, April 6, the United States declared war on the Central Powers.[11]

[10] Insull, "Memoirs," pp. 124–27.
[11] The general succession of events narrated here is well known and to be found in almost any textbook in American history. On Wilson's battle with his conscience, the most recent major work is Arthur S. Link's *Wilson: The Struggle for Neutrality* (Princeton, 1960), which unfortunately does not cover the war years, but is sympathetic and extremely illuminating. See also Tansill, *America Goes to War*, pp. 631–59; John L. Heaton (ed.), *Cobb of "The World"* (New York, 1924), pp. 268–70. On Wiseman and House see Viereck's *Spreading Germs of Hate, passim,* and his *The Strangest Friendship in History* (New York, 1932), and Charles Seymour (ed.), *The Intimate Papers of Colonel House* (2 vols.; Boston, 1925). On Insull and Tumulty see Tumulty's *Woodrow Wilson as I Knew Him* (New York, 1921) and Tumulty's remarks quoted in the *New York Times,* Aug. 11, 1935. Apparently the origin of Insull's friendship with Tumulty was their mutual friendship with Roger Sullivan. In the twenties, Tumulty was on Insull's financial syndicate lists; See *Chicago Tribune, Chicago Daily News,* Sept. 30, 1932. On Morgan and the war see the Nye Committee investigations: *Hear-*

Now Insull could go to work with official sanction. His formal role was established within a week after the declaration of war. In August, 1916, Wilson had established the Council of National Defense, and as soon as war was declared he asked the state governors to create state councils of defense to work with and under the direction of the national council. Immediately, Governor Frank Lowden telephoned Insull from Springfield and asked him to serve as head of the council. Insull accepted and pledged all his time to the job, a pledge he fulfilled.[12]

At a Washington conference early in May, he learned that the job was not what he had expected. The state councils were designed to be little more than officially organized and sanctioned vigilante committees to police persons suspected of disloyalty, particularly German-Americans. Insull, disappointed and unwilling to play so negative a role, decided to do far more on his own.[13]

Under Insull's command, the State Council of Defense of Illinois was transformed into a dynamic instrument of war, and other state councils followed this lead. Insull began by forming a full council, for which he picked men who combined standing with willingness to work long and hard, men who represented a balance between all groups in the state whose co-operation was sought. Insull and Lowden selected four Chicago businessmen, J. Ogden Armour, John A. Spoor, Fred W. Upham, and Charles H. Wacker; one physician, Dr. Frank Billings; one woman, Mrs. Joseph T. Bowen; three men from downstate, John H. Harrison, banker B. F. Harris of Champaign, and Lieutenant Governor John G. Oglesby; two labor leaders, John H. Walker and Illinois Federation of Labor Secretary Victor Olander; Democrats John P. Hopkins and Roger Sullivan and Republicans Oglesby and Speaker of the Illinois House David E. Shanahan to represent the two major parties; and Levy Mayer, of the

---

ings before the Special Senate Committee on the Investigation of the Munitions Industry (74th Cong., 2d sess., Parts 25–32 [Washington, 1937]), and Peterson, *Propaganda for War*, Appendixes A–C, pp. 333–41.

12 *Final Report of the State Council of Defense of Illinois, 1917–1918–1919* (Springfield, n.d., ca. 1919), pp. 7–9; Insull, "Memoirs," pp. 116–17; William T. Hutchinson, *Lowden of Illinois: The Life of Frank O. Lowden*, I (2 vols.; Chicago, 1957), 329–30; Marguerite E. Jenison (ed.), *The War Time Organization of Illinois* (Springfield, 1923), pp. 29–66.

13 Illinois Council, *Final Report*, p. 7; interview with George R. Jones (who worked on the council), Chicago, Dec. 29, 1959.

largest Jewish law firm in Chicago, to serve as counsel. Insull commanded this diverse group as if they were so many subordinates in one of his companies; with the spur of his own example, he drove them to work, and to work together.[14]

Soon after they were appointed, Insull assigned the council members to a set of three-man committees, one for each of the major tasks he foresaw. Then he provided each committee with a ready-made organization, recruited mainly from his own companies—Munroe, Budd, Gilchrist, William A. Fox, Frank Baker, L. E. Myers, Martin Insull, E. W. Lloyd, E. J. E. Ward, John Gulick, and every other key subordinate he could spare from their jobs—and this group of men became the working executive department for the committees. In turn, members of the executive department formed their own staffs, often consisting of men who drew salaries from an Insull company while working for the council.[15]

Having created the mountain top, Insull rapidly built a mountain under it. Drawing on the council's political members for lists of local politicians and on the labor members for skilled organizers, he recruited volunteer workers until he had reproduced the central organization, in miniature, in almost every neighborhood in every community in the state. Simultaneously, he launched the first active phase of the council's work as he conceived it: planning, organizing, and executing a campaign to mobilize public opinion. In retrospect, the brilliance of the planning and organization is breathtaking; the ruthless precision of the execution is terrifying. In a world without radio, sound films, television, or any other instantaneous mass media, Insull and his organization infused the people of Illinois with a zeal that many thought excessive; he produced a band of militant enthusiasts whose momentum never allowed patriotic fervor a moment's rest.[16]

---

[14] Illinois Council meetings, May 8, May 12, 1917 (in the two-volume manuscript minute book of the council, in the Insull Papers); Jenison (ed.), *War Time Organization of Illinois*, pp. 29 ff.; *Journal of the Senate of the Fiftieth General Assembly of the State of Illinois*, pp. 801–2.

[15] Illinois Council, *Final Report*, pp. 82, 83, 96–97, 104, 164, 181–83, 187, 216, 219, 246, 249, 259, 268, 272; *Minutes*, State Council meetings, May 12, May 19, June 2, June 9, June 23, 1917.

[16] *Minutes*, Illinois Council meetings, May 26, 1917, *et seq;* Illinois Council, *Final Report*, pp. 15–17, 27–28, 159–61. For reflections of fanatical patriotism see Chicago newspapers throughout the war.

President Wilson had established the official national propaganda agency, the Committee on Public Information (CPI), during
the first week of the war. Under the zealous direction of George
Creel, the CPI ultimately became as effective as Wellington House
had been. But while others were sometimes disturbed by Creel's
speed—his CPI was in full and effective operation by the fall of
1917—he moved much too slowly for Insull. Insull's propaganda
agency was in operation three months before Creel's; and when the
CPI was ready to begin operations, Insull's agency co-operated with
it—and even taught it a few things.[17]

For the working head of his "publicity department," Insull borrowed from his political friends a brilliant publicist and former
newspaperman, Bernard J. Mullaney. Mullaney immediately established a news and editorial service through which, by mixing patriotic appeals with political and economic pressure, he enlisted the
state's editors as active propagandists, disseminators of information
on Illinois' part in the war, and publicists for the State Council of
Defense. Simultaneously, believing with Insull that word of mouth
propaganda was far more effective than the printed word, Mullaney
set out to recruit a statewide force of public speakers. To beat the
drums until Mullaney could establish permanent speakers' bureaus
in every county, Insull enrolled a small army of ministers, fraternal
orders, labor organizations, nationalistic societies, mayors, and civic
and commercial groups to stage a host of Fourth of July celebra-
tions.[18]

Once the speakers' bureaus were established, mobilization and
war fever cascaded downstate like an avalanche. By the end of the
summer, local committees were holding daily, sometimes hourly
meetings in public buildings, schoolhouses, churches, and private
homes in virtually every neighborhood in the state, to promote
"appreciation of the ideals of true patriotism and love of country"
and "a proper war spirit." Small meetings were addressed by local
speakers, "neighbor talking to neighbor"; for larger meetings, the
"neighborhood committee" of the "publicity department" worked

[17] George Creel, *How We Advertised America* (New York, 1920); Harold D. Lasswell,
Propaganda Technique in the World War (New York, 1927); *Minutes*, Illinois Council
meeting, May 26, 1917; Illinois Council, *Final Report*, p. 159; all Chicago newspapers,
June-September, 1917.
[18] Illinois Council, *Final Report*, pp. 25–35, 159–61; all Chicago newspapers, June-July,
1917.

with the Chautauqua association to form a bureau that promised to supply as speakers war heroes and other celebrities. In time, this bureau arranged programs for almost 7,000 public meetings.[19]

(For the working head of the "neighborhood committee," Insull appointed the self-styled curmudgeon, Harold Ickes. At first Insull was amused when Ickes—whom he called "an unsuccessful newspaper reporter who married money," and whom his aids called "that man Itches"—asked to become a member of the state council and rewarded his "presumption" by refusing to appoint him to anything. Insull disliked Ickes personally and thoroughly disapproved of his perennially unsuccessful campaigns as a reform politician. He made Ickes head of the "neighborhood committee" only after Ickes had pestered council members Sullivan, Olander, and Hopkins for several months. Under Mullaney, Ickes did a creditable job—though somewhat slower than his counterparts in other states—until he resigned in April, 1918, to be replaced by L. E. Myers. But Ickes had been dissatisfied with the assignment, and he never forgave Insull for the initial snub. From that snub was born a lifelong enmity, for which Insull would one day pay dearly.) [20]

One of Insull's propaganda activities spawned a national agency: the "Four-Minute Men," a venture in broadcasting without radio. The method, which Donald M. Ryerson of Chicago conceived and suggested to Insull, was to enlist a huge team of speakers to deliver, simultaneously, four-minute speeches to audiences in motion picture theaters and other places of public amusement. On trial in Chicago, the idea proved an immediate success, and it was quickly adopted by the CPI for nationwide use. Under the leadership of Chicagoans— notably Ryerson, William McCormick Blair, and George R. Jones, secretary of Insull's Public Service Company of Northern Illinois— the Four-Minute Men thrived throughout the war and were considered one of the most effective voices of the CPI. By the end of the war the organization had 75,000 speakers. In Illinois alone there

[19] *Minutes,* Illinois Council meetings, Aug. 16, Aug. 28, 1917; Illinois Council, *Final Report,* pp. 28–29. All these activities can be traced in the several Chicago newspapers and such downstate papers as the *Waterloo Journal,* the *Urbana Daily Courier,* the *East St. Louis Daily Journal,* and the Springfield *Illinois State Register.*
[20] Ickes, *Autobiography of a Curmudgeon,* pp. 189–90, *passim;* Berry, "Mr. Samuel Insull," p. 50; Illinois Council, *Final Report,* pp. 27–29, 83, 90–91; interview with Charles A. Munroe, New York, May 16, 1956; interview with George R. Jones, Chicago, Dec. 29, 1959; Frederick L. Allen, "The State Councils of Defense," in *Century* (Dec., 1917) ; see especially the map.

were 2,000 speakers who addressed more than 700,000 people a week.[21]

The Illinois Council had two additional tasks, as Insull saw it: raising money and policing the economy of the state. So adept was Insull at fund-raising that the citizens of Illinois enjoyed saying that if he had been running the war, he would have run it at a profit. While other state councils accomplished much less with appropriations as high as $5,000,000, the Illinois Council began with only $50,000, spent several times that sum, raised some $24,000,000 for war relief, and returned a profit of more than $450,000 to state and federal treasuries. Equally important, it assumed unofficial responsibility for the selling of Liberty Bonds in Illinois, and to do so staged spectacular shows like the Chicago War Exposition in September, 1918, at which 2,000,000 spectators watched 3,000 servicemen and a squadron of British and American planes engage in mock battle.[22] Using high-pressure, razzle-dazzle salesmanship the council induced patriotic citizens to spend more than $1,300,000,000 for Liberty Bonds in a period of eighteen months. This sum, half again the national per capita average, was half the value of the annual manufacturing output of the entire Chicago area. This well-publicized financial record established Insull in the public eye as a miracle worker with a Midas touch. (For a time, this popular image was invaluable, for it made possible the financing of utility expansion on an unprecedented scale, and enabled Insull to break the grip of the bankers on the nation's utilities.)[23]

Insull's third self-assumed function as head of the Illinois Council

[21] There is no published history of the Four-Minute Men; their history is summarized in the Illinois Council *Final Report*, pp. 30–31, 164–83; for brief accounts see also Creel, *How We Advertised America;* Lasswell, *Propaganda Technique;* and Viereck, *Spreading Germs of Hate.* The Four-Minute Men were housed at first in the offices of Commonwealth Edison Company; Illinois Council, *Final Report*, pp. 166, 168. In an interview cited earlier (notes 13 and 20), George R. Jones provided much valuable information.

[22] All Chicago newspapers, Oct. 20–22, 1917, Feb. 17, Feb. 18, March 8–10, May 25–29, June 13–14, Sept. 1–16, 1918; Illinois Council, *Final Report*, pp. 184–86; *Minutes,* Illinois Council meetings, Sept. 6, Sept. 17, 1918; George Creel to Insull, July 27, 1918, and Insull to Creel, Aug. 1, 1918 (bound in Minute Book II of the Illinois Council, pp. 342, 343) ; "U.S. Government War Exposition" folder, in the Insull Papers.

[23] The financial record of the council is summarized in its *Final Report*, pp. 19–21. Much additional information is in Insull's *Public Utilities in Modern Life,* pp. 166–77. See also the *Chicago Tribune* and other Chicago dailies, Jan. 19, 1919.

was to encourage all segments of the economy to co-operate in the war effort. When his volunteer army reached full force, he commanded more than 380,000 workers, who formed an efficient team that regularly astounded Washington by its speed in carrying out government requests. Counties that required more than a day to execute an assigned function, such as meeting their quotas for war relief, apologized for the delay, and even when requests from Washington were unpopular, Illinois responded.[24] But Insull had no intention of confining himself to the execution of orders from Washington. He had in his hands one of the most powerful semiofficial organizations in the history of the state, and he made his own decisions as to how to use it. In the main, his independent actions anticipated government action; but in several crucial areas the national government moved only in response to the example of Illinois.

Thus even as Insull marshalled his might, he began to wield it. His first action was a bold stroke against war profiteering in coal. Across the board and across the nation, the prices of basic commodities started creeping upward as soon as war was declared; but the price of coal took an astronomical leap. The cost-plus contracts Insull had signed with Peabody protected his companies from this kind of inflation and proved to Insull's satisfaction that the spectacular rise in coal prices on the open market was artificial. To be sure, natural pressures—higher wages, increased demand, and local shortages arising from the dislocation of rail transportation— pushed up the price of coal by as much as 20 per cent. But in the inflation a host of brigands saw the chance for easy profit. Speculators began to buy in the expectation that by winter the price of coal would be much higher. Then some asked, why wait for winter? Finding no reason, they began to manipulate the market, driving prices skyward. Then the coal operators, previously guiltless but long hungry for profits after several lean years before the war, capitalized on the rise: they stopped contracting for over half their

[24] Bernard M. Baruch to Insull, July 3, July 19, July 22, 1918; Insull to Baruch, July 18, July 19, 1918; Baruch to Secretary of War, Aug. 22, 1918; Edwin B. Parker, War Industries Board Circular No. 21 (Sept. 3, 1918) ; Josephus Daniels to Baruch, Sept. 7, 1918; Arthur H. Fleming to Insull, Sept. 11, 1918 (all bound in Minute Book II of the Illinois Council, pp. 352–60; duplicates of Insull's letters are in the Letter Book of the council, in the Insull Papers) ; Illinois Council, *Final Report*, pp. 56, 242–45; *Chicago Tribune*, Sept. 18, 1918.

output and started selling the rest in the open market for all it would bring. Immediately the mine workers, eager to share in the windfall, demanded a wage increase, and rather than jeopardize profits the operators granted raises without delay. After sixty days of war, the price of coal had trebled.[25]

Shocked and outraged, Insull thundered down upon the coal men. Through the publicity arm of the Illinois Council, he saw to it that they were denounced in press and pulpit as "profiteers" and takers of "unconscionable profits." Through his official affiliations and every political friend at his disposal, he urged that Washington immediately establish a fuel administration with absolute power over the price of coal from mine to furnace. And to the coal operators themselves, he issued a demand that inflation be brought under control.[26]

Embarrassed by the sound and fury and fearful that, because of Insull, they might have carried a good thing too far, operators froze prices late in June and then reduced them a little. But the price of coal was still two and a half times normal, and when Insull demanded further cuts the operators balked. Whereupon Insull summoned before the Illinois Council leading operators and officials of the mine workers union and told them that if prices were not slashed he would, in the name of the council, seize the mines and operate them himself. Operators and miners alike were shaken by this pronouncement, and a brief recess was held so that all sides could run to their lawyers and find out whether Insull could carry out his threat. By the time they reconvened, Insull was armed with sanction from both Washington and Springfield.[27]

But this power he did not have to exercise, for the nationwide publicity attending Insull's fight dramatized the problem and

[25] Illinois Council, *Final Report*, pp. 44–45; *Minutes*, Illinois Council meetings, May 12, May 26, June 9, June 16, June 23, 1917; *Minutes*, Commonwealth Edison directors' meeting, Aug. 21, 1917. This entire episode is summarized—with enthusiastic kudos for Insull and the Illinois Council—in many newspapers and magazines; see, for example, F. L. Allen, "The State Councils of Defense," in *Century* (Dec., 1917); New York *Evening Post*, Aug. 17, 1917; Hutchinson, *Lowden*, pp. 335–37.

[26] See the various Chicago newspapers for June and July, 1917; Illinois Council, *Final Report*, p. 45; *Minutes*, Illinois Council meetings, June 23, June 30, July 17, 1917.

[27] Illinois Council, *Final Report*, pp. 45–48; *Minutes*, Illinois Council meetings, July 17, July 21, July 31, Aug. 7, 1917; Insull and others to the Illinois Council of Defense, July 24, 1917; Franklin K. Lane to F. S. Peabody, June 28, 1917 (two letters); and F. C. Honnold and others (Illinois Coal Operators Committee) to Insull, July 31, 1917 (all bound in Minute Book I of the Illinois Council, pp. 89–95).

alcrtcd domcstic consumcrs. Thcy bombarded Congress with letters and telegrams, and Congress responded in August with the Lever Act, creating the Federal Fuel Administration. This agency immediately ordered the price of coal cut approximately in half, and thenceforth, until the end of the war, coal prices ceased to be a problem.[28]

Meanwhile, Insull and the Illinois Council struck out at others who sought undue profits from wartime dislocation. In some instances they employed the powerful weapon of exposure; in others they employed naked force. The most explosive problem arose in May and June, when race riots erupted in East St. Louis. Upon investigation the council learned that the fault lay at the door of certain industrialists who, under the pretense of increasing their labor force for war production but in fact to break the power of local labor unions, had imported droves of southern Negroes to work in the factories. This was stopped forthwith, and though race relations and the importation of Negro labor remained a difficult problem, the council was able to exercise some control over it and prevent further rioting during the war.[29]

All over the state, the council went about forcing businesses to comply with federal regulations; when there were no regulations, the council made its own and thereby served as a conscience for businessmen. By indirection, it also acted as a conscience for the people at large. Months before the national government began to urge "meatless Tuesdays" and "porkless Thursdays," the Illinois Council of Defense had taken practical steps to conserve food. Instead of asking consumers to give up bread one day a week, the Illinois Council persuaded bread distributors to discontinue the practice of taking back unsold day-old bread, and this saved more wheat than all the "wheatless Mondays" during the war.[30]

But lashing was more vital than leashing: while curtailing un-

---

[28] Allen, "The State Councils," in *Century* (Dec., 1917); *Chicago Tribune, New York Times,* Aug. 10–22, 1917; Woodrow Wilson to Insull, Aug. 27, 1917, in the Insull Papers; *Minutes,* Illinois Council meetings, Aug. 13, Aug. 23, Aug. 28, 1917.
[29] Frank W. Mollman (mayor of East St. Louis), telegram to Insull, June 2, 1917 (in Illinois Council Minute Book I, pp. 35–36); *Minutes,* Illinois Council meetings, June 2, June 30, 1917; Hutchinson, *Lowden,* pp. 338–40; *Chicago Tribune, St. Louis Post-Dispatch,* May 28–July 2, 1917.
[30] *Minutes,* Illinois Council meetings, June 30, July 17, 1917; Illinois Council, *Final Report,* pp. 36–37. The latter contains a misprint, citing July, 1918, as the time of this episode.

desirable activities in the economy was important, driving the rest of it was vastly more so. Insull and the council simultaneously stimulated it, drove it, and streamlined it, and when they were through they had became of great importance to the economy.

The council invaded agriculture by recruiting and training, through the college of agriculture of the University of Illinois, a volunteer army of 20,000 boys who were sent from the cities to farms to prevent a labor shortage; and when, during the winter of 1917–18, a study sponsored by the council forecast the impending failure of the corn crop unless measures were taken, Insull arranged to borrow $1,250,000 to finance the purchase of new seed corn and thereby saved the day.[31]

In industry, the Illinois Council formed a coalition of thirteen state councils (with Insull as chairman) and untangled a major production snarl created in Washington. In its haste to mobilize, the federal government had placed most of its orders for war materials in eastern states. These plants were overworked and understaffed, while factories in the Middle West, deprived of war contracts and curtailed in non-war production, were idle. Early in 1918, as a result of the pressure of the thirteen-state coalition, the federal government began a wholesale redistribution of war contracts.[32] Furthermore, the Illinois Council worked effectively to streamline the state's industrial production, anticipating the work as well as the methods of Bernard Baruch's War Industries Board. By the time the war ended—on November 11, 1918, Insull's fifty-ninth birthday—the council had set in motion a rationalization process that continued throughout the twenties.[33]

With war's end came a deluge of tributes; Insull was as highly praised for his war work as any other civilian outside government

---

[31] Illinois Council, *Final Report*, pp. 38–41, 191–93; interview with Peter Fleming (a member of the council's several committees on agriculture), Middletown, New Jersey, Jan. 1, 1958; *Minutes*, Illinois Council meetings, March 15, May 3, May 17, 1918; Hutchinson, *Lowden*, pp. 350–51. See also the letters from Herbert Hoover to Insull scattered through Vols. I and II of the Illinois Council's Minute Books.

[32] Illinois Council, *Final Report*, pp. 55–56, 262–63; *Minutes*, Illinois Council meetings, March 15, April 19, 1918.

[33] The council's rationalization work is evident from its *Final Report*, pp. 36–61, its *Minutes* for the last nine months of 1918, and its letter books for the same period. On Baruch and the War Industries Board see Baruch, *American Industry in the War* (New York, 1941); compare the chronology cited there with the chronology evident in the Illinois Council's *Final Report* and Minute Books.

service. The President and a score of governors sent telegrams and letters of commendation, foreign governments sent decorations and letters of gratitude, and the nation's press, newspapers and magazines alike, published reams of accolades.[34]

And then, feeling much as a Roman dictator might have felt upon relinquishing his emergency powers, Insull began to dismantle the efficient war machine he had created. But as he was doing so—or perhaps long before—he determined to perpetuate its two most important powers and adapt them for his own purposes. The machinery for raising money and for shaping public opinion was so efficient that, given Insull's instinctive love of anything that worked well, he might have been tempted to preserve them on the slightest pretext. As it happened, he had abundant reason for converting both to his own use.[35]

Ironically, at the very moment Insull's personal prestige was reaching its zenith, utility companies were under attack. This curious circumstance arose from a variety of causes, principally a wild new twist in the kaleidoscope of Chicago politics.

In 1914, the regulatory agency which Insull had worked so hard to establish, the State Public Utility Commission of Illinois, began operations. It had hardly opened its doors when a strong movement was launched to destroy it and replace it with "home rule," the new slogan for a return to municipal political regulation of utilities in Chicago. The most ardent opponents of utilities in Chicago and the most vocal agitators for home rule were three disparate groups: (1) the strong Democratic faction controlled by former judge, former mayor, now Governor Edward F. Dunne, who had a vested political interest in local control and who had never forgotten the sting of the defeat Insull had given him in 1907; (2) the reform faction of the Republican party, headed by Alderman (and Univer-

[34] See, for example, *Chicago Tribune*, Nov. 23, 1918; Jan. 19, Nov. 22, 1919; *Electrical Review*, May 17, 1919; Chicago *Economist*, May 24, 1919; *London Times*, May 3, 1919; *Survey*, XL (August 17, 1918), 556–59; *American Magazine*, XCI (March, 1921), 36 ff. An assortment of these commendations, including Insull's decorations from foreign governments, is in the Insull Papers, as is Lowden's letter of tribute, dated Nov. 21, 1919. Tributes to Insull for his war work appeared frequently through the twenties, and even after his financial collapse in 1932.

[35] That Insull was reluctant to close down the council, and particularly that he so appreciated the publicity machinery that he would have been tempted to preserve it for its own sake, is clear from general study of the man, but it was explicitly stated to me in an interview with George R. Jones, who was intimately involved in Insull's wartime publicity work.

sity of Chicago professor) Charles Merriam, which had opposed all efforts to establish a regulatory commission on the logically impeccable ground that it removed control from "the people" and was therefore undemocratic; and (3) the few remaining politicians of the Gray Wolves school, who opposed state regulation out of hope for the return of the good old days of bribes and other favors from utilities.[36]

Toward the end of the 1915 session of the state legislature, when these groups persuaded the state House of Representatives to appoint a committee to study home rule, Insull was not alarmed. The situation seemed safer than safe: Medill McCormick, one of Insull's closest friends, was chairman of the committee; the *Chicago Tribune*, the most powerful newspaper in Illinois, strongly opposed home rule; and in addition to all his other political friends, Insull now had a friend in the mayor of Chicago, William Hale Thompson. For his own reasons, Thompson was a devout enemy of each of the three leading anti-utility groups. Too, his principal financial backer during his twelve years as mayor was Samuel Insull and, to make affairs more binding, Thompson's corporation counsel and closest henchman was Samuel Ettleson, the law partner of Daniel J. Schuyler, Insull's close personal friend and his political lawyer. To be sure, Thompson could denounce utility barons or advocate municipal ownership with as much bombast as the next fellow, but he was rarely disposed to reinforce his words with action. And to make the certain doubly certain, Insull soon had a friend in yet higher station: Governor-Elect Frank O. Lowden. Hence even when, in January, 1917, the House committee unexpectedly issued a report favoring home rule, Insull saw no cause for alarm.[37]

Then came a strange turn of the wheel. Soon after his election in 1915, Thompson had cast about for issues which would increase his local popularity and serve as steppingstones to national politics. The

[36] This development has been traced by reading the *Chicago Tribune* for 1914–15 and by reading the various important secondary works on Chicago politics, such as Wendt and Kogan's *Big Bill of Chicago*, Hutchinson's *Lowden of Illinois*, and Stuart's *Twenty Incredible Years*. Also useful are Stuart's biography (unpublished) of State Senator Richard Barr and the *Majority and Minority Report of the Special Committee on Public Utilities* (Springfield, 1917).

[37] *Majority and Minority Report of the Special Committee on Public Utilities, passim;* Insull, "Memoirs," p. 131; Berry, "Mr. Samuel Insull," p. 3; Wendt and Kogan, *Big Bill,* pp. 86, 134; Hutchinson, *Lowden,* pp. 400–402.

ideal issue, he felt, was the European war. At the time—before British propaganda had done its work—the war was unpopular all over the country, particularly among Progressives, more particularly in the Middle West, and most particularly in Chicago, where more than half the voters were foreign-born and most of the foreign-born were either central Europeans or British-hating Irishmen. Thompson seized upon the issue, and anti-interventionism served him well until 1917 and the declaration of war, whereupon he suddenly found himself out on a precarious limb. To divert attention from his embarrassing position, he joined his erstwhile enemies in the home rule movement, and by the end of the year he was its principal leader. With great dexterity, he turned an unpopular position into a popular one. Posing as a vigorous opponent of war profiteering, he regularly made a point of placing utilities at the head of the list and asserted that home rule would have held them in check. As the squeeze of inflation became tighter, and as every major electric, gas, and transportation utility in the country—except Commonwealth Edison Company—requested and received rate increases from the new regulatory commissions, such attacks gained in effectiveness. By the summer of 1918 the number of supporters of the home rule movement in Chicago was enormous.[38]

Three other groups in Chicago and elsewhere followed a path strikingly similar to Thompson's. Progressive leaders all over the Middle West—LaFollette of Wisconsin, Borah of Idaho, Wheeler of Montana, Norris of Nebraska—had vehemently and sincerely opposed intervention in Europe. When war came, they too turned their oratorical batteries against war profiteers, and by the beginning of 1919 they too had begun to attack public utilities. Less numerous and less powerful were American Socialists, who had split into two violently opposed factions over the war issue in 1917. The antiwar faction attacked profiteering, but when they saw utilities emerging as a favorite target, they thought they saw a foot in the door toward government ownership of American industry. Thenceforth, they abandoned international bankers and munitions makers and directed all their energies against bloated utility barons and in favor of

[38] Wendt and Kogan, *Big Bill*, pp. 149–71, 181–90; Stuart, *Twenty Incredible Years*, pp. 36–74. See also Stuart's columns in the *Chicago American* for this period; Stuart was devoutly pro-Thompson.

government ownership of public utilities. The Socialists and pacifist Progressives were publicized and supported by the Hearst papers, probably the most powerful American newspaper chain. Like Thompson, the Hearst papers (two of which were in Chicago) first opposed the war, then attacked war profiteers, international bankers, munitions manufacturers, and public utilities, in that order.[39]

As the war ended, circumstances caught up with utilities, threatening their existence and placing them in public disfavor. In 1917 the cost of rendering utility service had increased alarmingly, sometimes to twice prewar levels, and utilities began to request emergency rate increases. Almost immediately, the newly formed state regulatory commissions were deluged with such applications; and as commissions failed to act, utilities began to falter and fail. Transportation companies, in which labor was a more important part of total costs than in other utilities, were hardest hit; by January, 1919, seventy-one of them had collapsed into receivership, and many others tottered on the brink of failure. Unfortunately for other utilities, local transportation companies affected more people more directly than did other forms of public service. As the war ended, the commissions began to catch up with their backlog of requests for rate increases, and early in 1919, while other prices began to fall, utility rates began to swing upward. The combination of less efficient service at higher cost, coming at a time when other businesses were improving service and lowering prices, added highly combustible fuel to the furnaces of the various anti-utility groups.[40]

In Chicago, a ludicrous turn of events epitomized the situation. Toward the end of the war the Peoples Gas Light and Coke Company, caught in a curious economic, technical, and political trap, veered within an inch of complete collapse. Needing an emergency rate increase to stay afloat, it found itself entangled instead in a legal

[39] The N.E.L.A.'s *The Radical Campaign against American Industry* (Washington, 1930), although biased, is nonetheless a useful summary of this development. It consists largely of photographic reproductions of newspaper clippings. I have traced the development carefully in various Chicago newspapers and in those published in Madison and Milwaukee.

[40] The generalizations about costs are based upon study of the corporate records of thirty or forty utility companies in the Middle West and the published histories of companies cited earlier; general price statistics such as those in the *Historical Statistics of the United States* do not fully reflect the increases; *Chicago Herald and Examiner,* *Chicago American, Chicago Tribune,* throughout late 1918 and 1919; Federal Trade Commission, *Utility Corporations,* II, 102.

battle to keep its rates from being cut. For several years Donald Richberg, a young attorney and dedicated reformer, had led a long and fruitless fight to force the company to cut its rates. Richberg, like Insull's father, was the one kind of person Insull could never understand: the zealous, uncompromising idealist. "Their case was hopeless and they were bound to lose," Insull said later, but "I saw no reason why the services of that earnest young attorney should go unrewarded." In an act of "impetuous and misguided generosity," he called Roger Sullivan and arranged that Richberg be officially engaged and paid by the city as a special counsel to fight the case, replacing the city's corporation counsel, Insull's man Samuel Ettleson. Richberg interpreted the gesture as a contemptuous display of power by Insull as well as an attempted bribe, and though he accepted the appointment he was privately furious at Insull. Soon he and Insull were in a public hassle in which Insull accused Richberg of having a "crooked mind" (the newspapers quoted him as calling Richberg a "crook"), and Richberg denounced Insull as a "gold-plated anarchist." Customers knew little and cared less about the details of the case, but such was the growing hostility toward utilities that, in spite of Insull's great personal popularity, public sentiment was with Richberg.[41]

To a man of Sam Insull's prowess and influence, the political aspect of the problem involved no more than a fancy bit of political sleight of hand. If the people demanded home rule through the abolition of the Illinois Public Utility Commission, he simply had to abolish the commission. Insull called together Republican Mayor Thompson, Democratic boss Sullivan, Republican House Speaker Shanahan, Democratic State Senator Richard Barr, gubernatorial aspirant (and soon governor) Len Small, and a handful of others,

[41] Berry, "Mr. Samuel Insull," pp. 49–50; Donald R. Richberg, *My Hero: The Indiscreet Memoirs of an Eventful but Unheroic Life* (New York, 1954), pp. 102–11; *Chicago Herald and Examiner*, May 24, 1918; *Chicago Daily News*, June 11, 1918; *Chicago Tribune*, July 24, July 26, 1918. Insull's account of the episode is accurate but naïve. Richberg's account is interesting but thoroughly garbled. He asserts, for example, that though he lost the case he won a major victory by causing the valuation of the company's property to be reduced from the $140,000,000 claimed by the company to around $85,000,000. According to contemporary newspapers and company records, Insull had claimed that the company's property should be fairly valued at between $90,000,000 and $100,000,000, approximately the figure ultimately allowed. Details of this dispute and of the gas company's problems are narrated in the following chapter.

and together they worked out the plan to give the people what they demanded. When the legislature convened in the spring of 1920, the Illinois Public Utility Commission was heartily and loudly denounced—especially by those in on the plan—and then abolished, with appropriate fanfare. Later in the same session, the legislature quietly established an agency called the Illinois Commerce Commission and clothed it with assorted powers over common carriers. They also clothed it, through clauses buried deep in the details of the act, with all the powers to regulate utilities that the original commission had held.[42]

But solving the more basic public relations problem was less simple. As he returned to harness at the end of 1918, Insull snorted fire at every subordinate in sight for having so badly bungled public relations, but fire would not solve the problem. In March, 1919, he called all his executives together, told them just how bad public relations were, and commanded them to "Get busy and do something about it." What they did about it was to pick up the propaganda machinery of the State Council of Defense, man for man, from Bernard J. Mullaney on down, merely changing the name of the Committee on Public Information to the Committee on Public Utility Information. In so doing, they gave birth to modern industrial and commercial public relations.[43]

In creating the Illinois Public Utility Information Committee, Insull was never more astute. To combat opponents of utilities who

[42] This sequence of events has been traced in the several Chicago newspapers, especially the *Chicago American* and the *Chicago Tribune,* and in the *Journals* of the Illinois legislature; the working out of the arrangement is inferred from study of the principal sources of Insull's political dealings, especially Hutchinson's *Lowden,* Stuart's *Twenty Incredible Years* and his unpublished biography of Richard Barr, Wendt and Kogan's *Big Bill,* Wooddy's *The Case of Frank L. Smith,* and interviews with several persons, particularly Samuel Insull, Jr., Francis Daily, George Lennon, William Sexton, Nate Gross, and William H. Stuart.

[43] The development of the Committees on Public Utility Information has been studied in the multivolume F.T.C. *Utility Corporations* investigation; the indispensable volumes are Vol. II, Vol. II of the published *Exhibits,* and Vol. LXXXIII, the *Index to Propaganda Activities of Public Utilities.* Several books have been written on the subject, the best known being Ernest Greuning's *The Public Pays* (New York, 1931) and M. L. Ramsay's *Pyramids of Power* (New York, 1935). Ramsay's work is sensational and unreliable. Greuning's is sometimes overenthusiastic in its denunciations of utilities, and it fails to distinguish between the activities of the committees before and after investment bankers seized control of holding companies and thereby rendered much of the propaganda a mockery (a distinction that the F.T.C. also failed to make); but factually it is a generally reliable and useful book.

had used opposition to war as their springboard, Insull borrowed the propaganda machinery he had used during the war and sought to equate patriotism with a favorable attitude toward utilities. He began by reproducing and circulating an address President Wilson had made in 1916 to the American Electric Railway Association, thereby furnishing rationalization, official sanction, and impeccably Progressive indorsement of what he was about to do. Wilson had said, in part:

There are, therefore, I suppose, certain rules of the game. . . . First of all is the rule of publicity: Not doing anything under cover; letting the public know what you are doing and judge of it according as it is. There are a great many businesses in this country that have fallen under suspicion because they were so secretive, when there was nothing to secrete that was dishonorable. The minute I keep everything in my pocket and will not show anybody what is there, they conjecture what may be in my pocket; whereas, if I turn my pocket inside out, the conjecture is, at any rate, dissipated. There is no use inviting suspicion by secretiveness. If a business is being honorably done and successfully done, you ought to be pleased to turn it inside out and let the people whom you are inviting to invest in it see exactly what is done and with what results.

To the Illinois Gas Association on March 19, 1919, Insull said, repeating statements he had made for two decades:

I am a great believer in publicity. I believe it is our duty to the properties we manage, to the stockholders who own them, and to the communities they serve, that we should enlighten those communities on the situation. I believe in doing it not in any gumshoe way, but openly and boldly. I believe in presenting the facts to the employees, whose interest is just as vital as that of the managers, to the citizens of the State who are owners of the properties, to every customer of a gas company, and electric light and power companies, or a street railway. . . . We have to bring home to [our own 45,000 employees, our own 50,000 stockholders and bondholders, our own 1,700,000 customers] that rate making in our business is not a simple matter of fixing a flat price for a service; that a proper system of rates has to be adjusted to varying classes of service and to the condition under which that service is rendered; that proper systems of rates can not be worked out scientifically when politics enter; and that an enormous field [exists] for development alike to industry and to ourselves by proper systems of rates.

To every newspaper in the state, he sent a circular letter stating frankly what he was about, offering a regular weekly news letter giving utility information, and soliciting from all editors their frank opinion of the plan. Most editors accepted it, and most also printed a public notice saying so.[44]

To Mullaney and his committee, Insull issued a warning and two basic rules, which Mullaney reiterated in his own speeches. The warning was that seeking "to 'put over' something—to promote a one-sided viewpoint, to spread 'propaganda,' to 'mold public opinion,' or to grab free puffery space in the news and editorial columns that ought to be paid-for space in the advertising columns— is unsound; in the long run, it defeats itself" and serves only to enrich public relations men. The rules were a concise summary of Insull's principles of public relations:[45]

Practically everything that a public-utility company does, or that any of its employees do, directly or indirectly affecting contacts and relations between the company and its customers . . . is an item in public relations. Hence, furnishing satisfactory service at satisfactory rates—best possible service at lowest practicable rates—is the first objective in public-relations work, because that is of greatest interest to the public. This is in strict accord with the principle quoted earlier: "If the rights of the public are properly taken care of in producing lower costs and in steadily improving the service, the rights of the stockholders will take care of themselves."

But the public is in no position to judge service and rates when it knows nothing about the multitude of details involved in furnishing service, and nothing about costs and other factors that determine rates. If to this lack of knowledge by the public you add an appearance of mystery or secrecy, or even extreme reticence, in the operations of the business, you inevitably breed suspicion that the service is poorer and the rates higher than they ought to be. Hence, the second objective in the public-utility industry's public-relations work is: a public well informed on the tangible details, as well as on the social and industrial significance of the industry in all of its ramifications.

So successful was the Illinois Public Utility Information Committee that utilities everywhere began to set up identical agencies;

44 F.T.C., *Utility Corporations*, II, 100–101.
45 *Ibid.;* F.T.C. *Utility Corporations Exhibits,* Vol. II, exhibits 199, 202, and *passim.*

before long there was a general committee of the National Electric Light Association, co-ordinating the state committees. By 1923, these agencies were turning out a stream of utility publicity that almost matched the volume of patriotic publicity during the war; one could hardly go anywhere or read anything without encountering the fundamentals of utility economics.[46]

As Insull was launching his public relations campaign, he was starting another campaign that would ultimately have far-reaching effects. He had decided during the war that the best way of winning friends for the "cause" was to get them to invest time and work in it; now he decided that the best way to win friends for utilities was to get them to invest their money in it. If, Insull reasoned, every customer had a financial stake, however small, in the utility that served him, he might consider the company's interest to be synonymous with his own. As a director of Pacific Gas and Electric Company, Insull had seen experiments in "customer ownership" drives just before the war, and a few of his own companies had ventured into it with some success. Now, in a companion campaign to the work of the Public Utility Information Committee, Insull set each of his companies to work selling its preferred stock to as many customers and employees as possible. (At first, customer ownership meant no more than that, a secondary public relations effort. But lurking in Insull's mind was the memory of having sold more than a billion dollars worth of government bonds on a similar basis. It would soon occur to him that he could do the same with utility securities and thereby raise capital on an undreamed-of scale.)[47]

The two instruments Insull borrowed from his wartime armory accomplished their purpose. By the mid-twenties, hating utilities was, in Chicago, as rare as hating mother and the flag. But as the use

[46] For the effectiveness of the campaign see the sources cited in note 44, above. The Illinois Committee compiled monthly reports of the number of speeches and newspaper stories; several of these are included in the F.T.C. *Exhibits,* Vols. I–III, which contain similar documents for other states as well. See, for example, Vol. II, exhibit 168, reporting activities in Illinois, county by county, speech by speech, for the month ending Sept. 25, 1927.

[47] The public relations origin—and the subsequent development—of customer ownership was elaborated by Insull in testimony at his trial in 1934; *U.S.* v. *Insull,* transcript, pp. 4278–80 (Nov. 1, 1934). Its development is easily traced in the annual reports of the several Insull companies, files of most of which are in the Insull Papers. For interesting evidence of the way customer ownership was received, see Samuel

of the techniques spread, it did far more than Insull had intended to do. The public relations campaign evoked from business a new view of the public it served and, because businessmen began to believe their own propaganda, a new concept of the social responsibility of corporations began to emerge. Insull's praises were sung by high and low. Later, when overzealous publicity men began to misuse it, and when cynical bankers who had seized utilities began to abuse it, Insull's public relations campaign backfired and evoked from government punitive legislation that made many businessmen devoutly wish that Insull had never been born.[48]

One further venture in the wake of the war was not strictly business: Insull tried his hand at President-making. By the summer of 1919 most seasoned political observers, viewing widespread postwar letdown and disillusionment, were convinced that the elections of 1920 would bring a Republican landslide. Whoever won the Republican nomination seemed almost certain to succeed Woodrow Wilson as President, and the contest for the nomination was wide open. Insull determined to win it for his friend Frank O. Lowden, "the best governor Illinois ever had," and in a conference held on his yacht in August, 1919, Insull initiated a campaign for Lowden. Subsequently, he planned and directed much of the campaign and financed more, and the effort almost succeeded. Lowden won considerable support from organized labor, a large corps of progressive businessmen, and the political bosses in a number of key states. When the Republican national convention opened, the number of delegates pledged to him was second only to General Leonard Wood. On the fourth ballot in that heated convention, Lowden came within 179 votes of capturing the nomination, but a deadlock developed, to be resolved by the celebrated conference in the "smoke-filled room" that put Warren G. Harding in the White House. Had Insull had his way, the course of American history might have been considerably different, for Lowden was as progressive as Harding was corrupt,

---

Crowther's article on Insull, "He's the Public's Hired Man," in *Colliers,* LXXV (Jan. 17, 1925) , 12 ff.

[48] See note 44, above, and pp. 262–71, 336–37, below. The rise and fall of Insull's own reputation in this regard has been traced in a multivolume collection of newspaper clippings in the offices of Commonwealth Edison Company. For a good example of the way the campaign backfired see Greuning's *The Public Pays.*

and morally and intellectually he was as strong as Harding was weak.[49]

But Insull had little time for conjecture and less for regrets. President-making is for people who feel they have nothing better to do, and Insull had something better to do: As the presidential campaign began, he was confronted with the most severe crisis in his entire business career.

[49] An excellent account of Lowden's campaign is in Hutchinson's *Lowden*, pp. 408–83. Occasional details of Insull's role in it are given in Chicago newspapers throughout 1919.

CHAPTER VIII   *The Crisis: 1917–23*

The trouble Insull's companies had in surviving the war and postwar crises depended on how long they had been Insull's companies. Commonwealth Edison Company (vintage 1892) breezed through. Public Service of Northern Illinois (1901–11) had a bit more difficulty, and Middle West and its subsidiaries (1912) were in and out of trouble but never in serious danger. The elevated railways (1911–14) were in difficulty at all times. At war's end, Peoples Gas Company (1913) tottered on the brink of collapse. On the one extreme, Commonwealth Edison was so well prepared and so well managed that it became the only major steam-powered electric company in the world that neither raised its rates nor cut its dividends during this period. At the other extreme, Peoples Gas was so ill-prepared and so badly managed that its history could well serve as a manual on how not to run a utility company.

But across the board, the crisis was of immense proportions, and it was aggravated by Insull's neglect of his companies while he headed the State Council of Defense. When he resumed their active command, he had to deal with hundreds of problems, many of a kind he had rarely or never faced before. There were five principal varieties. The first three were shortages and cost increases in labor, coal, and money. Another was the regulatory bottleneck and its companion, the decline in public relations; still another was a sudden and huge increase in the demand for power. Insull dealt with each problem on a day-to-day basis, but this called for increasingly radical measures. By 1923, when all his companies were thriving again, he had once more introduced a revolutionary set of changes to American business.

Labor alone could have been a devastating problem: The war brought shortages and sharp increases in wages, and the postwar years produced one of the most turbulent periods of labor unrest in American history. Most utilities were especially pressed, being unable to raise rates at will to offset rising wages. They held their workers for a time by promising long-range employment security as an inducement, but as the war boom continued, the workers found high wages in other industries difficult to resist. By mid-1918 many utilities could expect a 100 per cent turnover in workers every eight or nine months.[1]

Commonwealth Edison had little difficulty during the war. It was already paying somewhat higher wages than were paid in the industry at large and much higher than in most industries. In addition, its fringe benefits were a considerable attraction, a fact sharply dramatized when employees entered the armed forces: From the beginning of the war until January, 1918, when the national government began paying allowances to the dependents of soldiers and sailors, Commonwealth Edison supported the families of all its employees in the services. Consequently, the company was able to hold its workers in competition with increasingly attractive wage scales in other industries. Furthermore, its operating efficiency, measured in terms of output per man hour, was extremely high. Thus while in the utility industry as a whole average wages doubled and the total labor cost increased about 80 per cent between 1917 and 1920, Commonwealth Edison's over-all labor bill rose by only about half, and much of that was absorbed by increased production.[2]

Nonetheless, labor unrest during the period afforded Insull some bad moments. On the eve of the war, in late May, 1916, the Edison Company had undergone a brief wildcat strike, the only one in its history. It was settled quickly, and throughout the war the Middle West was virtually free of strikes of any kind because of the patriotic

[1] *Historical Statistics of the United States,* p. 68; *Minutes,* Milwaukee Electric Railway and Light Company directors' meetings, May 15, Oct. 16, 1918, and its *Annual Report,* 1918 (files in the offices of Wisconsin Electric Power Company, Milwaukee) ; Minute Book of Wisconsin-Minnesota Light and Power Company, 1917–18 (in the offices of Northern States Power Company, Eau Claire) ; Miller, *Kilowatts at Work,* pp. 183–86; Middle West Utilities Company, *Annual Reports,* 1917–19.
[2] *Historical Statistics of the United States,* p. 68; *Minutes,* Commonwealth Edison directors' meetings, July 8, 1916; April 13, Dec. 20, 1917; Commonwealth Edison Company, *Annual Reports,* 1917–19; *Electrical World,* July 10, 1920.

response of labor leaders, the persuasion and force of such agencies as the State Council of Defense, and, after the United States entered the war, the pressure of the national government. But immediately after the war, and throughout 1919, industry after industry was hit by an unprecedented succession of long and bitter strikes.[3]

Among Insull's companies, the Edison Company alone was unaffected by the postwar labor turbulence that shook all Europe and America. The first trouble came in Peoples Gas Company, where employee morale collapsed a month after the end of the war. In June, 1919, wildcat strikes swept across Illinois coal fields. Late in July, just as Chicago exploded with the bloodiest race riots in its history, elevated railway and streetcar workers went out on a brief strike, and the city was paralyzed. In October, just after the beginning of a country-wide steel workers' strike, the nation's coal miners went out again, this time on a month-long strike called by the United Mine Workers. In December, all outside and plant workers of Peoples Gas went out on strike. In the summer of 1920 Illinois coal miners again staged a series of brief, unauthorized walkouts.[4]

There was less to this than met the eye: The situation was not nearly so out of hand as it appeared. In the gas company, for example, Insull had long had an understanding with Big Tim Murphy, the boss of the gas workers' union. Insull knew that to preserve peace with the gas workers at least a modest raise would be necessary, but he also knew that since the company was near bankruptcy, he would have considerable difficulty with his stockholders and directors if he should openly and voluntarily grant a wage increase. Murphy understood and sympathized with Insull's predicament, but he would be equally embarrassed to have to go before his men and propose that they should forego a raise for the sake of the stockholders. Privately, Insull and Murphy worked out a deal. First, they agreed upon the amount of the wage increase—a happy

[3] *Minutes*, Commonwealth Edison directors' meetings, May 23, Nov. 9, 1916; *Chicago Tribune*, May 18–June 6, 1916; for the negative information, minute books and annual reports of Middle West and Commonwealth Edison, 1917–18; State Council of Defense minute books, *passim*.

[4] *Chicago Tribune, Chicago American*, April–December, 1919 (especially June 27–July 4); *Minutes*, Peoples Gas Company, directors' meetings, Oct. 23, 1918, July 2, Dec. 24, 1919; Jan. 24, 1920; Wendt and Kogan, *Big Bill*, pp. 173–74; Hutchinson, *Lowden*, pp. 400–401; Cecil Carnes, *John L. Lewis, Leader of Labor* (New York, 1936), pp. 19–37.

balance between the most the company could safely afford and the least Murphy could afford to settle for. Then they agreed that for public consumption Murphy should demand a somewhat larger figure and Insull should counter with a refusal to grant anything. Then they would vehemently denounce each other, so that the newspapers could ring with accounts of a battle to the death between capital and labor. A deadlock would ensue, whereupon the union would issue an ultimatum, the company would hold firm, and the workers would go out on strike. The company, forced to its knees, would capitulate and offer a compromise settlement: It would propose a raise smaller than the union demanded but sweetened by being made retroactive, and the union would accept. (The payment of the retroactive bonus would be spread over several succeeding months to enable the company to catch its breath and be in a position to afford the raise.)

Everything was played according to plan through the formal negotiations and denunciations, and then, on the eve of the well-staged crisis, Insull's son came down with appendicitis. So that Insull could devote himself to his son, whose illness took an unexpectedly serious turn, the strike was postponed for two weeks; during the "truce," the city's newspapers cheered what they took to be a new turn and a ray of hope in the negotiations. Once Junior recovered, negotiations were allowed to break down again, and the rest of the program, strike and settlement, was staged as it had been written.[5]

Even so, there was abundant cause for concern, particularly since strained labor relations came just as public confidence in utilities hit rock bottom. Too, two new labor problems arose. During the war Insull's companies for the first time hired females on a large scale, to replace men leaving for military service. When the European war began in 1914, the company had about 200 female employees; by April, 1917, it had 375, and by the end of the war the number had soared to almost 1,000. Women filled jobs they had never filled

[5] The external aspects of these negotiations are easily traced through the *Minutes* of the directors' meetings of Peoples Gas Company, especially the meetings of Dec. 24, 1919; Jan. 24, and April 1, 1920; and the various Chicago newspapers, Dec., 1919–April, 1920. Details on the inside arrangements are derived from interviews with Charles A. Munroe (who was a vice-president of Peoples Gas at the time), New York, May 16, 1956; Francis L. Daily (former attorney of the company), Wilmette, Nov. 18, 1957; and Samuel Insull, Jr.

before—as technicians, meter-readers, even as substation operators —and everywhere they went they took new problems with them. (One elementary example: in the massive, eighteen-story Edison Company building there was but one ladies' rest room.) [6]

The second was Insull's promise to workers who joined the armed forces that they would have their jobs back upon their return. In 1918 more than 25 per cent of Edison's employees joined one branch or another of the armed forces. To make up for the temporary shortage in jobs women could not fill, the company adopted a practice resorted to by many other Chicago concerns, and began to import small numbers of Negro workers from the South. When the war ended and employees began to return to their old jobs, Insull did not feel he could dismiss the imported Negroes. After all, he had induced them to come to Chicago and work for him. If employers all over Chicago dropped their Negro workers at war's end, a possibly dangerous racial problem might ensue. He kept them employed and thenceforth made it a practice to employ Negroes as meter readers and appliance store clerks in the growing Negro sections of the city. [7]

At one time Insull might have coped with each of these problems as it arose and let it go at that. But after the war he began to exhibit a new kind of paternal attitude toward his employees. He had always felt some responsibility for his people, but the feeling was impersonal, and in direct relations formality had been a strict rule. Employer-employee relations were strictly business: He treated his workers fairly and generously and in return expected obedience, diligence, and hard work. He, as president, was to be viewed with respect by his employees, and none except members of the upper echelon were to have any personal contact with him. But in the hot, helter-skelter, shirtsleeve world of the State Council of Defense, where dedicated volunteer workers from all ranks and all his companies worked long, hard, and effectively for a common cause, all formality collapsed, and he learned a new respect for his employees. [8]

[6] Interview with Helen Norris (former Dean of Women for Commonwealth Edison Company) , Chicago, July 16, 1958.
[7] *Minutes,* Commonwealth Edison directors' meetings, July 18, 1916; Dec. 20, 1917; and *Annual Reports,* 1918, 1919; Seymour, "History of Commonwealth Edison," pp. 524–29; interview with Helen Norris.
[8] Insull's prewar attitude toward his employees is implicit in many of his speeches and has been confirmed during interviews with thirty or forty of his former employees, many of them obscure, some, like Britton Budd, Charles A. Munroe, and Edward J.

And Gladys taught him another lesson. She too was extremely busy with war work, and to carry it out she borrowed workers freely from Insull's companies. She got to know the employees she borrowed, and she was quicker than her husband in spotting talent in unexpected places. For example, for the Allied Charities Bazaar she needed a small staff to handle tickets and money and took it from the Edison Company. One of these was an obscure bookkeeper named Philip McEnroe. On the day McEnroe returned to his regular job, she spoke to her husband: "Sam, there's a very nice young man in the bookkeeping department who worked at the bazaar. I don't know his name, but he has honest eyes and he is very nice. You'd better have him in your office." Insull took his wife's advice, and McEnroe soon became Insull's personal bookkeeper. Throughout the remaining years of Insull's career, as his personal fortune increased to fantastic proportions, McEnroe was entrusted with the whole of it; and he proved to be one of the most able and faithful members of Insull's personal staff.[9]

To these several elements was added one more, a deeply personal one. As he and Gladys grew further apart, and as Gladys and Junior grew closer together, Insull found himself increasingly alone. In this circumstance he turned to what Gladys always regarded as her one rival, Commonwealth Edison Company. As he did so, he came to a striking realization: His employees were as much a part of his family as his brothers and sisters had been, as important to him as his wife and son. Furthermore, as his sense of security in great power increased, the need to protect himself by maintaining formality decreased. His changed attitude was recognized by all who had even the most casual contact with him. Said one: "Now he felt that he belonged to his people."[10]

Doyle, high-ranking and members of Insull's inner circle. The reference to the visible change during the Illinois Council days is derived from an interview with George R. Jones, who was with Insull almost daily throughout the war.

[9] Mrs. Insull's war activities are occasionally recorded in Chicago newspapers and regularly recorded in the *Edison Round Table;* additional information was derived from interviews with Helen Norris and Samuel Insull, Jr. The story regarding McEnroe is from an interview with him in Chicago, Aug. 7, 1957. See also Insull's testimony in *U.S.* v. *Insull,* p. 4307 (Nov. 1, 1934).

[10] Insull's relations with his wife Gladys at this period have been studied in his correspondence with her and in various other sources; the subject is discussed more fully below, pp. 232–36. The other generalizations here are based on conclusions reached during interviews with former employees. The quotation is from Helen Norris.

Guided by this view, Insull embarked on a new course in dealing with postwar labor problems. Without stopping to ponder what he was doing, he set out to create a new kind of employee, a kind that would one day be styled the organization man. It was not so much that he sensed the highly organized and democratized world that was aborning; rather, he decided, out of his own experience, to create his portion of it. He would create the Insull man.

This involved (in addition to his earlier principles, including his policy of handling unions by negotiating privately with their leaders) three courses of action. First, employees were subjected to a barrage of material intended to increase their loyalty to the company and their pride in their work—from Insull in countless personal appearances, from other company officials, from regular bulletins, and from a lively company magazine. Everywhere they turned, employees would be reminded that they were in the service of the public and that they worked for the best public service organization in the world.[11]

Second, they were showered with fringe benefits. Some of these were increased benefits of the kind Insull had pioneered before the war. To the existing programs providing pensions and disability compensation, medical care, education, and the like, Insull now added a variety of new benefits, ranging from the installation of a huge cafeteria for employees of Edison, Public Service, and Middle West to free life insurance policies and an optional group plan for additional insurance. (Employees were sometimes singularly short-sighted in these matters. Commonwealth Edison first offered life insurance—policies ranging from $500 to $1,500, depending on length of service—when it was learned that insurance could be offered for little more than the cost of the Christmas turkeys employees had been receiving for years. At first the employees voted for the turkeys instead, and an intense campaign was necessary to change this habit of mind.) Whenever possible, the new benefits were designed to stimulate group consciousness. The company studiously promoted group recreational activities: Edison teams

[11] The principal publication was the *Edison Round Table;* various relics of the other publications are in the files of the company. Here as elsewhere when employee relations are discussed in this chapter, former employees were an important supplementary source; I have interviewed meter-readers, line crewmen, elevator operators, clerks, engineers, vice-presidents, statisticians, janitors, typists, and many others.

participated in every manner of amateur competitive sports, and the company bought a large and elegant resort area on Lake Delevan, Wisconsin, where employees could spend their vacations at nominal cost. Employee organizations abounded: new savings and loan associations and mutual benefit associations, both underwritten by the company; an employee representation plan in which final appeal was to the courts, not to the president of the company; the Electra Club for female employees; a Commonwealth Edison post of the American Legion. Above all, employees were urged to become stockholders, both individually and through group installment purchases. They were persuaded not by pressure but by terms so advantageous as to be irresistible, and soon the overwhelming majority of Commonwealth Edison's employees owned stock in the company. They were also urged to enlist their friends and neighbors on the "team" by selling them stock in Insull companies. For this, the persuasion was the earning of commissions.[12]

Third, all Insull employees were besieged with demands that they take up, on their own time, some form of community service activity. In this the persuasion was neither subtle nor sweet. Insull himself set the pace, and no top-ranking employee was safe in his job unless he was actively and conspicuously engaged in such work. The subordinate executives, in turn, demanded community service of their underlings, and so on down the pecking order. And from the top, Insull preached incessantly: "You represent your company and your community. Be a credit to both."[13]

All these devices—propaganda, pressure, example, appeals to pride, and, after a fashion, bribery—were skilfully devised methods of group persuasion, skilfully executed. But their great success was due

[12] These activities are clear from the files of *Edison Round Table*, 1919–23; see also Seymour, "History of Commonwealth Edison," pp. 524 ff.; the annual reports of Commonwealth Edison, Middle West, Public Service, Peoples Gas, Wisconsin Power and Light, and other Insull companies throughout the 1920's; *Minutes*, Commonwealth Edison directors' meetings, Dec. 16, 1919; June 22, Dec. 21, 1920; Jan. 4, Feb. 19, March 21, 1921.

[13] Insull's own community service activities are discussed below, pp. 240–45; the pressure on subordinates was attested by all those I interviewed; Miss Sophie Goetz, of the publicity department of Commonwealth Edison, supplied me with biographical data on about two dozen of Insull's upper echelon subordinates, including an extremely impressive array of community service activities. Further data was obtained from Britton Budd's scrapbooks, in his possession. For samples of his talks to employees see Insull, *Public Utilities in Modern Life*, pp. 33–39, 198–206, 250–51, 316–21, 351–61, 396–403.

to Insull's own personality. For one thing, it was easy enough for him to inspire employees; after all, he was the electric industry's Great Man and he was rapidly becoming Chicago's Great Man. He exuded confidence, confidence so all-pervasive that it was difficult to avoid believing him infallible.

And yet, although he would fire a man on the spot for failing to recognize and greet him ("Good morning, Mr. Insull"), he almost invariably managed to convey a personal interest in his dealings with employees. He made it a standing rule that his door was always open. In practice, he could hardly encourage the janitor to drop in for a visit, for in a normal working day he had as many as fifty appointments and as many different subjects to consider, affecting thousands of lives and involving millions of dollars. To filter complaints, he devised an elaborate heirarchy, through an industrial relations department established in 1921, and staffed it with persons highly trained and highly skilled in dealing with the problems of employees. But if an employee, no matter how lowly his station, complained that he was not getting adequate attention along the chain of command, Insull would see him, and the employee generally found Insull to be a soft touch. Too, Insull took pains to see that what he deemed desirable for the group did not crush the individual. In 1922, for example, Commonwealth Edison launched an "Americanization program" and exerted pressure on employees who were not yet citizens. Those who did not apply for citizenship were denied the benefits of the company's retirement program. But when Insull learned that on the company payroll were seven Filipinos, one Japanese, and one East Indian, none of whom were eligible for citizenship, he called a special meeting of the board of directors and gave these workers full benefits.[14]

Thus encouraged, Insull men developed an *esprit de corps* seldom equaled in modern industrial history. They believed with all the passion of life insurance salesmen in the worthiness of what they were doing. If they learned that some other company was doing anything bigger, better, faster, or cheaper than they were doing it, they plunged into work to take up the slack. They were aggressively

[14] Interviews with Helen Norris, Britton Budd, Edward Doyle, A. G. deClercq, Philip McEnroe, John Evers, and others cited earlier; *Minutes,* Peoples Gas directors' meeting, March 21, 1921; *Minutes,* Public Service directors' meeting, March 21, 1921; *Minutes,* Commonwealth Edison directors' meetings, March 21, 1921; Dec. 8, 1922; and special meeting, Jan. 4, 1923.

dedicated to public service; throughout the twenties Insull men were in the center or at the top of virtually every important community service activity in Chicago, and they continued to be so long after Insull was gone. Whenever volunteer workers were needed— as when Insull set out to democratize opera in Chicago—they would spread over the city like a cloud of benign locusts, and the job would be done. Finally, they were fiercely proud and intensely loyal; thirty years after Insull was evicted from business with a reputation as black as sin, men who had worked for him spoke his name with reverence.[15]

(Throughout the twenties other utilities increasingly emulated Insull's program, sometimes with a success approaching his. The idea spread rapidly among utilities and gradually to other industries. But in the main Insull's employee relations program—prewar and postwar—was ill-designed to win him imitators and admirers amongst the moneyed. Most frowned upon such innovations as too generous, too personal, or simply dangerous. Relatively few of them discovered their employees were human until their workers demonstrated their humanity by flourishing clubs bearing the union label.)

To every utility in the country save Insull's, coal supply was the most vexing wartime problem. With Insull it was no problem at all during the war; it became a problem to him only when the war ended and the coal problem became a labor problem. This labor problem did not lend itself readily to "Insullization" for, as one of John L. Lewis' biographers put it, "Coal mining, like starving to death, is a primitive business."[16]

During the war, while other utilities suffered shortages and high prices, Insull's companies could count on a steady supply of coal at a stable price. Throughout the war Commonwealth Edison normally had about 400,000 tons of coal on hand, a three months' supply. Indeed, so well stocked were the company bins that late in 1918, when

[15] These generalizations are based upon the sources cited in notes 5–14, above. The almost awesome way Insull's employees took over and made successful charitable and civic ventures has been traced in Commonwealth Edison's files of newspaper clippings for 1925–32.

[16] Carnes, *John L. Lewis*, pp. 95 and *passim*. On all subsequent discussions here of the postwar coal situation this book is useful, as are Saul Alinsky's *John L. Lewis* (New York, 1949), Arthur E. Suffern's *The Coal Miners' Struggle for Industrial Status* (New York, 1926), and Louis Block's *Labor Agreements in Coal Mines* (New York, 1931).

an impending shortage threatened a cold winter for millions of householders, Insull sold his coal to domestic consumers at cost, considerably under the market price. On into 1919, Commonwealth Edison and other Insull companies fared so well that no problems seemed to exist.[17]

Insull's farsighted coal policy also paid off in another way. Before the war virtually all electric utilities in the Middle West had burned anthracite from eastern mines, hard coal having about half again the heating value and only a third the moisture of Illinois bituminous, which Insull used. During the war, when the coal problem became essentially a transportation problem, Federal Fuel Administrator Harry A. Garfield ordered an emergency rerouting of coal distribution, and central stations in the Middle West had to switch from eastern to middle western coal. It was found that steam-electric generator boilers, designed for anthracite, suffered enormous loss of efficiency when bituminous coal was substituted. Even when utilities were able to get coal in what would otherwise have been considered adequate quantities, they were still short. Thus, too, the price rise— doubling to around four dollars a ton during the war, then skyrocketing to six and then twelve and then eighteen dollars a ton when federal controls were removed in 1919—was even greater than it appeared, and it was almost devastating to utilities all over the Middle West. Rationing of power was the common result. Insull, because he was already using local bituminous, was unaffected by these problems. The only power rationing in territory served by his companies came when he chose to divert his own supply to domestic heating.[18]

But the stability of price and supply afforded by the Peabody con-

[17] *Minutes,* Commonwealth Edison directors' meetings, Aug. 21, 1917; Aug. 22, Dec. 17, 1918, and *Annual Reports,* 1917–19; Public Service, *Annual Reports,* 1917–19; Insull, *Public Utilities in Modern Life,* pp. 140–41, 156, 161–62; Seymour, "History of Commonwealth Edison," p. 524.

[18] McDonald, *Let There Be Light,* p. 206; interviews with W. E. Schubert and Fred Dornbrook (engineers who were engaged in 1919 in research that would lead to the development of the use of pulverized coal for firing steam-electric furnaces), Milwaukee, 1954; *Historical Statistics of the United States,* p. 236. The latter volume indicates an increase in coal prices of only about 100 per cent between 1915 and 1920; that it was, as a practical matter, far more than this is clear from study of secondary accounts, minute books, annual reports, and sometimes purchase orders for utilities in New York, Providence, Chicago, Milwaukee, Minneapolis, Detroit, Green Bay, Appleton, and the several companies that made up the Middle West Utilities Company system.

tracts vanished suddenly in 1919. That summer, sporadic wildcat strikes in the Illinois fields were portents of troubles ahead but did not directly affect the mines operated by Peabody for Insull. The troubles came in October. The Insull-Peabody mines had always averted labor problems by relatively generous treatment of workers and by *sub rosa* deals with union leaders, but now the second device ran into a solid brick wall named John L. Lewis. In 1919 Lewis had advanced to the presidency of the United Mine Workers, and he immediately set out to effect his long-range goal of industry-wide unionization and industry-wide collective bargaining. In October, taking advantage of a huge international coal demand resulting from the disruption of mining in Europe, Lewis called a nationwide strike, demanding nothing less than a six-hour day, a five-day week, and a 60 per cent increase in wages. As far as the mines in Illinois were concerned, Lewis overstepped himself, for the ensuing crisis in Chicago provoked state action. By early November many Chicago factories had shut down, 25,000 men were out of work, most business houses were operating on a six-hour day, and coal rationing was necessary throughout the area. Governor Lowden turned the problem over to the Illinois Public Utility Commission, which settled the dispute at far less than the union's demands. But the nationwide character of the strike signaled the end of local control of collective bargaining in the industry.[19]

In the summer of 1920 a new ray of hope emerged in the form of an Illinois rebellion against Lewis' control. Frank Farrington, whom Insull had met when he ran the State Council of Defense and who had spearheaded organized labor in the drive to nominate Lowden for President, at the outset resisted Lewis' program. In mid-1920, for no apparent reason except to flaunt Lewis' authority, Farrington led his mineworkers in a series of brief strikes unauthorized by the national union. Here was obviously a man who might listen to Insull's arguments. Two years, more or less, of delicate negotiations with Farrington were required to effect a suitable arrangement, but in the end a deal was made which placed Illinois miners in a more favorable position than any others in the country, solved Insull's coal

---

[19] Hutchinson, *Lowden*, pp. 416–19; Alinsky, *Lewis*, pp. 29–35; Carnes, *Lewis*, pp. 28–37; *Chicago Tribune, Chicago American, Chicago Daily News,* throughout October and November, 1919.

problems, and eventually led to Lewis' loss of control of his union.[20]

Temporary private deals with Farrington sufficed until 1922, when a wave of strikes, called by Lewis, turned violent: A group of strikers in Herrin, Illinois, lynched several scab workers. From April to August of that year, the Insull-Peabody mines were closed, and for the first time Insull utilities had to buy coal on the open market at greatly advanced prices. Commonwealth Edison alone lost more than $1,600,000. This, Insull reckoned, was going too far, and he approved a new deal, though he did not initiate or negotiate it, and probably deliberately remained unaware of its details. Peabody negotiators offered Farrington an entirely different arrangement. Farrington would have to settle for the Illinois workers independently of the national organization, and cope with the politics of maintaining his status in the union while in fact breaking with its authority. As compensation, Farrington would receive two things: a $7.50 basic day wage—half again the pay prevailing elsewhere—for all his miners, and a personal gratuity from the Peabody Coal Company in the amount of $25,000 a year. Farrington accepted both. Thenceforth, Insull was not plagued by coal miners again.[21]

(In 1927, Lewis was able to unseat his archenemy Farrington by obtaining documentary proof of the $25,000 annual payment, and Farrington was immediately thrown out of the union. But at the same time the Illinois workers lost their favored position, and their day wage fell to the $5.00 level prevailing in the rest of the country. When Farrington's successor, Harry Fishwick, proved to be as amenable as Farrington had been, Insull-Peabody and the Illinois Coal Operators Association held the Illinois day wage at $5.00, while elsewhere it was slipping still lower. Ultimately, Farrington was able to lead a group which dethroned Lewis, and one of his most potent weapons was the charge that, to preserve his own power, Lewis had sacrificed the Illinois workers.)

Labor was explosive and expensive. Coal supply was capricious and costly. Politics was politics. And money was even worse: It became scarce, then it became dear, and then it all but disappeared.

[20] Carnes, *Lewis,* pp. 50, 60–61, 81–85; Illinois Council *Minutes, passim;* Hutchinson, *Lowden,* pp. 345, 416, 418–19.
[21] Carnes, *Lewis,* pp. 218–19; interview with Samuel Insull, Jr.

The wartime scarcity of investment capital is hardly a mystery: The war cost more money than there was on the planet. In thirty months America spent more on the war—fielding and equipping its fighting force, girding its industrial loins for battle, and lending money and supplies to its allies—than all its corporations had invested in the previous century. The postwar scarcity was somewhat more complex, involving the disruption of the machinery of international finance and the staggering tasks of refinancing war debts, settling international loans, and working out reparations, but it was no less effective. Commercial paper, available at just over 3 per cent interest on the eve of the war, soared to 8 per cent by 1920, the highest rate since the Bryan Panic of 1896. By 1919 industries rated as AA credit risks by Moody's Investment Service were unable to sell securities bearing less than 7 per cent, and by 1921 many well-managed, reputable utilities were finding it difficult to borrow at 8, 9, and even 10 per cent.[22]

The problem was aggravated by a sudden, enormous, and permanent increase in demand for power. In 1919 and 1920 the increase in sales by Commonwealth Edison Company amounted to as much as its total sales had been five years before the war. In the smaller companies the leap in output was even more spectacular: In such Middle West subsidiaries as Central Illinois Public Service and Kentucky Utilities Company, output almost trebled between 1916 and 1920. When the war began the combined electric output of all Middle West's subsidiaries was less than 200 million kilowatt-hours; when the money drought ended in 1923, output was approaching a billion kilowatt-hours. Meeting this demand required capital on an unprecedented scale at a time when money was unprecedentedly scarce.[23]

Staying afloat under these circumstances was, for Insull, a matter of

[22] *Historical Statistics of the United States*, pp. 278–79, 346–47; McDonald, *Let There Be Light*, pp. 184–85, 216–20; Milwaukee Electric Railway and Light Company, petition to Wisconsin Railroad Commission, Jan. 20, 1920, in Wisconsin State Archives; and the sources cited in note 18, above.

[23] Commonwealth Edison, *Annual Reports*, 1914, 1919, 1920; Liddle and Evers, "History of Commonwealth Edison," p. 172A; Middle West Utilities, *Annual Reports*, 1917–23; Central Illinois Public Service Company, "Integration Data Prepared for the Securities Exchange Commission," Exhibits I to X, and Kentucky Utilities Company, "Historical Data and Growth of Company," Exhibit I (copies of both manuscripts in offices of Central and South West Corporation, Chicago).

continuously juggling credit. As a group, his network of companies was strong enough to ride out virtually any adversity, but because it was made up of many corporations, some strong and some weak, a multitude of transactions was involved, and on paper they left a confused, almost chaotic record. Insull borrowed wherever he could, often on his personal credit, and shifted the available money from one of his companies to another, using the credit of the strong to aid the weak. In many respects it was the late 1880's all over again, with a hand-to-mouth existence, and with the humilating experience of begging, hat in hand, from bank to bank. (There were two differences: now, when personal credit was used it was his own instead of Edison's, and now the stakes were fifty times as high; where he had borrowed $100,000 for Edison, he now borrowed $5,000,000. A decade later he would go through the same mill a third time. Again there would be two differences: The stakes would be yet ten times higher, and he would lose.)

In raising capital, as in other matters, Commonwealth Edison was the strongest link in the chain of Insull companies, though even it caused some uneasy moments. Enabled by its huge reserve capacity to curtail construction during the period—Insull always anticipated what the demand for service would be three years hence—and enabled by good bank credit to avoid permanent financing at high interest rates, the company minimized the damages of the money scarcity. But the only issue of semipermanent securities floated, a note issue of June, 1920, cost more than 8 per cent interest. And on the opposite end of the scale, the elevated railway companies simply could not make out at all; they survived only by failing to pay their power bills. Commonwealth Edison, as their *de facto* parent, bore their losses for them. Public Service of Northern Illinois was able to carry itself, but no more. To carry Middle West Utilities Company (which in turn carried its subsidiaries), Insull used his personal credit. Between the outbreak of the war in Europe and 1921, Insull borrowed personally and lent to Middle West a total of more than $12,000,000; in 1920 alone the accommodation was more than $3,500,000. Too, during most of the period he carried the entire payroll of Middle West with his own funds. In 1920, to facilitate financing by making the company's securities more flexible, he ordered a complex reorganization that resulted in considerable personal loss.[24]

The money crisis began to ease late in 1921, and by midsummer of 1923 it was over. All Insull's companies had survived, and the group as a whole had displayed great strength in so doing. But the crisis had been a warning: In periods of prolonged financial duress, even the strongest could buckle. As things worked out, Insull emerged from the storm with a pair of new financial devices that seemed to promise perpetual security.

The first was customer ownership: What began as a public relations device Insull transformed into a major innovation in corporate finance. At about the time the war broke out Fred Scheel, the young district manager of the Joliet district of Public Service Company of Northern Illinois, asked Insull for a badly needed improvement. Insull said the improvement would have to wait, for it would cost a couple of hundred thousand dollars, and he saw no way of raising it. Scheel asked and was given permission to try to raise it himself by selling the preferred stock of the company to customers in his district. The sale was an immediate success. When the postwar money shortage developed, Insull recalled this experience and the experience of selling more than a billion dollars worth of government bonds, and the two clicked in his mind. It occurred to him, as it had to Jay Cooke after the Civil War, that if he could sell vast quantities of government securities by high-pressure retailing, he could sell good corporate securities the same way.[25]

He established, in each of the major companies, a security-selling department, co-ordinated by John Gilchrist but run by Scheel; these

[24] *Minutes*, Commonwealth Edison directors' meetings, May 29, 1916; April 29, Aug. 22, Sept. 17, 1918; Feb. 24, March 18, 1919; May 18, June 22, Dec. 21, 1920; Feb. 19, June 8, June 14, June 19, Nov. 15, 1921; *Minutes*, Public Service directors' meetings, 1917–22; *Minutes*, Middle West Utilities directors' meetings, Aug. 28, Sept. 25, 1917; March 25, May 27, Aug. 26, 1919; Jan. 23, April 21, June 30, Aug. 30, Dec. 18, 1920; Nov. 15, Dec. 12, Dec. 29, 1921; "Middle West Utilities Company, Settlement Made with S.I. Acct. Use of His Personal Credit and Resources from 1914 to 1921 Incl.," an envelope of documents in the Insull Papers; *Minutes*, Peoples Gas Company directors' meetings, 1919–22; annual reports of the several companies, throughout; F.T.C., *Utility Corporations*, XXXVIII, 438–40 and *passim*.
[25] Insull, *Public Utilities in Modern Life*, p. 167; Insull's testimony in *U.S.* v. *Insull*, pp. 4278–80 (Nov. 1, 1934); interview with Fred Scheel, New Lenox, Illinois, Sept. 3, 1959.

were soon consolidated as a separate corporation (Utility Securities Company) and owned by the companies it served. Scheel developed and trained a force of salesmen, and they in turn transformed hordes of employees, from department heads to meter-readers, into stock jobbers who sold preferred (and, to a lesser extent, common) stocks to friends, neighbors, and customers. The friends, neighbors, and customers responded eagerly: Middle West and its subsidiaries, for example, had scarcely 6,000 security holders at war's end, 54,000 by 1923, and almost 250,000 five years later. In every Insull company, the same thing happened. By 1930, a million people would own the Insull companies.[26]

The second major financial innovation was the senior-security counterpart of the first: large-scale retailing of corporate bonds. Ever since 1902, when a truce and alliance was forged between New York's Jewish banking power (headed by Kuhn, Loeb) and its non-Jewish banking power (headed by the House of Morgan), the investment banking business in the United States—the key to American industrial growth—had been almost exclusively the domain of New York. But through shortsightedness, the New Yorkers left two gaping weak spots in their control, and in the decade before the war a young Chicagoan had increased the size of both. The weak spots were in electric utility issues and in retail distribution; the Chicagoan was Harold L. Stuart of Halsey, Stuart and Company. Inspired by Insull's belief in the future of rural and small urban utility systems, Stuart set out to build a market for their bonds; lacking the rich institutional connections which underlay the power of the major houses, Stuart cultivated smaller outlets. In so doing he discovered, long before customer ownership was heard of, the advantages of mass marketing: a million dollars is a million dollars, whether it comes from a thousand buyers of a thousand dollar bond or four buyers of a quarter-million in bonds. And while the thousand investors were more unwieldy, their potential was vastly greater; and besides, with

---

[26] Interview with Scheel; interview with Frank Evers (who worked directly under Scheel), Los Angeles, Sept. 10, 1958; interview with J. D. Scheinmann (a former broker who did various business for Utility Securities Company), Los Angeles, Sept. 11, 1958; annual reports of Commonwealth Edison, Public Service, Middle West, Peoples Gas, Wisconsin Power and Light, Lake Superior District Power Company, Kentucky Utilities Company, throughout the 1920's; Insull Utility Investments Company, *The Insull Group, Public Utility Properties* (Chicago, 1930).

four investors the seller was at the mercy of four men, while with a thousand the seller was at the mercy of no man.[27]

From 1907, when he first sold a small amount of Insull's bonds, until the end of the war, Stuart was useful to Insull primarily as a house through which to sell the senior securities of his small rural companies, and Insull was useful to Stuart as a kite-tail on which to ride. But during the postwar money drought, Insull learned to appreciate Stuart's brilliance and his organization, for Stuart seemed able to sell bonds in a market that other financiers told him did not exist. In 1922 Insull turned, for the first time, to Stuart for large-scale financing, and Stuart responded by selling $27,000,000 of bonds at little over half the interest Insull had been paying. Thenceforth Stuart was Insull's bond man. The amount of bonds Stuart sold for Insull leaped spectacularly: soon he would sell almost two hundred million dollars' worth in a single year. Thenceforth, too, investment banking was a new and fiercely competitive business—and thereby hangs a tale, or a hundred tales.[28]

These two innovations can scarcely be overrated. They temporarily broke the stranglehold New York investment bankers had fastened on the economy, which was revolutionary enough; and they did far more than that. As their use spread, they brought about gigantic corporations that were owned by everybody and therefore owned by nobody, and thereby created a new managerial class, replacing old-style owner-management with new-style hired-management. Capitalism would never again be the same. Nor would Insull.

With nothing to do but handle a labor crisis, revolutionize public relations, finance a few gigantic corporations during a money drought, manage several dozen companies, and run a presidential campaign, Insull took on the most challenging task he had met: staving off the almost certain collapse of Peoples Gas Light and Coke Company.

[27] Fritz Redlich, *The Molding of American Banking: Men and Ideas* (2 vols.; New York, 1951), pp. 380–81; Insull's testimony in *U.S. v. Insull*, pp. 4296–301 (Nov. 1, 1934); several interviews with Harold L. Stuart.

[28] Insull's testimony and interviews with Stuart, previously cited; interview with William Bauer (formerly a salesman for Stuart), Chicago, Oct. 22, 1958; untitled statistical summary of sales of bonds of Insull companies by Halsey, Stuart, and Company, in the Insull Papers; Insull, "Memoirs," pp. 171–73.

The decline of the gas company was precipitated by both internal rottenness and external pressure. The main trouble on both counts was political. Long a sower of the seeds of political corruption and often a beneficiary of its fruits, after 1906 the company came increasingly to be a victim of its poison. When the owners induced Insull to accept the chairmanship of its board in 1913, they did so hoping that he could perform his political magic on their behalf. He did not even try. Instead, he modified its methods of finance, ordered a few changes in grosser matters of mismanagement, and allowed the company to continue to run itself more or less as before.[29]

As the war approached, Peoples Gas badly needed to build a new gas plant. There were two principal ways of manufacturing gas, in "water gas" plants, which produced gas from coal and a great deal of oil, and in coal gas plants. The former had once been more desirable because water gas burned more brightly and because oil was cheap and abundant. Then technical changes rendered water gas obsolete. First the gas mantle, which produced incandescent light from heat yielded by burning gas, made the illuminating power of gas inconsequential. Then the automobile ended the era of cheap oil, both by creating increased demand and by stimulating new refining processes that eliminated so-called waste oil, which had been the main source of the supply of inexpensive oil. At the same time, a new and extremely efficient kind of coal gas plant (the by-product coke oven) was being developed, and it soon became the only sensible kind of plant to build.

The trouble was that the new kind of coal gas had an illuminating power of only twenty-two candlepower, and an ancient city regulation required that gas be of twenty-six candlepower. Candlepower requirements had been obsolete since the introduction of the mantle, and most cities had long since changed over to a heat-content requirement. So Chicago might have done, in view of Peoples Gas Company's urgent need to build a new plant, but for the war between city and company over rates. A rate dispute, involving a potential $10,000,000 refund to customers of the company, had been pending since 1911, and the company had fought the case up the tortuous legal path

[29] See pp. 158–61, above, and the sources cited therein. Study of the minute books of the company for 1914 to 1919 confirms Insull's statement in his "Memoirs," p. 184, that he "had no idea whatever of taking part in the details of management of the property." Indeed, in 1913 he thought—not having looked closely—that the company had been well run.

toward the Supreme Court. Had the company been willing to give an inch—say by cutting its rates a nickel per thousand cubic feet—it could doubtless have induced the city council to accede to its perfectly reasonable request regarding the candlepower requirement. But it would not give an inch, and neither would the city council, and the deadlock dragged on until 1917.[30]

By then it was a new world. The huge wartime demand for gas made the new plant imperative, wartime inflation doubled the prospective cost of the plant, and the leap in oil prices made it impossible for the company to break even in daily operations with existing facilities and existing rates. The State Public Utilities Commission, already under attack from utilities for being so slow about increasing rates and from public and politicians for being so fast about it, was hardly anxious to incur further wrath by granting a rate increase to what was probably the least popular utility in the state. Thus it did not get around to granting an increase to Peoples Gas until near the end of the war. By that time, the company had cut out all dividends and for more than a year had failed to earn the interest on its bonds. In the first eight months of 1918 it operated at a deficit of $1,500,000. Credit disappeared; to raise $1,200,000 to meet maturing demand notes and to meet its bond interest due on September 1, 1918, it had to pledge liquid assets worth $2,996,607, in addition to its whole supply of coal, oil, and coke. Six months later it had to pledge collateral worth more than $3,000,000 in order to borrow less than $500,000. The First National Bank discreetly installed one of its own men on the premises to insure that not so much as a pencil was expended without bank approval.[31]

And going broke was but a fraction of the trouble. In the early fall of 1918, employees in the accounting department discovered that a large number of meter readers had decided it would be simpler to read meters from the corner poolroom—to turn in rough guesses

[30] *Minutes*, Peoples Gas directors' meetings, Feb. 15, 1906; June 8, June 21, July 12, 1911; April 17, 1912; Feb. 10, 1916, and *Annual Reports* for 1911, 1912, 1915–18; Charles Twigg (chairman of the City Council Committee on Gas, Oil, and Electric Light) to Peoples Gas Company, June 1, June 9, June 15, 1911; L. A. Wiley (secretary of Peoples Gas) to Twigg, June 7, June 22, 1911; Insull to the Committee on Gas, Oil, and Electric Light, Feb. 10, 1916 (all correspondence in the files of Peoples Gas Company); *Chicago Examiner*, June 20, 1911; interview with Francis Daily, Nov. 18, 1957.
[31] Insull, "Memoirs," pp. 184–85; Peoples Gas, *Annual Reports*, 1917–19; *Minutes*, Peoples Gas directors' meetings, July 9, Oct. 9, 1917; March 16, April 30, Aug. 29, 1918; March 24, July 2, 1919; interview with Charles A. Munroe, New York, May 16, 1956.

based on consumption during preceding months, less a small discount to prevent complaints. For six months or more, no one in Chicago had been properly billed; in September alone some 38,000 customers were not billed at all. The entire accounting department walked out in disgust, taking with them their account books, which they unceremoniously dumped in open manholes around the city.[32]

Nor was that all. Irate bondholders, bankers, employees, and customers might somehow be fended off, but there was one whose toll was inescapable: the tax collector. By April 1, 1919, Peoples Gas, devoid of cash, devoid of unpledged assets, devoid of credit, had to come up with a million dollars or be sold for taxes.[33]

This was the company Insull faced when he returned to business after the war. Doubtless his first instinct was to abandon it. His economic stake was small, it was not his own company, the mess was not of his making, and he had more to do than any three other men would have liked to undertake. Furthermore, the chances of success appeared remote, and he had little to gain and his reputation to lose if he should fail. On a cold, bleak Sunday at the turn of the year, he and John Mitchell met to decide what to do about it. All afternoon they wandered the dirty streets of the Loop, unable to think of a way to save the company, even less able to think of a reason why they should. Finally, as if struck with sudden realization, Mitchell turned and said, "Sam, do you realize what a black eye it will be for Chicago if we let a utility this size go under?" Thus to save Chicago a black eye, Insull determined to undertake the impossible.[34] (The timing could hardly have been more ironic. This was 1919, the year of the race riots in which hundreds of Negroes were butchered; the year of the Black Sox scandal; the year a young man named Alphonse Capone came west to seek his fortune in Chicago.)

[32] *Minutes*, Peoples Gas directors' meeting, Oct. 23, 1918; interviews with Francis Daily, Charles A. Munroe, J. E. Davis, and Walter McElligott. The interviews with Daily (long-time attorney for the company) and Munroe have been cited previously; that with Davis, an old-time employee, was in Chicago, Nov. 20, 1957; there were many with McElligott. The latter, a personal aid of Insull, Jr., in the twenties, went to work exclusively for the gas company in the thirties. As I worked in the records of the company, I saw him almost daily, and he very kindly spent many hours with me, explaining and narrating events in the company's history.
[33] *Minutes*, Peoples Gas directors' meeting, March 24, 1919.
[34] The generalizations in this paragraph are from the sources previously cited; the incident of the walk with Mitchell was told me by Charles A. Munroe and Insull, Jr., in separate interviews.

Gladys Insull as Lady Teazle in her own production of Sheridan's The School for Scandal *in 1925.* (INSULL COLLECTION)

Senator William B. Mc-Kinley, the traction magnate, long Insull's favorite business enemy. (CHICAGO TRIBUNE)

(Bottom left) Senator James Reed of Missouri, head of the Reed committee which investigated Insull's campaign contributions in 1926–27. (CHICAGO TRIBUNE)

(Bottom right) Fred Scheel, Insull's security salesman par excellence, revolutionized corporate finance in a customer-ownership campaign. (CHICAGO TRIBUNE)

To

COMMEMORATE

THE

FIFTIETH ANNIVERSARY

OF THE ARRIVAL

IN AMERICA OF

MR. SAMUEL INSULL

FEBRUARY 28
1881 - 1931

Scroll presented to Samuel Insull in commemoration of the fiftieth anniversary of his arrival in the United States.
(INSULL COLLECTION)

To Samuel Insull

In the fifty years that ends today, your civic contributions have bettered Chicago. You have become the first citizen of the youngest great city in the world.

In the fifty years that ends today, your technical triumph put cheap and abundant power at the elbow of America. You championed a true democracy of welfare.

In the fifty years that ends today, your economic daring set mechanical power free from physical confinement. You became an outstanding servant of humanity.

These are of your marks upon the yesterdays of the half century that has passed since you came to the country of your choice.

As you go up the tomorrows, we who believe you and believe in you salute you. We are proud of what you have done; we are glad that you chose us to follow you. Your honor is our heritage; your fame is our banner.

As you go up the tomorrows, it is enough for us if our admiration, our respect and our devotion may minstrel their music to your brave heart.

(SCROLL PRESENTED TO MR. INSULL)

Cyrus S. Eaton, of the Cleveland investment banking house of Otis and Company, who acquired large blocs of stocks in Insull companies. (CHICAGO TRIBUNE)

Edward Eagle Brown, vice-president of the First National Bank of Chicago. (THE FIRST NATIONAL BANK OF CHICAGO)

Abner J. Stilwell, vice-president of the Continental Illinois National Bank and Trust Company. (PHOTO BY BLACK-STONE-SHELBURNE NEW YORK; COURTESY OF THE ESTATE OF ABNER J. STILWELL)

Gladys Insull: portrait of the thirties. (INSULL COLLECTION)

Three generations: Insull, his son, and his grandson. (CHI-CAGO TRIBUNE)

A birthday party for Insull's grandson. (INSULL COLLECTION)

Insull and his grandson.

Insull and his wife and son.

Insull visiting the "Black Forest" at the Century of Progress Exposition.

Insull, en route to Cherbourg. (ACME)

Insull, under escort, leaves prison in Istanbul for the voyage home. (ASSOCIATED PRESS)

Insull arriving in New York harbor aboard the S.S. "Exilona" in May, 1934. (ACME)

Insull began the task in January, 1919, by sending a four-man advance team from the Edison Building to the Gas Building: Fred Sargent, his ace engineer; Charles Munroe, his right arm; George Mitchell (no kin to John), his private secretary; and Bernard J. Mullaney, his new-found public and industrial relations man.[35]

Mullaney's sole assignment was to pave Insull's way with employees and customers, which, to suit Insull, involved nothing less than transforming their discontent into a fighting *esprit de corps*. In January the task appeared well-nigh impossible, but before the year was three months old it was done. With the dexterity of a demagogue handling a mob, Mullaney sold everybody. His essential tack was to inspire confidence by repeatedly suggesting—never quite saying—that everything was going to be all right, for now the Great Man was coming. (Mullaney's words were reinforced by the speed and the manner in which Mitchell and Munroe executed their first task, streamlining office practices. They aimed, and truly, at making things work well, not at cutting payrolls—except at the very top. In this way they fulfilled every disgruntled bureaucrat's dream, for while no office worker loves a time-study man, he does like a new management that promises to [a] shake up the petty tyrants in the office, [b] remove bureaucratic stupidity, and yet [c] not seriously threaten anyone's occasional prerogative to loaf. Nor did Insull hurt anyone's feelings when he cut his own salary in half.) At the same time, Mullaney went immediately to work on a long-range "Insullization program" similar to that in the Edison Company. By late March, when Insull assumed active daily command as president of the company, Mullaney, Mitchell, and Munroe had created a work force prepared to work for and not against him.[36]

Insull's own rescue job involved the simultaneous application of four supreme talents—as political operator, as efficient administrator, as creative rearranger of the ingredients of a complex situation, and as financier.

The most immediate problem facing the gas company was the tax

[35] *Minutes,* Peoples Gas directors' meeting, Jan. 4, 1919; interview with Munroe. A file of clippings preserved in the Insull Papers contains a large portion of the newspaper coverage of this and subsequent events relating to Insull's rescue of the gas company.
[36] Interviews with Munroe, Daily, McElligott, and Davis, previously cited; *Minutes,* Peoples Gas directors' meetings, Jan. 4, July 2, 1919; April 7, 1920; March 21, 1921; and *Annual Report,* 1919.

crisis, and it appeared insoluble, for taxes were due and the company had no way of raising the money to pay them. But the day Insull arrived the crisis vanished: For six months the county treasurer forgot the company's address. (Munroe, recalling this phenomenon many years later, explained it with eloquent simplicity: "Mr. Insull spoke to some of his political friends.") [37]

Simultaneously, Insull went to work slashing operating expenses. This was no mean feat, for the tried and true way of reducing costs in times of trouble—wage cuts—was closed by the delicate labor situation and the tremendous pressure for wage boosts. Unerringly, Insull sensed the probable causes of the greatest removable waste. Given the company's political and managerial history, it seemed certain to him that many of its contracts for procuring fuel and supplies had been arranged on terms more advantageous to particular individuals than to the company. His hunch was right: Within four months he was able to renegotiate contracts and effect annual savings of $750,000. Various streamlined procedures ran the total savings to $1,000,000 in the first year. The rate increase put into effect near the end of the war added $2,000,000 in gross revenues in 1919. Thus, though the cost of everything rose during the year, in 1919 the company managed to break even for the first time in three years.

But these measures were like tiny fingers in a bursting dike. As a gas utility company Peoples Gas was still operating at a great deficit; it was in the black in 1919 only because it earned large incidental profits as a renter of office space and as a merchandiser of gas appliances. Insull had a long-range solution in view: building one of the new kinds of manufacturing plants that combined the best features of coal gas and water gas and would yield a host of lucrative by-products in the process. But it would take time and credit that the company did not have. As Insull put it, "Bankers will lend you umbrellas only when it doesn't look like rain."[38]

In 1920 it began to appear increasingly likely that the company would fail, drowned in the inflationary flood. No further operating economies could be effected, and though another rate increase was

[37] Interview with Munroe, previously cited.

[38] *Minutes*, Peoples Gas directors' meetings, March 24, July 2, Dec. 24, 1919, and *Annual Report*, 1919; interviews with Insull, Jr.; interview with Charles Stuart, New York, July 30, 1957; Insull, "Memoirs," p. 185.

granted by the utility commission in June of that year, the cost of wages and materials increased so fast that the rate increase was nullified by the time it went into effect.[39]

Then, between them, Munroe and Insull hit upon a brilliant idea. All around Chicago were industrial plants that produced coke oven gas in the process of making steel and other products. Much of the gas was burned off as waste. Seeing the Gary sky reddened by these flares, Insull wondered whether enough gas was being dumped to be worth buying, and whether the companies would sell. He sent Munroe to find out, and Munroe returned with a contract with Wisconsin Steel Company for eight to ten million cubic feet of gas a day, about one eighth of People Gas Company's total output. The price, including the necessary pipelines, was 38.4¢ per thousand cubic feet, 20¢ under Peoples Gas' manufacturing cost. The contract saved the company almost $600,000 a year.

And then Munroe made an equally important discovery. Most mills, he learned, closed down on weekends and left ovens running, burning as waste all the gas produced then. Peoples Gas had several huge gas holders which could be pumped full on the weekends and drained during the week, if a suitable deal for dump gas could be negotiated. Munroe talked with the management of the Mark Manufacturing Company and audaciously offered them 10¢ per thousand cubic feet for ten million cubic feet a week. They accepted. Then Munroe tried Inland Steel and offered 5¢. They also accepted. Before the year was over, Munroe had arranged to buy enough dump gas, at an average of around 15¢ per thousand cubic feet, to fill a quarter of Peoples Gas Company's total needs. The annual saving was around $2,000,000, and the company was once more in the black, this time to stay.[40]

But a way of financing the building of a new, $20,000,000 gas manufacturing plant had yet to be arranged. Soon after taking over the company Insull began negotiating with H. B. Rust, president of the Koppers Company, virtually the only organization in the world capable of building the kind of plant Insull had in mind. They

[39] *Minutes,* Peoples Gas directors' meeting, Sept. 24, 1920, and *Annual Report,* 1920; Insull's oral report to the stockholders, at the stockholders' meeting, Feb. 10, 1921; *Chicago Tribune, Chicago American,* Feb. 11, 1921.
[40] Interview with Munroe, previously cited; *Minutes,* Peoples Gas directors' meetings, April 1, 1920; Jan. 5, 1921.

worked out a foolproof plan to make the plant pay for itself; the only problem was that neither Rust nor Insull could think of a way to raise the money to build it. Rust was anxious to oblige, for he had respect for Insull, and, furthermore, a twenty-million-dollar contract was not something he was anxious to lose. But Peoples Gas had absolutely no market for its securities—indeed, preliminary inquiry indicated that not even a subsidiary, operating under its own first mortgage and controlled by Koppers, would be able to sell bonds, simply because of the connection with Peoples Gas.

The talks continued for about a year, to no avail. Finally, Rust took up the matter with his boss, Andrew W. Mellon, then one of the richest men on the continent and soon to be the Secretary of the Treasury. Mr. Mellon, whose properties included the Aluminum Corporation of America, Gulf Oil Company, a bank or two, an assortment of utility companies, and half of Pittsburgh as well as the Koppers Company, informed Rust that he would like to talk to this fellow Insull. They had met a few years earlier, though apparently Insull had made but small impression; but Mellon had been hearing much of Insull of late, not only from Rust, and he wanted to know the man he was dealing with. One afternoon in April, 1920, Rust telephoned Insull, saying Mellon would like to see him. As it happened, Insull was going to New York the next day. He arranged to stop off in Pittsburgh and go with Rust to visit Mellon in his home. For three hours they talked of international politics, postwar financial problems, labor—of ships and shoes and sealing wax—everything but the matter in hand. As Insull left, Mellon called Rust aside for thirty seconds; on the drive to the station, Rust told Insull he need worry no longer about financing the new plant. Construction began that month, and the plant was completed in October, 1921. The day was saved.[41]

(The financial details of the arrangements were immensely complex, but in essence Mellon guaranteed all the securities of the new subsidiary by pledging securities from his personal portfolio. When the subsidiary earned its way out—as it did in six years, all the while effecting huge savings for the company—it could redeem all the

[41] Insull, "Memoirs," pp. 185–87; Berry, "Mr. Samuel Insull," pp. 60–61; *Minutes*, Peoples Gas directors' meetings, March 24, Oct. 19, Dec. 24, 1919; Jan. 26, Jan. 30, Feb. 6, 1920; and *Annual Report*, 1921; Rust to Insull, Sept. 30, 1919 (in Peoples Gas Company files).

securities in question and become a wholly-owned property of Peoples Gas.) [42]

By the time the new plant was in operation, Insull was able to announce that the company was resuming the payment of dividends on its common stock. In another two years, dividends would be at an annual rate of 8 per cent, the highest in the company's history, and there they would remain.[43]

Many of the thousands who were induced to bet on Insull also bet on his venture into Peoples Gas. Those who did were able to buy gas company stock at $29 a share. In a decade they would see it rise to more than $400. (It fell calamitously in the summer of 1932, but never to less than double its price on the day Insull arrived.) [44]

The storm had its beneficent effects. Under pressure of emergency, Insull learned newer and better ways of doing things and ruthlessly pared from his several companies every ounce of fat. Each became better organized, more efficiently managed, and more solidly financed than it had ever been before. Too, in the process of surviving in a period of increasing demand for service, they had grown much larger: by 1923 their combined property was worth approximately three-quarters of a billion dollars. And because they were better managed they were more easily managed, and thereby more securely held in Insull's grasp.

But there was another side to it. Even as his grip on the reins of great and growing power had tightened, their grip on him had become inescapable. Whatever the extent of his commitment to his newly assumed power and responsibility before the crisis, it had now become absolute. His hands and the reins had become one: whatever happened, he could no more let go than they could slip loose.

Hence, just as there was, during the crisis, nothing he could do but fight and try to keep his companies afloat, in the boom that was coming there was nothing he could do but expand as the American economy expanded—even had he wanted to do otherwise.

[42] Peoples Gas, *Annual Reports*, 1921–27.
[43] Peoples Gas, *Annual Reports*, 1923, 1924.
[44] *Chicago Tribune*, Dec. 31, 1919; Dec. 31, 1920; Dec. 31, 1921; Aug., 1929; July, 1932; *Moody's Public Utilities*, 1932–40.

CHAPTER IX *The Empire and Its Marshals*

The postwar crisis was a man-killing ordeal, and when it was over Insull was sixty-three years old. As soon as it seemed safe to do so, he responded as he had after a similar ordeal with Edison: He had a thoroughgoing nervous breakdown. For himself, he had the strength to survive it and the wisdom to know what to do about it. He took a slow boat to Europe and, with Junior, tramped about in northern Scotland and emulated a vegetable until he was ready for action again.[1]

Some others in his organization were less fortunate. Whether because of the postwar pace or some other cause, six of Insull's most trusted associates and advisers died during the period: Fred Sargent, the brilliant Scotch engineer who, with Insull, had pioneered virtually every major advance in power production for a quarter of a century; Arthur Young, a British-born accountant who worked out much of the complex bookkeeping system that reflected Insull's way of doing business; William G. Beale, the wise old lawyer who had drafted for Insull the original open-end mortgage and the man whose advice Insull was likely to accept before that of any other; Roger Sullivan, the Democratic boss and Insull's closest political friend and adviser; Stuyvesant Peabody, Insull's coal man; and Frank Baker, the engineering and operations head of Public Service Company, the man who had first persuaded Insull to expand into the suburbs, and a pioneer with Insull in the early experiments in electrification of rural communities.[2]

[1] Interview with Samuel Insull, Jr.
[2] Insull, *Public Utilities in Modern Life*, pp. 133 n, 143 n, 184 n, 346 n; Commemorative address on Sullivan, in the Insull Papers.

Great as these men were in their specialties, and important as they were to Insull, they were not irreplacable. Besides, three giants of the Chicago business world remained to advise Insull: John J. Mitchell, James A. Patten, and John G. Shedd. Each of these men appreciated the creative value of Insull's daring and radical ventures, and each was conservative enough to sense when he was going too far or too fast. And because Insull respected their judgment, they could keep him in check when his daring threatened to be merely dangerous and his radicalism merely reckless.

Nevertheless, these deaths made a fundamental change in the nature of the Insull organization. Before, Insull's direct subordinates had been considerably outweighed by former outsiders who had stature and power in their own right. Now, despite the presence of Mitchell, Patten, and Shedd and despite the arrival of a few new outsiders, Insull was surrounded by men who had grown up under his direct tutelage and command. These were men of great ability, and on the whole the new organization was far better trained, far more skilled, far more efficient than the old; it could do in areas in which the old could not even dream. Yet it had a weakness that the old had not: The inside men so idolized Insull that they rarely disagreed with him, and they so feared him that they rarely ventured to say so when they did disagree. And because Insull's power was becoming awesome, this weakness could be fatal.[3]

The basic weakness was Insull's own, and it had two aspects. He had too much ability for his own good. Thus he could recognize the need for men who could think independently, and he developed a masterful skill at flushing the yes-men by playing devil's advocate.

[3] This and subsequent generalizations about Insull's men are based largely upon interviews. Particularly revealing in this regard were interviews with Charles A. Munroe, Britton Budd, R. H. James, Edward Doyle, John Evers, Fred Scheel, A. G. deClercq, Philip McEnroe, Francis Daily, Harry Reid, Helen Norris, and C. A. Turner. Samuel Insull, Jr., recorded his impressions of each of the marshals in a lengthy tape-recorded interview, a transcript of which is in the Insull Papers. I have also studied the men in the various records pertaining to Insull, in biographical sketches preserved in the files of Commonwealth Edison's publicity department, in *Edison Round Table,* and in Seymour's "History of Commonwealth Edison." Insull's own comments about his men are in his "Memoirs," pp. 174–84 and *passim,* and in his testimony in *U.S.* v. *Insull,* pp. 4296 ff. Objective appraisal may be made by studying the papers and discussions of these men at the conventions of the industry associations, as recorded in the N.E.L.A. *Proceedings* and the A.E.I.C. *Minutes.* These several sources underlie this entire chapter, whether additional documentation is cited or not.

He asserted an absurd proposition with solemn conviction, and any employee who fell into the trap and rushed to agree underwent a verbal thrashing that stung for years. But this very talent illustrated and aggravated the problem, for what he needed least were men he could manipulate. On the opposite side, though he recognized his weakness, he had never been able to resist the temptation to play the benevolent tyrant, to run other people's lives for their own good, and he had forgotten how to resist his compulsion to run things. His psyche flatly refused to listen to his reason. He consciously sought subordinates who would say him nay, yet all the while he continued to surround himself with Irish Catholics and to shun Scots and Jews. In his system of stereotypes, the Irish were persons who learned respect for authority as the first principle—good Catholics do not overthrow the Pope—and Scots and Jews were quite the opposite.

The weakness was shown clearly by an incident that occurred just after his return from the rest cure in Europe. Insull imported a man to survey the problem of co-ordinating his several companies: Lieutenant Colonel R. H. James, recently retired from the British army and a man whose prestige, ability, and experience had been far more than his rank would suggest (he had, for example, been in command of Home Defense during the war). Though he knew James well, Insull sent him on a trial run before giving him his major assignment. He asked James to investigate the intercompany coal supply system. Insull knew there was considerable waste in this area, but he also knew that its reform involved adroit movement among an assortment of vice-presidents who jealously guarded every prerogative. James quickly passed the test; in short order he came up with a series of changes that saved large sums without offending the *amour-propre* of the vice-presidents.

Upon undertaking his major assignment, James quickly became aware of Insull's too-tight hold on the reins, but he put it to Insull in a circuitous way. "Mr. Insull," he said, "you work too hard."

For a moment, Insull must have thought he had blundered in calling in this man. With an air of exaggerated patience, as if to a child, he answered: "I have a lot of work to do, James, and it takes time."

James said, "You begin your day at six-thirty and work long into the night. But look at your friend, Mr. John Mitchell. He runs a big bank, and he's on boards of directors all over Chicago, and yet he comes into his office at ten in the morning and goes home at three. He gets his work done."

"I know," said Insull. "How do those fellows do it?"

"They delegate authority."

Insull sat silently for a long time, staring out the window. At last he turned back to James. Almost in a whisper, he said, "Jamie, I haven't got the men."[4]

And he was right. Rarely has a man been surrounded by such a dazzling array of talent, and yet, because he lived in a world he had made, he did not have the men. He had many who could do one thing brilliantly, and some who could do many things brilliantly, but only a handful who had learned—or who had been allowed to learn—how to be a decision-making executive.

First among the men around Insull was the remaining triumvirate of outside advisers: Mitchell, Patten, and Shedd. On this level only one newcomer was added after the war. Stanley Field, the English-reared nephew of Marshall Field I, was a man whose abilities in some areas—particularly the building and management of office buildings—nearly measured up to his social standing. Insull found Field valuable for a variety of reasons, and increasingly he brought Field into his major companies in the dual capacity of director and personal adviser. Slim, handsome, and courtly, Field looked his part, and in lesser company he would have been a major figure. But he was in the company of giants, men of character and caliber beyond his ken. The difference between Field and the old triumvirate was vast. The others were equals, and Field, despite his status and stature, was simply not on their level.[5]

Also on the outside were, of necessity, Insull's lawyers. The situation with the lawyers represented, in miniature, the changed atmosphere under which Insull worked after the war. No one could ever quite replace Beale; he was an all-purpose lawyer, and his stature equaled Insull's own. Instead, Insull drew from four firms to gather

[4] Interview with Ralph H. James, Chicago, May 20, 1958.

[5] Here as elsewhere in this chapter the documentation offered is only supplemental to the sources cited in note 3, above. In addition to those sources, information about Field was derived from an interview with him in Chicago, Nov. 20, 1957; from a number of newspaper clippings in the possession of Commonwealth Edison Company; from Marquis (ed.), *Who's Who in Chicago*, 1931, p. 315; and from interviews with H. L. Stuart, Mrs. Bertha Baur, and Abner J. Stilwell.

about him a group who could match talents with any lawyers in the country. Isham, Lincoln & Beale continued to be (as it had been from the beginning) counsel for the Edison Company. The firm had always been burdened by its own respectability: It was almost too proper to be of much use to anyone who seriously needed a lawyer. It was ideal for a company of the proven stability of Commonwealth Edison, but in the dynamic world of Insull's other activities it was, frequently, beyond its depth. Fortunately, just as Beale had made it a vital firm during his lifetime, two younger men, Gilbert Porter and Waldo Tobey, revitalized it in the twenties.[6]

Complementing Isham, Lincoln & Beale were Cooke, Sullivan & Ricks, whom Insull inherited as counsel for Peoples Gas Company. Cooke was George A. Cooke, former chief justice of the Illinois Supreme Court; Sullivan was Boetius Sullivan, son of Roger; and Ricks was Jesse T. Ricks, who left the firm about the time Insull took over. The Edison lawyers wore white shirts, the gas company lawyers wore blue; but the Gas House Gang was superior in ability, if inferior in prestige. The reason was Cooke, a man who, like many of the men around Insull, startlingly looked his part. His manner, his mass, and his twinkling eyes set in seamed skin gave him away as a country lawyer who had come to the city by way of politics, and remained there because he was wiser and shrewder than his city cousins. After Beale died Insull depended upon Cooke more than on any other lawyer; he was the nearest to being Insull's personal attorney.[7]

The third lawyer was Ralph Bradley, whose official function was as counsel for the suburban North Shore Line but whose real job was in labor relations. Bradley had a rare talent for getting along with people of any background or status, and an even rarer talent for disagreeing strongly with people and yet befriending them in the process. He became such a friend of the labor leaders around Chicago that they often requested him to act as impartial arbitrator in disputes. (Occasionally, vice-presidents complained to Insull about

[6] Marquis (ed.), *Who's Who in Chicago*, 1931, pp. 783, 979; interviews with David Taber and Harry Dunbaugh (members of the firm), Chicago, Nov. 19, 1957. Dunbaugh had been with Isham, Lincoln & Beale since 1903 and was unofficially its historian. The appraisal made here is my own, of course.

[7] Marquis (ed.), *Who's Who in Chicago*, 1931, p. 209; interview with Judge Floyd Thompson, Chicago, Aug. 31, 1959.

Bradley's decisions, but not once in the twenties did labor protest.)

The role of the fourth lawyer, Daniel J. Schuyler, was harder to define. He was Insull's "political lawyer": As general counsel for the Chicago traction companies (the perennial happy hunting ground of local politicians) and as the law partner of Samuel Ettleson (officially the corporation counsel and unofficially the brains of Mayor William Hale Thompson), it was inevitable that he should be. But he was too able, too broad, and too farsighted to be only a political lawyer. Schuyler came to be, in all matters of general human relations, Insull's closest adviser—almost an extension of Insull himself. The role is illustrated by their work together for Chicago Negroes newly arriving from the South. In 1922 Schuyler and Insull, with the help of a few friends and associates, established a community center for Negroes, and a year later they formed the South Side Boys' Club for Negroes. Both were large-scale, well-financed ventures; both provided badly needed facilities for vocational training, recreation, miscellaneous guidance and aid, and a wholesome environment.

Neither man needed to explain to the other why this should be done; both understood, though the reasons were so complex and varied that neither could have verbalized them. The obvious reason was human decency, but that was not the sole reason. Another was civic pride: Negro immigrants, arriving in droves from the rural South, would clearly bring a blight upon the city and turn it into a vast slum unless something were done to help them adjust to their new circumstances. Still another was the memory of the race riots of 1919: Neither man wanted to live in a city where that was likely to recur, and both knew that in Chicago it would be a long time before blacks and whites learned to live together in peace. Again, it was simply good business (Insull, like most businessmen, needed that rationalization) : Let a large area of the city run down and a large segment of its population be impoverished, and the market for electric light, power, gas, and public transportation would fall as the city fell. Then there was politics: The quarter of a million Negroes who poured into Chicago in the twenties would inevitably become a powerful voting bloc—already Oscar DePriest was laying the foundations for his reign as the Black Boss of Chicago—and it was only prudent to befriend such a group. All these considerations, and more, Insull instinctively grasped. And in such matters, Schuyler's hypersensitive social antennae were perfectly attuned to Insull's own.[8]

(Schuyler had a Democratic counterpart as a "political lawyer": Patrick J. Lucey, a man who, like Judge Cooke, had come to Chicago through politics and stayed through superior ability. Lucey had been mayor of Streator, Illinois; then attorney general under Governor Edward F. Dunne, 1912–17; then the minority member of the Public Utilities Commission under Lowden. When he returned to practice in 1921, he joined Insull, working particularly with the gas company. The advantage of the connection to Lucey was obvious. The advantage to Insull was that Lucey had talents and a reputation for integrity that matched his political influence.)

Seven other outside specialists regularly served Insull. Three were financial men, Stuart, Edward P. Russell, and Walter Brewster. Since 1907 Stuart had been one of Insull's bond men, after 1922 he was nearly the only one, and in 1927 he became Insull's principal financial adviser. Russell, an old, trusted friend, had originally suggested the formation of Middle West. Brewster was the son of Edward L. Brewster, one of the two men Insull had contacted when he first went to Chicago. Together, as the firm of Russell, Brewster and Company, the two were—in the public's mind—for Insull's stocks what Stuart was for his bonds, until the companies inside the Insull system developed their own marketing machinery under Fred Scheel, and even then Russell, Brewster remained intimately associated with Insull. Two were engineers, William Monroe, the able successor to Fred Sargent in Sargent and Lundy, and Charles Merz, the British engineer who, with Insull, had been lobbying since 1903 for a quasipublic, unified British power system. Insull called on Merz regularly for two kinds of services: when he wanted to make use of

---

[8] Interview with John Richert (formerly of Schuyler's firm), Chicago, Nov. 20, 1957; interview with George Lennon (formerly of Schuyler's firm), Aug. 21, 1959; interview with Edward J. Quinn (Insull's tax lawyer), Chicago, Nov. 21, 1957; Wendt and Kogan, *Big Bill of Chicago, passim;* Stuart, *Twenty Incredible Years, passim;* Insull, "Memoirs," p. 177. Schuyler was Insull's personal counsel throughout the investigations following the disputed election of 1926, which is narrated below, pages 264–70. Documentary data regarding Insull's work on behalf of Negroes is contained in a file concerning his charities, kept by Samuel Insull, Jr., in his office; much information is contained in the files of newspaper clippings preserved in the offices of Commonwealth Edison Company.

a radical improvement developed by European manufacturers but which General Electric was reluctant to adopt, and when he wanted a fresh look at an old problem. In both capacities, Merz made major contributions on the occasions he was consulted. Another specialist was, like Monroe, a replacement of a predecessor. Stuyvesant ("Jack") Peabody, Jr., lacked the range of his father but was probably even better as a coal man. The seventh was Donald R. McLennan, the active partner in Marsh and McLennan and one of the ablest insurance men anywhere, a man who saved Insull huge sums by devising innovations in reinsurance and became a welcome director in many of the major Insull companies. McLennan, unfortunately for Insull, wanted everybody's insurance business, and that ambition soon set the stage for catastrophe.[9]

Next came the inside experts, men who specialized in operations, engineering, power distribution, cost accounting, public relations; men who in their specialties had few peers on earth. Most were in the three big operating companies (Edison, Gas, and Public Service) and the hard core was in the Edison Company. There was Louis Ferguson, prematurely grayed and stooped and scarred by a near-fatal illness in 1914, now nearing sixty and beginning to snarl sometimes when he spoke, but still blazing trails in urban distribution and still pioneering methods that utilities in some large cities would not begin to use for two and three decades. There was John F. Gilchrist, the human freight train, a man who could sell anything, promote anything, administer anything. And there was Gilchrist's low-pressure counterpart, Ed Lloyd, the one man in the world who knew more about the economics of industrial power sales than Insull did, a man who in a quiet way could convince any potential customer that the only sensible way to run his business involved, as a first step, buying power from Insull. There was John Gulick, tall, courtly, quietly charming; the man, of all the executives, whom Gladys was likely to choose as a partner for a formal dinner; a man skilled in finance and, in the broadest sense, accounting. There was E. J. Fowler, the first

[9] Russell, Brewster, *Stock and Bond Circulars, 1901–1913, 1914–1921* (two bound volumes in the Insull Papers); Insull, "Memoirs," pp. 103, 164–66, 170, 178–79; Insull, *Public Utilities in Modern Life*, pp. 154–55; Insull, *Central-Station Electric Service*, pp. 215–33; several interviews with Abner J. Stilwell and Harold L. Stuart; interview with Edward Eagle Brown, Chicago, Oct. 21, 1958. Some of Merz's reports of studies made for Insull are preserved in the Insull Papers.

and still the foremost industrial statistician in the land; and Bernard Mullaney, the former newspaperman who was revolutionizing public relations in the Public Utility Information campaign; and Fred Scheel, the former division manager who was revolutionizing corporate finance in the customer-ownership campaign. Then there was Ed Doyle, a man who began as Insull's office boy and became his private secretary, company secretary, then vice-president; a man with no special talents or special skills, but one who had been so close to Insull for so long that in almost any situation he knew how Insull would think and what he would decide; the man to whom everyone, irrespective of rank, turned when they did not know what to do and Insull was not there to tell them. And under each of these men were one or two or ten men almost as good.[10]

If these men were too specialized to be given complete authority (only Doyle became the executive head of a major company), Insull was nonetheless able to use them to broad advantage. Each was likely to be a vice-president of a dozen Insull companies as well as Commonwealth Edison, and each, directly or through his own subordinates, was regularly dispatched to lend his expertese to smaller companies in the Insull system. Thus tiny utilities in the sticks of Texas and Nebraska and Vermont had the advantage of managerial talent that otherwise none could have afforded. Thus, too, Insull multiplied himself by extending his way of doing business.

But an emperor cannot rule through his marshals alone; to run an empire one needs viceroys as well. Insull had only six, of one sort and another, and one of them was soon to go. The first was Doyle, who would soon (when Insull moved up to the chairmanship in 1929) leap beyond all the other vice-presidents and succeed Insull as president of Commonwealth Edison. The second was George Mitchell, who followed Doyle as Insull's private secretary and was his counterpart in the gas company. Mitchell's cherubic appearance and jovial manner belied his fierce independence and shrewd talent, and in later life a toxic goiter submerged his independence; but he was, withal, one of the ablest executives in Insull's organization, and in 1929 he became president of Peoples Gas Company, as Insull became chairman. The third was Britton Budd, a man able to do most

---

[10] The sources for this and the two following paragraphs are those cited in note 3, above, supplemented by Britton Budd's scrapbooks, in his possession.

everything and ready to dare most anything. Budd first ran the tractions; when the interurbans around Chicago came under Insull's control, he ran them, too. When Insull needed a man to replace Frank Baker as operating head of Public Service Company of Northern Illinois, Budd added that to his many chores; and when special assignments in labor or politics or general management were to be undertaken, Insull turned them over to Budd. More than any of the Insull men, save one, Budd seemed a lesser Insull incarnate.

The lone exception was Charles Munroe, the erstwhile young man on the make, and the only man who left the ship while it was still afloat. For Munroe's ability, no amount of praise is extravagant: He was imaginative, daring, and resourceful, yet thorough, careful, and prudent, and Insull could entrust to him any function and count it done. For Munroe's character, more restrained adjectives suffice. While Insull was abroad, Munroe learned that the Laclede Gas Company in St. Louis was verging on collapse and that working control could be purchased for about $1,500,000. Quick investigation showed him that it could be saved in the same way Peoples Gas had been saved, and that the profits would be enormous. Here was the main chance at last, and he seized it. On his own, and in Insull's absence, he borrowed Insull's credit, so to speak, and bought the company for the joint account of Insull and himself. Upon his return, Insull exploded and, in spite of the profits the venture promised, summarily dismissed Munroe. Thus after almost a quarter of a century the two parted company. Munroe took the deal with him, and cleared $26,000,000 profit in three years. (They would cross paths once again a decade later, when Munroe would have occasion to demonstrate that he was a man of superior quality, after all.) [11]

The two other viceroys were the most important, for they were of the imperial family: Sam's brother Martin and his son, Junior.

It was in Martin Insull's hands that the fate of Middle West Utilities Company ultimately rested. He never held the top office in the company—that was reserved for Sam—but as it grew larger and as Sam grew increasingly occupied with other things, Martin came

[11] Interview with Charles A. Munroe, New York, May 16, 1956 (in which Munroe was extremely frank about the entire affair) ; interview with H. C. Orton (onetime partner with Harley Clarke in a holding company system that later bought Munroe's St. Louis holdings), Chicago, Nov. 20, 1956. The incident referred to here is mentioned on p. 314, below.

more and more to be its driving force. And because Middle West itself grew so enormous, Martin Insull became a key factor in the ultimate success or failure of Samuel Insull. This fact was compounded by the fact that in Sam's eyes Martin could do no wrong.[12]

Many though Martin's virtues were, Sam's unqualified belief in him was in some respects unfortunate. Martin was a man of integrity, courage, intelligence, and imagination, but in two respects he was a far lesser man than his brother. First, he was his father's son, not his mother's; that is to say, he was long on enthusiasm and imagination and short on practicality and toughmindedness. Though he had a Cornell degree in electrical engineering and had brilliant theoretical understanding of the subject, his practical knowledge extended little beyond the ability to replace a burned-out light bulb. Where Sam, like his mother, reasoned from particulars to generalities, Martin, like his father, reasoned from generalities to particulars, and tended to think in straight logical lines, even when common sense should have told him that the path to truth is variously curved. Like a certain type of intellectual—some economists, for example— he thought in terms of models and concepts rather than pragmatically. He mastered the principles of utility management that Sam had worked out, but he failed to recognize, as Sam recognized, that the principles were simply useful guides, not infallible rules.

Second, living as he did under the colossal shadow of his brother, Martin had a strong, though probably unconscious, drive to prove that he could do great things independently of Sam. His own achievements were large and his talents would have qualified him for the presidency of any of several huge corporations, without Sam's

[12] The following sketch of Martin Insull is based upon the sources cited in note 3, above; a long study of the corporate records of Middle West Utilities Company; a large file of newspaper clippings covering his career, in the Insull Papers; a file of his public addresses and about twenty of his letters to Insull, all in the same collection; and interviews with several persons who were intimate with him in one way or another or had occasion to make special observations about him. The most important of these were his daughter, Virginia Insull Rafferty, in an interview in Morocco, Indiana, Aug. 20, 1959; Rose McKee Earley (his private secretary from 1912 to 1926), Chicago, March 14, 1957; Harry Reid (one of his principal marshals), Lexington, Kentucky, Jan. 6, 1957; Grover C. Neff (another marshal), Madison, Wisconsin, several interviews, 1953–54; C. A. Turner (Middle West's chief statistician), Chicago, several interviews, 1958–59; Ralph Stephenson (attorney for Middle West throughout its life as a corporation), Chicago, Nov. 19, Nov. 28, Nov. 29, 1956; H. C. Orton (see note 11, above); and Morse Dell Plaine (marshal to Insull, Jr., in Indiana), Chicago, Dec. 6, 1958.

influence; and yet he was never quite able to convince himself of that. (Hence, as late as 1924, when he noticed a newspaper article about an executive whose salary was $50,000 a year, he could say, sincerely and ingenuously to his secretary, Rose McKee, "Think of that, Rose. Fifty thousand dollars a year. Could any man really be worth that much money?") In spite of Martin's ability and his genuine admiration and unquestioning devotion to Sam, his latent jealousy sometimes led him to rash acts which required a major effort to undo.

Too, Martin had his own marshals, and they were hardly of the sort to encourage caution. Though Martin himself was in both appearance and manner the epitome of decorum, he had a particular affinity for audacious, colorful, free-wheeling, hard-trading types, and he surrounded himself with them, both in Middle West and in his personal friendships. In Kentucky, his marshal was Harry Reid, in New England it was Walter Wyman, in Illinois and Wisconsin it was Marshall Sampsell; and in the outside world, he did not fraternize with the John Mitchells and the James Pattens, but with men like Burt Howe of Grand Rapids, Victor Emmanuel of New York, and Harley Clarke of Chicago, free-wheelers all.

Sampsell epitomizes the lot. At war's end he was still a young man —forty-four—though he had conducted high-level business for some years. Shrewd, energetic, and ambitious, Sampsell was extremely clever at arranging deals and richly endowed with a talent for salesmanship and promotion; but sometimes he promised more than he could deliver. His methods were safe and even creative as long as he had Samuel Insull and Middle West Utilities Company behind him; but should Insull or Middle West get into trouble, his way of doing business could jeopardize the whole structure of the empire.

Thus, for example, Sampsell's acquisition of the strategic Janesville Electric Company on behalf of the burgeoning Wisconsin Power and Light Company, one of Middle West's major subsidiaries: Just after the war, William C. Durant was making his second attempt to mold a conglomerate of automotive companies into the gigantic General Motors Company. In 1919 he sought to buy the Sampson Tractor Company of Janesville—one of the city's largest industries—with a view toward expanding it into large truck production. But Durant told the town fathers that he would buy the tractor company only if he were assured of an ample supply of electric power. The owners of the small local electric company were more interested in bringing Durant's plant to the city than they were in their little company, and they doubted their ability to raise the capital and properly supervise the necessary expansion. They turned first to the Wisconsin Gas and Electric Company, a subsidiary of The North American Company, which aspired to extend its own system in the direction of central Wisconsin. Negotiations there were stalled because Wisconsin Gas and Electric Company was deeply involved in its own postwar shortages of power and capital.[13]

Sampsell learned of the situation and quickly capitalized on it. In separate interviews, he approached the Janesville businessmen and Durant. To the Janesville men he pointed out that he had the power supply and claimed he could get the capital to extend a transmission line to Janesville, if they would sell him the Janesville Electric Company in exchange for Middle West stock at a favorable price. To Durant he pointed out that he had the power supply and claimed that he could buy the Janesville Electric Company, if General Motors would advance him the cash to build the transmission line. Each accepted and the deals were made, contingent upon Sampsell's ability to fulfil his promises to both groups. Middle West then dispatched a corps of skilled engineers to do the necessary construction, and by 1924 the Janesville company was part of a system that would extend electricity to villages and farms all over central Wisconsin.

Sampsell and Martin Insull's other marshals were to Martin what Charles A. Munroe was to Insull, except that Sampsell and the others, across the board, fell a little short of being of Munroe's caliber. The danger lay not in their shortcomings but in the fact that Martin, across the board, fell a good deal short of being of Insull's

---

[13] This incident is narrated in McDonald, *Let There Be Light,* pp. 236–37. It is derived largely from corporate records of Janesville Electric Company and the correspondence bound therein, preserved in the files of Wisconsin Power and Light Company, Madison; see especially the *Minutes,* directors' meetings, Sept., 1919—Jan., 1921; *Minutes,* directors' meetings, 1921, 1922, and 1923; and a contract dated Sept. 19, 1919, between Janesville Electric Company and General Motors. A biographical sketch of Sampsell is contained in Marquis (ed.), *Who's Who in Chicago,* 1931, p. 849; Carter Harrison's *Stormy Years,* 242–47, and Ickes' *Autobiography,* pp. 111–14, make it possible to draw some interesting inferences regarding Sampsell. Otherwise, sources used for Sampsell are the same as those used for Martin Insull.

caliber. Insull found Munroe and others like him useful because he himself was stronger and more able than ten Munroes, and Munroe knew it. But Martin was only little stronger and more able than Sampsell and others like him, and both they and Martin knew it.

The built-in weaknesses were compensated, in large measure, by some built-in checks. Martin's affinity for free-wheelers was balanced by a keen eye for more down-to-earth men at the operating level. On this level, few holding companies had a collection of system operators as able as Grover Neff and Walter Hodgkins in Wisconsin, J. Paul Clayton in Illinois, J. C. Kennedy in Texas, Fred Insull in Oklahoma, and John A. McPhail in Sault Sainte Marie. Another built-in source of strength was the basic design of Middle West, to profit by long-term building, not by exploiting subsidiaries, as some holding companies did. It never developed the two institutions—privately held construction and security marketing companies—by which some holding company operators bled their operating subsidiaries.[14]

Thus the same attributes that could lead to folly could also lead to great creative achievement, and the Middle West system, as a whole, was immensely constructive, albeit never in comfortable circumstances. Witness the great Southwest: In spite of Insull's repeated protests that the area would never be more than a cactus patch, Martin poured money into its development and ended by building the vast Central and South West Utilities Company system, one of the largest non-urban utilities in the country. Witness Wisconsin: During the sixteen years Middle West operated there under Insull management, it raised and invested $14,500,000 in developing the territory. Middle West took out in dividends a total of $5,700,000; but in practice, every dividend check made out by Wisconsin Power and Light Company to the holding company was sent to Chicago, indorsed, and returned for reinvestment in additional expansion. Witness the extension of electricity everywhere: In central Texas, where in six years of operation the Insulls bought and modernized and interconnected plants that provided service—at high rates and usually part-time—to 46 small communities, extended service to 87 previ-

[14] Data on the commanders in the field are derived from a study of the subsidiaries in both corporate records and the F.T.C.'s *Utility Corporations* (especially Vols. XXXVIII and XLIV); considerable information about Neff and Hodgkins is contained in McDonald, *Let There Be Light, passim*. On the long-range purpose of Middle West, see note 23 chap. vi, above, and the accompanying text.

ously unserved communities, and in the process cut rates by an average of about 60 per cent; or central Illinois, where in eighteen years they bought and modernized and interconnected companies serving 185 communities, extended service to 210 unserved towns and more than 7,000 farms, and cut rates by more than 40 per cent; or Kentucky, where they acquired and interconnected 108 small plants, extended the first service to 206 communities, and cut rates by more than half; or west Texas, where they acquired plants in 32 towns with fulltime service and 18 with part-time service, extended the first service into 100, and cut rates in half. Before Middle West was through, its transmission lines would hum in 32 states and serve 5,000 communities.[15]

Insull's son was quite a different matter. Sam trained Martin but gave him the freedom to be himself, but both Sam and Gladys molded Junior as well as taught him. There was a difference in their aims: Sam sought to make him heir apparent to an empire and Gladys to make him a human being. The result was that he became something of both. As a businessman and in his relations with outsiders, persons whom circumstance thrust upon him, he was his father's son; with his intimates, friends he chose rather than those chosen for him, he was his mother's son. In the early twenties, when Junior first entered business, Sam's influence was more advantageous than that of Gladys. When circumstances were easy, Junior, like Gladys, had a tendency to be brilliant, quick, and charming, rather spoiled, and explosively temperamental. Sam held him in check and avoided charges of favoritism by demanding of Junior a standard of performance far higher than he expected of other men in the organization, and by withholding advancement until Junior more

[15] Annual reports of the several companies, 1912–32, minute books of Middle West Utilities for the same period, and the following documents pertaining to a 1940 investigation by the Securities Exchange Commission (copies of which are in the files of Central and South West Corporation, Chicago): Wisconsin Power and Light Company, "Historical Data"; Central Power and Light Company, "Historical Data"; Central Illinois Public Service Company, Exhibits I to X; Public Service Company of Oklahoma, exhibits submitted; Southwestern Power and Light Company, exhibits; Southwestern Gas and Electric Company, "Historical Data"; and Lake Superior District Power Company, "Historical Data." See also F.T.C., *Utility Corporations*, Vols. XXXVIII and XLIV, *passim*, and for the Wisconsin companies, McDonald, *Let There Be Light*, pp. 230–50, 275–97. On the extent of service at various times see the *McGraw Central Station Lists*.

than proved himself at each level. Later, when troubles came, Gladys' influence would be priceless. Junior had no way of knowing it, but he had, along with her flaws of temperament, imbibed her capacity for steel courage in the face of crisis.[16]

Junior took the Sheffield engineering course at Yale (his father had given him his choice of any college on earth save Harvard; Harvard was forbidden because Harvard graduates had snubbed Insull for his lack of formal education when he first came to Chicago). By the time Junior finished college, Gladys had resigned herself to losing him to business, but longed for one last period of intimacy: she wanted to take him on a grand tour of Europe in place of graduate training in engineering. Insull agreed, on condition that as they toured art museums and opera houses and concert halls and chateaus, he take time out to visit every important electric plant and meet every important electric man along the way. The trip was thus a dual education.

It also launched Junior into business with a spectacular achievement. In Milan, after visiting the renowned La Scala, Junior dutifully paid a call on the managers of the Pirelli Manufacturing Works. There he saw a revolutionary kind of underground cable, carrying electric current at almost unbelievably high voltage. The cable did not look like any Junior had ever seen. Conventional cable was wrapped in oil-soaked paper and permanently sealed in a lead sheath. The Pirelli cable lacked these trappings and had instead a hole in its center, through which oil flowed. The conventional type did not wear well against external damage, and when it heated up with an increase in the amount of electricity flowing, it was like a man trying to take a deep breath with his chest tightly strapped with adhesive. The new cable removed the adhesive; both cable and oil expanded under heat and contracted under cold so that the cable could breathe. Junior did not understand why this should make the Pirelli cable work, but he could see that it did work. And he knew that the largest conventional cable was rated at about 33,000 volts

[16] The following sketch of Insull, Jr., is based (in addition to the sources cited in notes 3 and 12, above) upon the several hundred letters between him and his parents, covering the years 1907–45, in the Insull Papers; upon Insull's comments in his "Memoirs," pp. 100–102, and at his trial, *U.S. v. Insull*, pp. 4284–86 (Nov. 1, 1934); upon the F.T.C.'s investigation of Midland United and Midland Utilities companies (*Utility Corporations*, Vol. LX); upon the testimony of Insull, Jr., before the Pecora Committee, *Hearings on Stock Exchange Practices*, pp. 1397 ff.; and upon interviews with a wide variety of his enemies and friends.

but could carry only about 23,000. This cable was carrying 80,000 volts, and Pirelli was prepared to deliver cable capable of carrying 138,000 volts.[17]

Junior at once informed his father of what he had seen, and Insull sent instructions to acquire a sample of the cable. Junior dispatched a one-foot piece of the Pirelli cable. After engineers at Commonwealth Edison had inspected it, Insull telephoned General Electric, who said it could not possibly work, and John Lieb of New York Edison, who agreed with Insull that it was worth investigating. Engineers from the two utilities went to Milan, and when the performance of the cable had been tested, Commonwealth Edison and New York Edison placed large joint orders. Pirelli licensed General Electric to manufacture the cable, and it was adopted almost immediately in all large American cities. For the third time, Insull had revolutionized urban electric supply.

After such an auspicious start, Junior might have expected an introduction into business at a fairly high level. Instead, he began as one of several clerks under C. A. Turner, the chief statistician of Middle West Utilities Company. From there he was shuffled from low-ranking job to low-ranking job, staying in each long enough to gain a working knowledge of an important aspect of the business.[18]

Then suddenly, before Insull was at all convinced that Junior was ready for it, there came an opportunity to test him in a major command, heading the properties in Indiana. Electrical development in Indiana had been unlike that in other states. By 1923 systematization had proceeded relatively far but in a helter-skelter way; about two-thirds of the state had high-line service from an assortment of loosely related or unrelated units. Of these, some were a partially integrated set of companies owned by the United Gas Improvement Company, an organization headed by Philadelphia financier Randall Morgan; a few of the rest were owned by companies outside the Insull system, the others by interests in or friendly to the Insull group. Middle West owned a number of utilities, principally in

17 This incident is narrated in Carlos Drake, *Mr. Alladin* (New York, 1947), pp. 196–97. It is such an excellent description that I have taken the liberty of following it, at one or two points, even to the exact language. Drake, a boyhood friend of Junior Insull, furnished valuable additional data on the family in an interview in Los Angeles, Sept. 11–12, 1958.
18 Interviews with C. A. Turner and Samuel Insull, Jr.

southern and central Indiana, that were in the final stages of inter-connection; Public Service of Northern Illinois and Commonwealth Edison owned a few fringe electric companies in northern Indiana; and Peoples Gas owned some old pipelines, gas wells, and some gas distribution properties. Altogether, forty or fifty companies were involved in the holdings of the two groups; in terms of value, Morgan-U.G.I. held roughly 25 per cent, Insull and associates held roughly 20 per cent, and the four major Insull companies held 55 per cent.[19]

In the early summer of 1923 circumstances induced Morgan and Insull to sit down together to rationalize the utility business in Indiana. They planned a series of corporate mergers and consolidations, but the necessary transactions were hopelessly complex. Finally, in the manner of a pair of European monarchs partitioning Poland, they simply agreed upon how it should come out and instructed their lawyers and directors to take the necessary steps. All the properties owned by both groups in northern Indiana would be put together under a single holding company, styled Midland Utilities, to be operated by Insull and owned in the proportions that the constituent predecessors were owned. The Insull management would rationalize electric and gas supply throughout the state and as rapidly as possible dissolve the corporate constituents into the parent company.

Heading Midland Utilities Company would be Junior's job. That is, it was Junior's job if he could handle it. Insull himself became president of Midland, and Junior became assistant to the president under an eminently sensible if overly cautious arrangement. Junior was given a list of persons to consult on special problems—Munroe, Lloyd, Gilchrist, and so on. He was also given four field marshals of his own: Morse Dell Plaine, inherited from U.G.I. as operating head of the northern part of Northern Indiana Gas and Electric Company; Samuel Emmett Mulholland, who was already in charge of the

---

[19] F.T.C., *Utility Corporations*, Vol. LX, is an investigation of the corporate history of Midland; the transactions regarding its formation are recorded in the minute books of the companies involved and in the annual reports of Midland; the details are recorded in full in *Minutes*, Peoples Gas Company directors' meeting June 15, 1923; personal aspects of the deal are derived from interviews with Morse Dell Plaine (who had long been a U.G.I. executive), Francis Daily (attorney for Peoples Gas), and Insull, Jr. Later, the Insulls began to buy out U.G.I. and to merge their southern Indiana properties with Midland's into a new corporation styled Midland United Company.

southern part of the territory; Charles Warren Chase, the man in charge at Gary; and Robert Feustel, who was running Fort Wayne. Junior was to make all decisions—provided his decisions were based on the suggestions of his consultants and did not conflict with the decisions of his subordinates. (As Junior put it, "I was nothing but a messenger boy. . . . They were working for me, and they could chase me out of the place.") [20]

The weakness in the arrangement was that while it kept Junior from making major mistakes, it also prevented Insull from learning whether Junior had ability. But a year later Junior proved himself in his father's eyes. He did it by making a single suggestion. A transmission line was badly needed in northern Indiana, but because of the complex of mortgages in the maze of companies that made up Midland, it seemed impossible to build it. Insull, his lawyers, and his advisers were stumped, whereupon Junior, with the practicality of the inexperienced, said, "Well, all you have to do is organize another subsidiary"; and then he spelled out a clever plan that was obvious once it was pointed out.

Insull snorted and said, "Who put that idea into your head?"

"Nobody did," said Junior. "I thought of it myself. I remembered something I learned while I was reading railroad histories, that's all."

Insull snorted again, and though Junior got no word of recognition for it, the plan was immediately executed. But from that day forward Insull began cutting the strings that bound his son. Junior had not ceased to be an institution, but now he was an institution on a higher level. Thenceforth, Insull began to allow him to assume command as a trusted executive.

And then there was Gladys. Now that Junior had entered business, Gladys was alone. She had a few close friends, and she had her two sisters, and she had Anna Nicholas, a superbly talented dressmaker and a person of serenity so sublime that she could calm even Gladys; but having these confidantes did not make her less alone, nor was she consoled because she had not lost her beauty and had a

---

[20] The remaining material on Insull, Jr., related here is derived from the transcript of a tape-recorded interview with him on Insull's marshals (see note 3, above) and on subsequent interviews.

country mansion in Libertyville, a palatial apartment in Chicago, jewels and furs and a yearly allowance in five figures to spend on clothes, and a blank check with which to buy anything else that money could buy. Impoverishment amid splendor, isolation amid a throng, boredom and frustration—these were her lot. Once she had been Somebody, and now she was merely Mrs. Somebody. Once, when they were young and on the rise, she and Sam had been together; later, when Sam was old and down, they would be together again. But in the intervening years, the years of Sam's greatness, they lived together but were miles apart, and she was nobody, a mere thing, and she was all alone.[21]

But even when she felt herself neglected, she was someone to be reckoned with. Sometimes this meant only that Sam had to cope with her capricious whims. Once, at the vast estate in Libertyville, he had planted in her absence a sizable group of trees, according to a careful design and at considerable expense. When she returned—he happened to be out of town—she saw the new trees and was incensed at what she considered their tasteless arrangement. She ordered them uprooted and rearranged.[22]

When Insull returned, he exploded. "Who in hell moved my trees?" he thundered at the grounds manager.

The manager, weakly: "Mrs. Insull told us to."

Insull, weak in turn: "Oh."

"Shall we put them back?"

"Of course not. If Mrs. Insull tells you to plant the damned things upside down, you do it."

Not all her whims were so capricious. About a year after Junior began his career in business, she began to toy with the idea of returning to the stage, and a year later she did. She formed her own company, hired seasoned professionals, and announced that she was leasing the Illinois Theatre for the first two weeks of June (1925), for a benefit performance for St. Luke's Hospital, long one of Insull's

[21] This characterization of Mrs. Insull's life during the twenties is based upon interviews with Anna Nicholas, Mrs. Tiffany Blake, Mrs. Bertha Baur, Edward J. Doyle, Ralph H. James, Philip McEnroe, Carlos Drake, Arthur Meeker, Jr., Samuel Insull, Jr., and Helen Norris, all previously cited; upon a file of newspaper clippings in the Insull Papers; and upon her extensive correspondence with Insull and their son, also in the Insull Papers.

[22] This episode was mentioned during an interview with Sam Alcover (former farm manager at Libertyville), Libertyville, April 20, 1960.

favorite charities. Thus far, it was simply another laudable civic venture, but the remainder was either colossal audacity or colossal foolishness: Gladys announced that the play would be Sheridan's *The School for Scandal* and that she would star as Lady Teazle, the lively, innocent eighteen-year-old country maiden who marries a man old enough to be her grandfather. At the time of the performance, Gladys would be fifty-six.[23]

Many were the Chicago socialites who squirmed in uncomfortable anticipation, knowing that, Society being what it is and Good Causes being what they are and Sam Insull being who he was, they would have to attend. The problem of age did not trouble those who knew Gladys. One New York reporter, covering the rehearsals (which were held at Belasco's Theatre in New York) summarized it succinctly: "Mrs. Insull," he wrote, "left the stage twenty-six years ago, when she married. She had play-acted for seven years [*sic*] as Gladys Wallis. So she must be more than thirty-three years old. But it is hard to believe so when one watches her play Lady Teazle in preparation for the Chicago opening." Yet it had, after all, been more than a quarter of a century since she left the stage.[24]

But those who attended out of duty departed in delight. In two weeks the play netted $137,749, and all Chicago was impressed by Gladys' performance. She was bombarded by telegrams and letters of congratulations, many of them from people who knew theater well and scarcely knew Gladys at all.[25] Arthur Meeker, Jr., perhaps Chicago's most hypercritical and hypersensitive drama critic, summarized the reaction in his review and in a personal note to Gladys:

"I have seen Ellen van Volkenburg, and Mary Young, and Ethel Barrymore [as Lady Teazle], but none of them could approach Mrs. Insull for delicacy of touch and humor. It is not only that she is the most beautiful of them all; she read the lines with so much archness and grace, and interpreted the varying moods of the charac-

[23] All Chicago newspapers, May 22–30, 1925.

[24] This story was carried in the several Hearst newspapers—for example, the *Chicago Herald and Examiner*—for May 23, 1925. See also *Drama*, XVI (November, 1925), 46; XVII (December, 1926), 68; F. L. Collins, "A Woman Whose Dream Came True," in *Delineator*, CXI (October, 1927), 12; *Chicago Daily News*, May 23, 1925.

[25] "The School for Scandal," a file of letters and documents in the Insull Papers; Insull to Chauncey B. Borland (secretary, St. Luke's Hospital), June 23, 1925; Insull to H. O. Edmonds (treasurer, St. Luke's Hospital), June 23, 1925; Borland to Insull, June 24, 1925; Edmonds to Insull, June 23, 1925; all in the Insull Papers.

ter with such a fine sense of values that . . . it was quite the most charming and exquisite and distinguished high comedy performance I've ever seen!"[26]

It was a glorious moment, and it was little tarnished by the indifferent outcome of her short-lived effort to organize a repertoire company, in which she participated largely as producer and director.[27] But it was only a moment, and when it was over she had to return to real life.

And real life, between Gladys and Sam, was not all whims and colliding temperaments and surface civility stretched tight and thin over an abnormally strained marriage. They were bound together by something stronger than the thing that separated them. In part, it was Junior; in part, it was that their love was as deep as it was unsatisfying. And, in spite of everything, neither completely lost sight of the quality of the other. So they went on together, like a pair of amnesia victims, each dimly recalling that he loved the other, and each having forgotten where the other lived. They tolerated one another, and he tried to amuse her, and she tried to amuse herself, and for almost twenty lonely years that was all there was.

Once, in the mid-twenties, she made a strong effort to interest him in one of her favorite hobbies. After their rift, she had gone through a long period of voracious reading. From her original first choice, poetry and plays, she wandered or groped through theology and philosophy, and then to history. For years she collected and read all she could find on Napoleon, until she became as well versed in the

26 Meeker's story in *Chicago Herald and Examiner,* June 2, 1925, and Meeker to Mrs. Insull, June 3, 1925, in the Insull Papers; see also all other Chicago newspapers for June 2, 1925. Meeker later wrote—in his book, *Chicago With Love* (New York, 1955) —condemning Mrs. Insull's performance, and in an interview with me, in New York, January 3, 1958, he said it was "awful." It is understandable that he might have been squeamish about condemning the performance in his review had his reaction been unfavorable, but his letter to Mrs. Insull is marked by unrestrained enthusiasm, enough to make one skeptical of his later denials. If the newspaper reports are biased because of fear of Insull—which seems unlikely, in view of the fact that Chicago newspapers showed no reluctance to attack Insull himself when they saw fit—obtaining an objective appraisal of the performance is difficult. I have attempted to do so by asking the opinion of a number of Chicagoans who saw the play, whose tastes in drama I trust, and who either did not particularly care for Mrs. Insull or did not know her (for example, Mrs. Bertha Baur and Theo Noel) , and the consensus seems to be that she gave a surprisingly brilliant performance.

27 On this venture, see, for example, *Chicago Herald and Examiner,* Aug. 19, Sept. 6, Sept. 9, 1926; Oct. 29, 1927; Oct. 2, 1932; *Chicago Journal,* Sept. 8, Oct. 4, 1926; *Chicago Tribune,* Oct. 25, 1926; April 23, Oct. 31, 1927; Dedmon, *Fabulous Chicago,* pp. 324-25.

subject as most experts. Insull had read widely in history, and had read one or two biographies of Napoleon, but there was so much to know, and he could see no reason for reading so much about one man. Repeatedly, she explained it to him: "Sam, you should learn about that man, and about what happened to him. If you don't, that's what's going to happen to you."[28]

[28] Interview with Samuel Insull, Jr. The observations regarding Gladys' reading habits prior to 1920 are from an interview with Helen Norris, former librarian for Commonwealth Edison Company, who supervised the establishment of the Insull library at the house in Libertyville.

CHAPTER X *The Enemies*

In the hero-worshipping postwar decade, Insull became the Babe Ruth, the Jack Dempsey, the Red Grange of the business world. The people—butchers, bakers, candlestick-makers who invested their all in his stocks—fairly idolized him, and even titans viewed him with awe. He measured up to America's image of itself: a rich, powerful, self-made giant, ruthless in smashing enemies, generous and softhearted in dealing with the weak. His doings, small and large, became a great spectator sport, and they were reported and followed accordingly.

Newspapers described his business deals and the behavior of his stocks on the market in the jargon of the sports page. Sample, from a day on which the stock trend happened to be downward:[1]

Shortly before midday . . . leading shares here were shriveling under a selling fire which at times approached white heat. As Commonwealth Edison broke through its previous resistance level of 230 and went reeling down 10 points it appeared as if the professionals had finally found the range of the Insull stocks. Insull Utility tumbled 5 to scrape a new bottom of 20 and other issues in the group were being similarly harassed. But when things looked their worst here the New York tape was streaming out a story of briskly advancing stocks. Short sellers here reversed positions, but not in time to avoid a good deal of squeezing. As the covering progressed Edison recovered half its loss and Insull snapped back to within a fraction of 25. Other issues followed.

When a generous act came to a reporter's attention—such as the time Insull sent a young Negro singer to Europe to study at his

[1] Thomas Furlong, in the *Chicago Tribune*, June 4, 1931.

expense or sponsored a European trip for his favorite Pullman conductor—the event was treated with all the reverence due Babe Ruth for hitting a home run to save the life of a hospitalized child. When the city room was dull, editors sent young reporters to interview Insull for words of wisdom or secrets of success. Sample questions and answers:[2]

Q: What are the most important elements in success?
A: Health, honesty, hard work, firmness of character, firmness of action, imagination, and keeping everlastingly at it.
Q: What is your advice to young men?
A: Aim for the top. There is plenty of room here. There are so few at the top it is almost lonely.
Q: What is your greatest ambition in life?
A: To hand down my name as clean as I received it.

Except when dealing with newspaper photographers (for whom he had a strong dislike acquired in Victorian London, where only royalty and criminals had their pictures in newspapers), Insull bore the demands of the role gracefully, even when it became extremely taxing. In the late twenties, for example, Chicagoans began to telephone him at home, and he handled the calls personally, with even temper, and never sought a private listing. ("Mr. Insull, I don't want to be rude, but some of us fellows got to talking, and we wondered, well . . . Are you Jewish?" Answer: "Not as far as I know. I have never had the inclination or the time to gather information about my forebears, but for four or five generations back we have been English nonconformists, chapel people." Or, "Mr. Insull, my husband has been out of work for two months, and we've got a notice saying they're going to cut off our gas, and I've got to have gas or I can't heat the baby's milk, and . . ." Answer: "All right, madam, give me your name and address, and if you'll send one dollar toward your bill, to show you are in earnest, I'll not let them cut off your service. Oh, by the bye: send your husband to the gas com-

2 See, for example, the *Chicago Tribune*, Aug. 31, Dec. 24, 1928; Jan. 16, Jan. 17, 1930; *Chicago Evening Post*, Nov. 12, 1927; Sept. 8, Dec. 24, 1928; Sept. 19, 1929; *Chicago Herald and Examiner*, June 8, 1928; Jan. 17, 1930; *Chicago Morning Mail*, Jan. 5, 1929; *Chicago American*, Sept. 18, Sept. 19, Nov. 27, 1929; Jan. 16, Jan. 22, 1930; the *Chicago Daily News*, Nov. 27, 1929; Chicago *British American*, July 17, 1927; Sept. 28, 1929; Chicago *Journal of Commerce*, Dec. 24, 1928; Jan. 22, 1930; *The Chicagoan*, Sept. 28, 1929. The interview quoted here is in the *Chicago American*, July 26, 1930.

pany employment office. Perhaps we can find something for him to do.") [3]

Among his peers, in that lonely world at the top, Insull was also celebrated. He had been decorated by foreign governments, awarded honorary degrees by American and foreign universities, and honored by a number of professional societies, and negotiations were pending to knight him. In the rarified atmosphere of British and continental aristocracy he was not always sure whether he should wear white tie or black tie, but he was accepted in that world, moved about in it with considerable ease, and had many friends there. His favorite European friends were men whose specialty was high-level international intrigue: among others, the celebrated Italian adventurer-patriot-poet Gabriele D'Annunzio, the influential Irish political leader T. P. O'Connor, the mysterious and fabulously wealthy Greek munitions maker Sir Basil Zaharoff. [4]

But not everybody loved Samuel Insull. No man ever started as an office boy and built a multibillion-dollar empire without alienating anyone along the way, and Insull was no exception. Over the years, three important groups developed a deep-seated hostility toward him. The first group, Chicago's Gold Coast social and economic elite, wore a face of friendship masking strong resentment; they— like the General Electric Company—resented the way he pushed them around and dragged them, kicking and protesting, into the twentieth century; but they would not become his active enemies as long as he was on top, for they feared and admired him and he had, after all, helped them make millions of dollars. The second group was the New York financial community. These men resented his

[3] Interview with James Kilgallen (a veteran Hearst reporter), New York, Jan. 3, 1958; interview with Nate Gross (a veteran Chicago reporter), Chicago, Dec. 19, 1958; the *Chicago Tribune*, Jan. 17, 1930; interview with Philip McEnroe, Los Angeles, Sept. 10, 1958; interview with Samuel Insull, Jr.

[4] The *Chicago Daily News*, May 4, June 15, 1925; the *Chicago Tribune*, June 19, 1925, March 7, 1926; the *Saturday Evening Post*, Aug. 1, 1925; *Forbes*, March 15, 1925; *Chicago American*, March 28, 1930; *Chicago Herald and Examiner*, March 30, 1930; *Chicago British American*, May 15, 1930; collection of honorary degrees, citations, and autographed photographs, in the Insull Papers; Marquis W. Childs, in the *New Republic*, Sept. 21, 1932, and Nov. 22, 1933; Berry, "Mr. Samuel Insull," pp. 27, 41–42; interview with Colonel Ralph H. James, Chicago, May 20, 1958. According to James, who had influential connections in London, Insull could have been knighted without difficulty but aspired to be given the Order of Merit, which was virtually impossible, there being, by design, only about twenty holders of the order at a time.

radicalism, his attitudes toward government and labor, his outspoken contempt, and his dependence on London instead of New York for financing; but they would become overtly hostile only if doing so gave greater promise of profit than did co-operation. The third group was made up of the perennially unsuccessful political reformers in Chicago, particularly those connected with the University of Chicago; they disapproved of Insull because they were convinced that no one who was not absolutely corrupt could be as successful in Chicago politics as Insull had been; they were continuously hostile and no more effectual than a single dissident stockholder. But in the late twenties, as Insull's stature and power waxed enormous and as his influence and reputation spread over the nation, the caliber and enmity of his foes grew apace.

Prior to 1922, the absolute ruler of Gold Coast society was Mrs. Edith Rockefeller McCormick. After the debacle of the McCormick divorce, Mrs. McCormick's logical successor as social leader was the wife of Samuel Insull; that is, it would have been so had Insull's wife been anyone but Gladys. Not that Gladys lacked the talent. She could dazzle appropriately, direct appropriately, and charm appropriately, but she had two characteristics that disqualified her for the role: She did not think it worth the doing, and she regarded most of the wives she knew as pretentious and shallow fools.[5]

Had Insull been free to do so, he might have emulated Gladys' example. But he had acquired—or to him had fallen—the task of running Chicago, and that included, to a large extent, the social life of the Gold Coast. He could demonstrate his contempt for the postures of high society in various ways, but he had learned and accepted the first burden of leadership: To rule one must accept the conventions of those one rules.

Insull's direct dealings with the Gold Coast were concerned largely with charitable and civic activities. In his personal charities he con-

---

[5] Dedmon, *Fabulous Chicago*, pp. 301–16; Mrs. Carter H. Harrison, "Strange to Say——" (Chicago, 1949), pp. 100–102; Meeker, *Chicago with Love*, pp. 251–53; interview with Mrs. Bertha Baur (who, after a time, did succeed Mrs. McCormick), Chicago, Dec. 7, 1957; interview with Mrs. Tiffany Blake (wife of the chief editorial writer for the *Chicago Tribune*), Chicago, Feb. 4, 1958; interview with Miss Anna Nicholas (the dressmaker for Marshall Field and Company, who was in a position to know the ins and outs of Gold Coast society), Chicago, Dec. 31, 1959.

tinued to specialize in individual cases; in the late twenties, when his total salary averaged almost half a million dollars a year, he gave away more than he earned, supporting his personal pension list and financing such unconventional projects as the Chinese Y.M.C.A. and the education of African doctors. But his seat of power obliged him to undertake charitable and civic ventures on a much larger scale than this, and in executing these undertakings he treated Chicago's aristocracy like so many subordinates. The ladies, particularly, thought him rude, but their complaints, even to their husbands, were uttered behind closed doors, and few dared complain aloud. Sometimes, as when he headed drives for the more fashionable and conventional charities, success elicited more than enough admiration to compensate for the resentment he stirred up. If Chicago needed a new hospital, for example, he pledged perhaps $50,000 personally, then picked up his telephone and called a score of Chicago's wealthiest to a conference at his convenience, at which he simply told them how much he expected them to contribute, and they obliged. When he demanded their support for a less popular activity, such as his work on behalf of Negroes, the city's aristocracy complied almost as quickly but far more grudgingly.[6]

(Either way, Insull's leadership cost them not at all. As often as he made demands of them, he lined their pockets with profits from his business dealings. The simplest and most lucrative means was to cut them in on an underwriting syndicate. In floating a new issue of securities, it is conventional to form a group to guarantee the sale. Doing so is normally no more than a formality, but a necessary one because security marketers cannot carry enough idle cash to guarantee the success of every issue. To the underwriters, the risk is nominal and the commission is high. Typically, a broker or investment banker made up a list of prospective underwriters and sent

[6] Charities File, in the Insull Papers; Insull's federal income tax returns, 1925–31, partly in the files of Murphy, Lanier, and Quinn, Chicago, and partly in the Insull Papers; interviews with Mrs. Bertha Baur, Mrs. Tiffany Blake, Stanley Field, Edward Quinn (Insull's tax lawyer), and Arthur Meeker, Jr., previously cited; several interviews with Harold L. Stuart and Abner J. Stilwell; interview with Herman Waldeck (former vice-president of the Continental Bank), Chicago, Dec. 8, 1957; the *Chicago Tribune*, May 25, 1925; Sept. 8, 1928, Jan. 17, Feb. 1, Oct. 1, 1930; June 13, 1931; *Chicago Journal*, Sept. 8, 1928; *Chicago American*, March 10, 1931; Chicago *Journal of Commerce*, Dec. 24, 1928; Jan. 22, 1930; *Chicago Herald and Examiner*, Jan. 17, Oct. 1, 1930; June 14, 1931; the *Chicago Daily News*, March 10, 1931.

each an unsolicited note, stating that he had been placed on the list to guarantee, say, $500,000 of the issue. If the recipient did not withdraw his name—and no one in his right mind would—he received a second note a few weeks later, announcing that the sale had been completed and inclosing a check for, say, $20,000 as his commission. Insull, like other large sellers of corporate securities, used this device, and like others he found that it made warm friends of many who might otherwise have remained aloof. He also adapted it to real estate deals, whenever he promoted a huge suburban development to furnish passengers for his interurban railways—another practice that was fairly common.) [7]

It was in civic musical ventures, particularly in opera, that Insull's actions epitomized his whole relations with Chicago's moneyed classes. His early associations with opera in Chicago were conventional enough, and a casual observer might have accepted his statement (as some did after a closer look) that "I am not in any sense an authority on Grand Opera, except as to what it costs." He attended regularly from his first days in Chicago, later bought a box every season, and after 1910, when Oscar Hammerstein's Manhattan Opera Company failed in New York and moved to Chicago, he became a minor guarantor. When Harold and Edith Rockefeller McCormick, the major guarantors, removed their support in 1922, it was inevitable that Insull (along with his friends Mitchell and Shedd) should inherit the responsibility. He began predictably enough: He rounded up a group of patrons who pledged a guarantors' fund of $500,000 annually for five years, introduced a rigid budget and cost control system, incorporated various economies in such areas as storage of scenery, and was able to expand the annual fare and remain well within the guaranteed deficit. [8]

But soon strange things began to happen, things that were rooted in Insull's childhood. As a poor working boy in London, he had gone

[7] For general descriptions of the way such things work see Judge Harold Medina's decision in *U.S.* v. *Morgan, Stanley, et al.* (1946) ; Reclich, *Molding of American Banking*, II, 304–423; Ferdinand Pecora, *Wall Street under Oath* (New York, 1939) , pp. 41–69. For abundant details see the Pecora Committee, *Hearings of the Subcommittee of the Committee on Banking and Currency . . . on Practices of Stock Exchanges* (Washington, 1933) ; Part V concerns the Insulls.

[8] Insull, "Memoirs," pp. 106–8; interview with Jesse D. Scheinmann (former auditor of the Chicago Civic Opera) , Los Angeles, Sept. 11, 1958; "Insull Tells Business Side of Opera," in *Chicago's Commerce*, Dec. 12, 1925; Dedmon, *Fabulous Chicago*, pp. 301–16.

without meals to afford a sixpenny seat in the upper gallery, and
though he grew up to sit with bejeweled ladies in the finest boxes,
his heart never left the gallery or the people in it. Opera, he believed, was for the people, and soon after he took charge of opera in
Chicago Insull set out to democratize it. Some of his actions could
hardly have offended aristrocratic patrons; for example, he saw to it
that increasing numbers helped pay the cost. He reduced the mini-
mum pledge for guarantors to $1,000, and later to as little as $100,
and increased the number of guarantors to 2,000, then to 2,500, and
later to more than 3,000.[9]

Other actions were less palatable. Opera performances were
deliberately set for the same nights as the performances of the
Chicago Symphony Orchestra, so that those of more aesthetic and
aristocratic tastes could consider themselves silently invited to attend
the latter instead. Most spectacularly, friction developed with Chicago's most celebrated opera star, Mary Garden, who preferred roles
sung in French. Given Insull's attitude, the friction was inevitable.
"There are," he said, "four hundred thousand German-Americans in
Chicago, and a quarter of a million Italian-Americans, and not a
handful of Franco-Americans." To him it made no sense to stage
more than one or two French operas a year. After one season under
Insull's management, Miss Garden left, insisting that Insull was
unable to comprehend modern opera. When she left, some of her
followers left with her.[10]

But the clearest expression of Insull's goal of democratatizing (or,
as Miss Garden would have it, vulgarizing) Chicago opera, and the
most blatant expression of his contempt for the Gold Coast, came
when he decided to give opera a new and permanent home. His plan
was to build a forty-two-story office building which would house, on
the street level, the Chicago Civic Opera. It would be financed by
selling $10,000,000 of first mortgage bonds to the Metropolitan Life
Insurance Company and $10,000,000 of preferred stock to the opera-
loving public, largely through Insull's employees and his agencies

[9] Interview with Scheinmann, previously cited; the *Chicago Daily News,* Oct. 19, 1931;
Chicago Evening Post, Nov. 13, 1931.
[10] Berry, "Mr. Samuel Insull," pp. 47, 48, 55–56; interview with John Panne Gasser (a
tenor who sang with the Chicago Civic Opera, as well as other major American and
European companies), Chicago, Aug. 17, 1959; Mary Garden and Louis Biancolli, *Mary
Garden's Story* (New York, 1951).

for selling the stocks of his companies. The common stock, representing ownership and voting control, would be held in trust for a non-profit organization called the Chicago Music Foundation. Rentals from the office building would support the interest and dividends on the bonds and preferred stock, and leave enough to finance the opera. Over the years, the bonds and the preferred stock would be retired, thus endowing the foundation with clear title to a huge office building whose rentals would pay for opera on a lavish scale and finance other musical activities, making Chicago the musical capital of the world.

As a financial scheme, the plan was brilliant, and its success seemed assured when Insull himself leased a large part of the office space for his own expanding enterprises. Construction was begun in January, 1928, and even when it turned out that the building would cost (as buildings always do) somewhat more than was anticipated, necessitating $3,385,000 in bank loans in addition to the planned financing, the plan seemed foolproof. It had only one flaw. The building was completed in the fall of 1929; the first opera in the new house was staged ten days after the stock market crash.[11]

The most striking thing about the building, however, was not the timing of the construction, but the opera house it contained. As one critic remarked (this was much later, for no one saw fit to criticize the plans as long as Insull was around), Insull had the architect visit every major opera house in the world and then return and build one unlike any of them. As construction proceeded, suspense mounted, for though the general plans were made public, the interior of the opera house itself was kept secret even from the executive committee of the opera. Not until opening night, November 4, 1929, when the audience began to arrive, did anyone see the interior. The sight was awesome, the design majestic. Accoustically the hall was superb. Visually it was excellent, every seat having an unobstructed view. The stage was huge, and it had power equipment that made possible almost instant changes of scenery. But design, view, acoustics, stage, and all went virtually unnoticed because of one astounding fact:

---

[11] The *Chicago Tribune,* Jan. 26, July 7, July 24, 1929; Oct. 28, 1930; *Chicago Herald and Examiner,* Jan. 26, July 24, Aug. 7, 1929; Oct. 28, 1930; *Time Magazine,* Nov. 4, 1929; *Chicago American,* Oct. 28, 1930; all Chicago newspapers throughout the summer and fall of 1929.

Insull had built an opera house without a single prominent box. Bejeweled and befurred ladies and their penguin escorts would have to sit in anonymous, proletarian darkness, just like people in the sixpenny gallery.[12]

No one has ever quite successfully described, or even identified, the inner circle of financial power in New York, "the Club." The Middle West, gifted with the insight of paranoia, always instinctively knew that it existed; and in the 1890's the Populists thought they knew what it was, as did, later, a long succession of others—William Jennings Bryan, the elder LaFollette, Henry Ford, Gerald Nye, a few of the Communists of the early thirties, Joseph McCarthy, Cyrus S. Eaton. To them, its outlines were shadowy and mysterious, its methods devious and conspiratorial. It could neither been seen nor touched, but its influence was everywhere; among its identifiable attributes were eastern seaboard aristocracy, the Ivy League (especially Harvard), Wall Street, Washington; the adhesives to its web were secret syndicate lists and blacklists, social connections, marriages; at its center was the House of Morgan.[13]

In truth, its outlines were clear. J. P. Morgan and Company, a

[12] The house had thirty-one boxes, set at the back of the theatre as a sort of middle balcony. Persons seated in the boxes can be seen only from the stage, the orchestra, and the first few rows of seats, and then only with difficulty. In connection with this subject, I have interviewed a score of persons, notably Mrs. Bertha Baur, who was a member of the most important women's group, the Friends of Opera; Stanley Field, who was more or less in charge of construction; John Evers, Insull's private secretary and the person to whom Insull delegated principal executive authority in the matter; Jesse Scheinmann, the auditor; Abner J. Stilwell, the banker who inherited responsibility for running the venture after Insull's financial collapse; Samuel Insull, Jr.; Arthur Meeker, Jr.; and John Panne Gasser. Later, many complained about the house; whatever their rationalizations, it is clear that the absence of the traditional horseshoe boxes underlay their feelings.

[13] The following description is based upon the multivolume senatorial *Hearings on Practices of Stock Exchanges* (the Pecora Committee) ; *Report of* [the Pujo] *Committee appointed . . . to Investigate the Concentration of Control of Money and Credit*, 62d Cong., 3d sess., House Report 1593 (Washington, 1913) ; Ferdinand Pecora, *Wall Street under Oath;* Redlich, *Molding of American Banking*, II, pp. 304–423; *J. P. Morgan and Company*, a mimeographed case study prepared by the Harvard Graduate School of Business Administration; the files of the *Wall Street Journal* from about 1900 to 1933 (from which I tabulated issues of bonds, by houses, for the 1920's) ; *U.S. v. Morgan, Stanley, et al.* (1946) ; and interviews with many financiers, bankers, and former bankers, investment as well as commercial, notably Harold L. Stuart, Abner J. Stilwell, Max McGraw, and Edward Eagle Brown of Chicago, Cyrus Eaton of Cleveland, and Arthur Taylor of New York.

private commercial and investment bank with branches and powerful connections in London and Paris, was at its core. There were
three other commercial banks in the Morgan group: The Guaranty
Trust Company, the Bankers Trust Company, and the First National
Bank.[14] Each of these had an investment banking affiliate, and these
seven, together with Bonbright and Company, another bond house,
formed the Morgan group. Allied with the Morgan group was the
Jewish investment banking community (there being no Jewish
commercial banking community), a group gathered around Kuhn,
Loeb and Company. The two gigantic Rockefeller banks—the
Chase National and the National City—and their investment affiliates were not quite in and not quite out of the Club; they remained
independent but had not engaged in any major conflicts with the
Morgan group since 1907, and had often co-operated with it. In a
general, spheres-of-influence way, Morgan dominated the financing
of industrial securities, Kuhn, Loeb handled railroads, and Chase
took care of oils. Government bonds were divided.

What held it together, though less concrete, was also clear. Essentially, the same kinds of fibers bound it as connected the Insull
empire, except that (after the elder J. P. Morgan died) it had no
single dominating personality. Admission to the Club was determined by social, family, business, and educational connections;
staying in it depended upon conformity to its highly formalized
proprieties; attaining power required talent at performing the essential work of the group.

The work was to make money from—and only from—legitimate
and necessary financial services, lending money and marketing and
trading securities. Obvious as that might seem, investigators and
politicians and students by the score overlooked it and read into the
workings of the New York financial community a sinister and devious
design to dominate all American business, either for the sake of
power or for the sake of the profits of running industrial and commercial enterprises. The evidence upon which this misreading

---

[14] The Irving Trust Company was sometimes reckoned as a Morgan bank, but though
it was always friendly it was apparently not one of the group. The First National was
actually an independent house but so intimately associated with the Morgan group—
originally because of the close personal friendship between its president, George F.
Baker, and the elder J. P. Morgan—that for all practical purposes it must be regarded
as part of it.

rested was the presence of Morgan partners on the boards of directors of multitudes of corporations. Their presence was, in fact, only an indication that the companies were among Morgan's accounts; when Morgan sold a company's securities, Morgan protected itself and its customers by placing a director, as a sort of private policeman, to make sure that the company was honestly and competently managed.

The group was rarely creative: It did not support the new, the radical, the different. Quite the opposite: It sought stability, order, rationalization—and financing by New York—in every major field of economic endeavor and opposed innovation as it opposed such other disorderly activities as embezzlement and competition. Because it regularly brought order out of chaos, its benefactions were large; but because in doing so it stifled creative nonconformity, the social cost of its benefactions was sometimes immeasurable.

For outsiders, it had two simple rules, and it neither forgave nor forgot transgressors: (1) Do not upset the order of things, and (2) Look to New York for financial leadership.

Insull violated both rules, and countless minor rules, regularly and on a huge scale. He upset everything—relations between business and labor, between business and government, between business and business. Worst of all, he and Harold Stuart had upended order in the financial world itself. And not only did he refuse to look to New York for leadership and financial backing, he expressed contempt for New York bankers in both his words and his deeds. As Charles Stuart (Harold's brother and the manager of the New York branch of Halsey, Stuart) put it: "Mr. Insull wouldn't let bankers tell him how to run his business, and when it touched his affairs he told them how to run theirs. He pushed bankers around. He said the only way to deal with them was to get so you could call them on the phone and make them come to your office to do business. Maybe you could do that in Chicago, but you couldn't do it in New York. These New York fellows were jealous of their prerogatives, and if you wanted to get along you had to be deferential to them and keep your opinions to yourself. Mr. Insull wouldn't, and that made bad blood between them. Real bad blood."[15]

[15] Interview with Charles Stuart, New York, July 30, 1957. That this was Insull's attitude toward bankers was attested by virtually ever banker or financier I interviewed

Bad blood became something more in 1928 as a consequence of two unrelated events. Until after the war, central station issues had constituted only a minor portion of the whole bond business and, indeed, New York had considered them as hardly respectable. The investment affiliates of some of the large commercial banks had marketed the bonds of large-city utilities, but otherwise Halsey, Stuart stood almost alone as a major house willing and able to market utility issues. After the postwar money drought ended in 1923, the nation's utilities began to expand with explosive force, and their offerings to investors suddenly became the most important segment of the total bond business. By 1926 new utility bonds and debentures approached a billion dollars a year, and Halsey, Stuart, together with lesser houses that participated in the bond business influenced or controlled by Insull, had by far the greatest share of the business.[16]

Utility bonds were unusually lucrative; they afforded hidden opportunities for profits that dwarfed the visible profits of commissions on initial sales. For one thing, because utilities issued bonds regularly and in relatively large quantities—at an average of about 10 per cent of a company's total capitalization every year—they made possible huge secondary market profits. The house that marketed the bonds of a particular utility had the exclusive function of protecting both buyer and issuer by "making a market" for the bonds: trading them on the open market to stabilize their prices within a certain range. Furthermore, it continued this function even when new issues were not being offered. Only small purchases were necessary; $50,000 daily might be all the trading in the bonds of a $100,000,000 corporation. But over a period of time the bond house could accumulate large holdings at the bottom of the permitted range, do everyone a service by running the price up to the top of the range, and then sell its accumulated holdings to a single institutional buyer at the market price and at a sizable profit. Over the life

---

—Harold Stuart, McGraw, Eaton, Stilwell, Brown, and Waldeck, previously mentioned, as well as several others—and by most members of Insull's high command whom I interviewed.

16 For an excellent brief description of this development see Redlich, *Molding of American Banking*, II, 380–81. The best way to trace it is by tabulating, from the files of the *Wall Street Journal*, participation by firms by classes of issue. Occasionally the *Journal* printed yearly and quarterly summaries—for example, in its issues of February 11 and April 21, 1928—but for most of the period tabulations must be made from weekly summaries.

of a bond issue, the investment bank that managed it could make as much in this manner as the entire face value of the issue. Again, utility issues offered another special source of profit. Utilities were being consolidated as rapidly as they were being expanded, and with every reorganization it was necessary to call in all the securities issued before consolidation and issue new ones. Reorganization yielded a double commission on the total capitalization of the consolidating companies. For these reasons, financing utilities was many times as profitable as running them. Few outsiders knew this, and to Insull's misfortune, he never learned it; he saw no more need to learn the inner economics of the bond business than to learn those of a law firm or any of a number of businesses that furnished him services. But by 1927 utility financing had become so large and so lucrative, even in the obvious areas of profit, that even the most myopic bond salesman could not fail to see it.[17]

As they discovered the utility business, bond houses scrambled to gain a share in its security marketing. Finding the field not entirely open to newcomers, they sought to capture control of utilities themselves. Starting in 1924 and 1925, and increasingly after 1926, minor bond houses began to invade the holding company world—some by creating new holding companies for the sole purpose of acquiring operating companies in order to get their security business, others by a more audacious (and twice profitable) means, the formation of investment trusts which sold their securities to the public and used the proceeds to acquire control of existing holding companies.[18]

In 1927 the House of Morgan determined to enter this happy pursuit and thereby eliminate waste, corruption, disorder, and an expensive oversight. Characteristically, Morgan set out to end the rivalry by bringing the entire electric and gas utility business under

[17] These operations are generally described in *U.S. v. Morgan, Stanley, et al.* Curiously, despite the abundance of materials on market operations, none of the investigations sheds much light on just how money was made thereby. For this description I am indebted primarily to Willis S. Baur (Chicago, Oct. 22, 1958), who was a bond salesman for Halsey, Stuart in the twenties and subsequently became a successful broker and market operator in his own right. For information on the growth and financing of utilities during the late 1920's see the F.T.C., *Utility Corporations, 72A*, especially pp. 23–39, 535–98.

[18] *Ibid.*, pp. 75–80. Although this volume is essentially a vitriolic polemic against the evils of holding companies, it considerably underrates the importance of investment banking houses in causing these evils.

the control of a single, Morgan-dominated super-holding company. The United Corporation was to be in the utility industry what American Telephone and Telegraph was in the telephone industry —whose bond business, by no coincidence, was under exclusive Morgan control. The United Corporation was the most ambitious venture ever undertaken by Morgan: Its capitalization would be twenty times that of United States Steel.[19]

As soon as this decision was made, all the impalpable might that was Morgan began to pervade the utility industry. Almost immediately, most of the major holding company groups controlled in New York came into the orbit of the United Corporation. Some came by way of formal corporate affiliations, but more came by way of the nebulous and informal means that characterized Morgan's operations—a complex of directorships involving somebody's son, somebody on a syndicate list, somebody else's brother in law, somebody else's former college roommate.[20]

Standing outside were three major groups and a handful of minor ones. The major groups were the Insull group, the Byllesby (Standard Gas and Electric) group, and the Doherty (Cities Service) group. By the middle of 1928 the latter two had ceased to count. The Byllesby group came under the domination of the New

[19] F.T.C., *Utility Corporations*, Vol. LII, *passim.*
[20] It should be understood that what was realized was not operating managerial control but only such control or influence as was necessary to capture bond accounts. Unified managerial control was apparently contemplated but never realized. The companies that formally came under the influence of the United Corporation were Columbia Gas and Electric Corporation, Consolidated Gas Company of New York, Niagara Hudson Power Corporation, Public Service Corporation of New Jersey, United Gas Improvement Company, and Commonwealth and Southern; these companies sold about 25 per cent of the nation's electric power. F.T.C., *Utility Corporations*, LII, *passim*, 72A, 38, 76, 176. The indirect influence covered even more. Two other groups, Electric Bond and Share and United Light and Power, were in the Morgan domain. For example, Electric Bond and Share was headed by S. Z. Mitchell, whose son, S. A. Mitchell, was an influential director of the company and many of its subsidiaries and also a director of Bonbright and Company, Morgan's "second-string" bond house, and of the Irving Trust Company (see note 14, above). The only evidence of the switch in dominant influences in some other holding company groups—for example, The North American Company —is that their bond accounts changed from non-Morgan houses to Morgan houses. Highly useful and reasonably complete and reliable tables of the Morgan web of directorships are contained in Anna Rochester's *Rulers of America: A Study of Finance Capital* (New York, 1936), Appendix D. Miss Rochester was an avowed Marxist, and much of her work reflects a semihysterical hostility toward all capitalists, but her tables were prepared carefully from evidence in the Pecora Committee hearings. See also the Pecora Committee, *Hearings on Stock Exchange Practices*, Part 2, especially pp. 370 ff.

York Jewish investment banking house of Ladenburg, Thalmann (one banker's explanation: "They were cutting the cake, and that was the only piece the Jews were going to be allowed.") The Doherty group was to remain outside, partly because H. L. Doherty was regarded as too rough-and-tumble to deal with and partly because he was clever enough to give a share of his most lucrative activities to the right people. Thus for all practical purposes Insull stood alone as the one great utility operator independent of New York—and he was the key to an annual bond business running into hundreds of millions.[21]

Just as New York was preparing to devour the Nation's utilities, Insull did something that must have appeared to eastern bankers as audacious if indeed not an open declaration of war. Early in 1928, Middle West Utilities Company made a pair of purchases—it was Martin Insull's doing, but Sam approved it—that were eminently logical but far from sensible: he bought the holding company systems controlled by A. E. Fitkin and by Victor Emmanuel. The properties of these companies were well situated for efficient interconnection with many of Middle West's properties and with each other, but they were extremely and dangerously pyramided. What was worse, they also operated in fourteen of the seventeen eastern

[21] F.T.C., *Utility Corporations*, Vols. XXXVI and LXVI, *passim;* 72*A*, 79–81; on Ladenburg, Thalmann, Byllesby, and Doherty. I have heard several bankers—for example, Abner J. Stilwell—assert that Ladenburg, Thalmann's control over Byllesby was "allowed" by Morgan as a part of "cutting the cake" to give the Jewish investment banking houses a minor participation in utility financing. As to outside houses, Halsey, Stuart was the principal house generally thought of as being completely dependent upon Insull's business, but there were others, including Howe, Snow and Co., E. H. Rollins and Company (these two became connected with Insull financing as a result of the Fitkin and Emmanuel purchases, as described in the following paragraph of the text), and Hill, Joiner and Co., which became a subsidiary of Middle West sometime in the 1920's. Howe, Snow and E. H. Rollins actually began to take over bond business formerly held by Morgan as Insull expanded into the East; Chicago *Journal of Commerce,* June 5, 1931; *Moody's Public Utilities,* 1930, pp. 1,912, 1,953. By the mid-twenties Halsey, Stuart was not dependent upon the Insull business, although it comprised about 25 to 50 per cent of the total business of the house at that time; interview with Harold L. Stuart, Oct. 30, 1958. The importance of Insull financing is clearly demonstrated by a tabulation published in the *Wall Street Journal,* April 21, 1928. For the first quarter of that year, the nation's twenty-nine largest bond houses had participations (including considerable overlapping participations) in a total of $800,000,000 of utility bond issues. Of this, almost half consisted of issues in which houses with a share of the Insull business participated. In 1927 Halsey, Stuart alone headed or participated in syndicates for $790,000,000 of bonds; J. P. Morgan's total business was $502,000,000; *Wall Street Journal,* Feb. 11, 1928. The Morgan total is greatly increased, however, when the flotations of its allied houses are included.

states. As a result of the purchase, Insull suddenly emerged as a major force in eastern as well as middle western utilities, operating in the very shadow of Wall Street. In the end, this invasion of the East proved to be as successful as Napoleon's invasion of Russia.[22]

As these events were taking place, Insull was also becoming the center of a national political controversy. It was an oaks-from-acorns affair, the acorn being the Chicago traction situation. The transportation issue, simmering for years, came to a boil in 1927; in that year, the twenty-year franchises of all the city's transportation companies expired.

Three major groups of companies were involved: the elevated railways operated by Insull, one set of streetcar companies operated by Henry Blair, and another set operated by Leonard Busby. These companies were kept unrelated by the franchise ordinances of 1907, but their managements were friendly; Blair, in fact, was a director of Commonwealth Edison Company. By the mid-twenties all the lines were badly in need of extensions and improvements, but several barriers precluded action. The companies had no credit: Some were in extremely shaky financial condition, and the average rate of return on the capital investment of all the properties was barely 3½ per cent, scarcely enough to support existing bond interest payments. The companies in greatest trouble needed fare increases; others, having issued twenty-year bonds after the 1907 ordinances were passed, were heading toward receivership in 1927 as the only way to conserve their property. And until a long-range solution could be worked out, all the companies would be in need of temporary extension of their franchises. Those involved agreed that the

---

[22] F.T.C., *Utility Corporations*, XXXVIII, 519–23, L, 212–334; *Minutes*, Middle West Utilities directors' meeting, Jan. 10, 1928, and *Annual Report*, 1928; *Chicago Herald and Examiner*, Dec. 16, 1927; *Moody's Public Utilities*, 1929. The F.T.C., in its *Summary Report* (*Utility Corporations*, 72A, 160), pointed to Insull's eastern holdings as an evil example of extreme pyramiding, without bothering to point out that such pyramiding was not typical of the Insull system—suggesting, in fact, the opposite—and without pointing out that this pyramid was bought by Middle West near the end of its existence. Francis Daily, one of Insull's lawyers, described the scene at which these purchases were consummated. Insull, Daily said, studied the figures, agreed that the underlying properties were excellent, and said "It will take us ten years to tear down this pyramid and make this a reasonable investment." But then he shrugged his shoulders, and signed the documents.

only long-range solution was to reorganize and unify all the companies. But for every need, major and minor, political action was
necessary.[23]

Political action for any need would be far from simple to obtain.
In spite of the relative peace that prevailed during most of the life
of 1907 ordinances, the tractions were never far removed from
politics. Despite the skilful public relations activities of Insull's
elevated company manager, Britton Budd, the tractions, as a whole,
had never fully recovered from the public hostility aroused by
Yerkes. And in spite of Insull's political influence, too many important local politicians, notably the former mayor, Big Bill Thompson, had too deep a vested interest in a show of hostility toward the
tractions to be able to approve favorable action toward them.[24]

Political action, of a sort, was attempted in 1924. The 1907
ordinances had, among other things, required that all the companies
pay the city a large annual "municipal compensation"; the plan was
that the city should accumulate these funds and use them to build a
subway system. In 1924 Democratic Mayor William E. Dever (who
had unseated Thompson the previous year) held extended hearings
aimed at making the subway a reality. Insull approved Dever's
plans, but only passively: He had no desire whatever to take on this
responsibility, for the rewards would be trifling and the burden
enormous, and he already had more than enough to do. Running the
elevateds was unpleasant enough; and he refused now to do anything
more, except to urge that the proposed subway be integrated with the
existing lines to form a single system, whether under city, private, or
joint ownership. Without Insull's active support, Dever's plans fell
through. Thereafter, no new action was politically possible until a
new round of elections took place. As a consequence, what happened

[23] For the general background of these events see Harry Weber, *Outline History of
Chicago Traction* (Chicago, 1936). Another useful summary is contained in the printed
Reorganization Plan and Agreement of Chicago Local Transportation Company, Dec. 1,
1930, a copy of which is bound in the *Minutes* of Commonwealth Edison's directors'
meeting, March 31, 1931. A brief history is contained in the *Chicago American*, Aug. 3,
1929. See also the *Chicago Daily News*, Feb. 28, 1928; Chicago *Economist*, March 3,
1928; and *Chicago Herald and Examiner*, June 13, 1929.
[24] See Wendt and Kogan, *Big Bill of Chicago, passim;* Stuart, *Twenty Incredible Years,
passim;* Berry, "Mr. Samuel Insull," p. 3; Insull, "Memoirs," pp. 192–94; editorial in
the *Chicago Tribune*, March 20, 1924; editorial in the Chicago *Union Leader*, Nov. 17,
1923.

to the tractions in 1927 would depend, in large measure, on what happened in the state, county, and congressional elections of 1926 and the municipal elections of 1927.[25]

As the elections approached, the political situation was roughly as follows: From the days in which each ward was a sort of feudal barony, Chicago politics had evolved toward a system of multi-ward principalities, separated and buffered by a few old war baronies. In the Democratic party, as a distinct minority party, factions were neither as numerous nor as strongly divided as in the Republican party. Indeed, Roger Sullivan and John P. Hopkins had presided over all Democrats in the city since the retirement of Carter Harrison, and after Sullivan's death in 1920 George E. Brennan kept the Democrats reasonably unified. In 1923 their unity and the help of the city's reform groups had enabled them to capture the mayorship, in spite of their minority position, from the faction-ridden and scandal-ridden Republican machine.[26]

On the Republican side, alignments were complex. One important faction, strong and long-lived albeit of modest size, was that headed by Senator Charles Deneen of Chicago. Deneen was not a key figure in the 1926 elections, for he was not up for re-election. His downstate counterpart, Senator William McKinley, was. McKinley, the traction magnate who had long been Insull's favorite personal and business enemy, was, in the jargon of the politicians, a "fat cat" —that is, he was fairly well liked, he made trouble for no one, he went along with the party wherever it went, and he had a great deal of money to spend as freely for his fellow politicians as for himself.

Two other downstate Republicans were major powers. The first was Governor Len Small, who had succeeded Lowden's simon-pure administration with one of the most scandal-plagued governorships in memory; while governor, Small himself had been prosecuted for mismanagement of state funds during an earlier term as state

[25] Stuart, *Twenty Incredible Years*, pp. 189, 223–25; the *Chicago Tribune*, April 19, 1923; Feb. 7, Feb. 26, July 12, Nov. 21, 1924; Jan. 20, February–April, especially March 31, April 1, April 7, 1925; the *Chicago Daily News*, Feb. 26, Nov. 21, 1924; February–April, 1925; *Electric Railway Journal*, March 1, 1924.
[26] The description of political alignments in this and the next four paragraphs is based upon Stuart's *Twenty Incredible Years*, pp. 248–320; Wendt and Kogan, *Big Bill*, pp. 191–251; Carroll H. Wooddy, *The Case of Frank L. Smith* (Chicago, 1931), pp. 1–18; study of all the city's newspapers, 1925–27; and interviews with veteran political reporters and observers, previously cited.

treasurer. Although acquitted in a criminal trial, he was held liable, in a civil trial on the same charges, for about a million dollars in missing funds. Even so, he was still a powerful man in downstate politics, and he would not be up for re-election until 1928. The other downstate power, and one who, had he been willing to wait, might have been Small's logical successor, was Frank L. Smith, chairman of the Illinois Commerce Commission. Smith, like McKinley, was independently wealthy, but he was more nearly a professional politician, having worked for the party many years and having held several offices, including a term as a congressman. A onetime ally of Deneen, Smith was now loosely reckoned as being in Small's camp. But that would depend entirely upon opportunity, for Smith had a burning desire for high public office. Among the high offices open in the 1926 elections, McKinley's senate seat appeared the most readily available.

In the city, in addition to Deneen, one major and three minor princes held sway. The major prince was Big Bill Thompson, mayor from 1915 to 1923, now aspiring to recapture the mayorship in the elections of 1927. Lesser but rising was the states attorney, Robert E. Crowe, a powerhouse in the west side wards, who aspired to be elected county judge in order to increase his patronage and solidify his existing power. Charles V. Barrett, another west side boss, had been slipping in the past two or three years, and he was anxious to regain lost ground by allying himself with a sure winner. Sometime in 1925, he and Crowe formed an alliance for the upcoming state and local elections. The third minor prince was Edward J. Brundage, north side boss and former attorney general of the state, the man who had prosecuted Small. Brundage was a Deneen man, but because Deneen planned to be relatively inactive in the upcoming elections, Brundage was casting about for winners, and he found and tentatively joined the Crowe-Barrett alliance.

Thompson was the crystallizing agent. In spite of the scandals of his last administration and his defeat in 1923, he was still the most powerful Republican in Chicago; but in 1924 he had broken with his former ally, Governor Small, and his former mentor, Fred Lundin, and without them he needed help. Surveying the various factional alignments in preparation for his attempted comeback, he made an overture to Deneen. When Deneen turned him down, he formed a coalition with the Crowe-Barrett-Brundage group in the city and then went downstate to lure Smith away from Small. To do so, he promised Smith the support of Crowe-Barrett-Brundage-Thompson in a bid for McKinley's Senate seat (McKinley had barely beaten Smith in the 1920 primary contest for the Senate). In exchange, Smith would, in both the county elections of 1926 and the municipal elections of 1927, lend all his support to the city coalition and bring along as much of Small's organization as he could. All these plans materialized, and this group was in power when the traction problem came to a climax in 1927.

Though Insull had no direct part in these doings—as a matter of policy, he did not interfere in the way politicians ran their business —he was fully aware of all the developments and, in fact, contributed large sums toward financing them. He contributed even more than usual for a personal reason, his long-standing hostility toward McKinley. Meanwhile, as the elections took place, one of the two major streetcar companies went into receivership. In the face of this, Henry Blair and John Mitchell, after several years of urging, succeeded in persuading Insull to take over the entire transportation problem. Not the least persuasive of their arguments was that the state and local political situation was a new one and that most of the present incumbents were both friendly and deeply indebted to Insull.[27]

After various consultations between businessmen and politicians, plans and means for executing them were worked out to rationalize local transportation—necessarily circuitous because of the posturing to which the politicians were committed. First came temporary expedients: receiverships where necessary, short-term extensions of franchises, and fare increases. Fare increases, especially, required some intricate mirror tricks. First, the traction companies applied to the Illinois Commerce Commission for the increases. Thompson, as the defender of the people against predatory interests, feigned furious opposition and assigned the corporation counsel, Samuel

[27] Wooddy, *Frank L. Smith*, p. 55; *Hearings of the Reed Committee on Senatorial Elections*, Part 6, p. 3407; virtually every American newspaper, Jan. 21–23, 1928; Insull, "Memoirs," pp. 161–62, 192–94; the *Chicago Daily News*, the *Chicago Tribune*, Feb. 28, 1928; *Chicago Journal of Commerce*, Feb. 29, 1928; Chicago *Economist*, March 3, 1928.

Ettelson, to fight the proposed increases. Ettelson fought without valid legal or economic grounds to stand on and without any intention of winning. His opponent, the attorney for the transportation companies, was his former partner, Daniel Schuyler, the lawyer Insull had chosen to be his "Thompson man." But it was a bit more involved than that. Because of the way a part of the 1926 campaign had backfired, it was now politically imprudent for the commission to grant the increase. Accordingly, it was arranged that the commission would refuse to allow the increase and that the companies would have to win it in the courts; but the company's case and the commission's refusal were phrased in such a way that no court was likely to reject the company's petition. Thus every company involved got what was needed, and every politician involved not only saved face but made capital of the incident.[28]

After these stopgap measures, the permanent solution was set in motion. Early in 1927 Insull asked Gilbert Porter, of Isham, Lincoln & Beale, to draw up enabling legislation in the form of five bills to be passed by the state legislature. These were openly and publicly company bills; they provided for unification, regulation by a local commission, extensions and municipal compensation, and the building of a city-owned subway system to be integrated with surface and elevated systems. The bills represented a rationalizing plan worked out by the best engineering and financial talent Insull could gather.[29]

The next step was passage by the legislature. The successful political coalition involved in the 1926 and 1927 campaigns backed the legislation, and Insull threw an additional force behind it. The Motormen and Conductors Union—whose friendship and support Insull and Budd had won in all the elevated and interurban companies in and around Chicago—wanted a wage increase as their share of the spoils. For public purposes they threatened a strike; privately, they agreed to influence all the labor members of the

28 The *Chicago Tribune*, April 15, 1927; Feb. 16, Feb. 21, Feb. 28, Feb. 29, April 7, Sept. 25, 1928; Chicago *Journal of Commerce*, June 27, 1927; the *Chicago Daily News*, May 7, Sept. 25, 1928; *Chicago Herald and Examiner*, Sept. 25, 1928; *Chicago Evening Post*, Sept. 25, 1928.
29 The *Chicago Tribune, Chicago Herald and Examiner*, the *Chicago Daily News*, May 21, June 12, June 15, 1927.

legislature to vote for the enabling legislation in exchange for the requested raise. Success appeared assured.[30]

But then, in February, 1928, the entire scheme collapsed. A bloc of downstate legislators, misled by the attacks of various enemies of the bills, misread the situation and assumed that Insull was in the venture because he wanted to be in it and because he and his associates expected to make huge profits from it. They sent word to him from Springfield that "legislation could be passed if he would provide a sum—not a very large sum for him—to grease a number of palms." They were a quarter of a century out of date. Insull exploded with anger; after all his efforts for something he had not wanted to undertake, something that would require great effort and entail great responsibility and offer virtually no reward, he was now being asked to bribe legislators for the necessary laws. He thundered his refusal, and the legislation failed to pass.[31]

But the traction situation was so bad, and its problems were so pressing, that the matter could not rest there. Too, despite the widespread and justifiable suspicion that various fancy political shenanigans underlay the confusion, Insull himself was so highly regarded that his protestations of disinterestedness were accepted by most Chicagoans, and most felt that only he could effect a permanent and satisfactory solution. Accordingly, numerous civic groups were formed to agitate until Insull was empowered to do so.[32]

One such group was immensely effective. James Wilkerson, the federal district judge in charge of the company in receivership, appointed a five-man committee of distinguished citizens, none of whom was connected with Insull or any of the involved companies, to study the problem and come up with detailed proposals. The committee, headed by James Simpson, chairman of Marshall Field and Company, made a thorough study of the problem and, early in 1929, emerged with a plan almost identical to the one proposed earlier by Insull. Under the plan, the city's transportation would become quasi-public in ownership and management. Existing bond-

[30] *Chicago Journal,* June 27, 1927.

[31] *Ibid.,* Feb. 29, 1928; the *Chicago Daily News,* the *Chicago Tribune,* Feb. 28, 1928; Chicago *Economist,* March 3, 1928; interview with John Richert (formerly a member of the firm of Schuyler and Ettleson), previously cited.

[32] The *Chicago Tribune,* May 27, June 25, 1928; Jan. 18, Jan. 21, Jan. 22, 1929; *Chicago American,* Dec. 8, 1928; Jan. 17, Jan. 18, 1929.

holders would be protected, Commonwealth Edison would retrieve a part of the losses it had sustained by keeping the companies afloat, and all lines would be consolidated as a private corporation under an indeterminate franchise. But the city would own the projected subway portion of the system, service in both private and public sectors would be provided at cost, the consolidated organization would be regulated by a special local commission, and many extensions, in addition to the city-owned subway network, would be built during the next ten years.[33]

Carrying out the plan involved giving a blank check—in the form of enabling legislation from Springfield, enabling ordinances from the city council, and approval by a popular referendum—to Samuel Insull and vesting him with near-dictatorial authority. Appropriate legislation was drawn up and introduced into the state legislature in the spring of 1929.[34]

And now entered the one political group which had always been hostile to Insull. This was a group of intellectuals and perennially unsuccessful reformers, particularly a group of professors in the economics and political science departments at the University of Chicago and a handful of lawyers who were especially friendly with them, who together constituted the city's only consistent dissenting political faction. The most important professors were economist (later Senator) Paul Douglas and political scientist (and sometimes alderman and candidate for mayor) Charles E. Merriam; the most important lawyers were Harold L. Ickes, whose antipathy for Insull dated from Insull's refusal to give him an important job with the State Council of Defense, and Donald Richberg, whose antipathy for Insull dated from his run-in with Insull in the rate suit against Peoples Gas Company. In August, 1929, this group organized the People's Traction League to fight the proposed enabling legislation.[35]

Their efforts might have received little attention but for another

---

[33] All Chicago newspapers, Jan. 18, 1929.
[34] The *Chicago Daily News*, May 2, 1929; the *Chicago Tribune*, May 14, June 13, 1929; *Chicago Herald and Examiner*, June 13, 1929.
[35] See above, pp. 177–78; *Chicago Herald and Examiner*, June 13, 16, Aug. 22, 1929; the *Chicago Tribune*, June 13, July 31, Aug. 22, 1929; the *Chicago Daily News*, May 2, Aug. 22, Aug. 26, 1929; Stuart, *Twenty Incredible Years*, pp. 361–62, 413–14. Neither Richberg nor Ickes mentions this episode in his autobiography.

and less idealistic factor. While no one concerned directly in the rationalization plan, either as manager, organizer, or owner, stood to make much money out of it, there was one ancillary activity in which profits would be sizable. If the plan should work out, there would be involved about a quarter of a billion dollars worth of refinancing of old securities and another quarter of a billion in financing the projected improvements. Given the distribution of commitments involved in the tractions, the bond business would go to Halsey, Stuart, to the investment banking affiliates of the large Chicago commercial banks, and to the National City Bank of New York. But Fred J. Lisman, an ambitious New York investment banker, saw in the activities of the intellectuals and reformers a possibility of capturing this huge and lucrative bond account. Lisman sent an attorney, John Maynard Harlan, to champion the people against the "Insull interests" and co-operate with and finance the activities of the People's Traction League.[36]

In June, 1929, the enabling legislation had been passed by the legislature. Insull, a committee of bankers, and a group of engineers then proceeded to work out the details of the plan while the city council debated the necessary ordinances. The People's Traction League attempted to head off the ordinances, but it soon became clear that they would be passed by an overwhelming majority. The final stage, the public referendum, was scheduled for July 1, 1930, and the league focused its entire energies on the referendum. They mustered every sympathetic intellectual in sight, brought in Carl D. Thompson, of the Municipal Ownership League, and other experienced fighters of utilities around the country and found support in the Hearst newspapers, which by this time were throughly committed to a pose of hostility toward all public utilities. Their campaign attacked the ordinances from a multitude of angles, but its essential theme was opposition to Insull. Such propaganda as he sponsored in behalf of the bills attempted to cast the issue in terms of its merits, but the league transformed the contest into personal popularity contest: Would Chicago give Insull the power to handle

[36] The *Chicago Tribune,* June 13, June 25, 1928; Jan. 21, Jan. 22, March 15, May 14, June 13, 1929; *Chicago American,* Jan. 17, Jan. 18, 1929; Chicago *Journal of Commerce,* March 15, 1929; *Chicago Herald and Examiner,* Jan. 28, 1930.

as he saw fit the city's longest-lived, most corruption-plagued political issue?[37]

Insull was confident that the referendum would pass, but he did not leave the matter to chance, for he believed that the issue of personal indorsement made it imperative to the success of the venture that the referendum pass with an overwhelming popular majority. In normal circumstances this would have been easy to arrange, for referendums were normally held concurrently with general city or state elections, and Insull could count on a wholesome portion of the machine vote. The traction referendum, however, was held in midsummer and at a time when no other elections were being held, and thus the professionals would not be "manning the polls." Manning the polls was an extremely expensive proposition; after all, there were several thousand precincts in Chicago, and conducting telephone and door-bell-ringing campaigns to get out the dependable vote in each ward cost $50 to $100 per worker per precinct. The expense had to be borne by someone. Accordingly, Insull required the bankers to produce $500,000, which his staff delivered to the appropriate politicians. The election was held on July 1, 1930; the outcome was 325,-468 votes in favor of the ordinance and 58,212 against. The way was now clear to rationalize and modernize Chicago's transportation facilities.[38]

Too—and no less important—the vote sharpened Insull's image as a special kind of folk hero in that land of Mammon called Chicago. (It mattered not that the machine vote had been employed, for people did not know this and could only see the results. Besides, Chicagoans being what they are, had they known they would have admired Insull all the more.) But while the political and popular battle was being won at home, a portion of the campaign was back-firing elsewhere and setting in motion events that would ultimately make Insull a national villain.

[37] The *Chicago Tribune*, June 13, July 31, Oct. 14, Oct. 16, Dec. 12, 1929; *Chicago Herald and Examiner*, June 13, June 16, Aug. 22, 1929; *Chicago Evening Post*, July 31, Oct. 16, 1929; *Chicago American*, July 31, 1929; the *Chicago Daily News*, Aug. 26, Oct. 14, 1929; Chicago *Journal of Commerce*, Oct. 14, Dec. 12, Dec. 15, 1929; and all these newspapers daily from March 1 to July 2, 1930, especially during the last week of the campaign.
[38] All Chicago newspapers, June 25—July 2, 1930; interviews with Philip McEnroe, John Evers, John Richert, George Lennon, and Samuel Insull, Jr., all previously cited.

When the 1926 political campaigns began, the public favor in which electric utilities stood—thanks largely to the propaganda work of the Committees on Public Utility Information—was probably unmatched by that of any business group in American history. In the platform of the Progressive party in 1924 almost everyone who even remotely could be accused of having any money was denounced as a "trust," but not one word was uttered against electric utilities. Throughout 1925, not even the Hearst newspapers, not even such magazines as the *New Republic* and the *Nation,* not even such crusading newspapers as the St. Louis *Post-Dispatch* and the Madison *Capital Times* had anything particularly unfavorable to say about electric companies. All the others sang their praises, national magazines and metropolitan dailies and country weeklies, labor newspapers, and sometimes even Socialist newspapers. But before the turmoil following the 1926 elections was all over, the situation would be completely reversed.[39]

In the 1926 campaign Insull followed his usual practice of contributing generously of his companies' money to all major factions. He had given $20,000 to Crowe; $10,000 to Barrett; $20,000 to George F. Harding, Thompson's candidate for county treasurer; $10,000 to Roy O. West, a member of the Deneen faction (and soon to be Secretary of the Interior) ; $20,000 to Charles F. Francis for the Small-Lundin organization; and $15,000 to George Brennan, the Democratic boss and candidate for the Senate. But he had gone much further: he had gone overboard on behalf of Frank L. Smith, head of the Illinois Commerce Commission and the man who defeated Senator McKinley in the Republican primary. Smith's record as a regulator of Insull utilities had been such as to lend credence to Insull's later protestation that he was motivated only by his long-standing personal enmity toward McKinley: in five years as head of the commission, Smith had allowed no rate increases to Insull companies and had, in fact, ordered or allowed cuts in the rates of five

---

[39] As a basis for this generalization, I have scanned not only the publications cited in the text but also a wide variety of other progressive and labor newspapers, such as the Pittsburgh Progressive, the *Bingham County News* (Blackfoot, Idaho) , the Nampa *Idaho Progressive,* the *Cleveland Citizen,* the Chicago *Union Leader,* and the Cincinnati *Chronicle.* For some notion of the almost breathtaking effectiveness of the C.P.U.I. see the *Index to Propaganda Activities* of the F.T.C.'s *Utility Corporations.* The 1924 platform of the progressive party is reproduced in the *Wisconsin Blue Book* for that year.

sets of Insull companies, cuts which effected savings to customers of over $42,000,000 during Smith's tenure. Nonetheless, Insull knew that to make a contribution to Smith's campaign would be indiscreet to the point of folly, but he allowed his hatred for McKinley to overcome his judgment. He contributed $125,000 directly and another $33,735 indirectly through propaganda against the World Court, that being Smith's principal campaign issue.[40]

It would ultimately come to light that McKinley had himself spent well over half a million dollars of utility money to defeat Smith, and that Julius Rosenwald, the multimillionaire head of Sears, Roebuck, naïvely appalled to discover the influence of big money in politics, had naïvely offered Smith a bribe of $550,000 to get out of the race and support independent candidate Hugh S. Magill. But these facts, like Insull's contributions, were unknown in 1926. Hence McKinley's complaints to his fellow senators might have gone unheeded, in spite of his popularity with his colleagues, but for another chain of events.[41]

In the Pennsylvania Republican primaries, also held in April, 1926, the controversy and spending dwarfed that in Illinois. The Philadelphia Republican machine had determined to root out the progressive Republicans, headed by Governor Gifford Pinchot, who controlled much of the state administration, and also to unseat Senator George H. Pepper, who was backed by President Coolidge, Secretary of the Treasury Andrew Mellon of Pittsburgh, and the Pittsburgh Republican machinery as well. They were successful, and Philadelphia Republican boss William S. Vare defeated Pinchot and Pepper in a three-way contest for the Republican senatorial nomination. Pinchot and the progressive Republican gubernatorial candidate, Edward Beidleman, charged that millions of dollars had been

[40] For a lengthy treatment of this matter see Wooddy, *The Case of Frank L. Smith;* see also the *Chicago Daily News,* July 27, 1926; Insull, "Memoirs," p. 161; and above, 154.

[41] Stuart, *Twenty Incredible Years,* pp. 248–65, which also constitutes a sharp and in some ways telling criticism of Wooddy's account of the incident. Wooddy was biased in favor of Rosenwald; Stuart was biased in favor of Thompson. Neither account should be read without the other. Rosenwald's semiofficial biographer, M. R. Werner, in *Julius Rosenwald: The Life of a Practical Humanitarian* (New York, 1939), pp. 295–315, not only admits Rosenwald's attempted bribery of Smith but also points out that Rosenwald financed and distributed Wooddy's books on the subject of the 1926 election. See also the *Chicago American* for May 17, 1931, and the *American,* the *Tribune,* and the *Daily News* for Aug. 17, 1931.

spent to defeat them. Pinchot, long a celebrated and controversial figure, was always good for newspaper copy, and newspapers the country over reported his charges.[42]

It was inevitable that some Democrat should arise to make political capital out of these charges of scandal in Republican primaries, and the rising Democrat was Senator James Reed of Missouri. Reed, a ruthless, shrewd, rebellious, and ambitious man, had considered himself a serious contender for the Democratic presidential nomination in 1924, and he considered himself an even more serious contender for 1928. But in his two most popular roles, as leader of the "wet" forces in the Senate and leader of the opponents of the League of Nations and the World Court, control was slipping from his grasp: the first to Democrat Al Smith and the second to progressive Republican Senator William E. Borah. In the Republican electoral scandals, Reed saw the chance for the kind of headlines that could lead him to the presidential nomination. Even before the primaries were over, he introduced a resolution calling for a special committee to investigate the elections, and in May such a committee was formed, with Reed at its helm.[43]

Had it been possible, Reed might have been disposed to concentrate on Pennsylvania and overlook Illinois entirely, for as a champion of isolationism he needed support in Illinois. He had effected an understanding with Big Bill Thompson, whose public posture also was that of the progressive and isolationist. But two developments made it impossible to skip Illinois. First, Pinchot, who had had several quarrels with Pennsylvania utilities over his program for dam-building in the state (Pinchot was a renowned conservationist and early advocate of government-owned multipurpose dams), charged that much of Vare's campaign fund had come from utilities and implied that utilities across the land were busy corrupting elections. Pinchot's charges alone made Illinois too promising a ground for Reed to neglect. Any hesitation he might have

---

[42] Pittsburgh *Gazette-Times*, *Pittsburgh Post*, *Philadelphia Record*, *Philadelphia Inquirer*, Philadelphia *Public Ledger*, April–June, 1926. Biedleman's charges first appeared in the *Gazette-Times*, May 24–25, 1926; by late fall, particularly during the general elections in November, the scandal was commented on by newspapers all over the nation.
[43] Frank R. Kent, "Senator 'Jim' Reed," in *Forum*, July, 1927; Wooddy, *Frank L. Smith*, pp. 23–36; *Congressional Record*, April 8, 1926.

allowed himself was dispelled in June when Senator Caraway of Arkansas, an intimate personal friend of McKinley's, made a spectacular and much-publicized speech charging that Insull had contributed half a million dollars to Smith's campaign and hinting that a twenty-million-dollar utility deal was involved. In the wake of Caraway's speech, Reed swooped into Chicago with such adroitness that one would have thought that he had intended to do so all along.[44]

The Reed Committee—which at this time consisted only of Reed and Robert M. LaFollette, Jr., the other members being at home campaigning for re-election—held hearings in Chicago from July 26 to August 5, 1926. Most of the important politicians in Illinois were embarrassed by the hearings, but the spectacular witness was Insull. Insull was in an awkward position. He was not at all squeamish about admitting large contributions to Smith's campaign—indeed, he was so frank about it that newspapers all across the country clucked editorially that he was "brazen," "insolent," and "arrogant." But Reed would not let the matter end there. On the ground that the Senate could not determine whether there was corruption without untangling the complex network of political alliances in state and local as well as national elections, Reed inquired as to Insull's local contributions. To give such testimony might wreck the hopes of his local political friends for the 1927 municipal elections, and on the advice of his attorney, Daniel Schuyler, Insull refused to answer. On that note the Reed committee adjourned its hearing until Congress reconvened in December. In the intervening months, hardly a day passed without some newspaper or another, from Maine to California, attacking political corruption in general and Insull in particular.[45]

By the time the Senate reconvened, throngs of Democratic and Progressive politicians had gathered to reap their share of the

[44] Wooddy, *Frank L. Smith*, pp. 24–26 and *passim;* all Chicago newspapers, June 27–30, 1926; Wendt and Kogan, *Big Bill*, pp. 230–31; Stuart, *Twenty Incredible Years*, pp. 74, 252, 257. Stuart suggests that it was George Brennan, Chicago Democratic boss, who urged Reed to move into Chicago.
[45] The *Chicago Tribune, Chicago American, Chicago Herald and Examiner*, the *Chicago Daily News, New York World*, the *New York Times*, July 26–August 6, and throughout October, 1926; Wooddy, *Frank L. Smith, passim* (containing a survey of scores of newspapers from all sections of the country); interviews with John Richert and Samuel Insull, Jr., previously cited; Insull, "Memoirs," p. 161.

political hay to be made of the Pennsylvania and Illinois elections. The Reed committee resumed its investigations in January and February, 1927, now in Washington. (Coincidentally, in January the Supreme Court issued its long-awaited decision in the case of *McGrain v. Daugherty*, in which for the first time it approved and defined the broad inquisitorial powers of Congress.) Insull again was subpoenaed by the Reed Committee, and this time he recited his contributions in detail, but he again refused to tell of his local contributions. (Under the authority of the McGrain decision, he was promptly cited for contempt of Congress. He avoided prosecution by supplying the requested information at a third session, in January, 1928, when doing so no longer threatened local candidates.) [46]

But in February, 1927, coincidentally, another pair of issues came to focus and set off an explosion from which Insull, the utility industry, and the nation never fully recovered. The first was the climax of a long, bitter, and complex dispute over the use of the Colorado River for power and irrigation. The specific issue was a proposal to build a federally owned dam on the river at Boulder Canyon. State administrations and various interest groups in California, Arizona, Utah, and Wyoming gathered to do battle over it. The other issue was the problem of disposing of the government's nitrate and power plant at Muscle Shoals on the Tennessee River, which had been built as a war measure and had remained the subject of controversy ever since. Several proposals were made— the most renowned being Henry Ford's offer to lease the plant for a hundred years—and rejected, largely because of the efforts of Senator George Norris and a handful of other progressive middle western senators, who wanted the plant to be expanded into a government power project along the lines ultimately incorporated in the Tennessee Valley Authority. Norris and his allies were determined that no utilities should be allowed to develop the area. Early in 1927 a proposal by the Alabama Power Company to lease the Muscle Shoals plant was under consideration, and senatorial debate on the proposal was scheduled for late in February. On both issues, the lobbyists for the National Electric Light Association were quietly

[46] Wooddy, *Frank L. Smith*, pp. 52–62; Madison *Capital Times*, the *Chicago Tribune*, the *New York Times*, *Providence Journal*, *Portland Oregonian*, *Milwaukee Journal*, *Washington Post*, Feb. 20–27, 1927; Jan. 21–22, 1928.

at work, but what could normally be done privately suddenly became no more private than a circus.[47]

Everything came to focus at once. The Senate, late in January, refused to seat Smith (it would later make the refusal permanent), and for a month the nation's newspapers had been publicizing the affair. Between February 22 and February 25 Insull testified again before the Reed Committee, this time evoking even more spectacular response in the newspapers. On February 25, in a full Senate session before a packed gallery, Reed gave his committee's report. The Senate was already in turmoil over the debate on the Boulder Canyon project, which had immediately preceded Reed's report. As soon as Reed sat down, the scheduled debate on the proposed lease of Muscle Shoals to the Alabama Power Company came up. Senator Norris was armed with maps and statistics to prove that the Alabama company was a part of a vast power trust headed by General Electric, and he planned to argue that the government should expand, not lease, its Muscle Shoals plant to combat the alleged trust. Norris was apparently caught off guard by the information in Reed's report, and he hastily made vague changes in his maps and altered his attack to include Insull in the trust. And "God only knows," said Norris, "how many Senatorial campaigns Mr. Insull has financed. . . . Are we going to turn this plant over to these interests?" Senator Walsh of Montana, renowned as a senatorial inquisitor for his exposé of the Teapot Dome scandal, seized the moment to demand an exhaustive senatorial investigation of the "power trust."[48]

Legion were the events that ensued from that turbulent day in the Senate. The efforts of both Norris and Walsh bore fruit in Congress a year later, though the immediate outcome was not quite what they had hoped for. In 1928 Congress passed Norris' bill to put the United States government in the electric power business at Muscle Shoals,

[47] Twentieth Century Fund, *Electric Power and Government Policy* (New York, 1948), pp. 496 ff., 573 ff.; *Congressional Record*, 69th Cong., 2d sess., p. 4742; Richard L. Neuberger and Stephen B. Kahn, *Integrity: The Life of George W. Norris* (New York, 1937), pp. 202–29; George W. Norris, *Fighting Liberal: The Autobiography of George W. Norris* (New York, 1945), pp. 245–59.

[48] The *New York Times*, the *Chicago Tribune, Portland Oregonian, Milwaukee Journal, Chicago Herald and Examiner, Providence Journal*, Madison *Capital Times*, Jan. 21–22, Feb. 20–27, 1927; *Congressional Record*, 69th Cong., 2d sess., pp. 4572–73, 4740. On Walsh as a crusading inquisitor see Josephine O'Keane, *Thomas J. Walsh: A Senator from Montana* (Francestown, N. H., 1955), pp. 109–47, 168–70.

only to see it vetoed by President Coolidge. Senator Walsh's resolution calling for an investigation of the electric utility industry by a Senate committee passed only after an amendment moved by Senator George, instructing the Federal Trade Commission to conduct the inquiry. (Five years later, Norris had his day, when the Tennessee Valley Authority was created. Walsh was equally successful, for out of the F.T.C. investigations came, directly and indirectly, some of the most far-reaching reform legislation in the history of the American Congress.) [49]

The F.T.C. conducted hearings for seven years. In the main, the commission's work was conducted by intelligent, able, and dedicated investigators, abetted by utility men themselves and obstructed only by state utility commissioners, jealous of their prerogatives, and by certain investment bankers, fearful of being found out. But the bankers need not have worried, for the situation was seized upon by newspapers seeking circulation and by politicians seeking votes, and in the shouting that ensued all possibility of clear understanding was lost. Almost daily from 1928 to 1935, increasing numbers of newspapers (notably, at first, those in the Hearst chain) and increasing numbers of politicians (notably, at first, Norris, Walsh, and Pinchot) blasted the utilities or Insull or other giants of the industry, and amidst the sound and fury the bond-house buccaneers who had invaded and were ransacking the industry escaped virtually unnoticed. And it was not the sober inquiry of the commission, but the public impression of the hearings as broadcast by those posing as crusaders, that formed the basis for subsequent political action.[50]

Typical of Hearst's coverage of the hearings was a story that appeared in his papers on June 15, 1929. The day before, two letters had been introduced in testimony before the commission. The first was one of March 6, 1928, in which Josiah T. Newcombe, a lobbyist

[49] Neuberger and Kahn, *Norris*, pp. 202–29; *Electric Power and Government Policy*, pp. 573 ff.; F.T.C., *Utility Corporations*, 72A, 1–6; *Congressional Record*, 70th Cong., 1st sess., pp. 788, 2771, 2893, 3054.

[50] F.T.C., *Utility Corporations*, Vols. 1–72A; otherwise, these generalizations can be verified only by reading Hearst newspapers and other newspapers throughout the period. See, for example, the Madison *Capital Times*, Feb. 22, Feb. 26, March 3, March 4, Nov. and Dec., daily, 1927; Feb. 3, Feb. 4, Feb. 16, 1928; 1930–31 and thereafter throughout, especially Jan. 12, 1931; *Chicago Herald and Examiner*, July 10, Sept. 23, Sept. 26, Nov. 17, Dec. 8, Dec. 9, Dec. 13, Dec. 14, 1928; Feb. 10, April 8, May 21, June 14, June 15, 1929; throughout 1930–31 and thereafter; and such newspapers as the St. Louis *Post-Dispatch*, and the *New York World* for roughly the same period.

for the National Electric Light Association, had written to Martin
Insull that Senator Carter Glass of Virginia was gaining a "totally
erroneous" view of the Muscle Shoals and Boulder Dam issues from
Senator Walsh and others, which he thought would "be very unfortunate" if it should continue. Martin Insull replied two days later
that he had written to Middle West executive Harry Reid, who knew
several Virginians who in turn knew Glass well, and had asked Reid
to ask his friends to give Glass "a more correct view of the situation."
That was all, and in the body of the story as written by Hearst reporter M. L. Ramsay, it was recorded more or less accurately. But
on the basis of the tried-and-true dictum that no one reads anything
but the headlines and lead paragraphs, the story was treated in this
manner. "SENATOR GLASS THREATENED BY POWER TRUST," screamed an
eight-column, front-page banner headline, and secondary headlines
read, *"Letters at U.S. Inquiry Show Pressure Planned; Name 3 Con-
gressmen as Friendly."* The first paragraph began, ominously, "A
bold attempt by the power trust lobby to influence the views of
Senator Glass of Virginia, former Secretary of the Treasury, and to
swing three representatives into line against the Boulder Dam project, was revealed before the Federal Trade Commission today."[51]

Typical of the politicians' attacks was a lengthy pamphlet Pinchot
issued—with front-page coverage in newspapers across the nation—
early in 1929. In "The Power Monopoly—Its Make-up and Its
Menace," Pinchot charged that six groups controlled thirty-five corporations that did most of the country's power business. He asserted
that through various systems of interlocking directorates, control was
even more concentrated. The six he named were General Electric
(which, as the F.T.C. investigation was demonstrating, had actually
been out of the power business since it disposed of Electric Bond and
Share Company in 1924), the Mellon group (which, according to the
F.T.C., had sold its holdings to Cyrus Eaton three years earlier),
the Morgan group (which, as the same investigations uncovered, had
begun its invasion of the holding company world only six weeks
earlier), H. M. Byllesby (who had died in 1924), H. L. Doherty, and
Samuel Insull. Among the sets of so-called interlocking directorates

[51] *Chicago Herald and Examiner* (and all other Hearst papers), June 15, 1929. Ramsay
later wrote a book using the same methods—*Pyramids of Power: Roosevelt, Insull, and
the Power Wars* (Washington, 1935).

cited by Pinchot were several groups of devout enemies, including one between the Insull and Morgan interests. Also typical was one of Norris' speeches in which he charged that electric companies were overcharging domestic consumers by some $750,000,000 a year. Martin Insull wryly remarked that Norris must have believed companies should pay their customers, for (as the F.T.C. was learning) the total annual bill for residential customers was only $650,000,000.[52]

(An era was dawning, the era of trial by newspaper, by smear and innuendo, by headline-hunting politicians who made spectacular hit-and-run charges, backed by impressive but inaccurate and irrelevant data. The episode constituted a crucial link in the development of the ruthless and irresponsible congressional inquisition as an instrument of demagoguery. The route from these events to McCarthyism and beyond was serpentine but it was sure: Once Walsh had blazed the trail, and Reed had demonstrated the tactics, and the Supreme Court had approved the function, the rest followed as a matter of course. The names of the inquisitors changed, from Walsh to Reed to Nye, from Pecora to Dies to Kefauver to Walter, and the avowed objects of their inquiry changed also, from trusts in the Department of Justice to war profiteers in the White House to hoods in local politics to Communists in the State Department, but the essence remained the same.)

As the din mounted through 1929 and 1930, the Insulls worsened the situation by committing three major blunders in their public and political relations—more than Sam had committed in the previous thirty years. In each their position was sensible but their action was foolish. The first was in Maine, where the Central Maine Power Company, a subsidiary of Middle West, involved itself in a spectacular and fruitless battle to repeal the state's archaic Fernald Law, which prohibited the export of power. The law was hardly a wise one, for it prevented the development of the rich water power resources of Maine, even for consumption in Maine, by precluding systematized utilization of the power. Too, in the opinion of Charles Evans Hughes, former justice and future chief justice of the Supreme

---

[52] The *Chicago Tribune*, the *Chicago Daily News*, *New York World*, Feb. 4, 1929; *Electrical World*, Feb. 9, 1929; *Chicago Herald and Examiner*, Feb. 4, Feb. 10, 1929; June 3, June 25, 1931; F.T.C., *Utility Corporations*, Vols. XXIII, XXIV, XXV, XXVI, XXXVIII, LIV, LXVI, 72A. Each of the F.T.C.'s volumes should be read with extreme care, and the *Summary Report* (Vol. 72A) should be read skeptically, cross-checking against the investigatory volumes that preceded it.

Court, it was unconstitutional. But outsiders are not welcome in Maine politics, and Insull and his men suffered many painful and well-publicized stings before they pulled out in embarrassment.[53]

The first blunder came about primarily through the actions of W. S. Wyman, one of Martin's lieutenants in the field, but the second was Sam's own. In June, 1930, at a World Power Conference in Berlin, the American ambassador, Frederic M. Sackett, was scheduled to give a speech in which he would attack American utility companies on the ground that the sale price of their product was fifteen times the cost of manufacturing it, and would charge that until that figure was brought in line with other industries, the electric industry was entirely unjustified in claiming that it rendered high-quality service at low cost. Insull happened to be in Germany at the time, and he learned of the speech before Sackett delivered it. Furious, he called on Sackett and talked for two hours, giving him an introductory lesson in the economics of electric supply—after which Sackett decided not to give the speech. But the story leaked out, and the furor in the international press was enormous, whereupon Insull called on Sackett again and asked him to deliver it. George M. Tidd, president of the American Gas and Electric Company and an old friend of Insull, spoke for the industry, trying to save its face. Sackett, he said, was being silly and showing complete ignorance of the economic facts of life. The cost of a banana on a tree, Tidd pointed out, was practically nothing, but its cost to consumers was several hundred times as much; and the cost of water lying in a lake was zero, but when water was piped to customers' faucets the price was infinitely greater than the "production" cost. In short, distribution costs as well as production costs varied from industry to industry, and different kinds of industries could not be compared by arbitrary and irrelevant statistics and ratios. But while the industry had the better of the argument, it had the worst of the publicity, and utility men everywhere squirmed in discomfort at what they considered Insull's rash action. Well they might, for the world press denounced the episode as an effort by a powerful businessman to "fix" an ambassador of the government of the United States.[54]

[53] Lincoln Smith, *The Power Policy of Maine* (Berkeley, 1951), is an excellent study of the Insulls and Maine.
[54] *Chicago American*, the *Chicago Daily News*, the *Chicago Tribune*, *Chicago Evening Post*, *Chicago Herald and Examiner*, and most large-city American and British dailies, June 18–26, 1930.

At almost the same moment, Martin Insull was committing the third and what would ultimately be the most costly blunder. He violated one of Sam's cardinal rules, that one never answered the attacks of politicians. Worse, he *attacked* a politician, and an extremely important one at that: Governor Franklin D. Roosevelt of New York. Roosevelt had been making speeches attacking holding companies with what seemed to Martin even less logic and factual basis than that underlying the attacks of Norris and Pinchot; and Roosevelt had also vigorously denounced, as being somehow unfair, the proposal of New York utilities to cut their rates to promote consumption. Utility men had difficulty following Roosevelt's unusual utterances on utilities. Had he been consistently Norris-like, they would have reckoned that he was simply making political capital out of a generally publicized situation, and had he stuck to New York companies, they would have reckoned that he was making particular capital out of a recent to-do over St. Lawrence River power projects. But he did neither consistently; his hostility seemed aimed at holding companies, not at utilities, and his position seemed to vary in accordance to no pattern. The most persistent explanation offered among holding company men and on Wall Street and LaSalle Street was that early in 1928, before he decided to run for governor, Roosevelt had approached his old friend Howard Hopson, head of the multibillion-dollar Associated Gas and Electric Company system, and asked for an executive job; the story went that Hopson virtually laughed him out of the room, and that Roosevelt never forgave the affront. Whatever the origin, Roosevelt impressed holding company people as a man with a grudge, not a cause. And whatever the governor's motivation, Martin Insull was most unwise in failing to hold his tongue. Many magazines and newspapers gave good play to his jabs at the politician. Two years later the politician jabbed back, and the Insulls paid dearly.[55]

[55] Franklin D. Roosevelt, "The Real Meaning of the Power Problem," in *Forum*, LXXXII (December, 1929), 327–32; Martin J. Insull, "The Real Power Problem," in *Forum*, LXXXIII (February, 1930), 88–94; Roosevelt, "The Revision of the Public Service Commissions Law," in *Academy of Political Science Proceedings*, XIV (May, 1930), 201–10; M. J. Insull, "Is Control of Operating Companies Sufficient?", in *Academy of Political Science Proceedings*, XIV (May, 1930), 81–89; see also the debates printed in this issue of the *Proceedings*; the *Chicago Daily News*, June 19, 1930; the *Chicago Tribune*, Aug. 11, Aug. 14, 1930; Sept. 16, 1931; Chicago *Journal of Commerce*, Aug. 14, 1930, Feb. 12, 1931; *Investment News*, Feb. 14, 1931; *Chicago Herald and Examiner*,

While Martin responded rashly to public attacks, Sam responded hardly at all. Sam's attitude was understandable. He had been conditioned by long experience to disregard all public statements of politicians, particularly those engaged in a crusade. Indeed, his rule of thumb was that the louder a politician barked, the less likely he was to bite. After all, among the most vocal denouncers were some of his best friends—even William Randolph Hearst paid a personal call on him and asked, in effect, "It's O.K., isn't it, Sam?"—and Insull understood that anti-business demagoguery was one of the tools of the politician's trade, one entirely unrelated to what they did in public office.[56] On the other hand, he had found that those who denounced and believed what they said, like his father in his day or the Chicago reformers in the twenties, were almost invariably politically impotent. As long as he was on top, he could handle the politicians. (Besides, the only visible result of the unfavorable publicity was that whenever people took seriously a politician's or a newspaper's wild statements about the extent of his power, they raced out and bought more of his stock, and it leaped upward.)

But there was danger in the situation, and in Insull's failure to recognize it lay the greatest danger of all. He saw no real threat—if he even recognized real enmity—from politicians, bankers, New Yorkers, Gold Coasters, or anybody else. He had made some mistakes, and he had suffered minor setbacks, but on major matters his ascent to the heights had been uninterrupted for more than three decades. Since his humiliation at the hands of Coffin and Morgan in 1892, he had been undefeated, untied, unscored-upon. He was Samuel Insull, by the grace of God, and the only thing that could beat Samuel Insull was the grave. And even on that score, he had a plan.

June 25, Sept. 16, 1931. For an example of the kind of reasoning on Roosevelt's part that baffled utility men see the report of his speech in the *Chicago Tribune*, August 11, 1930, in which he attacked a utility company's proposal to cut rates to promote increased consumption. I have heard the story about Roosevelt and Hopson from persons in the holding company systems of General Public Utilities Company, Associated Gas and Electric Company, and the North American Company. In an interview in Providence on November 1, 1961, Adolph A. Berle, Jr., formerly one of Roosevelt's closest advisers, said that it was possible but that it did not "ring true." The point is, however, that utility men were convinced that Roosevelt was acting out of some kind of personal grudge and that sometimes he acted as if this were the case.
[56] Berry, "Mr. Samuel Insull," pp. 20–21.

CHAPTER XI   *The Fall of the House of Insull*

On a Sunday afternoon in the autumn of 1926, Samuel Insull and Britton Budd went for a drive through the rich farm country
northwest of Chicago. Insull was a man who liked to see the visible
results of his labors—one of his favorite activities, at once relaxing
and exhilarating, was standing and staring out his office window at
dusk, watching the lights of the city come on—and on this particular
day he and Budd drove for miles just looking at the transmission and
distribution lines that interlaced the area.

After a while, they parked the car under a transmission tower,
and as the wires sang overhead Insull told Budd he was contemplat-
ing retirement. He was sixty-seven years old, and he had been a success, in his own Victorian terms, for two decades. Idly, he wondered
how wealthy he was. Budd fished out an envelope and wrote on the
back of it, as Insull recited: five thousand shares of this, ten thousand
of that, twenty of another. Then, as closely as they could recall market
prices, they figured it up. Not counting the farm at Libertyville, his
paid-up insurance, and an assortment of miscellaneous property, all
of which would total three or four millions, Insull's net worth was
about five million dollars. (His friends, and his enemies, would have
been shocked that it was so little; he could easily have made twenty
times that, had he been willing to work for the sake of acquiring it,
but since 1912—by which time he had a million pounds sterling—he
had simply not been interested in accumulating money.) [1]

---

[1] Interview with Britton I. Budd (Chicago, Aug. 26, 1956). I have verified this estimate
from Insull's account books, in the Insull Papers.

The narrative of events in this chapter is documented item by item, but a further
word may be apropos. A little more than half the data presented here was uncovered

The "empire," had they calculated it, would have been more impressive. By the end of the decade, growing at the ever-accelerating pace at which it had grown from the beginning, it reached dizzying proportions. It consisted, as it had for years, of five major and three minor parts. The major components were Commonwealth Edison, by then a $400,000,000 company, but still serving only electricity and only in Chicago; Peoples Gas, a $175,000,000 utility serving gas only in Chicago; Public Service of Northern Illinois, now a $200,000,000 company, supplying electricity and gas in 300 communities around Chicago; Middle West, whose several hundred subsidiaries, grouped into a half-dozen major divisions, now represented an investment of $1,200,000,000 and served electricity and gas in 5,000 communities spread over thirty-two states; and Midland, the Indiana holding company, whose subsidiaries now represented an investment of $300,000,-000 and served electricity and gas in 700 Indiana communities. The secondary components were the elevated railways in Chicago; the three interurban electric railways connecting Chicago with its suburbs; and North American Light and Power Company, an independent buffer property that had been formed to connect Insull's properties with, while separating them from, properties around St. Louis held by the North American Company. The total comprised nearly $3,000,000,000 worth of utility properties. Between them, the various companies had about 600,000 stockholders and about 500,000 bondholders; together, they served more than 4,000,000 customers and produced about an eighth of the electricity and gas consumed in the United States, and probably as much as the total consumed by any other nation on earth. This was the house that Insull had built, and this was the house he managed.[2]

in several government investigations of the Insull companies and the Insull system. These are to be found in the F.T.C., *Utility Corporations,* Vols. XXXVIII, L, LVIII, LX, and LXVII, and the Pecora Committee, *Hearings on Stock Exchange Practices,* Part 5, all of which I have read with care. The Federal Trade Commission's Vols. L and LXVII, especially, read like an indictment, and, indeed, form the basis of the government's indictment of Insull for use of the mails to defraud, a subject that is discussed at length in chap. xii, below. Although they are arguments rather than unbiased investigations, these volumes are extremely useful; but to use them with some perspective it is necessary to consult the other sources cited in this chapter, and particularly to read the transcript of *U.S.* v. *Insull* (1934), in which all the charges against Insull are analyzed, discussed, and debated at length.

[2] *The Insull Group of Public Utility Properties* (Chicago, 1930); *Annual Reports* and *Yearbooks,* Commonwealth Edison, Public Service of Northern Illinois, Peoples Gas, Middle West Utilities, and Midland United, 1926–30 (files in the Insull Papers);

It was one of those rare occasions on which he thought about the entire empire, and he was understandably proud of his accomplishment. He could retire in comfort and with all the sense of satisfaction a man could want. And now a new element had entered his calculations. At long last the British government had got around to doing what Insull and his friend Charles Merz had been urging for two decades: establishing a commission to build a government-operated unified power system for England—the British grid system. He had advised the Weir committee—the parliamentary committee that investigated the problem and set up the commission—on how to go about it, and the Weir committee proposed to model it after his own systems. Now, Prime Minister Stanley Baldwin had asked Insull to retire from his American businesses, re-establish his British citizenship, and move to London to become chairman of the commission.[3]

As much as he wanted anything in his life, Insull wanted to accept Baldwin's invitation. He weighed the matter a long time, but during that very summer his son had made up his mind for him. Since Junior's birth, Insull had geared all his long-range plans to him; had Insull, Jr., become a poet or playwright, as he dreamed of doing as a youth, Insull planned to provide him with an income for life and retire early. When the son followed the father into the utility field and, in 1926, married Adelaide Pierce of Chicago—thereby committing himself to a career in utilities in Chicago—Insull decided that he must himself stay in the city to consolidate the empire and groom his son for the role of heir expectant.[4]

During the five years after he made this decision, Insull would ascend higher and higher, until he attained power and prestige rarely if ever equaled by any businessman whose position rested on ability rather than wealth, and then come crashing to earth, to become less than a cipher, to degenerate into an arch-symbol of every manner of

Moody's Public Utilities, 1926–27; F.T.C., *Electric-Power Industry, Control of Power Companies*, 69th Cong., 2d sess., Senate Document 213 (Washington, 1927); *Electrical World*, Jan. 5, 1924; *Colliers*, Jan. 17, 1925; the *Chicago Tribune*, March 12, 1926; *Investment News*, Dec. 29, 1928.

[3] The first of Insull's recorded statements regarding his role in the formation of the British grid system is in Berry, "Mr. Samuel Insull," p. 12; Insull elaborated it in his "Memoirs," pp. 90–93, and stated it publicly in his trial, *U.S. v. Insull*, pp. 4293–95 (Nov. 1, 1934). It was subsequently confirmed by the British press; see the obituaries in the several London newspapers for July 17, 1938.

[4] Insull, "Memoirs," pp. 100–102.

corporate evil. He would see his personal fortune increase from around $5,000,000 in 1927 to $150,000,000 in 1929, and then tumble, by mid-1932, to zero and below, to a net indebtedness so large that, as one banker put it, he was "too broke to be bankrupt." With him—to the top and then to the bottom—went hundreds of thousands of stockholders who shared his faith in his own invulnerability.

The idea of founding a dynasty did not originate on Junior's wedding day. Long ago, it had crossed Insull's mind: so fleetingly at first that, like an ocelot, it almost left no tracks; and after 1912 he thought of it more regularly and more slowly. But there was no point in refitting a throne room for a son who might prove unable or unwilling to occupy it, and Junior's proof of talent and his choice of career and bride dissolved that barrier.

There was another barrier, equally strong: Insull's close friends whose status rivaled his own, those who could restrain him by merely saying nay. How can one say to even one's most trusted friend and adviser, a man like John J. Mitchell, "John, I think I'm going to establish a dynasty, and thereby render myself immortal"? Out of sheer embarrassment, it was impossible. But Insull's preoccupation, and his refusal to admit that a dynasty was on his mind, is silently attested by his exaggerated care in avoiding the honor of having things named after him—he called things the Edison this and the Edison that, but not the Insull anything. He had allowed the London Temperance Hospital to call his gift the Insull Wing in honor of his parents; and he styled the London firm that marketed his securities in Europe Insull and Son, Ltd., in conscious emulation of Dickens' *Dombey and Son.* Otherwise, however, neither company nor charity nor building nor shrine bore his name.[5]

But soon that barrier, the restraint imposed by having friends like Mitchell, dissolved as suddenly as had the first. John G. Shedd, John J. Mitchell, and James A. Patten, his remaining triumvirate of no-men, died in a period of two years. Mitchell's death counted most, and when he died—in a tragic automobile accident in October, 1927—Insull knew fear, the panicky fear a seaman knows when he loses

[5] The *Chicago Tribune,* March 5, 1931; Chicago *British American,* March 7, 1931; Insull, "Memoirs," pp. 200–203; "London Temperance Hospital," folder in the Insull Papers.

his rudder in a gale. (Before a low-ranking subordinate, who chanced into his office as he got the news of Mitchell's death, Insull wept and then, with foreboding wisdom, said, "It would be better for all of us if it had been me.") [6]

As serious—perhaps more so—was that between 1924 and 1927 virtually every old pro in the Chicago banking community died, leaving the banks in the hands of persons whose lack of seasoning prepared them ill for the financial storms ahead. Assuming command during the expansionist fever of the late twenties, they began throwing money at everyone who seemed prosperous; Insull they deluged with easy credit, begging him to accept it, for any purpose. At a party, the new president of the Continental Bank sidled up to Junior and, with the manner of a French postcard peddler, said, "Say, I just want you to know that if you fellows ever want to borrow more than the legal limit, all you have to do is organize a new corporation, and we'll be happy to lend you another $21,000,000." As Phil McEnroe, Insull's bookkeeper, said, "The bankers would call us up the way the grocer used to call my mamma, and try to push their money at us. 'We have some nice lettuce today, Mrs. McEnroe; we have some nice fresh green money today, Mr. Insull. Isn't there something you could use maybe $10,000,000 for?' " To an organization that had always been kept in check by the difficulty of raising capital for expansion, this new situation had the impact of three stiff drinks on an empty stomach. [7]

Having a reason to found a dynasty, and no longer having a reason not to, Insull now wanted only the occasion. The occasion arose in the late summer of 1928. Insull had become aware of the investment bankers' invasion of the holding company world soon after it began, and as more and more old-time operators lost control of their companies, Insull watched with increasing uneasiness. He did not know exactly where to look for the danger, for he did not understand that the stakes were ancillary to the main enterprise; and Morgan, whence danger might have been expected, had not yet entered the piratical race. Furthermore, Insull could recognize danger, as he

[6] *Minutes,* Commonwealth Edison directors' meetings, Nov. 9, 1926; Nov. 15, 1927; Dec. 18, 1928; all Chicago newspapers, Oct. 23, 1926; Oct. 30, 1927; Dec. 9, 1928; interview with E. H. Armstrong, Milwaukee, Oct. 16, 1957.
[7] James, *Growth of Chicago Banks,* II, 979–80; interviews with Abner Stilwell, Edward Eagle Brown, and Herman Waldeck (all of whom were vice-presidents of Chicago banks at the time) ; interviews with Philip McEnroe and Samuel Insull, Jr.

recognized accomplishment, only when it was tangible. But his every built-in warning mechanism stood alerted, lest someone attempt to unseat him. Then the inevitable attack came—or appeared to come —from an unexpected quarter.[8]

It was led by Cyrus S. Eaton, of the Cleveland investment banking house of Otis and Company. A creative capitalist in spite of his reputation as a financial buccaneer, Eaton was no newcomer to the utility business. Like Insull, he knew what it was to build utilities from the ground up, for he had built and successfully managed small utilities for almost twenty years. But he was a man of vast ambition and wily talent, and when he moved into the big leagues of utility operations in the early twenties, he had acquired tools to match his talent: a large investment bank and a holding company. Swiftly, silently, sharklike, he began acquiring enormous holdings. By 1925, through an investment trust called Continental Shares, he had obtained control of two holding companies that had been dominated by the Mellons. In 1926 he moved into Morgan country: His drive for a voice in the management of Detroit Edison failed, but he succeeded in obtaining for Otis and Company a participation in Detroit Edison's bond business, one of the few utility accounts then dominated by Morgan banks. And late in 1927 and on into 1928 he began quietly buying large blocs of stocks in Insull companies— Commonwealth Edison, Peoples Gas, Public Service, and Middle West.[9]

This appeared to be the kind of palpable, straightforward danger that Insull could recognize; but even so, he only gradually became aware that something out of the ordinary was going on. Eaton covered his purchases carefully, buying through various nominees, and his actions were additionally screened by the fact that other groups were making sizable purchases of Insull securities at the same time. Eventually, Insull learned that Eaton's holdings were disconcertingly large; indeed, by mid-1928 they were several times as large as Insull's own. As yet, Insull was not alarmed; but his cigar intake and his furious-paced, head-down walks through the woods at Libertyville

[8] Interviews with Philip McEnroe, Harold L. Stuart, and Fred Scheel; F.T.C., *Utility Corporations*, LII, 2–3.

[9] *Who's Who*, 1930; *Forbes*, April, 1956; F.T.C., *Electric-Power Industry, Control of Power Companies*, pp. 232–33; Miller, *Kilowatts at Work: A History of the Detroit Edison Company*, pp. 321–25; *Moody's Public Utilities*, 1930; Insull, "Memoirs," p. 205; interview with Cyrus Eaton, Cleveland, May 4, 1956.

doubled, a sure sign to the farm hands that the boss was disturbed, and mightily.[10]

(Eaton made no overt effort, then or later, to wrest control from Insull. Later he testified in court that if he had owned an overwhelming majority of the stock of an Insull company and Insull had owned but a small fraction, he would have wanted Insull to run the company; and, indeed, it would have been out of character for Eaton to seek control, for he believed Insull to be the best utility operator in the world. As someone put it, "Eaton wasn't really interested in running things. All he wanted was the money."[11]

(Insull, on the other hand, wasn't interested in the money. All he wanted was to run things—and, after a fashion, to continue to run them after he was dead. Consequently, he did not understand his adversaries' way of thinking; he thought from entirely different premises. In all that followed, he expected bankers to act like bankers and raiders to act like raiders. They did not, and Insull was never quite sure what his enemies were about.) [12]

His uneasiness increased proportionately as Eaton's holdings increased, and it was aggravated by associates who believed that Eaton was willing and might be able to overthrow him. After all, the empire had no adhesive of ownership, but was held together only by the brains and personality of the emperor; and mighty as these were, as weapons they would be to money as a slingshot to a revolver.

Insull became convinced of the danger during an ocean crossing in the late summer of 1928. Eaton made the same crossing, and with the gentle, blue-eyed innocence that he could affect so well, he was a most affable fellow passenger. But he smiled and whilst he smiled his agents increased their Commonwealth Edison holdings to 80,000 shares. Insull knew it, and Eaton did not know he knew it, and Eaton said not one word about it during the long, friendly voyage. This convinced Insull that Eaton was about to attempt a raid.[13]

[10] Insull, "Memoirs," p. 201; interview with Philip McEnroe; interview with Sam Alcover (Insull's farm manager) , Libertyville, April 20, 1960.
[11] *U.S.* v. *Insull*, pp. 5645 ff.; all Chicago newspapers, Nov. 12, Nov. 13, 1934; interview with Eaton, previously cited.
[12] This inference is drawn from Insull's description of the details of his collapse, in his "Memoirs," pp. 201–45, and the more detailed account in the first draft of the memoirs. By the time Insull wrote his memoirs—in the summer of 1934—he was aware of almost everything that had happened, but even then he did not understand it.
[13] Insull, "Memoirs," p. 205; interviews with Eaton and McEnroe.

Insull could see only one way to defend his group against a raid by Eaton or other banking groups, and to secure the continued management of his companies by himself, his son, his brother, and his organization. This was, in a word, to pyramid. He would do what he had long preached against: form an investment trust himself—one that he and his friends, after exchanging all their own utility holdings for its stocks, would control through direct ownership—and seek through it to buy enough of the voting stock of his four big companies to transform his control from that of manager to that of proprietor. (By thus entering the unfamiliar world of stock market operations, he also violated another of his preachings, the old saw that admonishes the shoemaker to stick to his last.) [14]

In December, 1928, he created an investment company styled Insull Utility Investments (commonly, I.U.I.) , "to perpetuate," as his press release baldly announced, "the existing management of the Insull group of public utilities." The Insulls turned over all their utility holdings to I.U.I. (taking the precaution, to insure that every step was above reproach, of setting the price below market value) , in exchange for common and preferred stock of I.U.I. As compensation for certain services to be rendered and dividends to be surrendered, the Insulls also received an option to buy, at a price set at 25 per cent above the initially established price, a large additional bloc of I.U.I. common stock. The ticklish problem was what initial price to set on the common; the object was to choose a figure that would represent a fair exchange for the securities turned in to I.U.I. by realistically reflecting the anticipated market price of the new stock. After considerable discussion, during which everyone in the organization who knew anything about stocks made his guess, a figure of twelve dollars a share was settled upon, and the price under the Insulls' option to buy the additional shares was accordingly set at fifteen. [15]

What no one anticipated was that the stock market was about to go

[14] Insull, "Memoirs," pp. 201–2; Insull, Jr., to Insull, Aug. 23, Sept. 4, Sept. 12, Sept. 18, Sept. 20, 1928; working papers for the formation of Insull Utility Investments, in the Insull Papers; F.T.C., *Utility Corporations*, L, 160–78.

[15] *Minutes*, Insull Utility Investments directors' meeting, Dec. 27, 1928; Chicago *Investment News*, Dec. 1, 1928; the *Chicago Tribune*, Nov. 28, Dec. 27, Dec. 28, 1928; Jan. 17, 1929; Chicago *Journal of Commerce, Chicago Herald and Examiner*, Dec. 28, 1928; Insull's testimony in *U.S. v. Insull*, pp. 4311–21 (Nov. 1, 1934) ; Insull Utility Investments, Inc., prospectus for 5 per cent gold debentures, preliminary copy, Oct. 24, 1928; I.U.I., *The Insull Group of Public Utility Properties* (Chicago, 1930) .

mad. On the first day of trading in the I.U.I. common, on January 17, 1929, the stock opened at 25 and closed at 30. As winter turned into spring I.U.I. common soared from its initial price of $12 a share to sixty, seventy, eighty, and beyond; and when spring turned into summer it shot beyond a hundred and then to a hundred and fifty dollars a share. Commonwealth Edison went from 202 in January to 450 in August; Middle West rocketed from 169 to 529 in the same period. In the fifty days ending August 23, Insull securities appreciated at a round-the-clock rate of $7,000 a minute, for a total rise of more than half a billion dollars.[16]

While others were losing their heads, Insull kept his, at least for a time. He thought stock prices had gone berserk, and he not only said so but entered the runaway market and, until it became hopeless, tried to hold it down. This policy was contrary to his immediate personal interest, for the boom sent his personal fortune (on paper) soaring to almost a $150,000,000. (Insull was not entirely immune to the intoxication of these figures. "My God," he said to Stuart in one of his money-drunk moments, "A hundred and fifty million dollars! Do you know what I'm going to do? I'm going to buy me an ocean liner.") But he reckoned that the bubble must inevitably burst, and that when it did it would be disastrous to his stockholders and detrimental to the companies themselves. More critical, the boom overinflated the prices I.U.I had to pay for Insull stocks, thus obstructing the realization of the purpose in forming I.U.I; and he did not propose to allow himself to be enriched but thrown out, as Villard and Edison had been forty years earlier. To solve this problem and to correct a technical oversight which made it possible for an outside group to seize control of I.U.I itself, Insull capitalized on the bull market and formed a second investment trust, known as Corporation Securities Company of Chicago (commonly, Corp), on essentially the same basis as I.U.I., except that Corp and I.U.I. partially owned one another and control of Corp was assured through a voting trust. The net effect was that after September, 1929, these twin investment trusts emerged as the throne room of the Insull empire. Their holdings were not yet enough to insure control against all comers, but they

16 The *Chicago Tribune*, Jan. 17, Jan. 18, June 21, July 20, July 23, July 31, Aug. 1, Aug. 20, 1929; Chicago *Journal of Commerce*, Jan. 18, 1929; the *Chicago Daily News*, June 21, Aug. 23, 1929; *Chicago American*, Jan. 17, 1929; *Chicago Herald and Examiner*, June 21, July 23, Aug. 15, 1929.

constituted large minority blocs in each of the four major Insull companies.[17]

Insull used the bull market to good advantage in a second important way: to refinance Middle West. Middle West had outstanding various note and preferred stock issues, floated during the money drought in the early twenties and bearing high interest and dividend rates. Furthermore, its common stock had grown so high priced that Insull's hope of a wide basis of popular ownership—which was necessary if he was to control it with a minority holding—was in danger of being defeated. Accordingly, in a huge refinancing operation, Middle West split its stock ten for one, retired all its secured and floating debts, called in its 8 per cent preferred stock and reissued only a small amount of 5 per cent preferred, and, to facilitate future expansion by its subsidiaries, changed its common from a cash dividend basis to a stock dividend basis. The net result was that Middle West emerged free of debt and was able to reduce its fixed cash charges to practically zero.[18]

As the fall of 1929 approached Insull's self-confidence was matched only by his strength and prestige. He demonstrated each when the great crash came in October. The first thing he did was to go to the rescue of his employees who were caught with marginal brokerage accounts by supplying, from his personal portfolio, whatever additional collateral they needed. Ten days later, as if nothing had happened, he proceeded with the long-planned opening of the palatial

[17] Insull to E. Ogden Ketting, Aug. 7, 1929, in the Insull Papers; the *Chicago Daily News,* June 29, 1929; interview with Harry Reid, Lexington, Kentucky, Jan. 6, 1957; interviews with Carlos Drake, J. D. Scheinmann, Frank Evers, and Philip McEnroe, Los Angeles, Sept. 11–12, 1958; interview with H. L. Stuart, Chicago, Oct. 30, 1958; Insull Personal Account Books, 1929; Insull's testimony in *U.S. v. Insull,* pp. 4321–30 (Nov. 1, 1934); *Minutes,* Corporation Securities Company directors' meetings, September–October, 1929; the *Chicago Tribune, Chicago Journal of Commerce, Chicago Herald and Examiner,* Sept. 26, Oct. 6, Oct. 18, 1929; F.T.C., *Utility Corporations,* L, 335–73, LXVII, *passim.* The technical flaw in the I.U.I. organization was that an active market developed in its stock purchase rights (see pp. 129–30, above, for an explanation of these rights), and by purchasing rights outsiders might gain control of I.U.I.'s common stock.

[18] The *Chicago Tribune,* the *Chicago Daily News,* Sept. 17, 1929; *Minutes,* Middle West Utilities directors' meetings, July 27, Sept. 17, 1929, and *Annual Report,* 1929; Insull to Martin Insull, March 18, 1928; Martin Insull to Insull, March, 1927; "Insull Utility Investments Corp., Middle West Syndicate," a packet of letters and documents, in the Insull Papers; F.T.C., *Utility Corporations,* XXXVIII, 440–45. In its *Summary Report,* 72A 77–78, 565–87, the Federal Trade Commission placed an entirely different construction on this refinancing. The F.T.C.'s position is that maintained by the prosecution in Insull's mail fraud trial; for details, see chap. xii, below.

new Civic Opera House. At about the same time, he undertook a huge new venture for the gas company: With others, he began the construction of the great natural gas pipeline from the Texas panhandle to Chicago, a project that would cost around $80,000,000 by the time it was completed, late in 1931. But for the reality of his strength, what he did next would suggest that he was possessed of delusions of grandeur. Flexing his financial muscles, he took on greater and greater burdens until it appeared as if he were attempting to carry the entire American economy on his shoulders. By year's end the list of persons and businesses he had saved with his own resources and credit was huge. In January the City of Chicago itself stood facing bankruptcy, and Insull took on the task—immediately involving 50 to 100 million dollars—of rescuing it and enabling it to pay its firemen, policemen, and schoolteachers. In March it was upper New England, where he set out to rehabilitate the textile and shipbuilding industries. In April it was again Chicago, where the popular referendum assigned him the task of bailing out, integrating, and modernizing the city's transportation system, a venture that would run to $500,000,000.[19]

Supremely confident that this depression would be neither longer nor more severe than those he had weathered in the past, Insull geared his own business operations to that expectation. As a result, in 1930 he did three things that considerably weakened his position: He expanded far more than turned out to be prudent, he returned to debt financing, and he bought Eaton's holdings.

While each of these steps turned out to have been a mistake, each was dictated by the circumstances of the moment. As for the expansion, his electric companies had to keep their generating and distribution capacity ahead of the maximum demand upon them, and the demand continued to grow by leaps and bounds throughout 1930 and for the first six months of 1931. This was particularly true of the companies in the Middle West system; having primarily rural and

[19] The *Chicago Tribune, Chicago Evening Post, Chicago Herald and Examiner, Chicago American*, Oct. 31, Nov. 18, 1929, Jan. 17, 24, April–June, 1930; *Financial World*, June 11, 1930; *Chicago Evening Post*, Nov. 13, 1931; Julianne Doane (Dean of Women of Peoples Gas Company) to Insull, Oct. 29, 1929; R. H. James to Insull, Nov. 1, 1929 (both in the Insull Papers) ; *Minutes*, Peoples Gas directors' meetings, May 26, 1930, to Sept. 4, 1931, and its annual reports for 1929, 1930, and 1931.

small town loads, they were slow to feel the industrial cutbacks that were quickly felt in urban areas. For this reason, and also because Insull took seriously the pledge he and other tycoons made at President Hoover's famous business-as-usual conference of November 27, 1929, Insull companies spent $197,000,000 on capital investment during 1930.[20]

This in itself would not have been a weakening agent but for the fact that financing switched from equity to debt—that is, from stocks to bonds and debentures. The big bull market had restricted normal investment; in diverting money to speculation, it had all but dried up sources of money for anything else. The stock market crash wiped out many speculators and many bankers and brokers along with them, but it also restored the money market, and debt capital became available again in large quantities at low rates. The availability of low-interest debt capital and the instability of stocks dictated the use of the former in 1930, and the vast majority of Insull's financing during the year was in the form of bonds, debentures, and notes. The various operating companies increased their bonded debts by about 10 per cent each, and I.U.I. and Corp, to complete the purchasing they had set out to do, each got out large debt issues—$60,000,-000 in debentures by I.U.I. and $30,000,000 in serial gold notes by Corp.[21]

The borrowing by the operating companies was necessary, as was

[20] The *Chicago Tribune, Chicago Herald and Examiner,* Nov. 28, 1929; April 17, May 7, Oct. 13, 1930; Feb. 4, Feb. 25, March 9, July 20, 1931; annual reports for 1930 and 1931 of Middle West Utilities, Wisconsin Power and Light, Lake Superior District Power, and Kentucky Utilities; Securities Exchange Commission, Integration Hearings, 1940, for Central and South West Corporation, Central Power and Light, Central Illinois Public Service, Public Service Company of Oklahoma, Southwestern Gas and Electric, and Southwestern Power and Light (copies of all of which are in the files of Central and South West Corporation, Chicago) ; the *Chicago Daily News,* Nov. 27, 1929; the *Christian Science Monitor,* Dec. 4, 1929; *Investment News,* Dec. 9, 1929; Insull, "Memoirs," p. 242; Berry, "Mr. Samuel Insull," pp. 28–29.

[21] For weekly fluctuations in the cost of money, 1929–30, see the Saturday editions of the *Wall Street Journal* for the period; summaries are contained in *Historical Statistics of the United States,* Series N; for examples of contemporary planning by businessmen that reflected changes of the cost of money on loan see the *Chicago Tribune,* Nov. 18, 1929, Chicago *Journal of Commerce,* June 6, 1930, Chicago *Economist,* June 7, 1930; for the remainder of the data in this paragraph see the *Chicago Tribune,* the *Chicago Daily News, Chicago Herald and Examiner, Chicago American,* Jan. 3, June 6, June 7, Aug. 1, Sept. 12, 1930; annual reports for Middle West, Commonwealth Edison, Peoples Gas, and Public Service of Northern Illinois, 1930; "Summary Statement of Financing for the Insull Group," a statement prepared by Halsey, Stuart in 1934, a copy of which is in the Insull Papers.

also, given their commitments, that by the investment trusts. But one part of the new financing was sheer folly. In Sam's absence in Europe, and against the urgings of several advisers, his brother Martin undid most of the good accomplished in Middle West's 1929 refinancing: He caused Middle West to issue $50,000,000 in five-year serial gold notes, maturing at the rate of $10,000,000 a year. Much of the proceeds were spent not on utilities but on ancillary activities, such as an effort to restore the textile industry in upper New England; though Martin knew the utility man's maxim, "There are not many kilowatts in a bolt of cloth," he carried to a logical extreme Sam's principle that a utility must do all it can to preserve the economic health of the communities it serves. Besides, the new-found ease of raising money, after so many years of strain in financing Middle West, was more than Martin could resist. But if it was an understandable blunder, it was nonetheless a major blunder.[22]

Insull's 1930 financing set Chicago observers gaping. And if Chicagoans were impressed by a man willing to take on more than two hundred million dollars of new debts in the wake of the great crash, the New York investment bankers must have ached with envy. Insull's credit was so good that buyers snapped up and oversubscribed almost every issue; for the most part Halsey, Stuart did not have to sell the securities, it had to ration them, and though no one knew what the house profit was, at typical New York spreads it would have been ten to twenty million dollars. And while the easterners looked on longingly, Insull did something hardly calculated to win their undying love. At the annual dinner of the Chicago Stock Exchange in May, 1930, he delivered an incendiary blast against the concentration of financial power in New York. The speech was sensationalized in the newspapers as being a call for the middle west to rally in a war of financial liberation against Wall Street.[23]

22 F.T.C., *Utility Corporations*, XXXVIII, 452–53; *Minutes*, Middle West Utilities directors' meeting, June 10, 1929, and its *Annual Report* for 1930; Chicago *Economist*, June 7, 1930; the *Chicago Tribune*, Chicago *Journal of Commerce*, June 6, 1930; *Financial World*, June 11, 1930; interviews with H. L. Stuart, Fred Scheel, and Philip McEnroe, previously cited.
23 The *Chicago Tribune*, Chicago *Journal of Commerce*, the *Chicago Daily News*, Jan. 3, June 6, June 7, Aug. 1, Sept. 12, 1930; Insull, "Memoirs," pp. 209–11; interview with H. L. Stuart; "Summary Statement of Financing for the Insull Group." See also the Pecora Committee, *Hearings on Stock Exchange Practices*, Part 5, *passim*. There was

But at that very moment Insull was taking a step which, though designed to render him permanently invulnerable to raiders from the east, actually accomplished the opposite: It delivered him firmly into the hands of New York. Early in 1930 Eaton made his move, but it was a surprising one. He offered to consolidate all his holdings with those of Insull, under Insull's exclusive management, no strings attached. The consolidation would have greatly strengthened Insull's group and furnished a considerable number of operating companies easily integrated with those of Middle West. But Insull knew Eaton's reputation, and he had many men around him to remind him of it, and he needed no one to remind him that nothing is free. He did not know what Eaton wanted (half of Stuart's bond business, costing Insull nothing, would doubtless have been more than suitable, though Insull's suspicions ran in another direction), but he was convinced Eaton wanted something, and the apparent generosity of the offer made him all the more suspicious. Accordingly, he turned Eaton down.[24]

Had Eaton offered to sell his holdings, he might have expected to find Insull more receptive, for Insull had, since Charles Munroe's attempted raid at the turn of the century, bought out a long succession of petty raiders. Offer to sell is just what Eaton did. The market price of his holdings—160,000 shares of Edison, Peoples Gas, and Public Service—was around $52,000,000; Eaton offered them to Insull for $63,000,000. With the offer, he presented the ominous hint that should Insull not want the securities, they could easily be disposed of to a syndicate of New York investment bankers. Insull did not fully appreciate the hint, for he did not, even yet, understand what the financiers were seeking, but the idea that Eaton might pass the securities on to even less friendly parties was disturbing enough. Like a

one exception to the eagerness of the buyers: Corp originally planned to sell $40,000,000 in gold notes, but found that the market would absorb only $30,000,000; Insull, "Memoirs," p. 211; interview with Stuart; F.T.C., *Utility Corporations*, LXVII, *passim*. The speech is preserved in the Insull Papers; reports of it are contained in all Chicago newspapers, May 13, 1930.

24 Interviews with Eaton, Stuart, Stanley Field, Samuel Insull, Jr., Britton Budd, and the testimony of each (except Budd) in *U.S.* v. *Insull;* "Memorandum of Conference with Mr. Eaton on September 14, 1934," in the Insull Papers; Insull, "Memoirs," pp. 205–14; all Chicago newspapers, Oct. 18, 1934 (reporting the testimony of government witnesses in *U.S.* v. *Insull*).

parent coping with kidnapers, he was at a loss as to the strategy of his adversary; in his perplexed fancy, it was conceivable to him that Eaton or the new buyers might dump the securities on the open market, thereby annihilating it.[25]

It was the most crucial decision in Insull's life, and he had to make it alone. The three persons whose opinions he asked had three different opinions. Junior, who was beginning to think that money grew on trees, took a rash position, favoring buying outright. Martin, who was inebriated with the magic of paper and credit, took an unrealistic position: He favored buying, but not for cash. Stuart, who suffered neither of these maladies, but did not know that New York was after his business, not Insull's, took a conservative gambler's position. "Let him sell to New York," Stuart urged. "They'll just have to break it up into smaller units, and that will mean we can buy it cheaper later." For the moment, Insull took a middle ground. He offered to buy, but only at a price he thought reasonable and on terms he could manage. Eaton refused, and the negotiations broke down. Stuart then sailed for a vacation in Europe, first extracting a promise from Insull that, should the question arise again, he would not buy without first consulting Stuart on the means of financing the purchase.

In Stuart's absence, Insull had no trusted financier to consult, save possibly the ghost of John J. Mitchell. Mitchell's ghost soon appeared, in the distorted form of the inheritors of his bank. For several years before Mitchell's death, the directors and officers of the Continental National Bank had sought a merger with Mitchell's Illinois Merchants Trust Company, a merger that would have created the largest bank under one roof in the world. They made a succession of attractive offers, all of which Mitchell rejected; but as soon as he was dead the directors and major stockholders of his bank sold out. Thereby, the new Continental Illinois National Bank and Trust Company came, by default, to be Insull's bank. Now one of its directors came, by design, to be Eaton's messenger boy.[26]

---

[25] Eaton to McEnroe, June 5, 1930, and the subsequent telegraphic correspondence between Insull, McEnroe, Insull, Jr., Stuart, Martin Insull, and Eaton, all in the Insull Papers; otherwise, the sources for this and the following paragraph are identical to those in the preceding paragraph (note 24).

[26] James, *Growth of Chicago Banks*, II, 949–51; *Moody's Banks*, 1928, 1929.

Donald R. McLennan, the insurance man, was a director of Commonwealth Edison; in that capacity, he had won much of Insull's insurance business by devising ingenious ways of saving money in reinsurance. He was also one of the most influential directors of the Continental and an ardent aspirant after Cyrus Eaton's insurance account. McLennan sold insurance by doing favors, and in the Eaton situation, owning not a whisper of understanding that he was playing with a bomb, he set out to do everyone, and especially Eaton, a favor.[27]

Four times in the months of May and June, 1930, McLennan urged Insull to buy, and assured him that there could be no risk, for the mighty Continental Bank would be behind him all the way. Four times Insull refused. Then McLennan called a fifth time, and Insull said yes. He did so without consulting Stuart about permanent financing. As it turned out, permanent financing, under the market conditions of the moment, was temporarily impossible, and the only way to finance the purchase was through bank loans, secured by stocks from the I.U.I. and Corp portfolios. Then after Insull had agreed to buy— for $56,000,000, a compromise between Eaton's asking price and the market—it developed that the Continental could not finance the entire purchase, nor could other Chicago banks. There was no time to go to London; and after borrowing $5,000,000 from General Electric, Insull had no recourse except to turn to New York. The details of the various loans were extremely complex, but the net effect was that by the beginning of 1931 I.U.I. and Corp owned Eaton's holdings, and they had increased their floating indebtedness by $48,000,-000, approximately $20,000,000 of which was owed to New York.[28]

[27] McLennan's way of selling insurance has been described to me by several persons who had firsthand knowledge of it, notably Abner J. Stilwell, former vice-president of the Continental bank. Details of this event were pieced together from interviews with Britton Budd, R. H. James, H. L. Stuart, Fred Scheel, Herman Waldeck, and Samuel Insull, Jr., and from Insull, "Memoirs," pp. 205–8.
[28] F.T.C., *Utility Corporations*, LXVII, 801–44, 72A, 413–14; interviews with Budd, H. L. Stuart, Charles Stuart, Eaton, and James, previously cited; letters and telegrams between McEnroe, Insull, Insull, Jr., Martin Insull, Stuart, and Eaton, June, 1930, all in the Insull Papers; all Chicago and New York newspapers, Oct. 18, 1934. The web of intercorporate loans involved in these transactions has been traced in the minute books of Middle West, I.U.I., and Corp; they are accurately summarized in Insull, "Memoirs," pp. 205–14. For summaries of the net change in the floating debts of I.U.I. and Corp, compare their annual reports for 1929 and 1930.

Even though the New Yorkers took collateral worth half again as much as the loans, and even though they took only voting stock of the three major operating companies, thus providing themselves with a potential wedge into the heart of the Insull system, still a $20,000,-000 piece of a $3,000,000,000 empire is not very much. To make it enough, the New Yorkers would have to break the market in Insull securities to a fourth or less of their 1930 levels. Doing so would whipsaw Insull's twin investment trusts into a hopeless condition. Since a sizable portion of their income was in stocks of Insull utilities, reduction of the market value of the stocks would proportionately reduce their earning power, thus preventing the retirement or permanent financing of their floating debts and keeping them dependent upon bank credit. At the same time, each drop in the market would force the investment trusts to put up more collateral against their bank loans. If the market were driven down far enough, the bankers would have as collateral the entire portfolios of I.U.I. and Corp, and with that, control of the whole Insull empire.[29]

Breaking the market would be no easy task. All utility stocks, and particularly those of the Insull group, had held up strongly after the 1929 crash. Insull securities, across the board, were higher in each of the first four months of 1930 than they had been in the same months of 1929. Toward the end of 1930 they sagged somewhat, and on December 31 the securities held by I.U.I. and Corp had depreciated from their book value (cost) by just over $100,000,000, out of a total of $400,000,000. But when the annual reports for 1930 began to appear, showing that the Insull operating companies' earnings in 1930 had exceeded by 15 per cent the record earnings of 1929, the market responded and in the first forty-two days of 1931 the market value of the securities held by I.U.I. and Corp increased by $86,000,000,

[29] According to their annual reports for 1930, about 40 per cent of the gross income of I.U.I. and Corp in 1930 was in the form of stock dividends, reckoned at market prices on the dates the dividends were received. The combined floating debts of the two companies totaled about $73,000,000, against which were pledged securities with a book value of about $140,000,000, of a total combined portfolio of $394,000,000. The companies together held 17.19 per cent of the stock of Commonwealth Edison, 29.21 per cent of the stock of Middle West, 28.78 per cent of the stock of Peoples Gas, and 11.45 per cent of the stock of Public Service. I.U.I. also owned 26 per cent of Corp's common stock, and Corp owned 14.8 per cent of I.U.I.'s common stock. "Fiscal History of Insull Utility Investments Company," and "Fiscal History of Corporation Securities Company of Chicago," manuscripts in the Insull Papers; F.T.C., *Utility Corporations*, 72A, 156–57; interviews with Stilwell and Brown, previously cited.

almost entirely wiping out the previous depreciation. Throughout the late winter and early spring of 1931, Insull securities remained higher than they had been at the same time in 1929. And the earnings of the operating companies continued to grow; for the first six months of 1931 they were again at all-time record highs.[30]

The impersonal pressures on the market in Insull securities were thus almost evenly balanced: All the forces of Depression combined to drive it down, and the popularity of the securities and the repeatedly proved earning power of the Insull operating companies combined to hold it up.

But the matter was not to be left to impersonal forces; it was in the hands of two quite personal ones. One set of hands was the razor-sharp paws of the bear: the New York financial club, abristle with excitement at the prospect of giving Insull his comeuppance, at last, and atremble with the prospect of all those millions the venture promised. They were well equipped. Their financial resources were enormous, and as an indiscreet partner was to testify before a Senate investigating committee, the House of Morgan had thirty-two experts trading on the floor of the New York Stock Exchange—comparable arrangements on the other exchanges—who had power to manipulate the market, up or down, as it suited Morgan's needs. All the weapons of the bear raid were at their disposal: short selling, tape advertising, wash and matched sales, life or death power over the liquidation of brokerage accounts, and the deadliest weapon of all, the Wall Street rumor (Insull has committed suicide; Insull has been seen leaving a New York bank in tears; Insull is ill and his mind has snapped; Insull and Eaton are locked in a battle to the death, and Eaton is winning) .[31]

[30] Market quotations from the *Chicago Tribune* and the *Wall Street Journal;* annual reports of I.U.I., Corp, Commonwealth Edison, Peoples Gas, Middle West, and Public Service, for 1930; *Investment News*, Jan. 10, 1931; the *Chicago Tribune, Chicago Herald and Examiner*, the *Chicago Daily News*, the *New York Times*, Feb. 4, March 9, 1931. According to these newspapers for July 20, 1931, Commonwealth Edison's gross income for the first six months of 1931 was down about 4 per cent from the same period in 1930, but net income was up more than 6 per cent; the other two big operating companies had comparable figures. The gross earnings of Middle West's subsidiaries for the year ending June 30, 1931, were up 4 per cent over the earnings for the year ending June 30, 1930, and Middle West's income was up 6 per cent; its 1930 net earnings, in turn, had been 25 per cent higher than those of 1929.

[31] Testimony of George Whitney (a Morgan partner) , Pecora Committee, *Hearings on Stock Exchange Practices*, p. 125; interviews with Scheel, Scheinmann, Charles Stuart,

The other set of hands were those of Fred Scheel, Insull's security salesman par excellence, the man who organized the customer-ownership campaign, a man who, some said, was the most skilful market operator in the game. Scheel's assignment was to hold the market up, whatever the cost. His means were sophisticated in the extreme, but in essence what he did was to buy Insull securities on the exchanges and sell as much of it as possible in small lots through customer-ownership machinery. He had a strong secondary support: Speculators, the big daily traders, learned the price at which Scheel was pegging a particular stock and snapped it up when it fell a fraction below that price, knowing they could resell to Scheel if their buying and his did not push it back above its pegged price.[32]

Skilled as Scheel was, and vast as his resources were, it was a losing battle—barring a miraculous recovery in the market—and Scheel knew it. ("It's very simple," he said. "You can't go on buying your own stocks forever. Sooner or later you run out of money.") That being the case, he devised a shrewd tactic that could not fail. New York could force the market down, but Scheel controlled its descent. Very well then, said Scheel; the thing to do was to sell short the stocks he pegged, drop the peg a couple of notches, and make money instead of losing it at each decline. (Hence, for example, if Peoples Gas was pegged at $300, Scheel could sell short twenty thousand shares at $295, stop buying, let the stock slide to $270, and buy his twenty thousand at that price to deliver at his short-selling price, clearing $500,000.) New York could drive the price of every Insull

William Bauer, Frank Evers, Harold Stuart, and Eaton, previously cited; Rochester, *Rulers of America*, pp. 94, 336; Pecora, *Wall Street under Oath, passim;* the *Chicago Tribune, Chicago Evening Post,* the *Wall Street Journal,* May 27, June 4, Sept. 16, Sept. 17, Oct. 6, 1931.

[32] Data on Scheel and his methods are derived from the several interviews cited in note 31, above; from Scheel's testimony in *U.S. v. Insull,* pp. 5881 ff., 5984 ff.; from the corporate records of Utility Securities Company; from study of daily trading, as recorded in the *Chicago Tribune* and the *Wall Street Journal;* the *Chicago Daily News,* Aug. 1, 1931; and from two government investigations—the Pecora Committee, *Hearings on Stock Exchange Practices,* Part 5, and the F.T.C., *Utility Corporations,* LXVII, *passim,* and 72*A,* pp. 565–87. The latter accounts contain much valuable information, but are not entirely reliable, for the investigators seemed intent upon proving that the Insulls used the same kinds of tactics that New Yorkers did. This allegation was thoroughly explored in Insull's mail fraud trial, and in my opinion it is unwarranted. That Scheel did not imitate New York was not a matter of ethical practices but of customary techniques; his method, given his superefficient retailing machinery, was simply more effective, and therefore to him more desirable.

stock all the way to zero; en route, Scheel could make a billion dollars in cash and break every bank in New York. (Said Scheel, likening his task to Marshal Ney's rear-guard action during Napoleon's retreat from Moscow, "There wouldn't have been a live Russian left on the battlefield.") [33]

In Insull's absence, Scheel got Junior's permission to give it a trial run: he sold short five million dollars worth of Commonwealth Edison. When Insull returned, he exploded. "What in God's name," he thundered, "do you think you're doing?"

In careful detail, Scheel explained the market situation, the resources and methods of the opposition, and his plan of counterattack.

"And what will happen to the market in our securities?" Insull asked.

"Well," said Scheel, "if New York is crazy enough to keep on fighting, we'll end up with all the money and the market will slide to nothing."

"Scheel, we can't do that," Insull said. "That would be immoral." He did not need to explain why: he was constitutionally opposed to making money by betting that things would get worse; and besides, his men were at that moment hawking securities to small investors who could not afford to lose. "We've got a responsibility to our stockholders," he added. "We can't let them down."

"Mr. Insull," Scheel said, "they're going to be let down anyway. Unless we go short, we can't possibly win."

"Well," said Insull, "we've got to try."

So for all his immoral dreams of immortality, Samuel Insull could not, when the occasion demanded, commit the single immoral act that would make the dream come true.

(Equally relevant was that in spite of everything he knew, Insull could not, as late as midsummer, 1931, bring himself to believe that he was in serious danger. Late in August, shortly before going on a brief business trip to Europe, he summoned Junior and McEnroe to Libertyville for a briefing. McEnroe brought along Insull's personal account books and those of I.U.I. and Corp, and they reckoned his financial position. "Well," said Insull when it was done, "I

[33] The entire episode is derived from an interview with Scheel, in New Lenox, Illinois, Sept. 3, 1959. Some of the details were confirmed by Samuel Insull, Jr., J. D. Scheinmann, and Frank Evers.

never owed so much money in all my life put together; but then, I never had so much collateral, either." Said Junior, impertinently, "What are you going to do if your collateral goes bad?" Responded Insull, eyes twinkling, "In that case, Chappie, I'll put on my fighting clothes.") [34]

But the end was near. Scheel had been able to keep the market up through the bankers' panic of the summer of 1931, but in September—while Insull was in London—England went off the gold standard, and the New York Stock Exchange reacted with complete hysteria. General panic was given focus by a rumor that Insull was dead or dying in London, and from the week of September 9 onward the bears controlled the market and they drove it down relentlessly. In that week the stocks of I.U.I., Corp, Commonwealth Edison, and Middle West dropped in value by $150,000,000, and in the weeks that followed they careened ever downward. As the market declined, I.U.I. and Corp had to put up increasing amounts of securities as collateral against their bank loans. By mid-December the well had run dry; every nickel of the combined portfolios of the two investment trusts was in the hands of bank creditors. [35]

The events of the ensuing six months were nightmarish. Insull, mistakenly believing that the creditors would behave like creditors —that is, do everything to protect their loans—frantically tried to negotiate standstill agreements or extensions; and as he had done in earlier crises, he borrowed to the limit on his personal credit in be-

---

[34] Interviews with McEnroe and Insull, Jr., previously cited. The trip to Europe is mentioned in the Chicago *British American*, Oct. 10, 1931, and in Insull, "Memoirs," pp. 215–16. The situation described is reflected in a monthly summary of Insull's personal finances, in the Insull Papers.

[35] Market quotations and descriptions of pressures on it are from the *Chicago Tribune*, the *Wall Street Journal*, and the *New York Times*, January–December, 1931. Information about the little-known bankers' panic of the summer of 1931 is principally from the previously cited interview with Charles Stuart. An excellent brief description of the international chain of events leading to England's abandonment of the gold standard is in James, *Growth of Chicago Banks*, II, 1007–19. Insull was in London at the time and returned to Chicago immediately; Insull, "Memoirs," pp. 215–16. That I.U.I. and Corp had no more unpledged securities after about Dec. 16 is attested by Insull in his "Memoirs," pp. 216–20, and was confirmed in interviews with Insull, Jr., Edward Eagle Brown of the First National Bank, and Abner J. Stilwell of the Continental Bank. The I.U.I. and Corp annual reports for 1931 show nominal amounts of unpledged securities in each portfolio as of Dec. 31, 1931, but these, according to Brown, Stilwell, and Insull, Jr., were only "cats and dogs" that the bankers would not accept as collateral. According to Brown, the Chicago banks were surprised to learn that I.U.I. and Corp were out of collateral.

half of his companies, shifted money around from one of the companies to another so as to use the strongest to shore up the weakest, and effected drastic reorganizations to reduce expenses. The effort was pathetically futile: Its only effect was to enmesh him deeper, and to leave a confused, disorderly record that would soon be used against him.[36]

The walls had tumbled down, and after December the very earth began to disappear under his feet. First the Chicago banks—whom he had counted on—defaulted leadership to New York. They could do no other. As a whole, the relative newcomers who controlled Chicago banking had neither the vision nor the understanding to perceive their responsibility to the community at large, and only two of them had the courage and the experience to cope with the crisis. Furthermore, they did not have clean hands. Their banks were overly and illegally extended, and some of the key Chicago bankers had, like Charles Mitchell of the National City Bank in New York, sacrificed their own independence by personally borrowing huge sums (as much as ten and fifteen million dollars) from New York commercial banks in the Morgan group. Again, New York was in a better strategic position: Having been more selective in their choice of collateral, the New Yorkers held more of the voting stocks of the three major Insull operating companies, and thus a bigger voice in their affairs, than did the Chicago banks. Finally, the New Yorkers, recognizing the deep involvement of Chicago banks in the Insull situation, almost as an afterthought determined to try to seize control of Chicago's commercial banks as well as its investment banks. Accordingly, the Chicago banks were in no condition to save Insull or even Chicago: They had to save themselves.[37]

As a result, from Christmas, 1931, onward, the New York bankers

[36] The Insull Papers contain several hundred documents—letters, memoranda, telegrams, notes—covering these chaotic transactions; many of them are described in the Chicago newspapers from mid-April to the end of July, 1932; Insull describes them accurately and in orderly fashion, though only in general, in his "Memoirs," pp. 217–30; the first draft of his memoirs contains many more details; the streamlining of Middle West after December is described in *Report of Edward N. Hurley and Charles A. McCulloch, Receivers, Middle West Utilities Company* (Chicago, 1933), though the receivers do not give credit to Insull and Insull, Jr., for the streamlining; see Martin Insull's handwritten critique of this report, in the Insull Papers. See also the *Chicago Daily News*, Jan. 23, 1932, and *Chicago Evening Post*, Jan. 25, 1932. The several government inquiries cited earlier also contain much data.

[37] James, *Growth of Chicago Banks*, II, 979–80, 1021 ff.; Pecora Committee, *Hearings on Stock Exchange Practices*, 1529–44, 1677–87, 1728–45; Pecora, *Wall Street under Oath*, pp. 12–13; interviews with Stilwell and Brown, previously cited.

were in the saddle. Almost as soon as this became clear, some more earth dissolved underfoot. Insull had counted on two powerful New York banks—the National City and the Chase National—to be at least neutral and possibly friendly in a crisis. President Charles Mitchell of the National City was an old Chicagoan who had co-operated in Chicago traction financing, and President Albert Wiggin of the Chase was one of Insull's oldest friends, one so close that he had once asked Insull to become a director of his bank. But, in effect, one of these was blackmailed and the other was bribed, and neither stood by, and that left only Morgan. Coolly and with finesse, the Morgan group moved in for the kill. The kill took about six months, for though the House of Morgan could be devastatingly predatory, it was never impatient and it was never messy.[38]

Having control of sufficient stock, the bankers could have taken over by voting power. But they had no desire to be cast in the role of cruel creditor—or outright pirate—that such action would have involved. This was 1932, and corporate rape had ceased to be fashionable. Millions of unemployed Americans were seething with an as-yet-unfocused anger and hungering for some tangible person or institution against which to aim their hostility. In this situation it would have been inexpedient, if not suicidal, for the banks to have appeared as a raiding party, gutting a corporate empire at the expense of half a million small stockholders. What the bankers had to do was reverse the facts and cast themselves in the role of man on a white horse, rescuing the widows and orphans from the clutches of a scoundrel.

[38] The *Chicago Daily News*, Sept. 11, 1926; the *Chicago Tribune*, June 2, 1927; Berry, "Mr. Samuel Insull," p. 29; Insull, "Memoirs," first draft. The "blackmailing" of Mitchell was that he had sacrificed his independence by borrowing $10,000,000 from J. P. Morgan and Company; Pecora, *Wall Street under Oath*, pp. 12–13. Wiggins' case is more complicated. Harry Reid, Insull's marshal in the East, the active executive head of National Electric Power and National Public Service, negotiated with the Chase National and obtained a promise of all the credit the eastern properties needed, but then the pledge was suddenly and mysteriously withdrawn; interview with Reid, Lexington, Kentucky, Jan. 6, 1957. In subsequent interviews with Stilwell, Brown, and Stuart, it developed that while they had no direct recollection of what had happened, it appeared probable that Chase National had been invited to partake of bigger things, namely participation in the $60,000,000 of refinancing of the three big Insull operating companies, and a promise of future participation. This suspicion is confirmed by the *Minutes* of the directors' meetings of Commonwealth Edison, July 19 and July 27, 1932; Chase-Harris-Forbes, for the account of the Chase National Bank, now had a participation equal to the biggest participant, the Guaranty Company, of the Morgan group.

They set out deliberately to shift the spotlight, and they succeeded, in large measure, by simply changing the accounting system. In March, 1932, ostensibly searching for a solution, the New York bankers put in a new auditor, to supervise all expenditures by the Insull companies and maintain the status quo of all creditors, thus keeping Insull in handcuffs (he might, with his juggling, bring off a miracle; New York knew he had done it before) and incidentally to report any "improper transactions" they might turn up. Under the circumstances it was necessary that the new auditors be a firm with high professional standing and one with no extensive connection with Insull and his companies. The new auditors substituted the straight-line depreciation system used in industrial accounting for the retirement reserve system used by Insull and most other utility operators. By a stroke of the pen Middle West became insolvent; and when the system was extended backward, Middle West became retroactively insolvent, never having earned any money and thus nothing but a worthless pile of paper that had been kept alive only by continuous impairment of capital, disguised by improper bookkeeping. This provided the New York bankers with an excuse for anything they chose to do.[39]

But Insull was still a mighty and a popular man, and something of a more personal and more fraudulent nature had to be turned up before anyone dared depose him. He had just had occasion to demonstrate his continued popularity: In February, 1932, at the annual meetings of the stockholders of his various companies, he had won enthusiastic applause and a rousing vote of confidence from thousands

[39] The new auditors were Arthur Andersen & Co. Details of their appointment and their actions are from Chicago newspapers, April–July, 1932; Insull, "Memoirs," pp. 224–26; interviews with Stilwell and Brown; "Minutes of a meeting of bankers and others, held in the office of Samuel Insull, April 13, 1932," in the Insull Papers. The changes in the accounting system were primarily two: 1) appreciation of the book values of securities and subsidiaries, resulting from determinations made by Insull's accountants of the earning power and market prices of the securities of the subsidiaries following improvements and interconnections made by Middle West, were made no longer reckonable as income; and 2) the depreciation method was switched from a retirement amortization system to a straight-line depreciation system. Both changes are clear in the statement of Arthur Andersen & Co., printed in the *Report of . . . Receivers, Middle West Utilities Company*, p. 74. These changes deprived Middle West of a principal source of income and considerably increased its expenses. For a persuasive critique of Andersen's accounting see Martin Insull's handwritten notes on the receiver's report; his defense of the retirement system is more persuasive than his defense of write-ups. On Insull's depreciation system see above, pp. 126–27.

of stockholders, many of whom had come to the meetings bitter and hostile. He had also just demonstrated his power: During the catastrophic days from October to December, Junior had taken time to head an emergency fund-raising drive for the relief of the city's poor and unemployed, and in the midst of the holocaust he had collected more than $10,000,000; and then at Junior's instance Insull called a half-dozen political friends, with the result that the Illinois legislature enacted one of the nation's first and largest statewide relief programs.[40]

Through March and into April, the auditors uncovered one corporate indiscretion after another—particularly in the form of intercorporate loans made during Insull's last-ditch efforts to save his companies—and some critics of Insull who had learned of the discoveries leaked them to the press; but they were hardly enough. At first the press was skeptical, and even after it began to sensationalize the disclosures, Insull's personal reputation remained untarnished. But it developed that late in 1931, Russell, Brewster and Company—which in addition to handling much of Middle West's security operations was also Martin Insull's personal broker—had been overextended and, with a routine audit by examiners from the New York Stock Exchange coming up, faced the possibility of suspension. Because Russell, Brewster was, in the public eye, intimately associated with the Insull empire—many thought it was an Insull company—Insull feared that its suspension would set off a final wave of panic selling that would wipe out all Insull stockholders. In a futile effort to prevent this, he had caused a subsidiary of Commonwealth Edison to make a large unsecured loan to Russell, Brewster. Meanwhile, Martin Insull's own account went under. The brokers tried, for a time, to save Martin, and they were slow about liquidating his account. By the spring of 1932 the loan from Edison's subsidiary was worthless, and the circumstances surrounding the transactions were just confused enough to smack of fraud. The bankers dropped the hint to various members of Chicago's powerful Gold Coast elite, and they in turn spread the rumor: The Insulls had been embezzling! Insull was

[40] The *Chicago Daily News,* the *Chicago Tribune, Chicago Evening Post,* Chicago *Journal of Commerce, Chicago Herald and Examiner,* Jan. 16–21, Feb. 16, April–May, 1932; interviews with Insull, Jr., John Richert, and George F. Lennon, previously cited.

now thoroughly and personally tainted, and the bankers could safely raise the ax.[41]

They made their move in April. On Thursday, April 7, Insull and Stuart were in New York to discuss means of financing Middle West's $10,000,000 note issue coming due on June 1. The New Yorkers had not yet revealed their plans; it was a foregone conclusion that I.U.I. and Corp would have to go into receivership, to attempt to save something for the bank creditors and the holders of I.U.I.'s debentures, but neither Insull nor Stuart believed that Middle West was in serious trouble. The company was hardly in shape to weather a financial hurricane, but Insull had worked furiously since December, and it was now in reasonably good condition. Its operating subsidiaries all seemed secure, and Harry Reid, the executive in charge of Middle West's eastern subsidiaries, had negotiated with the Chase National what he thought was a firm promise of all the support the eastern companies needed. In the afternoon, Insull talked with the representative of a British investment house that had financed many of his operations, and with an officer of the Sun Life Insurance Company of Canada, and tentatively arranged for their participation in a syndicate to lend the money to cover Middle West's note.[42]

The next afternoon a meeting was convened in the office of Owen D. Young, chairman of General Electric and the New York Federal Reserve Bank, who served as mediator. Besides Insull, Stuart, and Young, a handful of bankers were present: men from Chicago's two biggest banks (Abner Stilwell of the Continental and Edward Eagle Brown of the First National), representatives of Insull's New York creditors, and a sprinkling of others. The talks had not got underway before strange things began to happen. First one,

[41] Spectacular "revelations" appeared almost daily in the various Chicago newspapers from April through August, 1932, and in many other large-city dailies as well. Details of Martin Insull's case are derived from *U.S.* v. *Martin Insull and Samuel Insull*, which is abundantly reported in all Chicago newspapers in March, 1935; they were acquitted on one count of the indictment, and the state's attorney dropped the case. Other data in this paragraph are from interviews with Stilwell, Brown, Stanley Field, and Herman Waldeck, previously cited, and from Insull's undated notes on the transfers of securities, in the Insull Papers.

[42] Insull, "Memoirs," pp. 227–28; interviews with Stilwell, Brown, Reid, and Stuart, previously cited; the *Chicago Daily News*, Jan. 23, 1932; the *Chicago Tribune*, Jan. 12, Jan. 15, March 19, 1932; *Financial World*, Feb. 17, 1932.

then three, then five men from Morgan banks—ostensibly, in no way involved in the matter—began to file in. Then Insull was invited to wait in a small adjoining room while they talked, and Stuart was sent out with him. Soon even Stilwell and Brown were sent out, but they were later allowed to return. After an hour, Young appeared at the door. It had been decided, he told Insull, that no one was going to put up any more money for Middle West.

Unbelieving, Insull asked, "Does this mean a receivership?"

"It looks that way," Young said. "I'm sorry, Mr. Insull."[43]

In silence, Insull and Stuart left the building. They caught a cab to pick up their bags, and took the next train for Chicago. Hour after endless hour they sat facing each other, wordless, as the train raced into the night. Finally, halfway to Chicago, Stuart ventured to speak.

"Mr. Insull?" he said, almost timidly.

"What is it, Stuart?"

"Mr. Insull," Stuart said, "do you know what I'd do if I were you?"

"What would you do, Stuart?"

"The first thing I'd do is hire the Chicago stadium. And then I'd get Mullaney and all his publicity people together, and I'd announce in every newspaper and on every radio station around Chicago, I'd announce that I was holding a mass meeting of everybody who owns any kind of Insull securities. It would draw 50,000 people, at least. And I'd go before them and tell them exactly what these bankers are doing to you, and to them."

"What good would that do?"

"It might not work at all. But even if it didn't, you'd at least have your side of the story before the public, and it would stick, no matter how the bankers lied about it. But I think it would work, and if it did, one of two things would happen. What I believe is, that they'd get the money for you, and we could save Middle West. And if they couldn't, the next morning they'd pull such a run on the Chicago banks that they'd break every God-damned bank in Chicago, and maybe in New York too."

For an instant only, Insull's eyes lit up, charged by the audacity of Stuart's proposal. The Insull of old would have done it, or something

[43] Insull, "Memoirs," pp. 228–30; interviews with Stilwell, Brown, and Stuart, previously cited. On this episode see also Young's testimony before the Pecora Committee, *Hearings*, pp. 1507–29.

equally daring and dramatic, and he would not have needed Stuart to prompt him. But his spirit's sword was dulled by the long battle, and he had no fight left in him. He slumped back into his seat, and the fire in his eyes went out. "Aw, hell," he said. "Somebody would just shoot me." [44]

And so, for the want of ten million dollars, a billion and a half dollar corporation went under. The first ax had fallen.

I.U.I. and Corp were down, and so was Middle West. National Electric Power, Middle West's eastern division, soon followed, for the Chase National was invited to partake in bigger stakes, and it withdrew its support. Midland and the elevateds did not count; they were controlled by the other companies. All that remained was to shove Insull out of his three major operating companies—Peoples Gas, Public Service, and Commonwealth Edison. This was no trivial part of the job, for they represented, after all, a third of the empire, and from them Insull might one day be able to strike back; and besides, without them the coveted prize, Stuart's bond business, would remain out of New York's grasp. Furthermore, it would be a difficult undertaking, if Insull chose to fight and his men fought with him. Inside men—men who had grown up as Insull's employees—were in a majority on all three boards of directors, and folding up I.U.I. had taught the bankers that Insull could not be dislodged by calling the stockholders. (For tactical reasons, the bankers had wanted the receivership to originate in a suit by a private holder of I.U.I. debentures, and they had had to go all the way to Iowa before they found one who would do it.) Besides, the three companies were the essence of solvency; each was capable of enduring another decade of Depression without so much as skipping a common stock dividend or dipping into earned surplus to pay it. Finally, no one, inside the organization or out, believed anyone would dare attempt to dislodge Insull from the Edison Company.[45]

[44] Interview with Harold L. Stuart.

[45] See note 38, above; annual reports of the several companies, 1931; *Minutes*, directors' meetings, January–June, 1932, of Commonwealth Edison, Peoples Gas, and Public Service; interview with Abner Stilwell. The general comment regarding the solvency of the three companies is based upon study of *Moody's Public Utilities*, 1931–40. That no one believed that anyone dared depose Insull is clear from the general tone of Chicago newspapers in May and early June, 1932, and interviews with fifty to a hundred individuals who were close to the scene.

There was one hint of a weak spot in the three operating companies: Between them, they had $60,000,000 in notes falling due in July. This was, in fact, no weak spot at all, for Stuart was already set to market bonds, at favorable interest rates, to finance the notes. But it offered an appropriate pretext for the occasion; the bankers could maintain that in the wake of all the receiverships and all the scandal, the credit of the operating companies would vanish if Insull remained. So if Insull was to be dethroned, now was the time for a naked power play.[46]

Not quite naked: they planned it secretly and executed it stealthily. During the first week of June, Martin, Insull, Jr., and all the executives of the two electric companies would be in New Jersey at a convention of the National Electric Light Association, and Stuart would be on a brief vacation in West Virginia;[47] Insull would remain in town at his Lake Shore Drive apartment. In private, the outside directors of the three companies—the Gold Coasters and those who represented Chicago banks—met late in May with bankers from New York and Chicago and nominated Insull's trusted friend Stanley Field to carry their message. On Saturday afternoon, June 4, Field called upon Insull in his office. "Mr. Insull," he said, "we want your resignations, and we want them now." [48]

---

[46] *Minutes,* Commonwealth Edison directors' meeting, July 21, 1931; Chicago *Journal of Commerce,* the *Chicago Tribune, Chicago Herald and Examiner,* July 23, July 24, 1931; March 1, 1932; Insull, "Memoirs," p. 238; interview with Stuart; working papers for 1932 refinancing, in the Insull Papers. Edison had $20,000,000 in notes due on July 30; Peoples Gas had $15,000,000 in notes due on the same date; Public Service had $15,000,000 in notes due on that date and $10,000,000 in debentures due on August 1; Stuart proposed to sell $60,000,000 in bonds to refinance the maturities. He said at the time, and repeated in an interview with me, that he was able to sell the bonds at a considerably more favorable price than the New Yorkers were able to obtain, and that their profits were exorbitant. Judging by the statements of financial writers, no one anticipated difficulty in this financing.

[47] N.E.L.A. *Proceedings,* 1932; interviews with Edward J. Doyle, Philip McEnroe, Helen Norris, Insull, Jr., and other Insull executives, previously cited; interview with Stuart.

[48] This scene with Field is based upon details gained during an interview with him, previously cited. Insull, "Memoirs," pp. 235–38, narrates the incident, but without the dialogue. Otherwise, the two accounts coincide. The outside directors were Field, Sewell L. Avery, and Donald R. McLennan, all of whom were directors of the Continental Bank as well as the Edison Company; Solomon Smith, director of Edison and Public Service and president of the Northern Trust Company; the Chicago bankers were Melvin A. Traylor and Edward Eagle Brown of the First National and A. W. Harris of the Harris Trust. Insull, "Memoirs," pp. 237–38; interview with Abner J. Stilwell. I have been unable to learn for certain which New York bankers were present.

"The hell you do," Insull replied.

"Yes, we do," Field said, "and we're going to have them."

Insull stared at Field a long time. At last he answered. "All right, I'll resign from everything. But I won't do it through the back door on a Saturday afternoon. I'll do it properly. You call special meetings of all the boards for Monday, and you can have my resignations then."

But it could not end so easily, for he had yet to tell Gladys. It took all night. At six o'clock on Sunday morning, he finally got her to sleep, but only by making a promise: He would try.[49]

He did not know how the inside directors would react if he chose to fight. Stuart, he knew, would fight to the end, and Martin and Junior were certain, but of the likes of Budd and Gilchrist and Doyle and Ferguson he could not be sure; and loyal as they were, it was a terrible decision to impose upon them. As it happened, there was a testing ground at hand: by chance, Britton Budd, the ablest and most tenacious of the lot, had skipped the convention, and he was asleep in his apartment only a few blocks away. If Budd's instinctive reaction to the news was to fight, Insull would fight; if it was not, then so be it.

At six-fifteen Insull telephoned Budd and asked him to come over, and in a quarter of an hour Budd was there. Insull met him at the door and, whispering so as not to awaken Gladys, took him down to the far end of the great living room, overlooking Lake Michigan. Quickly he told Budd what had happened. He asked Budd no questions and did not explain his intentions, but he gave him a broad hint. "It's those bastards at the Continental," he said. "They got us into this. Four times they asked me to buy out Eaton, and four times I refused, but they kept insisting that they would cover us, and finally I did it. And now they're demanding that I resign."

With red eyes and poker face he watched Budd, waiting his answer. It came: "Well, Mr. Insull, I'm sorry. But you've built a monument that they can't tear down."

His face still blank, Insull sighed, and ended the conversation. "Thank you, Budd," he said. "I'm counting on you fellows to keep my memory green."

[49] The following scene with Budd is based upon details gained during an interview with him, Chicago, June 22, 1959.

On Monday, June 6, the deed was done. Insull dictated and signed papers all day, drafting resignations from chairmanships and presidencies and receiverships of sixty-odd corporations, and each time Insull resigned the directors framed suitable resolutions of commendation for his long and treasured services, and ordered them spread upon the minutes, and ordered that finely engraved copies be prepared and bound and sent to Mr. Insull as a token of their appreciation.[50]

All afternoon, as the orgy of resignations and resolutions went on, newspapermen swarmed around Insull's door. When it was over, and he emerged, they saw his face and a hush descended upon them. His statement to the press was a single sentence: "Well, gentlemen, here I am, after forty years a man without a job."

He shuffled off, then stopped and turned to a faithful flunky. "I guess you'd better call Mrs. Insull, and tell her." He started off again, then turned again and said, "But she may be asleep. Never mind. I'll tell her myself."

And he wandered off into the dusk, to watch the city light up one last time.

[50] The following episode is reported in all Chicago newspapers, June 7, 1932; some of the details of the scene were reported again at the time of his death, July 16, 1938; the transactions have been studied in the minute books of the several companies; the engraved copies of the resolutions are preserved in the Insull Papers; Insull's brief account of the incident is in his "Memoirs," p. 238.

Insull waiting to board the Manhattan Limited for re-turn to Chicago. (NEW YORK DAILY NEWS)

Insull on arrival in Chicago. (CHICAGO TRIBUNE)

Insull on way to Cook County Jail. (CHICAGO TRIBUNE)

Insull released from jail after posting bond. (CHICAGO TRIBUNE)

Insull in courtroom during trial for mail fraud. (CHICAGO TRIBUNE)

Martin Insull, Insull's brother, president and active head of Middle West Utilities. (MARTIN INSULL)

Federal Judge John C. Knox and Judge James H. Wilkerson (CHICAGO TRIBUNE)

Judge Cornelius J. Harrington (CHICAGO TRIBUNE)

Attorney Dwight H. Green (CHICAGO TRIBUNE)

Frank L. Smith, chairman of the Illinois Commerce Commission. (CHICAGO TRIBUNE)

The defendants in the courtroom of Judge Wilkerson. Back row, *Harold
L. Stuart, Waldo F. Tobey, Edward J. Doyle, Clarence W. Sills, Samuel
Insull, Sr., Fred Scheel.* (CHICAGO TRIBUNE)

Attorney Dwight H. Green and two assistants to the Attorney General,
Forrest Harness and Leslie E. Salter, examine the mountain of evidence
accumulated for the mail fraud trial. (CHICAGO HISTORICAL SOCIETY)

THE DARING OLD MAN

Insull's unremitting effort to clear his name, as caricatured by Vaughan Shoemaker in 1935. (CHICAGO DAILY NEWS)

n Criminal Court, December 21, 1934, Samuel Insull, Jr., Martin Insull, ohn E. Northrup, and Samuel Insull, Sr., await the verdict. (CHICAGO RIBUNE)

CHAPTER XII *The Trial*

When he was on top, almost everyone who counted had been on Insull's side, and out of fear, those who were not had held their peace. Then as the war drums began to roll and the battle shaped up, there were two sides. The coalitions were numerous and tenuous and shifting and confused, and no one could be sure where everyone stood, but it was clear that there were just two sides. Then Insull lost, and there was just one side again.

After Insull lost, his erstwhile enemies reacted in two ways. Those who had won—the financial enemies—wanted no more: Having devoured his flesh, they hungered not to pick his bones. Those who had been foes but not in the battle—the political enemies—had only had their appetites whetted. Insull's sometime friends, on the other hand, reacted in four ways. Some were opportunists, and many were passive friends, and a handful were fighting friends.

In 1929 and 1930 Royal F. Munger, the financial writer for the *Chicago Daily News,* was the chief yea-sayer among the financial reporters, singing Insull's praises to the point of idolatry. In 1931 he wrote as if he had been hired as chief apologist for the losses of the year, and even as late as February, 1932, he played the role of chief whistler in the dark. But as soon as Insull's empire collapsed, Munger was among the newspapermen calling for his scalp. Playing to both sets of victors, he began praising the bankers who had "rescued" the Insull companies and shouting for municipal ownership of all utilities in future.[1]

[1] See, for example, Munger's articles in the *Chicago Daily News,* Aug. 23, Oct. 31, 1929; Nov. 26, 1930; Dec. 24, 1931; Jan. 23, Feb. 8, Feb. 16, Sept. 14, 1932.

The opportunists were more devious and more destructive. Salivating with greed, hordes of once-friendly businessmen in Chicago and New York swarmed to join in the looting, but to Insull, personally, they proved to be less damaging, albeit more eager, than the political opportunists. Because Insull had nothing left worth stealing, plunderers could harm him only indirectly. They could pillage his companies and cover their doings with continued denunciations of his management, but since his reputation had already been made as black as sin, a little additional tarnish could scarcely destroy him. Furthermore, though perhaps as many fortunes were being made as had been lost in the collapse, theft by scavengers was kept relatively modest by the actions of two men, Edward Eagle Brown and Abner J. Stilwell, the trouble vice-presidents of the First National and Continental banks, who inherited the mess. They must at times have felt like a pair of policemen at a pickpockets' ball, and they often faced the embarrassment of catching important people from their own banks with hands in one Insull till or another, but they were tough, shrewd, incorruptible, and they held the thievery within reasonable bounds.[2]

Once-friendly politicians were slower to seize the opportunities afforded by Insull's fall, even though it was an election year. Capitalizing on the situation meant running against Insull rather than against one's opponent. Because the elections portended almost certain Democratic victories, it was only incumbent Republicans, fighting for their political lives, who might have to resort to such devices, and few of them were anxious to attack Insull, even in his exile. Almost all were sincere friends of Insull's; then, too, almost none could stir up scandal about him without fear of exposing their own involvement in it. Furthermore, there was a psychological barrier. For the first two or three months, no one except the bankers knew

---

[2] The pillaging is hinted at, from time to time, in all Chicago newspapers throughout 1932 and 1933, but the principal sources for this information have been interviews with persons who were in inside positions at the time, notably Stilwell and Brown, Samuel Insull, Jr. (who remained as assistant to the chairman of the three big operating companies), Ralph D. Stevenson (who was attorney for Middle West), Edward J. Doyle (who remained as president of Commonwealth Edison), and Philip McEnroe. Mr. Stilwell kindly furnished many facts, figures, and names, on condition that I use the information generally, not specifically. The judgment of the quality of Stilwell and Brown is my own, but it is shared by most members of the Chicago business and banking community.

how completely defeated Insull was. Chicago politicians were rather in the position the politicians of France had been in when Napoleon was first in exile: no one could be sure that he would not return from Elba.[3]

Meantime, Insull was quietly vanishing, at least temporarily. Nervous, exhausted, and at wit's end after his resignations, nonetheless he felt that he should stay in Chicago. But after two or three floor-pacing days, punctuated by regular and awkward visits from former subordinates who came to protest changes being introduced by the new management, he decided to leave. He would, as he usually did when he was badly in need of rest, go to Europe by way of Canada (that being slower and quieter than sailing from New York), and he would remain there until his nerves had healed and the Chicago climate was less frenzied. Not wanting to be hounded by newsmen along the way, he made no public announcement of his plans, but he made no particular secret of them, either. On Tuesday morning, June 14, he boarded a train for Montreal; the ever-loyal Phil Mc-Enroe kept him company. The next day McEnroe returned to Chicago, and Insull went on to Quebec, where he caught a ship for Cherbourg. A little later, Gladys joined him in Paris. After a brief flurry of headlines following his "discovery" in Paris by a Chicago newspaperman, the Insulls settled in a Paris apartment hotel to live in relative obscurity.[4]

He had no plans except to rest. After the long battle, every muscle, every brain cell, every nerve ending was exhausted, and he wanted only to be left alone for awhile. He expected to be consulted from time to time about the affairs of his companies; and in September he went to London to meet and discuss several problems with James Simpson, who had been brought in to succeed him as head of the three major operating companies. But in the main he spent an untroubled and inactive summer in Paris. He was even without financial worries. Under Illinois law, Gladys' dower rights consisted of one-

[3] Rumors were persistent that Insull had concealed a private fortune; the figure most often cited was $10,000,000. See all Chicago newspapers, July–August, 1932. Furthermore, many people knew of Insull's friendship with Sir Basil Zaharoff and even late in 1933 were fearful that somehow Zaharoff and Insull were up to something. See, for example, Marquis W. Child's letter to the editor in the *New Republic*, Nov. 22, 1933.

[4] Insull, "Memoirs," p. 249; interview with Philip McEnroe; interview with Mrs. Tiffany Blake, Chicago, Feb. 4, 1958; interview with Helen Norris, Chicago, July 16, 1958; all Chicago newspapers, July, 1932.

third of his estate, and though all his liquid property was lost in the collapse and he owed $16,000,000 more than he owned, she still had a claim to half the Libertyville estate, a paid-up life insurance policy, and an assortment of smaller items of property, the total value of which was close to a million dollars. He was not anxious to protect himself with his wife's skirts, and agreed in principle when his bank creditors argued that they had lent him money in good faith with th expectation that all his property was being pledged as collateral. But then, he was hardly able to go looking for a job to support himself and Gladys; it was her property, not his; and he expected that she would survive him many years. For these reasons, he balked. After several discussions, Abner Stilwell came up with a proposal. Insull had earned pensions totaling $21,500 a year from the three operating companies, and for a long time all the companies had made a practice of continuing pensions to widows of retired employees, usually at a reduced rate. In Insull's case, the directors of the three companies had voted, even as they asked for his resignations, to increase his pensions to $50,000 a year during his lifetime, and to pay Gladys $25,000 a year during the remainder of her life if she survived him. Stilwell suggested that in view of this Insull should induce Gladys to sign over her dower rights. Insull agreed, and the bargain was struck. (Said Gladys: "I'm a damned fool, but I'll do it.") [5]

But obscurity and comfort died with the summer, for Chicago politicians—first one, then almost all—finally succumbed to the logic of events. John Swanson, state's attorney for Cook County, an able and respected citizen, a friend and admirer of Insull's, a Deneen Republican, faced overwhelming odds in his campaign for re-election. As early as June his political advisers urged him to capitalize on Insull's collapse and ride the publicity and the scandal to political victory. The pickings, they said, would be easy: Everyone knew that a close look, such as only the state's attorney was in a position to take, would uncover enough dirt to smear political enemies in every faction in both parties. Only through such a crusade, they argued, could he dissociate himself from a political and economic order that the people were clamoring to repudiate in November. Day after day,

---

[5] Insull, "Memoirs," pp. 241, 250; interviews with Stanley Field, Edward J. Doyle, and Abner J. Stilwell, previously cited; *Minutes,* Commonwealth Edison directors' meetings, June 6, July 26, 1932; *Minutes,* Peoples Gas, directors' meeting, July 26, 1932.

through the long, sweltering, turbulent summer of 1932, Swanson's managers so advised him, and day after day, like every other important politician in Chicago, he refused. At first he even refused to admit that re-election would be difficult. Political insiders whispered that Swanson was confident because of a deal with Democratic Mayor Anton Cermak; Swanson had, it was said, executed a strategically timed raid in 1931 that had embarrassed fellow Republicans and insured Cermak's election, and Cermak had promosed Swanson the vote of the Democratic machine in 1932. It was even said that Cermak had allowed Swanson to choose his Democratic opponent. But early in September, Swanson suddenly began to "run scared," and wiseacres began to whisper that Cermak had withdrawn his support.[6]

On September 15, at about eight o'clock in the morning, Swanson rode into the Loop on a train built and, until three months before, operated by Insull. Across from him sat his son-in-law. The son-in-law, concerned by his harrassed look, asked what was the matter. Swanson summarized the situation for him and then paused, sadly, reflectively. "You know," he said at last, "Sam Insull is the greatest man I've ever known. No one has ever done more for Chicago, and I know he has never taken a dishonest dollar." Another pause, and then a faint, resigned shrug of his shoulders, as if to say, "But Insull knows politics, and he will understand," and then Swanson said, "But I've got to do it." At ten o'clock that morning, Swanson held a press conference, and soberly announced to the assembled reporters that he was launching an investigation of the scandals involved in the Insull collapse.[7]

For the next nineteen days, Swanson's swashbuckling investigation captured front-page headlines in every Chicago daily, and during those days politicians the nation over entered into competition with him, trying to run hardest against Insull. Democratic presidential nominee Franklin Roosevelt, campaigning on the west coast, needed little urging to induce him to join the fray, and he had urging in abundance, for he numbered among his campaign managers and

[6] William H. Stuart, *Twenty Incredible Years*, pp. 356, 362, 373, 376, 466, 488, 501; Stuart's columns in the *Chicago American*, July–August, 1932; interviews with Stuart and Nate Gross, previously cited; Wendt and Kogan, *Big Bill of Chicago*, p. 332; interview with Russell Olson (Swanson's son-in-law) , Chicago, Dec. 31, 1959.
[7] Interview with Russell Olson, Chicago, Dec. 31, 1959; all Chicago newspapers, Sept. 15, Sept. 16, 1932.

speechwriters Donald Richberg and Harold Ickes, two of Insull's oldest political enemies, and A. A. Berle, Jr., an economist who had run afoul of Insull's and the industry's propaganda machinery. On September 21, in one of the rare occasions in which he discussed personalities in public, Roosevelt delivered a long attack upon Insull before a large audience in Portland, Oregon. Within forty-eight hours Democratic candidates for public offices from alderman to governor, in virtually every state where Insull companies had operated, echoed their leader's sentiments. In Insull's home state, Probate Court Judge Henry Horner, Democratic candidate for governor, led his party's attack. And every day for another week, as he moved toward Chicago from the Coast, Roosevelt blasted Insull again.[8]

Swanson, not to be outdone, seized the banner headlines in the dailies of Chicago, New York, and points between by releasing to the press the first of two aces he had in the hole: the secret list of "insiders" who had been allowed to buy Insull Utility Investments common stock at twelve dollars a share in January, 1929 ("Half price!" said the *Tribune*). But for the circumstances, the list might have attracted little attention. It included a few newsworthy names, such as those of South Trimble, the clerk of the United States House of Representatives, Owen D. Young, chairman of General Electric and the author of the celebrated Young International War Reparations Plan, and Samuel Ettleson, Big Bill Thompson's erstwhile corporation counsel; but in the main it consisted of people everyone knew were Insull's friends and associates, ranging from opera singer Rosa Raisa to Insull's valet, T. W. Obee. But Swanson's success in releasing the list further stimulated politicians everywhere to join in the fun: On September 24, Progressive Republican Senator Peter Norbeck of South Dakota announced that he would personally launch an

[8] The *Chicago Tribune,* the *Chicago Daily News,* Madison *Capital Times,* the *New York Times,* Sept. 17–24, 1932; interview with A. A. Berle, Jr., Providence, Oct. 2, 1961. Berle's brilliant classic, *The Modern Corporation,* had been published in Chicago earlier in the year, and then suddenly and mysteriously suppressed. Because of the reputation the Committees on Public Utility Information had for such activities, Berle assumed they were responsible; in the heat of the political campaign, he had no time to find out for sure. Berle wrote Roosevelt's Portland speech and the celebrated Commonwealth Club speech, in both of which Insull was denounced. In Berle's draft of the latter, he had denounced only "the Ishmaels, whose hand is against every man's." Apparently Roosevelt himself added Insull's name, thus creating the widely quoted line, "the Ishmaels and the Insulls."

investigation of the Insull empire; the next day the regular Republicans countered with U.S. Attorney Dwight H. Green's announcement that the Department of Justice had commenced a full-scale investigation of the Insull companies; and two days later Norman Thomas, the Socialist candidate for President, ventured that he was probably more opposed to Insull than anybody.[9]

Swanson now played his second ace: He released another syndicate list, this one politically explosive and timed to do maximum damage to Democrats. Roosevelt, en route from the West to attend the New York state Democratic convention, had scheduled an important fence-mending stop in Chicago. During the last week in September, Roosevelt appeared to be headed for political trouble: New York Democrats, in a rebellion led by his erstwhile friend Al Smith, seemed about to slip from his grasp, and Mayor Cermak, the Illinois Democratic boss, had never been friendly—in fact, refused to support him at the national convention. It therefore seemed prudent, if not imperative, for Roosevelt to establish friendly relations with Cermak. Roosevelt apparently planned to do two things in Chicago: throw his arms around Cermak in fond embrace and climax his ten-day campaign against Insull with a major blast in Insull's home town. But when he debarked from the train in Chicago, he was greeted by newspaper headlines announcing Swanson's exposé of the second syndicate list. Heading the list of newly revealed Insull insiders was Mayor Cermak. Roosevelt hastily deleted Insull from the speech he had prepared, and for a time he dropped Insull as a subject for attack.[10]

But no one else did. The second list, dated August, 1930, was of an I.U.I. stock-selling syndicate, and it was embarrassing even to Swanson, for it included the name of Pat Roche, his own chief investigator. But it was too good to hold, and the opportunity was too great to permit squeamishness. On the list, in addition to Cermak and Insull's friends, associates, and employees, and celebrities from the

[9] The *Chicago Tribune,* the *Chicago Daily News, Chicago American,* the *New York Times,* Sept. 23–27, 1932; see also the *New Republic,* Sept. 21, Sept. 28, Oct. 5, 1932. The first syndicate list was published in the newspapers on September 23, 1932.
[10] All Chicago newspapers, the *New York Times,* Sept. 30, Oct. 1–5, and throughout October, 1932. The events related in these two paragraphs were covered most fully in Chicago newspapers, but in one form and another they were front-page stories in almost every newspaper in America.

business and musical worlds, was a virtual all-star team of politicians —the lieutenant-governor and a former lieutenant-governor of Illinois; a number of state and federal judges and their relatives; the speaker of the state House of Representatives; political boss Billy Lorimer; political operator Moe Rosenberg; Melvin Traylor, the candidate who had lost to Herbert Hoover in the Republican presidential nomination of 1928; and Joseph Tumulty, Woodrow Wilson's former private secretary. This was September 30. On the next day the Cook County grand jury convened, and Swanson asked them to indict Samuel and Martin Insull for embezzlement, larceny, and larceny by bailee. Three days later, on October 4, the grand jury returned indictments. Swanson's whirlwind performance was hard to top, but until election eve scores of politicians kept trying.

Meantime, even more clearly than Swanson had expected, Insull understood. Through friends and the Paris edition of the *Tribune,* he kept a watchful eye on events after September 15. As soon as Swanson released the second syndicate list and thereby violated the professional politicians' code (calling one's enemies crooks is legitimate but documenting it is unforgivable), Insull realized the full implications of the situation. Convinced that a political lynching was in the wind, and vaguely preoccupied with a fear of assassination that had haunted him since April, he decided not to return to Chicago until the political climate calmed. As it happened, Insull, Jr., had just arrived in Paris on a mission from his new boss, James Simpson—he was to persuade Insull that it would be wise to take a temporary cut in his pensions to $21,500, the earned amount—and he concurred in his father's judgment. After a day's conversation, Junior urged Insull to leave Paris. Junior suggested Milan as a destination, but they decided upon Athens because the influence there of Insull's old friend Sir Basil Zaharoff might be useful and because Judge George Cooke, Insull's most trusted lawyer, cabled that Greece had no extradition treaty with the United States.[11]

[11] Insull, "Memoirs," pp. 250–51; interview with Floyd Thompson (Insull's attorney in the mail fraud trial, 1934), Chicago, Aug. 31, 1959; interviews with Samuel Insull, Jr., previously cited; Berry, "Mr. Samuel Insull," pp. 31–32. The letter to the *New Republic,* cited in note 3, above, correctly mentions the Zaharoff connection, though the speculations in the latter are absurd. As to the fear of assassination, it was confided to Harold Stuart, as stated in chap. xi, above; to Insull, Jr.; and to Berry ("Mr. Samuel Insull," p. 53); and in the *Chicago Tribune,* Nov. 13, 1932, Insull is quoted as being fearful of assassination.

On October 4, at almost the same moment that the grand jury was returning its indictment, Insull and Junior entrained to Turin. After reporting to local police, registering under their own names in a hotel, and staying overnight, they went on to Milan, where Junior managed to charter an airplane to Salonika. On the eve of Insull's departure, the two men emptied their pockets in their hotel bedroom and counted what they had—between them, just under $3,000. Junior kept enough to get him back to Paris, and Insull took the rest. (Except for occasional loans and gifts from friends and such money as his son could scrape up, that was to be Insull's means of support for three years, for the bankers and Gold Coasters who dominated the boards of directors of the Chicago operating companies, fearing political criticism, broke their promise and cut off Insull's pensions.) Insull then flew to Greece, and with his arrival began one of the most bizarre international legal fiascoes in history.[12]

For the next nineteen months, the arena belonged to Insull, Jr., on one side and the governments of the United States and the state of Illinois on the other. Insull (and to a lesser extent Martin, who was in Canada, from which, as a British citizen, he could be ejected only by long and technical extradition proceedings) was the spectacular center of public attention, but the quiet, deadly drama was a legal battle between Junior and officialdom, backed by all the legal authority both sides could muster. Junior had one goal: to keep Insull abroad until the political tempest subsided. The governments also had one: to bring Insull back before the tempest subsided, and try him as a symbol of the discredited age he represented.[13]

Junior was not without friends. Newspaper reporters, sent from the outside to do feature stories on Insull, found among Chicago's com-

---

[12] Insull, "Memoirs," pp. 241, 253–54; Insull to Gladys Insull, Oct. 6, 1932; interview with Insull, Jr.; *Minutes,* Commonwealth Edison directors' meetings, Oct. 5, Nov. 22, 1932; interview with Abner J. Stilwell.

[13] Interviews with Leslie E. Salter (the chief prosecutor in the mail fraud trial), Flossmore, Illinois, Aug. 20, 1959; Floyd E. Thompson (Insull's attorney), Chicago, Aug. 31, 1959; and Samuel Insull, Jr. Said Salter: "For Insull to fight extradition was not only sensible, it was also courageous. He took upon himself all the odium of flight; had we got him back during the political climate of a year earlier, not only he, but half the businessmen in Chicago might have gone to jail." Copies of most of the documents covering the ensuing events are preserved in the Insull Papers, as are many newspaper clippings. Francis X. Busch, *Guilty or Not Guilty?* (Indianapolis, 1953), pp. 127–94, is an excellent and impartial account of the battle for extradition and the subsequent trial.

mon man—taxidrivers and schoolteachers and laborers, many of
whom had lost their life's savings in Insull's collapse—a surprising
number who bore no grudge and many who still believed Insull a
great man. Former employees, almost to a man, remained intensely
loyal, and sometimes they put Junior in an awkward position by
proposing to do something for Insull that would embarrass the new
management. Charles A. Munroe, to whom Insull had not spoken in
almost ten years, cabled $5,000 to him in Athens. One Chicago labor
boss, long impressed with Insull's fairness to union laborers, approached Junior and offered to shoot the businessmen he reckoned
were responsible for Insull's fall.[14]

But the general atmosphere had the heady, musty odor of a lynch
mob. (Said one anonymous note to Gladys: "You can get ready to
buy a cemetary lot as the gang will send you your crooked boys head.
you will pay as we have paid our good money. that has been stolen by
the dirty yellow crooked Insulls Jews. we will haunt you till we get
the whole crooked family.") Too, Junior's own circumstances were
hardly easy. He had a job as assistant to the chairman of the three
major operating companies—Simpson was abundantly able but without experience in the utility business, and Junior was the only available person capable of running all three companies—but his expenses were enormous and most of his $50,000 combined salary
was consumed in legal charges, support of his parents, and partial
support of his Uncle Martin. More important, he had to bear the
entire brunt of the political storm; it was he who had to look
Chicagoans in the eyes, he who had to undergo systematic harassment
from internal revenue agents, he who had to hold up his head, as the
only Insull around, when President-elect Roosevelt promised to "get"
the Insulls. And before his father returned from Greece in May, 1934,

[14] On the lack of hostility see, for example, the *New Republic*, Oct. 5, 1932, in which
Marquis W. Childs wrote in a feature article that there was "little apparent hostility
toward him"; see also Dedmon, *Fabulous Chicago*, p. 231. The other data in the paragraph are from interviews with Insull, Jr., Charles A. Munroe, and a dozen or more
former employees, and from a large file in the Insull Papers entitled "Trial Period."
See especially, in that file, the voluminous correspondence in folders labeled "Letters
of Encouragement" and "Offers Help Declined." The latter contains the correspondence of "The Friends of Samuel Insull, Inc.," an organization of persons independent
of Insull, Jr., and his lawyers and Insull companies. See also the *Christian Science
Monitor*, Sept. 2, 1933. On Christmas Day, 1932, scores of Insull's old employees sent
him a cablegram of greeting, and other such remembrances were often sent; they are
preserved in the Insull Papers.

Junior would himself be indicted twice by the United States government: in February, 1933, with his father, his uncle, Harold L. Stuart, and fourteen others, he was charged with using the mails to defraud, and in June, 1933, along with Insull and Stuart, he was charged with violating the Bankruptcy Act. He would also be called to testify before the renowned Pecora Committee of the Senate and treated as gently as left-wingers were later treated by the House Un-American Activities Committee. He would be sued for more money than he had ever seen. And then, as if the Fates wished to see how far he could be pushed, his young wife died of a sudden and tragic illness, leaving him a two-year-old son. And there was neither time nor opportunity for protest, for he had a battle to fight.[15]

The details of the battle to stave off extradition were immensely complex, but the general outlines were simple. The first action came on October 9, 1932, when the President of the United States asked Premier Mussolini of Italy to seize Insull when he passed through that country. Insul was already in Greece. In November, the Senate ratified an extradition treaty which had been pending for some time, and the battle for extradition began. Under the treaty, no person could be extradited from Greece unless, at a hearing before a tribunal of five Greek judges, substantial evidence was presented to prove the accused guilty of a crime under Greek law. Embezzlement, the charge for which Insull had been indicted in Illinois, was such an offense, and upon formal application by the United States Insull was tried in December before a board of judges, who refused, for lack of evidence, to order his extradition. By February, 1933, Insull had been indicted for use of the mails to defraud, but this was not an offense under Greek law, and the court again refused to extradite him.[16]

---

[15] The general atmosphere was learned from Chicago newspapers, the many interviews cited earlier, and the "Trial Period" file, in the Insull Papers; see especially the anonymous letter to Gladys Insull, May 2, 1933. Junior's continued employment was traced in the minute books of the three big operating companies. Other data are from the testimony of Insull, Jr., before the Pecora Committee (*Hearings on Stock Exchange Practices*, pp. 1397 ff.) ; copies of the several indictments as preserved in the Insull Papers; transcripts of the trials; and Busch, *Guilty or Not Guilty?*, pp. 132–33.

[16] Busch, *Guilty or Not Guilty?*, pp. 133–34; Insull, "Memoirs," pp. 255–60; the *New York Times*, the *Chicago Tribune*, Oct. 6–14, 1932; Nov. 1, 1932, to March 1, 1933; and the correspondence between Insull, Insull, Jr., Thompson, Messrs. Simmons and Simmons of London, Denis L. Lazaremos of Athens, Secretary of State Cordell Hull, and others, in the Insull Papers.

A temporary stalemate ensued, for under Greek law Insull could not be brought again before the court for the same indictments. The United States government countered in May, 1933, by indicting Insull a third time, now for violation of the Bankruptcy Act. In August, a special prosecutor was sent to Athens by the Department of Justice, but after hearing the prosecution's argument the Greek judges again dismissed the case for lack of evidence. Throughout 1933, Insull, provided with legal advice that Junior secured and forwarded from Chicago, and represented by Greek counsel paid for by Junior, was able to fend off extradition. All the while, he regularly asserted that he would voluntarily return as soon as he became convinced that a fair trial, not a political trial, would be held.[17]

In the interim, Gladys joined him in Athens, and Insull began to recover some measure of his former intellectual vigor. His mind, ever active, could not leave the power business for long, and after a few months, at the request of various important Greek businessmen and public officials, he found himself making a survey of the possibilities for electric power development in Greece. He offered a series of proposals which departed radically from conventional power systems and which he and his sponsors felt might launch Greece on an industrialization program that would restore it to its ancient grandeur. Insull also negotiated, through friends, an unwritten understanding with General Condylis, would-be dictator of Greece who lost the election to power by 700 votes. Had Condylis won the election, Insull would have become a Greek citizen and minister of electric power in the cabinet.[18]

But the new government in Washington, ever more determined by the frustration of its legal efforts to extradite Insull, resorted late in 1933 to extralegal means. There was in the United States an organization known as the Greek-American Merchants Association, whose

[17] In addition to the sources cited in note 16, see *U.S.* v. *Samuel Insull, et al.,* Indictment in the District Court of the United States of America for the Northern District of Illinois, Eastern Division, May Term, 1933; Insull to Simmons and Simmons, June 17, June 18, June 21, 1933; Stuart to Insull, May 29, June 18, 1933; Insull to Franklin D. Roosevelt, May, 1933; and the several legal opinions solicited by Thompson; all in the Insull Papers; and all Chicago and New York newspapers, May–December, 1933. A file of newspaper clippings from all Chicago newspapers from Nov., 1933, through 1935 is preserved in the Insull Papers.

[18] Insull, "Memoirs," pp. 263–68; Berry, "Mr. Samuel Insull," p. 52; Insull, "Some Possibilities for Greek Trade Development"; and the letters from Insull and Gladys Insull to Insull, Jr., throughout 1933; all in the Insull Papers. See also *New York Herald Tribune,* Sept. 17, 1933; *New Outlook,* Oct., 1933, pp. 56 ff.

importance to Greece lay in the fact that its prosperous members regularly sent large sums of money to relatives in the old country. The State Department approached the membership of this organization and told them, in effect, that unless they successfully exerted pressure to force the Greek government to surrender Insull, the United States would prohibit the exportation of further money to Greece. The association responded, and as a result of its pressure the Greek government yielded. Greece still refused to extradite Insull, but it ordered him to leave the country by January 1, 1934. Because of his bad health—general debility and a heart condition, complicated by diabetes—he was given a brief extension, but in February he was given final orders to leave by midnight, March 15.[19]

Convinced by the government's maneuver that the prospects for a non-political trial had hardly increased, Insull borrowed money from friends in London, chartered a Greek vessel, the S.S. "Maiotis," and prepared to sail from Greece. His departure was delayed when Greek officials learned what he was doing, but after a brief flurry of formalities he was allowed to leave. For two weeks Insull cruised the eastern Mediterranean, pondering whether he should accept an offer to go to Rumania and become minister of electric power or seek asylum in a country in the Middle East. But the United States was taking action that would end his deliberations. On March 22, at the urgent request of the State Department, both houses of Congress rushed through a bill authorizing the executive department to arrest Insull in any country in which by treaty it had extraterritorial rights. A week later, when the "Maiotis" put into Istanbul for provisions, the American ambassador, on direct orders from the State Department, demanded that the Turkish government arrest Insull. Though no extradition treaty or any provision of international law covered the action, the Turks complied by kidnapping Insull from the vessel. He was detained in Istanbul for a few days, subjected to a mock trial, then escorted under heavy guard to Smyrna and placed in the custody of Burton Y. Berry, third secretary of the American embassy in Istanbul. At Smyrna, Insull and Berry boarded the S.S. "Exilona" to begin the long voyage home. They stopped once en route, at Casa-

[19] The *New Republic*, March 28, 1934; Busch, *Guilty or Not Guilty?*, p. 133; Insull to Simmons and Simmons, Nov. 11, 1933; interviews with Thompson, Salter, and Insull, Jr., previously cited; Insull, "Memoirs," pp. 267–68; J. Mounzourides (Director of City Police, Athens) to Insull, March, 1933 (original in the Insull Papers, translation in Insull, "Memoirs," p. 269).

blanca, to take on cargo destined for the Chicago World's Fair, a venture Insull had directed and helped to promote as a means of combatting the Depression.[20]

As the "Exilona" steamed toward New York, Insull sank toward total despair. The reality of his disgrace and humiliation penetrated, like an icy winter, into the marrow of his bones. Several times he burst into uncontrollable tears—he was, as he described it, blubbering like a baby—and twice he thought of suicide. He displayed his weakness before only one person, Burton Berry, his State Department guard. Berry, impressed by Insull's aura of greatness even in utter abjection, soon became warmly sympathetic. It was he who talked Insull out of suicide: he told Insull that to kill himself would be to admit guilt and to blacken the name of his son.[21]

Insull passed each day by telling Berry and others anecdotes of his career. Four or five newspapermen had managed to get passage on the ship, and there was a handful of other passengers. Insull became friendly with one of the newsmen, James Kilgallen of the Hearst papers and International News Service, and he and Kilgallen prepared a press statement with which to greet the barrage of newsmen who would be waiting his arrival. After that Insull lapsed into a dull state that hovered between depression and vacuity. When the ship approached New York, it was difficult to tell whether he was a shell of a man or something less.[22]

But when the ship arrived and his son scrambled aboard to meet him and demonstrated his command by thrusting a press statement into his hands, Insull took heart again. He read the prepared statement with defiance and dignity; and even though, immediately afterward, federal agents whisked him by car across New Jersey to prevent any legal maneuvers on his behalf in New York, he was now prepared to fight, not to surrender.[23]

[20] The *New York Times,* the *Chicago Tribune,* and all other New York and Chicago newspapers, daily, March 14—May 8, 1934; Insull, "Memoirs," pp. 270–82; Berry, "Mr. Samuel Insull," *passim;* interview with James Kilgallen (reporter for the Hearst newspapers and International News Service who was on board the "Exilona" with Insull), New York, Jan. 3, 1958.
[21] Berry, "Mr. Samuel Insull," pp. 5–6, 8–9.
[22] *Ibid., passim;* interview with Kilgallen, previously cited.
[23] All Chicago and New York newspapers, May 5–8, 1934; *Time,* May 14, 1934. The original of the press statement is in the Insull Papers. See also the opening scene described in chap. i, above.

As soon as he arrived in Chicago, he had opportunity to demonstrate that his old toughness and shrewdness had not entirely deserted him. Insull, Jr., and his lawyers had been informally advised that Insull's bail would be $100,000, and Junior had arranged to have the sum ready. But when Insull was booked in Cook County Jail, bail was set at $200,000 instead. Pending the deposit of the sum, Insull was summarily thrown into a cell with vagrants, criminals, and a murderer, and only later transferred to a hospital cell. Judge Floyd Thompson, Insull's attorney—whom Junior had engaged, on Judge Cooke's advice, as a brilliant and respected trial lawyer who had had no prior connections with the Insulls—came to the cell to express his apologies. They had been double-crossed, he explained, but he would go right out and raise additional bail as quickly as possible.[24]

"You'll do no such thing," Insull snapped.

"But, Mr. Insull," said Thompson, "maybe you don't understand. If I don't raise the rest of the bail, you'll have to spend the night right here."

"That's exactly what I propose to do," said Insull.

A big grin spread across Thompson's face. "Mr. Insull," he said, "we'll get along just fine. That's just what I would have suggested, if I had had the guts to do so."

Both men recognized that, whatever the legal trappings with which the case would be surrounded, in large measure Insull would be tried at the bar of public opinion. The publicity attending the bail and jailing incident was the first step in transforming the popular image of Insull from that of an evil manipulator and swindler, brought back to face justice, into an infirm and aged sometime public benefactor persecuted for the sins of his generation. And on that issue—prosecution versus persecution—the defense was to rest.[25]

That was May, 1934. The first trial—on the federal indictment for use of the mails to defraud—was set for October. After the initial

[24] The *New York Times, New York Herald Tribune, Chicago Times,* the *Chicago Tribune, Chicago Herald and Examiner,* May 7–12, 1934; Insull, "Memoirs," pp. 283–84; interviews with Thompson and Insull, Jr., previously cited; interview with Howard Ketting (Insull's bodyguard-companion during this period), Chicago, Nov. 18, 1957. The press accounts vary in their bail figures, but they tell essentially the same story.
[25] Interview with Thompson, previously cited. Public opinion began to shift immediately, though the shift was far from complete. See, for example, the letters to the editor in the *New York Herald Tribune,* May 8, 1934, and the letters to the editors of the various Chicago newspapers through the summer of 1934.

burst of activity attending his return, and after a brief rest in St. Luke's Hospital, Insull settled for the summer at the Seneca Hotel. The Seneca, once a fairly fashionable apartment hotel, was at that time said to be populated by a different class of clientele. But it was clean, and there Insull could be reasonably comfortable. There were ten thousand things to do, but he left these largely to others, and spent most of the summer fulfilling, as well as circumstances permitted, a lifelong ambition: He dictated his memoirs.[26]

This was no flight of capricious egotism, but a well-calculated part of Thompson's strategy of defense. For one thing, the autobiography might command enough from a publisher to pay for the defense—which might run to $50,000 or more—and pay some of the debts Insull had incurred in fighting extradition. More important, it was a rehearsal for the trial. It was clear by the time Insull returned that the mail fraud trial would be the case on which the others would turn, and both prosecution and defense concentrated their whole energies upon it. In it the government would contend that the formation of Corporation Securities Company had been a scheme, concocted in 1929 and executed in 1930 and 1931, to use the mails and other media to unload worthless securities on an unsuspecting public. Thompson shrewdly and instantly saw that the best defense was to counterattack by placing Insull's whole life on trial. In the courtroom he would trace Insull's entire career, from London to Athens, showing the creative achievements, material success, and popular acclaim that had attended him, and then close with the obvious question: Could the jury take seriously a charge that this man—rich, powerful, respected, idolized after a distinguished career spanning five decades—decided to take up crime in 1929? In preparation for such a defense, to dictate his memoirs was the best thing Insull could do.[27]

[26] All Chicago newspapers, May 12–30, 1934; interview with Howard Ketting, previously cited; Insull, "Memoirs," pp. 284–85; affadavit of James J. O'Keefe (to whom Insull dictated his "Memoirs"), March 3, 1958.

[27] Thompson's plans for the trial I learned during an interview with him, previously cited; from interviews with two of his assistants, Carl Scholtz and Edward J. Fleming; and from the folder in the Insull Papers headed "Memoranda, Reports, Statements, Etc., gathered for Mail Fraud Case." Thompson believed that the government position would be as stated in the Federal Trade Commission, *Utility Corporations,* Vol. LXVII; a copy of his letter regarding it, and Insull's lengthy notes commenting upon it, are preserved in the "Trial Period" folder, in the Insull Papers.

Thompson, who represented Insull and his son, and the seven lawyers who represented the fifteen other co-defendants (Stuart, eight other officers, directors, and employees of Halsey, Stuart or Corp, four employees of Utility Securities Company, and an attorney and an accountant who had approved Corp's annual reports and stock-selling circulars) worked feverishly through the summer to familiarize themselves with the complex details of the case as well as with the intricacies of corporate accounting. But this was not Thompson's main focus of attention. The government, he reckoned, had to build its argument from a mountain of tedious, logical— sometimes only seemingly logical—detail. He must counter fact with fact, and logic with logic; but the trial, he sensed, would turn less upon logical than upon psychological pivots, and these, if he was shrewd enough to exploit them, were on his side.

He was able enough to exploit them, for in such a contest Thompson was superbly gifted. Like all great trial lawyers, he had hypersensitive antennae which detected the slightest shift in the mood of a jury, and a genius for improvising arguments, tactics, and lines of questions that would turn the jury's mood to his advantage. But he had more. Always generously endowed with self-confidence, he had acquired, during nine years as a justice of the Illinois Supreme Court, an air of authority which he could use to make a jury believe he had won a point even if he had in fact lost it. (Occasionally during the trial, when Judge James H. Wilkerson, a mere federal district judge, overruled one of Thompson's objections, Thompson shook his head and half-muttered, half-sneered, "In all my years on the bench, I never heard of such a ruling," and did so in such a way as to suggest to the jury that the judge was a bit shaky on the law.) But while he conveyed authority and wisdom, he also retained a folksy, farm-boy persuasiveness in his speech, and with this quality he could establish and hold the jury in close rapport. Finally, he had an actor's keen sense of rhythm, of pace, of touch: When the situation demanded it, he could fire his words crisply, sharply, brilliantly, or he could drawl them slowly, deliberately, ponderously.[28]

[28] This description and appraisal of Thompson as a trial lawyer is based primarily on the transcript of *U.S.* v. *Samuel Insull et al.* (the mail fraud trial) ; and, secondarily, upon Busch's account of the trial in *Guilty or Not Guilty?;* the newspaper accounts of the trial; and interviews with nine of Insull's sixteen co-defendants (Insull, Jr., Doyle, Field, McEnroe, Charles and Harold Stuart, O'Keefe, Scheel, and Frank Evers) , two of

Given these attributes and given the case, his job of preparation was mainly to study Insull. He did so, at great length, and as the trial approached, there seemed every reason for cautious self-confidence. Then suddenly something went wrong. The entire defense depended upon Thompson's skill in leading Insull through direct examination and upon Insull's ability to tell his life story interestingly, convincingly, and clearly. Through the summer, as Insull dictated his memoirs and Thompson regularly interviewed him about his career, Insull was reasonably sharp, but in September his memory began to grow hazy, and as he recited episodes he garbled events, forgot sequences, wandered off into irrelevant anecdotes, and forgot the thread of conversation. So alarming did this become that Thompson began to grope for an alternate defense should Insull prove unable to take the stand.[29]

Had he been able to spy on the prosecution, Thompson would have found consolation. The chief prosecutor was Dwight H. Green, U.S. attorney for the northern district of Illinois. Green was a Republican, appointed by Herbert Hoover and still holding his job under the new Democratic administration. Politically shrewd and ambitious (he would soon be governor of Illinois), he recognized the importance to his career of a conviction in the Insull case; it was, indeed, too important to intrust to his own indifferent talents as a prosecutor, or even to those of his capable assistant, Leo Hassenauer. They were aided by scores of brilliant investigators, sent from Washington by the Justice and Treasury departments, and these experts worked full time for more than two years to get the case ready, but Green was not satisfied. Long before Insull returned from Greece, Green called for extra help, and the Justice Department complied: It sent out Forrest Harness, the ablest special prosecutor it had in the Middle West. By the time Insull returned, Harness was in full charge, and throughout the summer he worked furiously, preparing and organizing the prosecution. A week or two before the trial, Green again grew nervous, and he asked Washington for a final bit of insurance. Attorney General Homer Cummings responded by sending Leslie E. Salter, the hottest special prosecutor he had in New York and

---

Thompson's assistants (Fleming and Scholtz), several persons who attended the trial, one of the jurors (Walter R. Valters), the prosecuting attorney (Leslie E. Salter), and Thompson himself.

29 Interviews with Thompson, Insull, Jr., and Ketting, previously cited.

probably the best in the country. By the end of September, the government was ready with one of the most thoroughly prepared cases it had ever put together. Then a minor catastrophe struck. On the very eve of the trial Harness, exhausted from his labors and the tension that surrounded them, was suddenly removed from control by Green.[30]

That left the case almost entirely in the hands of Salter, a man who had been called in only for moral support, for technical advice, and for occasional stints at spelling Harness in the prosecution. But this proved to be less calamitous than might have been expected, for though it meant that the prosecutor had to learn the case even as he developed it, it also meant that a nearly superhuman prosecutor was now in charge. Salter's career as a special assistant to the Attorney General had been breath-taking. After almost incredible success in Oklahoma, he was called to prosecute prohibition violators in New York, where convictions were all but unprecedented, and he responded by winning ninety-eight convictions in a hundred and one trials. Thereafter, he blazed a trail of convictions against overwhelming odds—a political boss in Rhode Island, an embezzling industrialist here, a mail-fraud violator there—that earned him a reputation as a virtually unbeatable man. His mind was as sharp as a rapier and as devastating as an ax; his oratory, like that of the statesmen of old, evoked biblical and historical imagery; his voice, a shrill, piercing Oklahoma whine, recalled the crusading vigor of Ingersoll, LaFollette, and Billy Sunday; and in the courtroom, as his brain crackled and his eyes blazed and his tongue lashed, accused and jurors alike trembled, as in the presence of a vengeful, wrathful, terrible God of the Old Testament.[31]

On Tuesday, October 2, 1934, at 10 o'clock in the morning, Judge Wilkerson rapped his gavel and the trial began. The bailiff an-

[30] A running account of the preparation of the prosecution may be obtained in the newspaper clipping file, in the Insull Papers; several documents relating to it are in the Insull Papers; it is attested to by the several expert witnesses for the government, as recorded in the transcript of the trial. Judging by the correspondence between Thompson and Harness, however, the government was extremely secretive in its preparations. The personal details in this paragraph were derived from an interview with Leslie E. Salter.

[31] Details of Salter's career were derived from a collection of newspaper clippings in his possession, which he kindly allowed me to study. This description and appraisal of him as a trial lawyer is based on the same sources as was the characterization of Thompson (see note 28, above).

nounced the names of the contestants: the United States of America versus Samuel Insull *et al.* These, however, were only aliases; their real names were the New Order and the Old. For the New, assembled before an awesome parapet of corporate records which had been arrayed, fortresslike, across the north wall of the courtroom, stood Leslie E. Salter, flanked by an elite guard of special prosecuters, F.B.I. men, Treasury agents, and experts, and reinforced by an army of witnesses, conscripted from villages and cities and farms across the land. For the Old, surrounded by a blank-faced jury on one side and a hostile prosecution on the other, a coldly impartial judge to the front and a hostile press and public to the rear, stood Floyd Thompson and seven co-attorneys, Samuel Insull and sixteen co-defendants.[32]

The Honorable Dwight H. Green opened for the prosecution by reading from the fifty-page, twenty-five-count indictment. The twenty-five counts were the same except as to the allegations of specific matter mailed and specific recipients. Together, they charged that Insull and the co-defendants had devised a fraudulent scheme whereby, through "false pretenses, representations, and promises," they defrauded thousands of persons of money by inducing them "to buy the worthless stock of this corporation [Corporation Securities Company of Chicago] at highly inflated and fictitious prices." Green then proceeded, in a two-hour speech, to state what the government intended to prove. It would be a tedious process, he warned, requiring many witnesses and "many, many books and records," but this was not, he insisted, a complicated case. "In the end," he said, "you will find this to be a simple conspiracy to swindle, cheat, and defraud the public."[33]

He led the jurors through a bewildering maze of corporate transactions, market quotations, accounting theories, offering circulars,

[32] This description of the opening scene is based upon accounts in several Chicago newspapers, Oct. 2–3, 1934; the interviews cited in note 28, above; newspaper photographs of the racks of records; and study of the courtroom itself.

[33] *U.S.* v. *Insull* (transcript in the Insull Papers) , pp. 3–66; Busch, *Guilty or Not Guilty?*, pp. 136–38. Busch's account is excellent, judicious, and impartial. Because it is more readily available to readers than is the transcript, I have cited Busch hereafter when I have followed his account exactly. The trial may also be studied in the *Chicago Tribune* and the *New York Times,* which gave detailed coverage, including verbatim reports of much of the testimony, and with less full coverage, in almost every other American newspaper. I have not cited newspapers in the following notes—though I have read the complete coverage in about fifteen different newspapers—but for convenience I have cited dates in the transcript, which readers may follow in newspapers.

syndicates, and the like, but the general outlines of the government's allegations were clear enough. In essence, the prosecution charged that Middle West Utilities Company had been in considerable trouble before 1929 and had, in fact, been able to remain solvent only through dishonest bookkeeping. In 1929, Green said, Insull, Stuart, and the others had hit upon a scheme for refinancing Middle West and making it more nearly solvent, but to execute the scheme they had to run up the market price of its stock. In doing so, they had purchased $13,000,000 of stock on the open market, and by August, 1929, they were stuck with these worthless securities. They then organized Corp as a dumping ground for the Middle West stock, and thereafter they repeatedly issued, through a high-pressure, nationwide selling campaign, false statements about Corp, rigged the stock market to support its stock, and juggled its books to give the illusion that it was a prosperous company. Along the way Insull, Stuart, and the others made huge profits, and thousands of "little people" lost their life's savings.[34]

The general plan of the prosecution was that, after Green finished his opening statement, it would launch a three-stage attack: First, it would introduce and verify the vast body of corporate records—including account books, minutes, correspondence, stock transfer books, memoranda, annual reports, and circulars—on which the government's case would be built; then it would introduce a collection of witnesses, mainly persons who would testify that they had bought Corp's securities in good faith after reading unsolicited mailed matter or listening to high-pressure salesmen, only to suffer large or total loss of their investment; and finally, it would work through a long, labored analysis of the records, using as witnesses to interpret them former employees of the companies, independent practicing accountants, college professors, and agents of the F.B.I.[35]

In a week the government called eighty-three witnesses, mainly employees of the several companies or of receivers, to identify and

[34] It will be observed that Green's statement is substantially identical to the accounts given in the F.T.C., *Utility Corporations*, Vols. LXVII, *passim*, and 72A, pp. 412–14, 502–4, 565–86. It differs somewhat—as does the F.T.C. *Summary Report*—from Vol. XXXVIII, which is a detailed investigation of Middle West Utilities Company before its collapse.

[35] This plan is clear in the transcript of the first two weeks of the trial, as well as in Busch's account of it.

authenticate the records and to lay the foundations for interpreting them in a way that would prove the guilt of the defendants. In spite of considerable bickering over technicalities—arising from the efforts of the defense to insure the validity of the documents and to lay foundations for possible error in the event of an appeal, as well as to harass the prosecution—Salter executed the task quickly, methodically, skilfully. But as he was beginning to gain the kind of momentum that was crucial if he were to hold the jury throughout the tedious details of the case, the defense struck its first telling blow.[36]

To introduce and begin interpretation of a collection of documents from Halsey, Stuart's files, documents that were particularly damaging to the defendants, Salter called Van Lamont, a disgruntled former comptroller of the company. In cross-examination, Charles Lounsbury, attorney for the Halsey, Stuart defendants, led Lamont through a set of carefully stated leading questions that seriously impaired the government's case before it could be made. It was developed that, as to the alleged running up of Middle West stock in 1929, all the purchases were made secretly so as to *prevent* a rise in the market; and as for dumping a $13,000,000 investment in "worthless" stocks by turning them over to Corp, the market value of the investment was, at the time of the transfer, almost twice what Insull and Halsey, Stuart had paid for the securities.

The cross-examination developed another effective point. The government alleged that Corp's initial offering circular had claimed that the company's assets were $80,000,000, whereas they were in fact only $7,000,000, against which $3,500,000 in bank loans were outstanding, and that the company made up the difference by juggling its books. The government's witness was compelled to admit that under prevailing commercial practice, it was customary to issue circulars representing the financial status of the offering company as of the completion of the proposed financing, and that on that basis, Corp had even more assets than it claimed. Finally, the cross-examination brought out that all the officers of Halsey, Stuart—including the witness—had voluntarily made large purchases of the securities at their offered price because they believed they were a sound investment, and that all had held the securities to the end and had taken large losses.[37]

---

[36] Busch, *Guilty or Not Guilty?*, pp. 138–39; *U.S. v. Insull*, pp. 84–706 (Oct. 4–9, 1934).
[37] Busch, *Guilty or Not Guilty?*, p. 152; *U.S. v. Insull*, pp. 729–1233.

On Thursday of the second week, after three days on the stand, Lamont stepped down. Just after he was dismissed, two critically important events took place backstage. During one of the numerous (and to the jury, infinitely boring) recesses, the jurors retired to the jury room while the lawyers argued over some technicality. One of the jurors, a former sheriff, spoke a thought that must have already been forming in the minds of some of the others. He remarked upon the bulk of the records that were being used in the case and observed that the government seemed to be basing its entire case upon their accuracy and reliability. He said that in all his years of dealing with crooks, he had never heard of a band of crooks who thought up a scheme, wrote it all down, and kept an honest and careful record of everything they did. The only crooks he knew about, he said, kept no records, falsified them, or destroyed them.[38]

The change in the jury's mood was subtle, but Salter was alert enough to sense it. Furthermore, by the time the week's hearings ended he had completed his study of the planned prosecution, and for the first time he realized how top-heavy with documents it was. Since the jury was already growing cold, he believed that it would be disastrous to attempt to present in its entirety the thorough but tedious case that had been originally planned.

Accordingly, on Sunday, October 14, he called a special meeting of the entire prosecution team: Green, Harness, Hassenauer, and F.B.I. agent Harold Huling, the man who had worked for more than two years directing the investigation on which the prosecution was based. Salter explained his feelings and then made a blunt proposal: that the government slash three weeks from the prosecution and try to pull the remainder together in a way that would present the essence of the evidence in a more dramatic fashion.

A major crisis ensued. Some agreed with Salter, and others were

[38] This and all comments regarding what went on in the jury room are derived from an interview with Walter R. Valters (the only surviving juror I was able to find), Nov. 8, 1961; and from interviews with Edward J. Fleming, Harold L. Stuart, and Philip McEnroe, previously cited. Fleming, Stuart, and McEnroe asserted—and juror Volters confirmed—that they talked with several of the jurors on several occasions after the trial and obtained the information they reported to me, as reported here. Volters confirmed most, but not all, of the statements made to me by Fleming, Stuart, and McEnroe. Some information on the jurors is reported in the several Chicago newspapers immediately after the trial (Nov. 24–26, 1934). These reports conflict somewhat as to details, but they do indicate the general attitude of the jury toward the case.

willing, albeit grumblingly, to go along with him, but Huling fiercely objected. The more Salter attempted to defend his position, the more enraged Huling became, and in a semihysterical outburst he accused Salter of planning to throw the case. Salter was a temperamental man, and his nerves were frayed by the enormous strain under which he labored, but he held himself in check. Carefully, patiently, he explained to Huling that he was trying to save the case, not throw it. Huling had prepared the case brilliantly, he said, and investigation and preparation were Huling's specialty. But without reflecting any discredit on the preparation, he, Salter, was the expert on trial work, and he knew that excessive documentation would alienate the jury. After a tense pause, Huling conceded.[39]

The next day—Monday of the third week—was spent in executing a subtle switch to the revised plan. On Tuesday, the new tack began. Salter's prosecution was brilliantly conceived and brilliantly executed. Dismissing all but the absolutely relevant details, he put on the stand half a dozen expert government witnesses, F.B.I. agents all, and led each through a summary interpretation of the records in a way that cast the most damning possible light on the documented doings of the defendants. After each day or day and a half of such testimony, Salter paraded a small band of widows and old folks and working people to testify that they had invested and lost their life savings in Corp's stock; then he put on another expert. In two whirlwind weeks, Salter brought the government's case to a climax.[40]

The defense was not defenseless during this dazzling performance. In addition to being effectively dilatory at two points, the defense impaired the effectiveness of two of the expert witnesses through skilful cross-examination.

One witness, F.B.I. agent R. A. Knittle, had testified damagingly as to market manipulations by the Insulls—wash and matched sales and other forms of fictitious transactions. On cross-examination, Thompson induced the witness to admit that his only training as an accountant had been through a correspondence course; that his only previous experience as an accountant had been for a small firm in

[39] This and the preceding two paragraphs are derived from the interview with Salter, previously cited. That the prosecution changed pace at about this point was attested by several of the interviewees cited in note 28, above; if the transcript is read with foreknowledge of the change, it is discernible in the transcript.

[40] *U.S.* v. *Insull,* pp. 1234 ff. (Oct. 15–26, 1934).

Casper, Wyoming; that though he recognized that the auditing of brokerage accounts was something that only highly trained experts dared undertake, he himself had never seen a brokerage account prior to the beginning of the investigation; that Huling, who had had no such training himself, had told him what to find and the *a priori* formula to use in finding it; and finally, the witness admitted that he never heard of an F.B.I. investigation "in which it turned out that the fellow was innocent."[41]

The second expert, F.B.I. accountant Wayne Murphy, testified that the companies had treated certain income and expense items—particularly stock dividends and organization expenses—improperly in keeping its books, and thereby gave a false and deceptive impression of its income. Thompson wrung from this witness a reluctant admission that, while he believed his testimony as to proper accounting practices to be sound, he recognized that the questions were controversial and that reputable accountants were divided on the matter.[42]

Even so, Salter had registered large gains, and when he put on his final witness, Huling himself, the prosecution had achieved great momentum. Huling took the stand on Friday, October 26, and he played the role of both star witness and summarizer. For the rest of that day and all the next, Huling testified, and so clear was his presentation that jurors lost in the details were able to regain a sharp understanding of the government's case. But Huling's testimony revealed a weak spot in the prosecution, a weakness which Thompson had been building toward and upon which he now dramatically seized. When the government's allegations were brought into focus during Huling's testimony, it was evident that the whole case depended upon the construction placed upon the company's account books. Having previously shaken the government's position on one of its two vital accounting procedures—the proper treatment of stock dividends—Thompson now smashed a substantial hole in the other, the proper treatment of organization expense. Huling had testified that Corporation Securities had improperly capitalized organization expense, instead of treating it as a charge against current income, and thereby falsely inflated its income statement. In cross-examination, Thompson compelled Huling to admit that he agreed with a professor of

[41] *Ibid.,* pp. 2477–82 (Oct. 19–22, 1934).
[42] *Ibid.,* pp. 3378–443 (Oct. 26, 1934); *Busch, Guilty or Not Guilty?,* pp. 153–55.

accounting at the University of Michigan and author of a widely used textbook on accounting who considered organization expense a permanent intangible asset. Even more damagingly, he admitted that the system used by Corp was that used by the federal government itself for income tax purposes. Upon that dramatic note Huling was dismissed as a witness, and the prosecution rested.[43]

For the next two and a half days the attorneys for all the defendants except Insull and his son filed and argued separate motions to direct the jury to return a verdict of not guilty. Judge Wilkerson listened politely, then denied all the motions.[44]

On November 1, ten days before his seventy-fifth birthday, Samuel Insull was sworn in as a witness, leading off for the defense. Around the world, from San Francisco to Boston, from London to Athens, from Montreal to Buenos Aires, newspapers covered Insull's testimony, and through them ten million—or fifty million or a hundred million—pairs of eyes watched the old man as he mounted the witness stand. In the Loop, business virtually stopped as almost every prominent businessman called upon influence or bribery or chance to get him into the courtroom. Inside the court, like an audience of Romans gathered to watch a lion devour Christians, the spectators waited with mixed feelings—some apprehensive, some vengeful, some merely curious, but all tense. And of them all, none could have been as tense as Thompson, for only he knew the enormous gamble he was taking, only he knew that in private Insull had been bumbling and befuddled in trying to recall his career.

Thompson's fears proved groundless, for once Insull took the stand he was the razor-edged Insull of old. He did more than tell his story —he wove a spell. Before he was through, everyone in the courtroom was entranced. He began by describing his childhood, his first job at $1.25 a week, the chance connection with Edison. At first neither Salter nor Judge Wilkerson was aware of what Thompson was about, and when they realized it, it was too late. By the time Insull began to talk about his years with Edison, Wilkerson himself was so

[43] *U.S.* v. *Insull,* pp. 3483–621, 3632–42 (Oct. 26–29, 1934) ; Busch, *Guilty or Not Guilty?*, p. 154.
[44] *U.S.* v. *Insull,* pp. 3657 ff. (Oct. 29–31, 1934) .

wrapped up in the story that he waved aside Salter's objections. Salter continued to try to block the testimony as irrelevant, but when Insull told of his early Chicago years, and described the working-out of the economics of the business, the early operating problems, the daring installation of the first steam turbine and the giant turbines that followed, Salter found the jury glowering at his every interruption, and thereafter he could only hold his peace.[45]

(Though it did not make his cross-examination any the less merciless, even Salter came under the spell. About two-thirds of the way through Insull's direct testimony, Judge Wilkerson ordered a short recess, and during the interval Salter and Junior found themselves at adjoining stalls in the men's room. Salter looked at Insull, Jr., with a puzzled expression on his face, and half-said, half-inquired, "Say, you fellows were legitimate businessmen." Said Junior: "That's what we've been trying to tell you.") [46]

The defense might have rested when Insull stepped down, but it dragged on for another two weeks. It focused on two things, a parade of distinguished character witnesses for all the defendents save Insull (who grandly refused to do any such thing) and expert accountants who gave affirmative indorsement to the way the Insulls kept their books, thus completing the weakening of the government's allegations on that score.[47]

Insull did have a character witness, in a way. In cross-examination, Salter used Insull's tax returns to show how huge Insull's personal income had been in the five years before the collapse—salaries totaling $500,000 a year. In further examination, Thompson brought out that the same returns showed that Insull's charitable contributions were also enormous, amounting in several years to more than his entire income from salaries. (When this testimony was entered Salter, who had been repeatedly urged by Huling to get Insull's income into

[45] For this description of Insull's appearance, I have studied all Chicago newspapers; those of every other large city for which there are files in the State Historical Society of Wisconsin, the Chicago Public Library, and the John Hay Library of Brown University; and the extensive clippings in the Insull Papers. Additional descriptions were provided by the interviewees cited in note 28, above. The testimony is from *U.S. v. Insull*, pp. 4234 ff. (Nov. 1–5, 1934) ; it is fairly summarized in Busch, *Guilty or Not Guilty?*, pp. 166–81.

[46] Interviews with Insull, Jr., and Salter, previously cited.

[47] *U.S. v. Insull*, pp. 4609 ff. (Nov. 5–16, 1934) .

the record, turned to Huling angrily and, in a whisper loud enough to be heard by the jury, snapped, "You son of a bitch. Why didn't you tell me that was in there, too?") [48]

On Friday, November 16, the defense rested. A week was consumed in motions, maneuvers, and counter-maneuvers, and then both sides summed up. Thompson's summary was cool and clear, emotional only where it would be most persuasive. Salter's was brilliant, eloquent, and impassioned, likening Insull's rise and fall to that of Napoleon, and charging that Insull, like Napoleon, had become intoxicated and corrupted by power. At 2:30 on Saturday afternoon, November 24, the jury retired. [49]

Behind locked doors, the jurors faced a curious problem. All were convinced that the defendants were innocent—some, it turned out, had been convinced even before Insull took the stand—and in five minutes they had reached their formal decision. But then the former sheriff posed a problem. In view of the magnitude of the trial, he said, and in view of the publicity attending it, if the jurors took only five minutes to return a verdict of not guilty, they would be inviting widespread suspicion that they had been bribed. So while defendants and prosecution and curious public paced their several floors, the jury dawdled for another two hours. It happened that one of them was having a birthday, so the jury ordered a cake and coffee and held a small birthday party. At 4:30 they re-entered the courtroom and solemnly announced their verdict: All defendants were innocent of all charges. [50]

Insull had been right in predicting his acquittal, but he was wrong about one thing. When his story was told in court, he had said, "My judgment may be discredited, but certainly my honesty will be vindicated." Many people saw it in a different light. The *Chicago Times,* an ardent supporter of the New Deal, summarized a more widespread attitude: "Insull and his fellow defendants—not guilty;

[48] *Ibid.,* pp. 6324–32 (Nov. 15, 1934); interviews with McEnroe, Thompson, Salter, and Insull, Jr., previously cited.

[49] *U.S.* v. *Insull,* pp. 6759 ff. (Nov. 16–24, 1934).

[50] Interviews with Volters, Fleming, McEnroe, and Stuart, previously cited (see note 38, above); all Chicago newspapers, Nov. 24–25, 1934. Said the *Chicago Tribune,* as the jury retired: "This verdict is not expected to be a hurried one, although the jurors may be anxious to get home for Sunday dinner."

the old order—guilty. That was the Insull defense, and the jury agreed with it."[51]

Two hands were yet to be played out, the state indictments for embezzlement and the federal indictments for violation of the Bankruptcy Act. In March, 1935, Insull and his brother Martin were tried on the first of the embezzlement charges, one alleging their embezzlement of $66,000. After a brief trial, they were acquitted, and the state's attorney dismissed the remaining charges. Three months later, Insull, his son, and Stuart were tried on the federal indictments. Judge John C. Knox of New York was assigned to hear the case. After the prosecution was finished, the judge instructed the jury to bring in a verdict of not guilty.[52]

For his fifty-three years of labor to make electric power universally cheap and abundant, Insull had his reward from a grateful people: He was allowed to die outside prison.

[51] *Chicago Times,* Nov. 26, 1934. The liberal magazine, the *Nation,* Dec. 5, 1934, was more outspoken: The acquittal, it said, "illustrates once more the difficulty of sending a rich man to jail, no matter how flagrant his crime."

[52] The subsequent trials are accurately summarized in Busch, *Guilty or Not Guilty?,* pp. 192–94; transcripts of the trials, and newspaper clippings covering them, are preserved in the Insull Papers. Judge Knox, in his autobiography, *A Judge Comes of Age* (New York, 1940), pp. 268–72, gives an interesting summary of the bankruptcy case.

Aftermath

During his eclipse, Insull was the subject of more magazine and newspaper copy than any other half-dozen businessmen, and virtually every article was condemnatory. But the several writers only appeared to agree; in actuality they were divided into two fiercely opposed camps. All charged that Insull was evil. The question was, was he the rule or the exception?

Those who were suspicious of or hostile to Business labored diligently to indict a whole system by pointing to Insull and saying, "You see? That's the way businessmen are." On the other side, businessmen the nation over pointed to Insull and said, "It's not the system, and it's not us; it was him, and men like him."

As John R. Commons put it, business "needed a scapegoat for the sins of capitalism," and Insull was ideally suited for the role. Thus the General Electric Company quietly expunged Insull from its official company history, and began to hint that G.E. had been for progress and low rates and quality service all along but had been hindered by certain scoundrels in the utility business. Thus such magazines as *Colliers*—on whose board of directors sat Thomas Lamont, a Morgan partner—published a series of articles and editorials denouncing Insull and certain bankers but carefully suggesting that their well-deserved downfall stemmed from their own personal corruption and not from the system or from external forces. (*Colliers* capped this performance by serializing a book by Lamont, singing the praises of the House of Morgan.) And thus the holding companies slyly dissociated themselves from Insull in several steps: first, he was a great man who had somehow gone wrong; then he was an operator who had been all right in some respects but always a bit shady; and finally he became (along with Howard Hopson and W. B. Foshay) the kind of scoundrel who had abused a trust and made it difficult for honest and constructive holding companies.

They might, with equal expectation of success, have been trying to prevent the Crusades by claiming that there were only a few bad infidels. These efforts helped stamp Insull indelibly as a symbol of business evils that led to the Depression, and they gave an anti-Insull coloration to much of the coming reform legislation, but otherwise they weighed nothing at all.

The two years following Insull's first federal indictment in 1933 saw some of the most far-reaching legislation in the history of the U.S. Congress, and a large portion of it was passed in direct response to Insull's real or alleged doings: the Public Utility Holding Company Act of 1935; the acts creating the Tennessee Valley Authority, the Securities Exchange Commission, and the Rural Electrification Administration; and significant portions of the Glass-Steagall banking act, the Corporation Bankruptcy Act, and the Wagner-Connery labor act.

Along the way, there were ironies in abundance. Not the least of these was that most of the reforms were measures that Insull had worked for or lobbied for or put into practice all his life. Doubly ironic was the particular case of the Tennessee Valley Authority. The sponsors of the T.V.A. were determined to use it as a means of demonstrating to American utilities how a unified power system should be run, and as a "yardstick" for measuring rates and standards of service. Before this could be done, however, the directors of the project themselves had to learn how to run a unified power system. The embarrassing fact of the matter was that American systems were easily the best managed in the world, but under the circumstances it would obviously be awkward to pattern the T.V.A. after one of them. Accordingly, director David Lilienthal and chief electrical engineer Llewellen Evans went to England to study the British grid system—which had the great political virtue of being government-owned—in order to pattern the T.V.A. after it. Meanwhile, Insull, who had taught the British how to build their system, was a fugitive from justice, and Middle West Utilities Company, whose subsidiaries had served as the model for the grid, was in receivership. (The facts and therefore the irony were unknown to the American press, but they were not overlooked by the British. Said the *Electrical Review* of London:

Though perhaps it may have no direct relation to their enquiry, we are somehow or other led to recall to the minds of some of our leaders the occasions, while the British grid was either in process of birth or in the stage of early nourishment, when the utility experience of another American visitor, Mr. Samuel Insull, of Chicago, was found helpful at Westminster. . . . Those who know the story of his early and remarkable work in the expansion of electricity production and consumption in the States will remember that it was the envy of students of such matters here. He is undoubtedly a man of "seasoned specialised judgment" such as [Mr. Lilienthal] regards as essential for determining future policy in the States, but circumstances have deprived the American people of his experience and of that of his associates.)

There was more. The New York banks had won the titanic battles of 1931–32, but in the end they lost more than anyone. As Samuel Insull, Jr., put it, year after year and generation after generation New York maintained its financial supremacy against all comers— Boston, Philadelphia, Pittsburgh, Cleveland, Chicago—until one day Washington won it all. The decisive actions were two features of the banking acts of 1933 and 1935: those divorcing commercial banks from their investment banking affiliates, and those requiring competitive bidding in the marketing of utility bonds. By these means the House of Morgan's stranglehold on the American economy was broken for all time. (The private irony in this instance was that the suggestions for these measures came not from anti-business crusaders or reform politicians, but from Harold L. Stuart and Cyrus S. Eaton.)

And the last episode was the most ironic of all. In 1935, Congress proposed to enact the celebrated "death sentence" for holding companies—section 11 (b) of the Wheeler-Rayburn or Public Utility Holding Company bill—and to inaugurate a new pattern of business regulation in America by vitalizing the Federal Power Commission (other sections of the same bill) . The investment bankers and financial buccaneers who had captured control of the holding companies had retained the massive and hyperefficient propaganda machinery that Insull and his men had created, and now they put it to work in a monumental effort to defeat the Wheeler-Rayburn bill. The machinery ground out the propaganda as profusely as ever: Congress was deluged with more mail and telegrams than it had ever received on any legislation, and radio, newspapers, magazines, pulpits, and even the schools echoed with denunciations of the bill. But the machinery had been so thoroughly perverted by its new masters, and its workings had been so thoroughly publicized by its enemies, that the campaign backfired magnificently. Each new attack on the bill was regarded as one more proof of the holding companies' power for evil, and the propaganda against the bill, as much as anything else, insured its passage.

For Insull himself, there were two consolations. The first, a personal consolation, Insull summarized succinctly in conversation with his State Department guard on his return trip from Greece. "I got a cable this morning that upset me completely," he said. "It was from my wife. She said: 'Hoping and thinking of you.' That said volumes. She thought that I had no money and perhaps no friends aboard. It shows that all her time, all her thoughts, are centered on me. Sometimes it is more than I can bear. I break down when I think of it, and again it is the thing that keeps me going—the closeness between the members of my family which has been brought about by this trouble."

The other was business. Insull never knew the details (they were not completely available until several years after his death), but in time his companies as a whole proved to be considerably stronger than American business as a whole. During the depression, close to 40 per cent of the securities of all American corporations were forfeited. Of all the Insull securities outstanding in the hands of the public in June, 1932—including those issued by predecessors in companies Insull took over when they were already on treacherous footing—just over one-fifth forfeited in any way. None of Insull's operating electric or gas companies went into receivership or bankruptcy, and people who had bought their securities lost only a fraction of 1 per cent of their investment. In time, even Insull's personal creditors made out well. The securities they held as collateral in 1932 were worth $16,000,000 less than his personal debts; ultimately, they were worth ten to fifteen millions more than the debts. And a quarter of a century after Insull's death, his companies were still producing about an eighth of the electric power and gas consumed in the United States; they were still selling it for much less than the national average; and though they were no longer related as corporations, many of them were still being managed by old Insull men.

The only remaining enemy was boredom. Like Napoleon on St. Helena, Insull was required to spend his declining years in well-fed inactivity. He had no problem of earning a living, for after his final trial his pensions were restored. He was even spared most of the barrage of civil suits that his son, Stuart, and the others were fighting (and winning) in the wake of the criminal suits, for all his personal estate and debts were placed in the hands of trustees for his creditors. But he was an exile in two ways: he was not only a man without a job, he was also a man without a home, for Gladys refused to live in Chicago or London, and so they settled in Paris.

In 1936 he made a brief and pathetic effort at a comeback. His idea was good enough: He proposed to start a network of radio stations in medium-sized cities in the Middle West. The economics of the plan also appeared sound: Two large companies promised (or so he thought) advertising contracts guaranteeing enough income to meet overhead and operating costs, and all local advertising that could be sold would be at a profit. He took on partners, obtained backing from old friends to finance his share of the undertaking, and launched the Affiliated Broadcasting Company. But the promised contracts failed to materialize, and local advertising failed to meet expectations, and finally some of the partners began to suspect that one of them (not Insull) had his hand in the till, as possibly someone did. Worst of all, Insull was not the Insull of old. He had all the old thunder, but none of the old lightning, and soon the venture collapsed.

For two more years, life dragged on. He followed the news of business and politics with keen interest, but there was rarely anyone with whom to discuss these subjects, and Insull was ill-equipped to play the passive spectator. A few times he went to Chicago to visit his son, and once in awhile he ran into old friends in Europe, and on those occasions his eyes lit up and his self-generating energy and enthusiasm briefly returned.

In the spring of 1938 he visited Chicago for the last time. On the return voyage to Paris, having crossed the Atlantic without incident more than two hundred times, he was in his first shipwreck. There were no casualties, and the worst thing that happened to him was having to sleep on a pool table on the rescue ship.

Two months later, on the morning of July 16, Insull entered a Paris subway, and while waiting for a train he had a heart attack and died. His body remained unidentified for several hours, and the official police statement reported that he had nothing in his pockets except a white silk handkerchief with the monogram "SI" and the equivalent of eight cents in francs. One last time, Insull was front-page news all over the world. Most newspapers garbled the circumstances of his death, and then played upon the fallen titan theme, contrasting his former might with death in anonymous poverty. "He was, after all, a man like other men," one reporter wrote.

But, as always, the circumstances were a bit more complicated than that. At the time of his death, Insull had about $10,000 and unless he had suddenly departed from his lifelong habit, he would have left his apartment that morning with a good deal of money—perhaps as much as $2,000 in cash—in his wallet. The Paris police reported that he had neither money nor wallet. Some bystander in the subway, or some Paris police officer, went home that day many hundred francs the richer.

And so in his death, as in his life, Samuel Insull was robbed, and nobody got the story straight.

INDEX